WAR AND UNDERDEVELOPMENT
Volume II

War and Underdevelopment

Volume II
Country Experiences

FRANCES STEWART AND VALPY FITZGERALD
AND ASSOCIATES

OXFORD
UNIVERSITY PRESS

OXFORD

UNIVERSITY PRESS

Great Clarendon Street, Oxford OX2 6DP

Oxford University Press is a department of the University of Oxford.
It furthers the University's objective of excellence in research, scholarship,
and education by publishing worldwide in

Oxford New York

Athens Auckland Bangkok Bogotá Buenos Aires Calcutta
Cape Town Chennai Dar es Salaam Delhi Florence Hong Kong Istanbul
Karachi Kuala Lumpur Madrid Melbourne Mexico City Mumbai
Nairobi Paris São Paulo Shanghai Singapore Taipei Tokyo Toronto Warsaw

and associated companies in Berlin Ibadan

Oxford is a registered trade mark of Oxford University Press
in the UK and certain other countries

Published in the United States
by Oxford University Press Inc., New York

British Library Cataloguing in Publication Data

Data available

Library of Congress Cataloging in Publication Data

Stewart, Frances.
War and underdevelopment / Frances Stewart and Valpy FitzGerald and associates.
p. cm.
Includes bibliographical references and index.
Contents: v. 1. The economic and social costs of conflict—v. 2. Country experiences.
1. War—Economic aspects.   2. Economic development.   I. FitzGerald, Valpy.   II. Title.
HC79.D4 S74 2001   338.9—dc21   00-060668

ISBN 0-19-924186-4 (vol. 1, hbk)
ISBN 0-19-924187-2 (vol. 1, pbk)
ISBN 0-19-924188-0 (vol. 2, hbk)
ISBN 0-19-924189-9 (vol. 2, pbk)

1 3 5 7 9 10 8 6 4 2

Typeset by Graphicraft Limited, Hong Kong
Printed in Great Britain
on acid-free paper by
T.J. International Ltd.,
Padstow, Cornwall

PREFACE

This study attempts to address a vital issue of our time to which development economists have devoted far too little attention. When embarking upon this research in 1994 we found very little academic literature or rigorous data, and few scholars focusing on the topic. This enabled us to make a fresh start and gave us the opportunity to build up a new multidisciplinary team of researchers, mostly young scholars completing their doctoral research or assuming their first research posts at Queen Elizabeth. This combination of a new start and a fresh team lead us down unexpected paths and generated an unusual degree of interdisciplinary debate, pulled together by a common sense of the seriousness of the task at hand.

The research programme that is reported on in these volumes was partly funded by the UK Department for International Development and the Swedish International Development Cooperation Agency. We are grateful for their support, and also the free hand we were given in the development of our own agenda. Valuable editorial assistance was provided by Kate Raworth and Maureen Hadfield. Finally, research at Queen Elizabeth House is greatly facilitated by the efficient and enthusiastic support given by our administrative and library staff—we would particularly like to thank Denise Watt, Wendy Grist, Roger Crawford, Sheila Allcock, and Julia Knight.

The results of the research programme are presented in two related volumes. Volume I is devoted to general analysis of the economics of conflict, derived from analytic and empirical work, while Volume II contains seven in-depth case studies of countries in conflict. The countries studied were Afghanistan, Mozambique, Nicaragua, Sierra Leone, Sri Lanka, Sudan, and Uganda.

EVF and FS

CONTENTS

ABBREVIATIONS AND ACRONYMS

AFP	*Agence France-Presse*
AICF	Action Internationale Contre la Faim
APC	All Peoples Congress (Sierra Leone)
ARDE	Democratic Revolutionary Alliance (Nicaragua)
BAAG	British Agencies Afghanistan Group
BCIE	Central American Bank for Economic Integration
CAFOD	Catholic Fund for Overseas Development
CARE	Cooperative for Assistance and Relief Everywhere (USA)
CEPAL	Comisión Económica para América Latina
CIO	(Rhodesian) Central Intelligence Organization
COARSA	Corporación Arrocera Sociedad Anónima (Nicaragua)
CONFAID	Conflict-Related Food Aid
CPI	Centro de Promoção de Investimentos (Mozambique)
CRIES	Coordinadora Regional de Investigaciones Económicas
CRS	Catholic Relief Services
CSAE	Centre for the Study of African Economies
DAC	Development Assistance Committee (OECD)
DEVFAID	Development-Related Food Aid
DHA	(UN) Department of Humanitarian Affairs
DP	(Uganda Catholic) Democratic Party
DUP	Democratic Unionist Party (Sudan)
EC	European Community
ECLAC	Economic Commission for Latin America and the Caribbean
ECOMOG	Economic Community of West African States Ceasefire Monitoring Group
EIU	Economist Intelligence Unit
ENABAS	Empresa Nacional de Abastecimiento
EPI	Extended Programme Of Immunisation
FAO	Food and Agriculture Organization
FDI	Foreign Direct Investment
FDN	Nicaraguan Democratic Front
FNI	Fondo Nicaragüense de Inversiones
FSLN	Frente Sandinista de Liberación Nacional (Nicaragua)
GDP	Gross Domestic Product
GNP	Gross National Product
HDI	Human Development Index
HIPC	Highly Indebted Poor Countries
ICG	International Crisis Group
ICRC	International Committee of the Red Cross
IDB	Inter-American Development Bank

IDS	Institute of Development Studies, Sussex
IMF	International Monetary Fund
IFPRI	International Food Policy Research Institute
IHCA	Instituto Histórico Centroamerícano
IISS	International Institute for Strategic Studies
ILO	International Labour Organization
IMF	International Monetary Fund
IMR	Infant Mortality Rate
JAMA	*The Journal of the American Medical Association*
KY	Buganda Kabaka Yeki
LDCs	Least-Developed Countries
LTTE	Liberation Tamil Tigers of Eelam
MMR	Maternal Mortality Rate
MNR	Mozambique National Resistance (Renamo)
MFEP	Ministry of Finance and Economic Planning (Uganda)
MSF	Médecins Sans Frontières
NGO	Non-Governmental Organizations
NPRC	National Provisional Ruling Council (Sierra Leone)
NRA	National Resistance Army (Uganda)
NRM	National Resistance Movement (Uganda)
OLS	Operation Lifeline Sudan
PHR	Physicians for Human Rights
PRE	Mozambique Structual Adjustment Programme
RN	Resistencia Nicaragüense
RUF	Revolutionary United Front (Sierra Leone)
SAP	Structural Adjustment Programmes
SCA	Swedish Committee for Agriculture
SCF	Save the Children Fund
SIDA	Swedish International Development Authority
SIPRI	Stockholm International Peace Research Institute
SLPP	Sierra Leone People's Party
SPLA	Sudan People's Liberation Army
TEEDO	Tamil Eelam Economic Development Organization
TRO	Tamil Rehabilitation Organization
TULF	Tamil United Liberation Front
UDCA	United Democratic Christian Army (Uganda)
ULIMO	United Liberation Movement for Democracy in Liberia
UNAG	Unión Nacional de Agricultores y Ganaderos (Nicaragua)
UNCHR	United Nations Centre for Human Rights
UNCTAD	United Nations Conference on Trade and Development
UNDCP	United Nations Drugs Control Programme
UNDP	United Nations Development Programme
UNDPI	UN Department of Public Information
UNHCR	United Nations High Commission for Refugees

UNHTDS	UN _Handbook of Trade and Development Statistics_
UNICEF	United Nations Children's Fund
UNLA	Ugandan National Liberation Army
UNLF	Ugandan National Liberation Front
UNO	Union Nacional Opositora (Nicaragua)
UNOCHA	United Nations Office for the Coordination of Humanitarian Affairs
UNSYB	United Nations _Statistical Year Book_
UPM	Ugandan Patriotic Movement
UPANIC	National Agricultural Producers' Association (Nicaragua)
UPC	Ugandan People's Congress
UPM	Uganda Patriotic Movement
USAID	United States Agency for International Aid
USCR	United States Committee for Refugees
WB	World Bank
WBDI	World Bank Development Institute
WIDER	World Institute for Development Economics Research
WFP	World Food Programme

1

Case Studies of Countries at War: An Introduction

FRANCES STEWART AND VALPY FITZGERALD

> For as the nature of foul weather lieth not in a shower or two of rain; but in
> an inclination thereto of many days together: so the nature of war consisteth not in
> actual fighting, but in the known disposition thereto during all the time there is
> no assurance to the contrary.
>
> Thomas Hobbes, *Leviathan* (1651) p. 1, ch. 13

1 Developing Countries at War

The frequent incidence of civil conflict in poor countries[1] and its tendency to recur
mean that it is responsible for some of the most serious aspects of underdevelopment—
including persistent malnutrition, endemic disease, poor education and lack of infrastructure as well as the absence of human security. However, analysis of the economic
and social developments of countries at war has been largely neglected by development
economists, while those authors who do address conflict tend to focus on the politics of
war, or on post-war reconstruction.[2] Yet the topic should be central to any analysis of
poverty and human development. This was the motivation for our study of poor economies at war, the results of which are presented in this book and its companion *War and
Underdevelopment: The Economic and Social Consequences of Conflict*. The first volume provides an analytical framework within which to consider the issues. It draws on the detailed
case studies presented in this volume, a wider statistical sample of countries in conflict,
and cross-section studies of topics ranging from fiscal policy to child welfare. *War and
Underdevelopment: The Economic and Social Consequences of Conflict* demonstrates that by
far the greater part of the economic and social costs of war is 'indirect' in the sense of
being caused by the dislocation of markets, the collapse of government, forced migration,
declining production, and foreign exchange losses rather than by battle deaths and material
destruction as such. It comes to some significant policy conclusions which if implemented
could contribute substantially to the reduction of human costs in conflict situations.

This second volume of our study contains eight case studies which examine seven
countries in depth, using primary sources. Important insights can be gleaned from
these case studies because they reveal the interaction between political and economic

---

[1] Of the 48 poor countries classified by the United Nations as 'least developed' half have experienced
significant wars in the last quarter of the twentieth century, while most of the others exhibit the signs of economic and social fragility which appear to worsen the effects of conflict (FitzGerald 2000).

[2] See Ch. 1, Vol. I.

developments, between external and domestic actors, between military and civilians, and between leaders and led. These interactions turn out to be invariably highly complex and sometimes counter-intuitive; they form an essential complement to the comparative analysis based on internationally available statistics and secondary documentary sources.

This chapter provides an introduction to our eight case studies. The analytical framework which provided the background to the case studies, set out fully in the first volume, is summarized in Section 2 of this chapter. Section 3 explains our selection of countries to be investigated and provides a comparative overview of the main findings of the country studies. Finally, Section 4 provides an overview of the conclusions of the study as a whole and our key policy recommendations.

2   The Economic and Social Consequences of Conflict

2.1   *Wartime Entitlement Loss*

Deaths as a result of physical force account for only a small proportion of the suffering induced by war in developing countries. Far larger numbers die indirectly from internal wars—from the famine and disease that results from the economic and social turbulence—than from the fighting itself. This is one of the major differences between wars between industrial countries and those within developing countries. To understand these indirect effects, the behaviour of the economy during conflict needs to be understood, and how this translates into dramatic changes in conditions of living for vulnerable populations.

The approach adopted in our study traces the consequences for the entitlements of vulnerable households of macro- and mesolevel[3] changes due to conflict. These household entitlements we divide into five categories: market entitlements derived from the purchasing power of income earned in the market, from paid employment, marketed goods and services, enterprise profits or financial assets; direct entitlements arising from subsistence production and household services;[4] public entitlements arising from goods, services or transfers supplied by the state; civic entitlements provided by the local community and NGOs; and extra-legal entitlements in the form of cash or goods taken by force, including looting and theft.[5] Generally, market and public entitlements, especially for vulnerable households, can be expected to decline as a consequence of conflict, while direct, civic, and extra-legal entitlements may rise as survival strategies emerge.

---

[3] We employ the term 'mesolevel' rather than 'sectoral' because the concept embraces not only production sectors as such (for example, agriculture) but also the fiscal sector, traded versus non-traded sectors, regional markets and so on—all of which have their own institutional structure which mediate between the macroeconomy (national and international) and the microeconomy (that is, the household or firm). The impact of a macroeconomic shift (for example, devaluation) on firms and households—and thus on production, distribution and accumulation—depends on the intervening mesoeconomic behaviour.

[4] Where much of women's work is concentrated, of course.

[5] In theory, market entitlements are distributed according to wealth, while in an ideal world, public entitlements are distributed equally among all citizens, and civic entitlements to particular membership groups defined by locality, religion, need, etc., while extra-legal entitlements do not exist. In practice, above all in developing countries in wartime, access to all five of these means of distribution is complex, uncertain, and above all unequal.

war

The interaction between war and the economy affects all these entitlements.[6] At the macrolevel, the mining of agricultural land and roads and the destruction of infrastructure such as power supplies and bridges, when combined with human flight, results in severe disruptions to production. Shortages of inputs are caused by the initial output loss and the subsequent decline in imports due to reductions in foreign exchange earnings; the impact on output is worsened by rising transactions costs as markets are dislocated, uncertainty among producers increases and 'social capital' in the form of inter-personal trust and administrative efficiency deteriorates. The fall in national income, often accompanied by a weakening in the administrative machinery and an expanding informal economy of smugglers, artisans, and petty traders, is likely to lead to a decline in government revenue at a time when public expenditure needs are rising due both to increased expenditure on the military and to the plight of vulnerable groups. The rising budget deficits which result, if not covered by foreign aid, lead to inflationary pressures which are increased by supply bottlenecks and lack of confidence in the national currency.[7] Relative price shifts and supply constraints are likely to lead to a switch in activities within the economy, towards less traded, transaction-intensive activities, such as subsistence agriculture, and away from manufacturing. Civil war also tends to result in heavy development costs. Not only is much existing physical, financial, and human capital reduced through deliberate destruction, capital flight, and forced migration, but also the routine replacement and long-term expansion of that stock are attenuated as uncertainty reduces investment levels, fewer children go to school, preventive health coverage shrinks, and market institutions break down.

These changes in the economy have serious implications for entitlements. Market entitlements can be expected to be reduced through loss of employment as well as the effects of rising inflation on real earnings, and public entitlements to social services are likely to be cut as total government revenue falls and a higher share of government expenditure goes to the military. However, direct entitlements would be expected to rise, as people retreat from the market and rely more on their own production. Civic entitlements may rise to compensate for the fall in public entitlements, but this depends on the responsiveness of communities and NGOs to the conflict situation. In general extra-legal entitlements rise in wartime—since the opportunities for such non-legal activities are much greater; however while some households gain from these opportunities, others obviously lose.

Apart from the effects of the actual fighting, human suffering thus arises from the decline in entitlements as well as an increased burden on the rest of the household when some family members go to fight, and may be killed, or disabled. Poor households suffer further when flight is necessary to avoid violence or find food, when they travel long distances on foot, and are exposed to contagious disease in camps. What few assets they have in the form of land, cattle, or housing is lost, as are their children's opportunity to acquire skills and confidence.

---

[6] See Ch. 1 in Vol. I.

[7] In terms of the simple monetary identity ($Mv = PT$), there is not only an increasing supply of money (M) but also a reduction in real transactions (T) and a rise in the velocity of circulation (v), the combination of which must therefore be accompanied by a rise in prices (P).

This general model, which admits of many variations, provided the background hypotheses for the detailed case studies in this volume. Our aim in these was to explore how these mechanisms worked in reality—whether in fact these *were* the main ways that the economic effects of war translated into human consequences.

2.2   Macroeconomic Behaviour in Wartime

Macroeconomic behaviour during war exhibits particular structural and behavioural characteristics that need to be taken into account in the design of policy.[8] Neither the policy approach of most wartime governments nor that advocated by the IMF are generally appropriate. Wartime governments tend to rely on deficit financing, price controls to suppress the inflationary consequences, and import rationing to contain the trade balance. However, such policies typically discriminate against small producers (particularly peasants), and undermine export incentives. Moreover, the controls are rarely effective in preventing inflation in the presence of severe monetary imbalances, and they encourage black-market trade. The foreign-exchange shortages which result have negative multiplier effects on production. Not only do the macro policies commonly adopted tend to reduce the possibilities of economic growth in the medium term, but they can fuel the conflict itself by causing discontent among the groups adversely affected, notably the peasantry and those whose employment and earnings possibilities have been undermined.

Bilateral donors can unwittingly contribute to such macroeconomic mismanagement by providing resources which disguise the negative distributive effects of these policies. IMF policies are rarely adopted in the midst of violent strife—but where they are the standard formula of government expenditure cuts, exchange rate liberalization, and abandonment of market interventions are grossly inappropriate.[9] As far as the macro-economy is concerned, excessive credit restrictions worsen the production situation, while any anti-inflationary effects are offset by currency depreciation. The severe cut-backs in government expenditure make it very difficult for the government to sustain essential health and education services, or provide food relief, all vital to prevent a sharp worsening in entitlements. The removal of import controls prevents the government channelling scarce foreign exchange into the maintenance of essential production (including exports) and priority consumption.

Clearly, an appropriate macro-adjustment package must be designed in terms of the specific needs of the economy: the country studies in this book demonstrate just how important the changing institutional context can be. None the less, the desirable alternative adjustment packages invariably contain two key elements: first, the avoidance of excess budget deficits by increasing revenue rather than by reducing social expenditure; and second, the maintenance of primary production (particularly by small farmers) through the maintenance of real prices and input supply. The inevitable need to reduce consumption in wartime should be accompanied by a vehicle for household savings

---

[8]   See Ch. 2, Vol. I.

[9]   The industrial economies, of course, have always applied extensive controls in wartime.

—possibly in the form of land distribution—so as both to preserve entitlements and strengthen the capacity for post-war reconstruction.[10]

2.3 The Functionality of War

War is often regarded as irrational and chaotic, an unreasoned aberration from 'normal' life. A closer examination of the political economy of war in developing countries[11] challenges this conclusion, arguing that despite the social costs the private benefits make war rational for key actors. Unless these incentives, and the mechanisms by which they develop, are understood it is impossible to comprehend the workings of the wartime economy. By extension, attempts at peace-making will be ineffective or impermanent unless the private functions of war are addressed.

This approach constitutes an important corrective to much of the literature on conflicts in developing countries, which tends to focus only on the 'losers' or 'costs' of war, ignoring the 'beneficiaries' or 'gains'. The gains are mainly economic: new profit opportunities that arise, for example, for import-substituting industrialists and makers of uniforms on the one hand and smugglers and soldiers on the other. However, they can also be social and psychological: previously marginalized individuals and groups may gain a new role and sense of purpose. The mechanisms of gain are both legal—such as the new opportunities in the informal sector—and extra-legal[12] such as theft and smuggling. Gains for some are matched by losses for others in many cases—directly in the case of theft and indirectly in the case of black-market trading—but in other cases the opportunity to develop labour-intensive activities (such as vehicle repairs) may actually add to the productivity of the economy. Careful exploration of the political economy of these gains and losses is essential not only to clarify the economic and social consequences of conflict but also to understand the motivations which shape and prolong wars.

2.4 Some Empirical Estimates of the Costs of Conflict

The incidence of war has increased since 1950, rising from 8 wars in which more than a thousand people died in any one year in the early 1950s to 27 in the first half of the 1990s.[13] Africa has been the worst affected region with 1.5 per cent of the population dying from direct killing or war-related famine between 1960 and 1995, while for the other regions the equivalent rate was about 0.5 per cent less. Low-income countries were much more severely affected than other developing nations. Careful examination of the available data for the 25 countries worst affected by war over these years—with over 0.5 per cent of their population dying between 1960 and 1995—reveals some common patterns.

Almost all countries showed negative effects on per capita income growth, food production, investment, savings, and exports. Most countries also showed worsening

[10] A parallel can be drawn with Keynes's proposals in *How to Pay for the War* for industrial remuneration in wartime Britain, see Ch. 2, Vol. I.

[11] See Ch. 3, Vol. I by David Keen.

[12] 'Extra-legal' (or 'non-legal') rather than 'illegal' because the rule of law itself no longer obtains.

[13] See Ch. 4, Vol. I.

budget deficits and accelerating inflation. However, economic behaviour did not always conform to our 'standard model' of the conflict economy as set out above. For example: tax revenue fell as expected in some countries—with very sharp falls in a few cases—but actually *rose* as a proportion of national income in others. There was also divergence of behaviour on social expenditure which also rose in a few cases, although it fell in the majority. Imports generally did better than expected, despite the near-universal fall in export earnings, reflecting continued foreign aid and countries' ability to borrow during conflict; in all countries external debt rose massively. People's well-being—as indicated by their access to basic services, nutrition levels, and infant mortality rates—generally worsened, but there were a few cases in which government managed to protect aspects of human life, despite the adverse circumstances.

Two summary variables provide a rough indicator of the economic and social costs of conflict in each country: the cumulative loss of national income and the accumulated increase in infant mortality, as compared with non-war economies in the region. The economic costs are summarized by the total loss in income from one year before the war started to five years after it ended, estimated as the cumulative difference between actual growth rates and the growth rate of the (non-war affected) region. The results of the calculations show considerable variation, with very high costs in some cases (for example, with cumulative income loss of 48 times 1995 national income in the case of Iraq during the Iran–Iraq war) and very low costs in others such as El Salvador which, in fact, grew faster than the regional average. The social costs are summarized by a similar calculation for the infant mortality rate (IMR), while here the decline (or rise) is compared with the downward trend in the (non-war affected) region as a whole. Additional infant deaths of over 3 per cent of the 1995 population occurred in Cambodia and over 2 per cent in Uganda, but no additional infant deaths were indicated for Mozambique, El Salvador, and Guatemala.

Children are among the worst victims of wars[14]—partly because nutritional deprivation of food, health services, education, and family stability in childhood can last a lifetime in the form of physical, intellectual, and psychological trauma. In the West at least, we tend to view children as a privileged group who should be protected from worldly cares: yet during wars, they are not only frequently deprived of their basic needs but also may be left to fend for themselves and perform 'adult' tasks ranging from farming and childcare to military service.[15] Humanitarian agencies tend to conceptualize childhood along Western lines, assuming that any economic or fighting role they undertake must be harmful. This view of childhood—which is not widely shared in many developing countries—leads many agencies to advocate the removal of children from war zones, often unaccompanied by their families, and even sometimes their removal from the country. The separation of these children from their families can be permanent, and even if temporary may be more damaging to children than if they stayed with their families or communities in the country at war. 'Targeting' children for relief within a country may be less harmful, but is likely to be ineffective as families balance their resources in

[14] See Ch. 6, Vol. I by Eric Greitens.
[15] Even the 'Western' view is relatively recent, of course; young men entered both the British army and navy as young as 12 in the nineteenth century.

Table 1.1 Cumulative losses in infant lives lost, and GDP lost in war-affected countries[a]

Country	Estimated cumulative loss in infant lives, 1965–94 (% of 1994 population)	Cumulative loss in income 1965–90 (as % 1995 GDP)
Angola	0.73	−1.48
Burundi	0.13	[b]
Ethiopia	1.57	−3.95
Liberia	1.76	−1.56
Mozambique	[b]	−2.83
Sierra Leone	0.57	−1.47
Somalia	1.1	−1.72
Sudan	0.1	−0.5
Uganda	2.03	−0.5
El Salvador	[b]	−5.67
Guatemala	[b]	[b]
Nicaragua	2.2	−13.5
Iran	0.93	−10.99
Iraq	1.5	−48.06
Lebanon	0.35	na
Cambodia	3.18	na

[a] Cumulative losses are estimated for war-affected years, defined to include the year preceding the war and the five years following the end of the war. Where wars have not yet or only recently ended the last year for which data are available is taken as the end of the war. The actual developments are compared with the average for the region excluding war-affected countries over the war-affected period.
  [b] Indicates that infant mortality rate fell more than the non-war regional average, or income grew more than non-war regional average.
na = not available.
Source: Vol. I, Tables 4.16 and 4.17.

the way they think best for family survival, which may involve giving priority to adult members of the family. The best way to support children physically and psychologically is to support the family and community as a whole.

2.5 *International Humanitarian Relief versus Global Market Forces*

Food aid is perhaps the most visible-and indeed symbolic-way in which outside donors interact with war economies.[16] The purported objective of the 'international community' is humanitarian. Yet numerous studies have shown that this objective is frequently not achieved despite large amounts of resources devoted to it. The normal 'humanitarian' view of food aid ignores its economic and political economy roles, and it is these functions which can undermine the apparently humanitarian intentions of donors. The impact varies according to the context, especially the political situation, as the histories of food aid to Afghanistan, Mozambique, and Sudan illustrate.

[16] See Ch. 7, Vol. I.

In Afghanistan its main role was *outside* the country in the refugee camps in Iran and Pakistan. Availability of food there facilitated the mass migration of nearly a third of the population, which seriously weakened production within the country. In Mozambique the food aid which permitted the survival of large numbers was distributed by the government and NGOs—much of it through camps. Food reached those in need because the Frelimo government facilitated its distribution throughout the country, including enemy-controlled areas. However, food supplies to camps meant that people left their own farms for long periods, undermining production and thus food security itself. In contrast, the political economy of Sudan meant that the vast inflow of food aid was mainly not used for its humanitarian objective but rather as an instrument of war. Food was used by the Northern government to prosecute the war, to feed their own soldiers and to force Southerners into camps where they were badly treated. Food supplies also became a source of private gain from war: it could be sold privately or used to maintain fighting bands. In Mozambique and Sudan, sales of donated foods contributed substantially to government finance. This in turn sustained military expenditure, and in the case of Mozambique also helped sustain basic needs expenditures. These cases clearly illustrate the multiple role played by food aid and the need to understand the political economy dimension, in particular, if it is to be effectively used as a humanitarian instrument rather than a weapon of war.

Whatever the efficacy of humanitarian relief, it appears that the ability to wage war in developing countries—and thus its human cost—depends on the operations and regulation of the global economy.[17] The international financial agencies claim that there is a positive relationship between integration into the world economy and the reduction of conflict. On the one hand, it is argued that the consequent increase in economic growth will generate more remunerative employment and permit greater expenditure on social services in the medium term. On the other hand, it is suggested that the process of privatization reduces the discretionary powers of the state, strengthens civil society and thereby reduces the likelihood of war. Conflict is seen as arising in cases of 'state failure' associated with corruption, rent-seeking behaviour, neglect of small-scale agriculture, government control over the economy, and financial repression. In other words the problem is domestic and political in origin, although aid donors can use conditionality appropriately in order to make the state more efficient and democratic.

In consequence, the application of orthodox stabilization and adjustment policies even *during* a conflict is seen as contributing to a peaceful solution. This view contrasts sharply with the view of others to the effect that rapid integration into the world economy can actually reduce social cohesion and intensify conflict, due to the creation of open unemployment as firms attempt to recover competitiveness by shedding labour, and governments reduce the civil service in order to service debt, on the one hand; and there is a reduction of social services coverage and neglect of vulnerable groups as the state is scaled back, on the other. The process of privatization increases inequality as state managers become private entrepreneurs, raise tariffs and

---

[17] See Ch. 8, Vol. I.

shed labour; while the deregulation of markets weakens solidarity within communities and neighbourhoods.

In practice, private finance for productive purposes is likely to dry up rapidly in conflict situations. Multinational firms cease new investment projects even if they are prepared to continue operations: their concern is to protect their existing assets, and to establish profitable relationships with the eventual victors in the conflict. In consequence, new private finance is likely to be linked to 'informal' activities such as arms supplies and illegal exports. Globalization itself creates trans-border markets which are independent of any one nation state, and are not subject to a system of international public or private law. Developing countries at war form part of an 'international informal sector' that is not subject to any set of rules other than short-term profit. This international informal economy works through new networks (such as the narcotics trade or through diasporas) and offshore centres established for tax and legal evasion purposes. These networks and centres create new opportunities for financing conflict because they can supply arms or foreign exchange needed to get them; and they can market smuggled goods, particularly those with a high unit value such as narcotics, timber, and gems. New financial groups emerge, often based on the extraordinary profits available from wartime trading and in some connection with armed groups, either supporting or opposing the government. Their financial power means that they may enjoy considerable official support despite the fact they often operate at the margin of the law. While finance is available from the private sector (albeit of a dubious legality) to finance the war, multilateral lenders rarely restructure—let alone suspend or cancel—debt for countries in conflict, even though this would release funds for development and protecting the vulnerable. Indeed, if multilateral debt is not serviced on time, further lending is suspended and the whole principal becomes payable. As a result, bilateral aid is often diverted to maintaining multilateral debt service rather than alleviating the economic burden of conflict on vulnerable groups. This reflects a more general problem, that debt renegotiation in conflict situations is an ad hoc arrangement responding to short-term liquidity problems rather than part of a comprehensive approach to peace building or the protection of vulnerable groups.

Official bilateral credits—mainly export credit guarantee facilities—are often used to place pressure on the governments in conflict economies; as are longer-term development loans and multilateral loan programmes. However, there is no evidence that this has affected the level of conflict in practice, while as in the case of trade embargoes it is probable that the economic cost of financial restrictions is likely to affect vulnerable groups disproportionately unless the debtor government makes special provision to protect them. Indeed if the development finance to be cancelled was properly designed in the first place—in other words that it followed DAC criteria and was clearly targeted at poverty reduction—then financial sanctions would affect vulnerable groups disproportionately.

Finally, at present humanitarian relief is usually mobilized *after* conflict has broken out, and thus has to face weakened administrative, production, and transport systems as well as large population movements leading to health and nutrition emergencies. Such intervention would be better used in preventing such emergencies from occurring in the first place.

3   The Country Studies

3.1   The Choice of Cases

Our choice of the seven countries to be studied was intended to reflect as broad a range of experience as possible. Hence we selected cases from each of the three main regions in the developing world: Mozambique, Sierra Leone, Sudan, and Uganda in Africa; Afghanistan and Sri Lanka in Asia; and Nicaragua in Latin America. We also included wars of different types: two in the last phase of the Cold War[18] where the divisions were largely ideological and related to geopolitics (Mozambique and Nicaragua); two largely instigated by governments attempting to suppress potential opposition to the state (Uganda and Sudan); two which occurred partly because of weak government which permitted rival groups to fight for power and resources (Sierra Leone and Afghanistan); two inspired by the separatist tendencies of groups located in distinct geographical areas (Sri Lanka and Sudan); and two in which ethnicity was the main mobilizing factor (Sri Lanka and Sudan). This list itself demonstrates how causal categories overlap which complicates analysis. In addition, different economic structures will affect the cost of conflict, so we took examples of countries that are extremely poor (Afghanistan, Uganda, and Mozambique); countries with mineral resources (Sierra Leone) or more modernized export agriculture (Sudan); and of countries with somewhat more advanced industrial sectors (Nicaragua and Sri Lanka).

Despite our best efforts, our relatively small[19] sample of developing countries in conflict and the large variance in experience mean that generalization is hazardous. Indeed it is for this reason that in Volume I we have supplemented the individual studies by wider statistical analysis and the exploration of 'cross-cutting' themes such as food aid and the plight of children. Moreover, we avoided the temptation to impose a single methodology on the case studies, deliberately building a multidisciplinary team of researchers so as to combine economics, sociology, anthropology, politics, and history in a single political economy approach. This means that the case studies demonstrate different ways of approaching reality.

For example, one of our two Mozambique studies (in Chapter 3) and the Nicaraguan study emphasize the macroeconomy and largely rely on national statistical sources; while the Sierra Leone and Sudanese studies take a social anthropology approach, drawing on contemporary documentation and interviews. The Sri Lankan and Ugandan studies combine statistical material and interviews, and focus on a particular war-affected area. Perhaps the most illuminating contrast is between the sociological view 'from below' in the second Mozambique study (Chapter 4), exploring the emergence of informal urban markets in detail on the basis of a survey, and the macroeconomic view of the same country 'from above' in Chapter 3.

Some characteristics of the countries and the studies are summarized in Table 1.2.

---

[18] When the geopolitical divide was already blurred and countries such as Mozambique and Nicaragua could trade with and receive aid from both East and West.

[19] That is, 7 out of the 25 significant cases identified in Ch. 4 of Vol. I.

Table 1.2 Some characteristics of case-study countries

Country case	Income level, 1981 (US$)	Agrarian sector (as % of GDP, 1981)	Manufacturing sector (% GDP, 1981)	% of total exports, 1980			Nature of war	Nature of state	Approach adopted in study
				Agriculture	Minerals; fuels	Manufactures			
Afghanistan	240[a]	60[b]	4[c]	74[d]	13[d]	13[d]	Low-intensity, pervasive; destruction of infrastructure	Post-Soviet, very weak	Economic and political
Mozambique	140[a]	45[a]	9[a]	86[d]	11[d]	3[d]	Low-intensity, pervasive; destruction of infrastructure	Strong	I. macroeconomic; II. sociological
Nicaragua	860	20	26	83	3	14	Regional focus; low-intensity	Strong	Macroeconomic; political economy
Sierra Leone	320	31	6	48[d]	8[d]	44[de]	Low-intensity, pervasive	Very weak	Political economy
Sri Lanka	300	28	16	65	16	19	Strong regional focus	Strong	Economic macro, meso, and micro
Sudan	380	38	6	96	1	3	Strong regional focus	Strong	Political economy
Uganda	236	75	4	99[d]	1[d]	0[d]	Centrally located	Became weak	Economic macro, meso, and micro

[a] 1978; [b] estimate in country study; [c] pre-war (1974/5) estimate for industry from country study; [d] 1977; [e] probably mainly unpolished diamonds.

Sources: World Bank, *World Development Reports* (various years); and country studies.

3.2   Afghanistan

In Chapter 2, Marsden and Samman show how the war in Afghanistan was marked by pervasive foreign intervention, the near-collapse of government institutions, and massive migration from the country. For nearly twenty years, foreign financial and military support helped prolong the struggle and worsen internal divisions. While conflict had domestic origins, it was rapidly absorbed into Cold War politics, with Western-supported groups fighting the Soviet-backed government. After this government had fallen and the Cold War ended, the war continued as an armed struggle between Moslem fundamentalists and more secular groups aggravated by ethnic divisions. External powers continued to supply arms and finance to different groups. National income fell dramatically following widespread destruction of infrastructure and massive forced migration: agricultural output and formal sector activities were worst affected. The negative effects of the virtual disintegration of the state and the resulting collapse of public services were to some extent offset by household survival strategies, including smuggling and opium production as well as migration across the frontier. Extensive NGO action also helped provide civic entitlements which partially substituted for lost public entitlements.

None the less, the war in Afghanistan inflicted severe economic and human costs. Per capita calorie consumption fell from 2,186 in 1980 to 1,573 in 1992 and malnutrition increased sharply. With the decline in sanitation and health services, the incidence of communicable diseases rose dramatically. Yet there was not extensive starvation of the kind experienced in Sudan and some demographic and health-related indices actually improved over the course of the conflict. There was also a wide disparity in the impact of war between and within groups. For example, the better-off were most able to flee overseas; while the worst-affected appear to have been urban households headed by widows and the elderly or disabled. Women were particularly badly affected by the Taliban take-over in 1992, which reversed the social gains they had made in the two previous decades of conflict. The conflict in Afghanistan also inflicted long-term development costs through its destruction of many forms of capital. Human, institutional, and cultural capital—vital for economic growth and social development —sustained particularly heavy costs from the insecurity bred by the type of warfare pursued, notably the indiscriminate use of violence against civilians and the extensive deployment of landmines.

3.3   Mozambique

Except for a brief period of relative stability shortly after independence in 1974, Mozambique experienced almost continuous civil war for nearly twenty years. The Renamo rebel force, with the logistical and military support of South Africa, waged a low-intensity conflict aimed at destabilizing the government in Maputo. Tactics of sabotage and terrorism against civilians were adopted by Renamo, as was the deliberate destruction of physical capital and food production. The undermining of agriculture was particularly damaging, as over 80 per cent of the population worked in agriculture prior to the war. The conflict in Mozambique proved extraordinarily destructive in terms both of human costs—with nearly a million deaths, and many more displaced—and economic destruction. By 1986, real GDP was below 60 per cent of its level in 1980.

Starting from the assumption that war can be modelled as a shock to the economy, in Chapter 3 Bruck explores how one might expect different economic agents to alter their behaviour in conflict conditions, and tests his conclusions against actual developments. He predicts that war will reduce output, long-term growth, consumption, and welfare, and increase government debt, as a result of direct effects arising from the physical destruction of capital and increased government deficit finance, as well as indirect effects stemming from increased uncertainty and higher transaction costs. Although data deficiencies in Mozambique make it difficult to test this model, most of the evidence supports his theoretical predictions. There was massive destruction of capital during the civil war; export agriculture suffered more damage than the subsistence sector, and, in general, the formal, tradable sectors were more vulnerable than informal, non-tradable activities. High levels of uncertainty had adverse consequences for social organization and transactions efficiency, and private investment collapsed. Schools and hospitals were destroyed, families displaced and traumatized, and the network of rural commercial structures such as warehouses, shops, and trading posts eradicated as part of the insurgency strategy.

Public finance also suffered: the real value of tax receipts fell by half during the 1980s and fiscal deficits increased each year as military expenditure rose, even though public investment expenditure fell significantly during the 1980s. The destruction in capital, the increase in uncertainty, the rise in transactions costs, and the increased fiscal deficit led to falling output and growth, as predicted. There was a consequent deterioration in welfare, with a worsening in most social indicators—particularly mortality and literacy rates. However, contrary to the model's predictions the savings ratio fell. The combination of producer uncertainty and dislocated markets meant that the economy initially recovered very slowly even after peace was achieved in 1992.

Chingono explores a key aspect of Mozambique's war economy at the household level in Chapter 4—the emergence of large informal urban markets. As violence deprived people in the countryside of their previous means of subsistence and drove them from their homes, they sought new ways to survive in the cities to which they moved. Given the virtual collapse of formal-sector opportunities, most became 'barefoot entrepreneurs', creating a burgeoning informal economy. The chapter documents this process in Manica Province in south-west Mozambique, where a large range of activities was actually stimulated by wartime strategies: these included peri-urban agriculture and horticulture, pottery, handicrafts, metalworking, food processing, transport, and petty trading. Activities were clearly stratified by gender and class: the more lucrative activities (such as trade in second-hand clothing and manufactured commodities) were largely the domain of men; while women traded mainly in the less profitable basic consumer goods and agricultural products. Children also participated, working for themselves or to supplement family income, by trading or producing simple products.

The 'grass-roots economy' thus involved considerable income differentiation: many of those engaged in illegal activities made huge profits from bypassing the restrictions enforced by conflict, while others managed to obtain only bare subsistence. Chingono comes to the controversial—yet compelling—conclusion that in part civil conflict played a constructive economic role in Mozambique not only by permitting large numbers of households to survive but also by unleashing an 'entrepreneurial ethos' which benefited the economy as a whole. In contrast to Bruck's conclusion in Chapter 3, Chingono thus finds that the war may have ultimately had a beneficial effect on the organizational capacity of Mozambique by fostering new forms of social capital and relations while destroying the old ones. This helped to offset some of the negative economic impact of war and may also have provided a basis for post-war reconstruction.

3.4 *Nicaragua*

In Chapter 5, FitzGerald and Grigsby examine the impact of macroeconomic strategies on Nicaragua's wartime economy. The Sandinistas' economic policies emphasized the provision of basic needs, and the state enlarged its economic role through the nationalization of the properties of the pro-US elite and the distribution of essential commodities. Peasant resistance, however, was aroused by the failure to redistribute land and poor rural terms of trade, and formed the backbone of the Contra rebellion of 1981 which was strongly supported by the USA. The rebels' strategy was one of low-intensity conflict, aimed at political de-legitimization of the government and the promotion of economic chaos, involving heavy economic costs. Macroeconomic imbalance was worsened by the war, with the destruction of productive inputs, particularly in the export agricultural sector. There was a large decline in national income, with cumulative losses over the 1980–90 period estimated at some US$2 billion. Inflation also accelerated as a result of deficit financing to support the ambitious basic needs projects and greatly increased military spending. The conflict also had a heavy indirect impact through the 'multiplier' effect on domestic production of lost foreign exchange, which resulted not only from declining export production but also from the effects of the US trade embargo and the cessation of loans from international financial agencies.

Despite the rise in military expenditure, social-sector expenditure rose during the war and the basic-needs strategy meant that, apart from the large number of war casualties, effects on households were comparatively mild. Most social indicators, including literacy, infant mortality, school enrolment, and life expectancy, improved up to 1987. However, the orthodox stabilization programme adopted in the late 1980s failed to stimulate production while inflation undermined the distributional objectives of the reforms. International aid flows contributed to the economic crisis by allowing the government to postpone tackling the underlying economic problems of peasant production. The long-term development costs of war in Nicaragua were also large with destruction of both physical and institutional capital, with high uncertainty leading to very low levels of private investment. The erosion of trust between social actors may have had even more negative effects, associated with the marked decline in the effectiveness of Nicaraguan institutions. The authors conclude that in both wartime and post-war reconstruction, macroeconomic strategies must incorporate the special structural features of an economy in conflict.

3.5 Sierra Leone

The civil war in Sierra Leone has imposed considerable costs, as Keen shows in Chapter 6. Tactics on both sides involved indiscriminate violence against civilians, causing major disruption and displacement. By 1995, nearly 900,000 civilians had been displaced and 300,000 killed out of a total population of 4.3 million. During 1985–94, GNP per head is estimated to have declined at an average rate of 1.9 per cent in real terms. However, the economic decline in the Sierra Leone economy cannot be solely attributed to the effects of war. Before the conflict a pattern of economic development based on the elite's exploitation of Sierra Leone's considerable mineral wealth, combined with widespread corruption, rendered the country one of the world's poorest. Economic activity increasingly fell outside official control: diamond production, in particular, was controlled by a small group of Lebanese traders, who were Presidential allies. By the mid–1980s, 70 per cent of all exports left the country through clandestine channels, leading to a sharp decline in state revenue.

The purported war aims of the Revolutionary United Front (RUF) were to seek political changes and in particular to reduce government corruption. However, once the war started a new economic logic took over. In the context of severely constrained economic and educational opportunities generated by decades of underdevelopment and corruption, the RUF provided a vehicle for a wide variety of groups to make money. Previously marginalized groups, particularly youths with little opportunity for formal-sector employment, benefited economically from looting and participating in trading networks that had earlier been tightly controlled by the elite, particularly the illegal trade in diamond production. Aid resources also constituted an important additional wartime benefit for those elements of the government able to 'cream off' a substantial share for their private business ventures.

With key groups on both sides gaining from the civil war, a perverse logic ensued in which the warring factions took actions that seem calculated to perpetuate conflict, with the great majority of violent acts being against unarmed civilians. Keen concludes that there may be little chance of engineering a lasting peace in Sierra Leone unless the underlying economic and psychological functions of war are properly understood. Simply aiming to secure an end to the violence without addressing the nature of the peacetime political economy that generated conflict in the first place, including the limited economic opportunities available to young people, may doom the viability of peace-making schemes.

3.6 Sri Lanka

In Chapter 7, O'Sullivan seeks to account for Sri Lanka's success in maintaining robust growth and household entitlements during war, in strong contrast to the other cases studied. Violence erupted between the Liberation Tamil Tigers of Eelam (LTTE) and government forces in 1983; the LTTE then gained control of the northern and some parts of the eastern provinces, creating a *de facto* state. Violence was mainly confined to these areas, but the conflict produced very limited macroeconomic dislocation. In fact, the Sri Lankan economy actually grew faster than in the pre-war period and foreign exchange earnings were largely maintained.

One explanation for the limited aggregate impact of the war is the restricted geographic area subject to direct combat. A strong government also lessened insecurity and uncertainty which helped to sustain investor confidence. Moreover, at the outset of the civil war, the Sri Lankan economy possessed a relatively high level of human development, which, together with structural adjustment programmes from the late 1970s, led to a flexible production sector which helped Sri Lanka to avoid heavy macroeconomic costs. There was actually a *decrease* in the measured incidence of poverty, and a continued improvement in human indicators outside the war zone. O'Sullivan attributes these surprising trends to the key role of public policy, which continued a long-standing commitment to universal provision of health and education services. Within the war zones there was some worsening of social indicators, but even there some indicators actually improved over the course of the war. The limited damage to household welfare in the war zone was largely due to the emergence of a complex network of official and quasi-official providers. Throughout the war period, the government continued to provide a steady proportion of expenditure to education and health in rebel-held areas. In the north-east, alternative societal structures developed to complement government initiatives, the LTTE ensuring that the supply of goods was distributed progressively favouring vulnerable groups. Local and international NGOs also helped to sustain welfare.

3.7   Sudan

While ethnic and religious tensions contributed to the outbreak of civil war in Sudan, economic motives also help to explain the recent violence. In Chapter 8, Keen highlights the material motives behind the Sudanese civil war. He argues that war represents the culmination of long-standing conflicts over resources (such as land, cattle, labour, and oil) and, more importantly, a means for certain groups to maximize the benefits of economic transactions through the exercise of force. The war in Sudan was thus shaped by the peacetime political economy.

For two centuries northern Arab interests have continually exploited the non-Muslim peoples of the south, plundering their material and manpower resources, and effectively denying them means of representation within the state. This pattern of uneven development persisted in the post-independence era, as southern groups were further marginalized economically and politically. Successive governments attempted to prop up this highly inequitable political economy, permitting powerful groups to exploit natural or human resources through the use of violence. By dividing and manipulating civil society government policy greatly aggravated ethnic and religious tensions; and the southern rebel Sudan People's Liberation Army (SPLA) was formed in 1983.

Khartoum used the war that followed to justify a strategy of violence aimed at maximizing extraction of resources from southerners. This not only led to famine, but also deprived victims of relief. The famine benefited northerners by forcing southerners to leave their homes in search of food, facilitating control over the territory for the expansion of mechanized farming, while the migration of famine victims provided a source of cheap or even slave labour for Sudanese Arab farmers. The economic and political practices underlying the civil war thus both perpetuated violence and undermined the efficacy of emergency aid. Keen concludes that neither humanitarian interventions nor peace-making will be successful unless the international community recognizes and addresses the rationality of violence.

3.8   Uganda

In Chapter 9, Matovu and Stewart and show that economic and social costs of conflict were particularly heavy in Uganda not only as a result of the direct destruction and death generated by combat, but also from the generalized instability generated by the Amin dictatorship. Indiscriminate state-sponsored violence was a primary cause of massive deaths, estimated at around 300,000 people during Amin's era, and 500,000 in Obote's second regime—some 4 per cent of the population. The prolonged political instability—including the whole Amin era as well as the war episodes—largely account for the heavy macro costs. Growth was negative during the years of fighting, and fluctuated around zero during the Amin years of instability. There was a large decline in exports and imports and an acceleration of inflation. Tax revenues dwindled to almost nothing.

Econometric analysis confirm these effects, indicating that the prolonged political disturbances had a larger impact than the specific war episodes. With the disruption of markets and rising transactions costs, subsistence agriculture rose and industrial activities declined. Within the public sector, defence spending crowded out expenditure on social services as a portion of the minimal government expenditure. There was a steady decline in both education and health as a percentage of GDP from the early 1970s. The combination of declining social expenditure and falling GDP translated into damaging declines in household welfare. Most social indicators worsened during the 1970–80 period, including calorie intake per person, primary enrolment, the ratio of doctors to people, and access to safe water. The results of a retrospective survey of people who had lived in the worst-affected war area give graphic expression to many of these negative microlevel effects of war.

One reason for the heavy costs was that no strong quasi-official or NGO response arose to counteract the collapse of revenues and reduced government health and education services, as occurred elsewhere. Informal survival strategies did develop but the range of activities appears to have been more limited than in Mozambique, geared towards trade and smuggling rather than production. In the 1990s, war continued in the periphery of the country, much of it related to disputes in neighbouring countries. These peripheral wars are still costly, perpetuating the state of underdevelopment in the areas affected, and involving a large rise in the share of military expenditure in the government budget which crowds out social and economic expenditures. However, the peripheral conflicts have not impeded economic growth for the country as a whole, and have been associated with some aggregate social progress.

4   Some Conclusions

4.1   Protecting the Poor

Taken as a whole, the case studies demonstrate that, as expected, conflict has heavy economic and social costs, arising from both direct and indirect effects of the wars on the economy. Few countries managed to contain the economic costs but a number managed to offset or even, to a considerable extent, to prevent the social costs by government action, while in some countries new household survival strategies, often supported by NGOs, helped to moderate the costs. Variations in the costs of conflict were due to three factors: first, the nature of the war—with prolonged and geographically pervasive conflicts being most costly; second, the nature of the government itself, with stronger and socially committed governments able to protect the poor, and ill-intentioned or weak governments unable to do so; and third, the offsetting actions of alternative governmental structures, communities, NGOs, and people themselves.

Strong governments committed to social progress were most effective in reducing the social costs of war—for example, in Sri Lanka, Mozambique, and Nicaragua. Alternative rebel government structures (as in Sri Lanka) and effective NGOs were also able to ameliorate the costs (as in Afghanistan). People's own survival strategies also made a contribution—with the development of a huge range of new income-earning activities, many exploiting the opportunities arising from the war economy—exemplified especially in Afghanistan and Mozambique. Flight was another survival strategy which protected very large numbers of people in Afghanistan—made possible by the refugee camps in Iran and Pakistan. The worst cases occurred where the government collapsed and no alternative structures developed (Uganda and Sierra Leone), or the government itself deliberately withheld services from particular areas (Sudan).

The economic costs were more difficult to avoid, since the physical destruction, market dislocation, raised uncertainty, reduced trust, and higher transactions costs are all intrinsic aspects of war. The costs were less where war was localized, and where the government sustained authority (as in Sri Lanka). Moreover, alternative structures, such as those of the LTTE in Sri Lanka, could provide a sufficiently stable structure for some economic activities to flourish. Alternative methods of exchange also developed to substitute for the structure of formal markets—for example for the transmission of money and goods in Afghanistan through informal networks. Macro policies were also important, often by default, particularly by permitting or preventing hyperinflation and the undermining of export incentives. Only Sri Lanka, among our sample of countries, succeeded in this regard. Avoidable macropolicy mistakes were partly responsible for economic collapse in Nicaragua and possibly Mozambique, which eventually undermined the social policies as well.

4.2   Drawing Policy Lessons

Some general policy findings do emerge from our studies, despite—or perhaps because of—their variety. One is that appropriate macro strategies can be devised in order to reduce the human cost of war. These include avoiding excess budgetary imbalances and price incentives and controls which discriminate against the productive sectors, especially exports. Revenue raising is an essential part of an appropriate macro wartime strategy as large expenditure cuts and premature market liberalization can be both socially and economically damaging in wartime—socially damaging because of the loss of public entitlements that typically ensue and the increasing inequality of incomes and market entitlements often associated with such changes; and economically damaging because markets cannot reach a stable equilibrium due to supply constraints, transactions costs, and high uncertainty. It is also necessary for governments to retain the ability to steer scarce imports to priority sectors. Investment is almost unavoidably reduced during war, although since the economic dislocation cuts deeply into the already low consumption levels of the bulk of the population, some reduction in the saving share may be desirable. Key reconstruction and maintenance projects need to be given priority, but the nature of the projects may need to be redesigned to a smaller scale and for ease of repair—which itself would increase their value to the rural population.

Ensuring adequate access to food and health services are the most important factors in supporting vulnerable groups, although mechanisms for doing so vary depending on the situation. In the case of nutrition not only are adequate food supplies necessary, but entitlements must also be sustained through employment, food subsidies, and monitoring and controlling food prices. The movement of rural people into camps clearly reduces domestic food-supply capacity, particularly for household subsistence; although this forced movement is sometimes unavoidable, it can also be a result of food aid being delivered late and only to camps. Effective health (and education) services need both sustained government expenditure and the redesign of service provision in order to fit wartime needs, including, for example, introducing mobile clinics and immunization campaigns.

Such policies, however, are only feasible in a context where there is a capable government which is committed to social and economic development. External agencies which wish to reduce the costs of war should, therefore, support such governments, avoiding undermining them by their economic or political policies. In practice, the opposite often happens: major powers deliberately supported rebels against the Nicaraguan government; the adjustment policies imposed on Mozambique by the Bretton Woods institutions weakened government capacity to support vulnerable groups; and in many African cases the channelling of aid through NGOs has undermined public-sector institutions. Of course, where the government is itself the source of vulnerability, or so weak itself that it cannot contribute to a solution, a different approach is needed. This may involve external agencies supporting alternative administrative structures (including rebel structures or local governments where they exist), or local NGOs and communities. None the less, such approaches need to be adopted with caution because they are likely further to weaken government structures upon which vulnerable groups ultimately depend.

4.3 The Political Economy of War and Peace

A recurring theme of our study has been that no solution to any of the war-related problems will be effective or lasting unless it incorporates a full understanding of the political economy of war. Wars are caused by deep horizontal inequalities in access to political and economic resources, and are likely to continue unless these are addressed. Wartime policy may do the reverse of what is needed in this respect, deepening existing inequalities, or creating new ones. In addition, the economic functions of war provide a powerful impetus to its initiation and prolongation. So long as those who orchestrate and carry out the violence gain much more from this than any realistic peacetime possibilities, war is likely to continue, or, if it stops the cessation will be temporary. This means that wartime policies should aim to reduce the economic gains from war and improve alternative opportunities. Some of the policies needed to sustain the economy and social conditions can be designed to contribute to this objective as well. For example, the less the opportunities for black-market activities, the fewer the war gains. Appropriate macro policies can reduce such opportunities by reducing excess demand and thus opportunities for speculation. Public-employment schemes are also justified not only by the need to ensure adequate food entitlements and to restore damaged infrastructure but also the more alternative jobs are available, the less the incentives for joining the fighting to make a living through extra-legal activities.

Finally, external actors—aid agencies, the international financial institutions, the NGOs, and the private sector—are themselves as much subject to forces of political economy as domestic actors. Their own private or institutional motivations—which include economic gain and political power—determine their actions in conflict economies as much as any professed desire of the 'international community' for peaceful development.[20] To be effective, policy proposals must also take into account the political economy of humanitarian assistance, international trade and foreign investment.

[20] See, for instance, de Waal (1997).

2

Afghanistan: The Economic and Social Impact of Conflict

PETER MARSDEN AND EMMA SAMMAN

1 Introduction

In most respects Afghanistan closely conforms to the model of a war-torn society. It exhibits all the expected features of macroeconomic decline, following the near-collapse of its political system. Conflict has lasted nearly twenty years in parts of the country, marked by periods of heavy fighting, the loss of nearly 1.5 million lives, and the displacement of some 8 million people. Central government, never strong, has occasionally been on the verge of collapse and often had to cede control over large areas of the country to local warlords. At present, although the Taliban controls most of Afghanistan, it is still challenged by rival heavily armed militias, entrenched through many years of fighting.

Government spending has fallen in all sectors except the military. Household entitlements have been correspondingly adversely affected. While certain groups of people—primarily families headed by widows and the disabled in cities—were particularly hard hit, several factors prevented the collapse of the formal economy from translating into devastating human costs: the ability of most of the population to retreat into subsistence production and/or the informal economy; the use of coping mechanisms including movement into adjoining countries; and NGO action to uphold the collective welfare.

This chapter attempts to measure the cost of war at macro- and mesolevel, and to assess its impact on individual households and communities. Throughout we have tried to draw comparisons between Afghanistan's pre-war and wartime performance. To establish counterfactual points of reference, Afghanistan has been compared with Nepal —which in many ways resembled Afghanistan prior to the war—and with the least-developed countries (LDCs) as a whole.

For data, we relied primarily on the United Nations (UN) and World Bank. The analysis also draws on fifteen visits one of the authors made to the region between 1989 and 1998 to assess humanitarian needs and operating conditions for NGOs.

2 Afghanistan pre-conflict

Afghanistan is a largely mountainous desert situated at the western edge of the Himalayan massif. The country's economy has relied largely on a subsistence base and

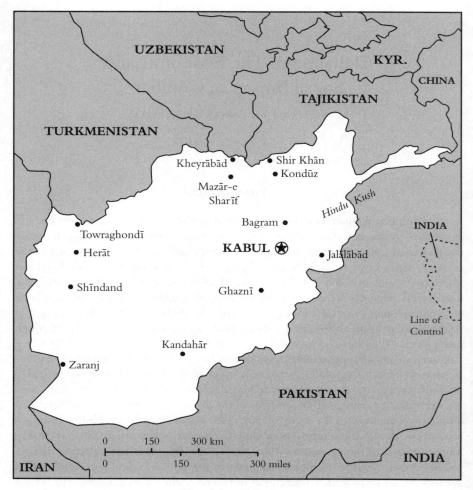

Map 2.1 Afghanistan

the cash economy has been slow to penetrate. In 1978, an estimated 85 per cent of the population lived in rural areas. The extended family served as the major economic and social unit, characterized by residential unity within a village or compound. After World War II, there was a growing trend for young people to seek work in the cities, breaking this residential unity. Traditional obligations, none the less, persisted. Adherence to Islam remained important.

Ethnically, Afghanistan is complex. There are six major ethnic groups: the Pushtuns; Tajiks; Uzbeks; Turkomans; Hazaras, and Baluch. These mostly have a common ethnic affinity with neighbouring populations. However, ethnic identities were not well established except among an elite; at the local level, relationships based on kinship and patron–client relations prevailed (Rubin 1997: 11). Prior to the Soviet invasion, the political system was characterized by non-Pushtuns' attempts to reduce the Pushtun stranglehold on government, which it had enjoyed since the eighteenth century.

The strategic interests of other countries have led to significant interference in Afghanistan's internal affairs. For centuries, present-day Afghanistan was a major trade route, and Russia had long sought to gain access to the Indian Ocean through it. This resulted in a tradition in Afghanistan of taxing transit traffic, of selling goods to passing traders, of banditry, and of Afghan traders themselves engaging in trade within the wider region. Britain became militarily involved in the country during the nineteenth century, and was twice defeated. The Soviet Union invaded in 1979 and remained for ten years. With the end of the Cold War, Pakistan, Iran, Saudi Arabia, and Russia have vied to exert influence and control.

Pakistan has long sought to establish a sympathetic Islamic government in Kabul with the objective of creating an Islamic axis stretching from Central Asia to its border with India, so strengthening its relative power. India sought to counter Pakistan's efforts by seeking influence with the government in Kabul, when possible, by providing material support. With the Taliban take-over of Kabul in 1996, India shifted its support to the opposition alliance in northern Afghanistan. Iran, concerned to avoid the emergence of a strong Sunni Islamic bloc, backed the elements resisting Pakistani influence and control. Saudi Arabia, in turn, provided funding for military initiatives aimed at reducing the power of Shi'a groups.

3 Nepal as Comparator

Like Afghanistan, Nepal is a small geographically remote country characterized by inhospitable terrain. Its population is nearly the same as that of Afghanistan, although Afghanistan is far larger and, therefore, less densely populated. Both countries are primarily agrarian, with a heavy emphasis on subsistence and handicraft production. Further, both are situated between much larger powers, which have historically tried to control them. Nepal is located next to India and China, and during the Cold War was of interest to both the USA and USSR. Nepal is ruled by a monarchy, as was Afghanistan until 1973. Until it adopted liberalizing reforms in the late 1980s, Nepal's economy was governed by centralized 5-year planning, as was Afghanistan's until 1992. Moreover, where the countries differ, Afghanistan would have had a clear developmental advantage: a larger economy; greater volume of trade; natural gas and mineral deposits; and much larger inflows of foreign aid.

4 Overview of the Conflict

Despite tension between the ruling Pushtuns and the other ethnic groups, the recent conflict had its origins in growing differences between those clinging to traditional customs and creeds and those espousing external ideologies.

At the turn of the century, this struggle surfaced with traditionalists opposing a minority who wished to modernise Afghanistan, following Western philosophies and technologies. The reformist agenda, which while remaining within the Islamic fold included the emancipation of women, provoked a conservative reaction from religious and traditional leaders. The reform movement went into abeyance until the 1960s, when those affiliated to universities again challenged the status quo. Two ideological movements gathered support: socialism on the USSR model; and radical Islam, advocating a new political ideology based on religion. The latter had close links with a similar movement in Pakistan. At first, the socialist movement, with strong Soviet backing, was in the ascendant. Indeed during the 1960s and 1970s, Afghanistan became increasingly economically and politically dependent on the USSR.

The King, Zahir Shah, responded positively to calls for reform but the pace of change was slow. In 1973, he was ousted in a coup by his cousin, Daoud. Initially, Daoud furthered the socialist aims, but when disagreements broke out he imprisoned some of their leaders. This internal split between the traditionalists and the modernists was aggravated by the actions of outside powers. Owing to its proximity to the Persian Gulf, Afghanistan assumed a position of importance in Cold War politics after the rise in oil prices in 1973. Both the USSR and USA increased their aid to the country; the Soviets also trained the army that launched a successful coup in 1978.

The People's Democratic Party of Afghanistan, the major socialist party, overthrew Daoud in April 1978 and embarked on a process of accelerated reform. The often brutal methods used and the nature of these reforms provoked a massive backlash throughout the country. The situation became chaotic, and the USSR feared that its economic and political interests might be threatened.[1] In December 1979, Soviet forces entered Afghanistan and took control of key centres. Their arrival strengthened resistance to the government and provided an opportunity for the radical Islamist parties to increase their following. The Soviet invasion provoked a massive exodus of refugees to Pakistan and Iran, as people fled the military onslaught of the Soviet army.

Major resistance, therefore, was organized from Pakistan. The radical Islamist parties regrouped in Pakistan, from where they planned military incursions into Afghanistan against the Soviet troops. Other resistance groups remained in Afghanistan, with only a nominal link to a Pakistan-based group. Iran also accepted a number of Shi'a Mujahedin groups. In time, these formed a single party, known as the Hisb-e-Wahdat, which after the departure of the Soviet troops, took control of central Afghanistan. Resources, particularly from the USA, and to a lesser extent from Saudi Arabia, were given to certain radical Islamist parties in Pakistan, to help their resistance fight against the USSR.

By February 1989, the Soviet government had withdrawn its forces. However, the USSR continued to provide military and financial support to the socialist government in Kabul, which still controlled the urban areas. Following the disintegration of the USSR, the government lost power in 1992. Fierce factional fighting broke out between the proliferation of heavily armed Mujahedin groups with rival ideologies. In April 1992, the leading radical Islamist parties took Herat, Kabul, and Kandahar, leaving

---

[1] Rubin (1997: 14) notes that directly after the coup, US and USSR aid increased perhaps fiftyfold.

Mazar-i-Sharif in the north under the control of a militia leader, Dostam, who had supported the socialist government. Dostam virtually established his own independent fiefdom there. In Herat, the local resistance leader managed to operate a reasonably effective administration and imposed a certain stability. Central Afghanistan had been stable for two years under Hisb-e-Wahdat leadership. In Kabul and Kandahar, conflict broke out between rival radical Islamist parties, leading to significant human casualties, major destruction of buildings, and the exodus of a further half million people from Kabul.

In October 1994, a new group known as the Taliban emerged. Much of their support came from young people educated in *madrasahs* (Islamic religious schools), with a creed that drew heavily on conservative religious tradition and the puritanical beliefs of the Wahhabi movement in Saudi Arabia. They were even more radical than the Mujahedin groups, but because they were untainted by past atrocities soon gained a considerable following. Their effectiveness in providing security and removing bandits from the areas under their control increased their popularity. The Taliban, entering from Pakistan, took Kandahar easily and then moved north. The next year they succeeded in taking both the south-eastern provinces and western Afghanistan, including Herat. In October 1995 they reached the outskirts of Kabul, where they took control in September 1996. Between May 1997 and August 1998, they made significant advances in the north.

It is rumoured that the Taliban received substantial backing from Pakistan and Saudi Arabia, as well as the USA—although all deny it. India supported the Rabbani government (1992–6) in Kabul, together with Iran and Russia; these three have continued to support the northern alliance under Rabbani, its titular head. Taliban-controlled areas lack administrative infrastructure. This is in part the legacy of earlier instability, followed by the flight of officials to Iran and Pakistan. In addition, the Taliban paid little attention to the administration of public services, concentrating on the conquest of new areas and the disarming of the population.

The Taliban had a dramatic influence on the provision of basic services to the population. They placed major restrictions on female access to education, employment, and health care. This resulted in the closure of large numbers of girls' schools, the end of employment for thousands of female teachers, and serious obstacles to maternal and child health care. NGOs and UN agencies have had limited success in countering these developments, but it has largely been ad hoc and dependent on the attitude of local Taliban leaders. At the national level, there is no discernible improvement in female entitlement to services and there are many examples of growing rigidity on the part of the Taliban.

5 Refugees

During the course of the war, 6 million Afghans—more than one-third of the population[2]—fled to Pakistan or Iran, while a further 3 million persons, according to UNHCR

---

[2] No complete population census has ever been carried out. The first attempt in 1979 was interrupted by the war. Population estimates are, therefore, to be treated with caution.

(1999) and Rubin (1997: 28) were displaced internally. Over 3 million refugees fled to Pakistan during the Soviet occupation, where they were placed in designated camps, and provided with tents, a regular food ration, and basic health and education services. Many benefited from skills training and income-generating projects. The Mujahedin parties had recruiting offices in the camps and ran their own schools. They organized incursions into Afghanistan from the camps.

Most refugees returned from Pakistan in 1992 when the government fell. They were helped by NGOs and UN agencies to restore their agricultural base through the provision of improved seed, fertilizer and pesticides, repairs to their irrigation systems and flood-protection structures, and veterinary care. Subsequently, the failure of the Mujahedin to bring stability to Kabul slowed down the return of refugees.

At the end of 1999 approximately 1.2 million refugees remained in Pakistan. These include the new waves of refugees from Kabul in 1994 and 1996. While new arrivals still received food assistance, the older groups of refugees had to become largely self-sufficient; rations were stopped in September 1995, and they had to organize and pay for their own services. Well over two million refugees are thought to have fled to Iran. In Iran, they were permitted to work, given free access to health and education facilities, and allowed the same subsidies on food and other staples as Iranians.[3] They were generally expected to find their own accommodation. Refugees started to return from Iran in 1993, and some 800,000 returned in the first year. From then, the rate of return slowed. In fact, many refugees returned to Iran following the Taliban take-over of Herat in September 1995. In 1999 an estimated 1.4 million refugees were still living in Iran, although the Iranian government imposed increasing restrictions on Afghan migration and employment.

Although hailed by the UNHCR for their exemplary treatment of refugees, both Iran and Pakistan began to feel the strain of coping with this refugee population. UN workers were concerned at Pakistan's plans to restrict refugees to camps in the Northwest Frontier, according to Reuters (11 March 1999). In Iran, early in 1999 there was renewed pressure on refugees to return to Afghanistan. In 1998, between 60,000 and 100,000 Afghans were forcibly repatriated from Iran, and in May 1999, the Iranian government announced that it would repatriate Afghan refugees in the south-east province, blaming them for the high level of drug trafficking there (*Agence France-Presse* (AFP) 17 May 1999). UN agencies and NGOs were concerned because they lacked the capacity to cope with this new influx.

6 Women and Gender Issues

Since the 1920s, the status of women has been a politically charged and highly divisive issue. Indeed, it has been one of the most important and visible symbols of the struggle between the modernizers and traditionalists. Successive reform programmes advocated the unveiling of women, and their education and employment. Because of strong

---

[3] The UNHCR (1997) commended both countries' treatment of refugees: Pakistan for using its own food stocks to feed them in 1982–4, and Iran for not asking for any external assistance until 1986.

resistance from the traditionalists, until the late 1970s the modernizers concentrated their efforts in the cities, which widened the chasm between urban and rural women (WB 1999; DHA 1997; Moghadam 1994). In the 1970s, the communist-led government enacted a series of national reforms, including land reform, a literacy campaign and marriage reform—ending the tradition of the 'brideprice' and making it illegal for girls under 16 years to marry.

Reaction to these reforms focused not only on the reforms, but also on the violent and heavy-handed manner in which they were introduced.[4] During the Soviet period, the government took radical steps to include women in its education and employment reform programmes (UNDP 1993, ii. 77). Progressive views on the status of women were equated with communism, the modernizing agenda became a 'military programme', and the urban–rural divide grew. To quote the DHA (1997) 'for many rural Afghans, the achievements in the field of education and gender took on a definite political colour under Soviet occupation', and today rural Afghan women refer to urban–educated females as 'Russians'.

Throughout the war competing factions used the role of women as one of the defining elements of their agenda; Rubin (1996: 4) noted 'that the principal role of women in Afghan politics over the last 18 years has been to function as symbols of legitimation for political groups led by men'. Radical Islamic groups reaffirmed the traditional role of women as the hallmark of Islamic virtue.[5] In 1992, a coalition of Mujahedin groups issued a series of decrees banning women's education and employment, and making veiling compulsory. At first, in the fragmented political climate, they were too weak to enforce these measures.

The situation changed when the Taliban took over government, because then they could enforce their decrees. Rubin (1996: 2) wrote that when the leader, Mullah Omar, first came to power:

he immediately attacked Afghanistan's most pressing problem by issuing new regulations about proper dress for women. . . . Tragicomic as it may seem for the alleged leader of a country whose capital city has been demolished by rockets (largely his own) and which has the lowest literacy rate and the highest rates of both infant and maternal mortality in the world, this incident illustrates the importance of control over women as a highly charged symbol of political and social legitimacy in Afghanistan, a symbol that assumed new importance.[6]

Women were required to wear the full *burka*, and forbidden to work or appear in public without a male guardian. Girls' schools were closed and girls' schooling prohibited, with the exception of Koranic training for girls under 8. In effect, the Taliban reversed

---

[4] Maley (1996) noted that in the 1970s the content of literacy materials was highly political. Attendance at classes was made compulsory and sometimes backed by violence. As a result, some literary workers were killed and some rural people fled to Pakistan (Moghadam 1994). The campaign led to a rejection of government teaching, particularly that aimed at girls (Maley 1996).

[5] Rubin (1996: 3) writes that control over women 'reasserted the honour of Pushtun men and legitimated their power with an Islamic symbol'; for the 'chasteness of women' is 'central to the Taliban image of superior Islamic virtue' (UNHCR 1997).

[6] Non-gender specific decrees banned flying kites, playing chess, music, television, and the possession of photos of living creatures.

earlier socialist attempts to impose an urban liberal culture in rural areas, and instead imposed a particularly harsh rural culture on the cities (UNHCR 1997). Accordingly, the change in policy was most dramatic, and dictates were rigorously enforced in the cities—particularly Kabul, which comprised 8 per cent of the population according to DHA (1997)—where by and large women's activities have been suppressed, often with severe abuse of transgressors. In some rural areas, Taliban policies were 'in line with the traditions and . . . *modus operandi* of the local rural population', and the most extreme edicts, such as the wearing of the *burka*, were ignored (DHA 1997). Barker (1999) commented that regulations were enforced unevenly throughout the country and over time.

Occasionally, external organizations have persuaded the Taliban to relax certain measures: for example widows have been allowed to collect relief food unchaperoned; a few women doctors and teachers have been allowed to continue working; and some girls have been allowed to attend school.[7] In April 1999 the Swiss-based Terre des Hommes signed an agreement with the Taliban allowing Afghan women to work with the agency on childrens' health issues (AFP, 23 April).

Seventy-five per cent of refugees were women and children. Conditions in Pakistan and Iran affected the status of women in different ways. In Pakistani refugee camps, refugees from the same village tended to be concentrated together; this increased the practice of purdah. To quote from UNHCR (1997, internet) 'whereas a woman would have gone out quite freely in her home village, with her face uncovered . . . in the refugee villages she was surrounded by strangers, and became much more confined to her family's compound for fear of endangering the all important family honor'. Local Pakistani attitudes reinforced this conservatism. Conversely, in Iran, most women were assimilated into the wider society, and their status improved 'both in their eyes and those of their male relatives. The peer pressure of Iranian society, where most girls go to school and many women work, had an unquestionably beneficial effect' (UNHCR 1997, internet).

7   The Impact of Conflict on the Macroeconomy

Assessing the economic impact of the conflict presents two major methodological problems: first, a lack of reliable, comprehensive statistics, and second, the rapid pace of change that must be factored into any analysis. Even before the war, statistics were sparce. From the beginning of the conflict, the government in Kabul's capacity to collect data was reduced even further. Soviet-issued statistics tended to be propaganda, minimizing the impact of conflict (EIU 1989: 55). In April 1992, when the Soviet-backed government fell, data collection ceased altogether. The major sources of information are now the data compiled by outside organizations, mainly the UN and NGOs, drawing on microlevel studies in various localities and government data where

---

[7] Barker (1999) reports that 35 per cent of students in CARE-supported schools and 14 per cent in Swedish Committee schools are girls. The Ministry of Justice has allowed widows and married women with their husband's permission to work, if modestly dressed.

possible. There are no regular comprehensive national data covering the whole country. The data used here, therefore, frequently show wide discrepancies in absolute values and trends. We used the sources that seemed the most logical and compatible with anecdotal evidence. Furthermore, the situation is volatile, and has changed dramatically over the past two decades, making it difficult to draw reasonable conclusions and impossible to project into the future.

In order to identify the effects of war on the macroeconomy, one needs to consider how the economy would have performed in the absence of conflict. One way was to compare performance with pre-war trends. A second way was to compare the Afghan performance with that of a similar country that did not experience conflict, Nepal in this case. We also compared conditions in Afghanistan with those in LDCs as a whole, which of course, included countries in conflict.

7.1   *The Pre-war Situation*

From the 1950s, the state became increasingly involved in the Afghan economy. The close alliance with the USSR included the adoption of centralized 5-year plans. In the mid-1970s, the government nationalized banks, mining, and heavy industry. Between 1960 and 1970, World Bank figures estimate that the economy grew at 2.0 per cent a year. The growth rate increased to 3.7 per cent a year over the next decade; this compares to GDP growth of 2.7 per cent in Nepal and 3.5 per cent for LDCs generally. Afghanistan's growth rate in the 1970s—close to that for LDCs overall—can be attributed to several factors: improved export performance; initiatives to boost agriculture; emphasis on mining and industry; and increased foreign assistance and investment.

Other macroeconomic indicators were robust. International reserves grew at an annual rate of 27 per cent between 1970 and 1979. Gross domestic investment as a share of GDP rose from 5.5 per cent in 1970 to 14 per cent in 1978, while domestic savings as a share of GDP grew from 3.3 to 10.8 per cent in the same period. UNCTAD statistics report that manufacturing grew at 4.6 per cent a year during the 1970s and accounted for 9 per cent of GDP in 1980. Exports also grew rapidly during the 1970s, and the trade deficit was moderate during these years. Regardless of the context, it is unlikely that these growth rates could have been sustained. In centrally planned economies embarking on import-substituting industrialization, growth tends to slow down after an initial period. Moreover, the war began at a time of global recession, marked by high oil prices and interest rates, so that economic performance could have been expected to worsen in any event.

To estimate the likely degree of change attributable to global economic conditions, we compared Afghanistan's performance with that of Nepal and the LDCs. These data are set out in Table 2.1. GDP in Afghanistan fell by 0.3 per cent a year between 1976 and 1981, compared to growth of 2.6 and 2.8 per cent a year in Nepal and LDCs respectively. This fall is probably attributable to political instability during those years. In the early 1980s, Afghanistan's growth was slightly above that of the LDCs but well below that of Nepal.

Table 2.1   Afghanistan: Percentage change in GDP, 1970–1985

Country	1970–80	1976–81	1980–5
Afghanistan	3.7	−0.3	2.9
Nepal	2.7	2.6	4.1
LDCs	3.5	2.8	2.0

Source: UNCTAD, *The Least Developed Countries.*

7.2   Sectoral Effects

We examined data on output and physical infrastructure, and services by sector—in order to estimate macroeconomic performance. Following this sectoral examination of change, we considered the effects on human capital and social institutions, by which we mean the system of rules governing society and relationships between individuals that underpin economic activity.

7.2.1   Sectoral output: agriculture

During the war the greatest fall in output was in agriculture, which accounted for the largest share of the economy and the majority of exports.[8] During the war agricultural production fell by as much as 50 per cent, as a result of military destruction, displacement, and government neglect. The pre-war economy was overwhelmingly rural: agriculture and pastoralism accounted for 60 per cent of GDP, while rural trade and handicrafts comprised another 25 per cent. Owing to the limited penetration of the cash economy—just 48 per cent of GDP in 1972—inequality was not marked. A Swiss ethnologist commented on visits to the countryside in 1972: 'we do not find the exterior forms of deprivation which characterize certain regions of Pakistan and India' (cited in Rubin 1997: 7). Wheat[9] comprised over 40 per cent of crop production, sizeable quantities of barley, corn, rice, vegetables, and fruit were also produced, and farmers owned considerable numbers of livestock.

Just under half of Afghanistan's cultivable land was farmed, nearly 70 per cent of which was irrigated. Lack of irrigation was the main constraint to further expansion. Production varied between regions; before the war, Johnson (1997:10) estimated that the average farm produced three times subsistence needs; however, in the deficit areas such as Badakhshan in the mountainous north-east, local production met only 50 per cent of needs. D'Souza (1984) reported that the central areas, such as the Hazarajat region, also experienced shortages because of their remoteness and dependence on rainfed agriculture.

---

[8] Dupree (1980) estimates that agricultural exports were nearly 90 per cent of the total in 1968–9. The SCA gives 65 per cent for 'just before the war', while UNCTAD gives 46 per cent in 1980. Some of this difference may result from the categorization of processed agricultural commodities.

[9] Before the war, Afghanistan had one of the highest levels of per capita consumption of wheat in the world, providing nearly 80 per cent of the calorie intake (UNDP 1993, iv. 10).

Table 2.2 SCA findings on destruction caused by war in Afghanistan

	1978	1980	1985	1986	1987
Percentage of farmers reporting:					
Destruction of irrigation system	0	13	24	20	12
Bombing of crop	0	4	11	8	4
Bombing of village	0	23	53	38	22
Destruction of grain store	0	7	13	10	3
Livestock shot	0	9	23	13	6
Livestock killed by mines	0	2	6	5	2

Source: SCA 1988: 37.

Beginning in the 1960s, the introduction of chemical fertilizers and green revolution technology in wheat, coupled with government efforts to supply inputs—such as improved seeds, fertilizer and pesticides—helped to improve agricultural output. World Bank data show a sharp rise in cereal production and yields during the 1970s. The strongest evidence of improvement was the elimination by 1974 of cereal imports, which had previously averaged over 115,000 tonnes a year, and the increase in exports (SCA 1988).

The SCA provided detailed agricultural sector estimates for the Soviet period. It estimates that the area cultivated fell 30 per cent between 1978–9 and 1990–1; the average size of holdings fell by 63 per cent; and per capita grain production and livestock by 50 and 40 per cent respectively. Cereal imports increased 50 times during the same period. SCA data suggest a substantial decline in yields from 1978 to 1987 of 33 per cent for irrigated wheat and 50 per cent for dry-land wheat. However, these data should be treated with caution as farmers tend to give misleading information on yields, and prewar figures were considered rather high (SCA 1988).

During the war, production was affected by military destruction and population flight. Interviews between 1978 and 1987 with 20,000 farm families (nearly 10 per cent of all farmers) in Afghanistan and Pakistan refugee camps point to considerable destruction of villages, irrigation facilities, and livestock through acts of war, as shown in Table 2.2. For instance in 1985, the year of greatest destruction, 53 per cent farmers reported bombing of their villages; 23 per cent bombing of their grain store; and 23 per cent the shooting of livestock. The SCA concluded that Mujahedin areas 'were the target of a carefully planned and systematic destruction of agriculture'.

Landmines also jeopardized agricultural production. According to CARE (1996, internet) an estimated ten million landmines were buried in Afghanistan, of which, UN estimates, perhaps only 200,000 have been removed in ten years (UN Mine Action Programme for Afghanistan: Workplan 1999). In 1998, the UN (internet) identified 725 sq. km as contaminated, of which 45 per cent was classified as high priority. *The British Medical Journal* (September, 1995)[10] claimed that agricultural production could have increased between 88 and 200 per cent without land mines.

---

[10] Cited in War Child Landmine Programme (1998, internet).

In addition, marketing networks were disrupted. The Soviet-backed government put pressure on farmers to grow cash crops to be sold to government factories, instead of the subsistence crops that would increase rural autonomy (Rubin 1997: 27). At the same time, Mujahedin commanders expected farmers to stop producing for the market and to store their surplus in case of shortage.

The SCA survey identified a number of likely indirect reasons for agricultural decline:

1. *A reduction in the availability of family and hired labour.* The mass departure of farmers as refugees reduced crop production, and the ability to maintain irrigation systems. The refugees tended to be the better off inasmuch as they had the resources to leave. However, these farmers seem to have experienced the most destruction, because their farms were often near roads, which were the *foci* of fighting. Not only did they lose their homes and farms, but canals, access roads, and fields were often mined.

2. *A decline in livestock numbers.* When production fell, livestock were sold to buy food, or to finance journeys to refugee camps and expenses there. The survey reports that farmers remaining in Afghanistan claimed a 70 per cent decline in sheep; 40 per cent in draught oxen; 45 per cent in horses; and 6 per cent in donkeys or mules. Donkeys and mules were the last to be sold as they may have been kept for travel and/or to provide cash when hired to Mujahedin or refugees.

The decline in cattle had two main consequences. First, the buffer of animal ownership was reduced to near zero for many farmers, and the risk of destitution in the event of crop failure was therefore high. Second, the number of draught oxen, and therefore the ability to cultivate land, was reduced to a low level in most zones.

3. *A substantial decline in the genetic potential of wheat seed.* In 1978, a high proportion of farmers used government wheat seed, but by the end of the 1980s its use was negligible. According to the SCA survey: 'In order to maintain the *status quo* of genetic potential of (at least) the four major crops of Afghanistan, there is no alternative to centralized plant-breeding facilities.' (p. 24). Such facilities were not available in the Mujahedin controlled areas. The Ministry of Agriculture used to receive 10,000 tonnes of seeds a year from the USSR which it distributed only to its supporters.

4. *Government failure as provider.* The government effectively ceased to provide resources to the rural areas to maintain seed and soil quality (for example fertilizer and pesticides) and to keep roads under repair. The proportion of farmers using fertilizers fell by about 20 per cent over the decade. World Bank estimates suggest that fertilizer consumption per hectare fell from 1.9 kg from 1980 in the early 1980s to 1.1 kg in the early 1990s.

So far we have considered the actual change, but it is also interesting to consider what might have happened if the improvements begun in 1970 had continued. Azam Gul (1992 cited in UNDP 1993, iv. 1) suggested that, if green revolution technology had been fully implemented, wheat yields might have increased from 1,150 kg per hectare to 2,300 kg per hectare, an increase of more than 15 per cent. The actual fall in production, estimated at nearly 40 per cent, should be set against a rise in population. UNDP estimated the population at 20 million in 1995 compared to 15.5 million in

1979, an increase of under 2 per cent a year. It is reported by FAO (1997, internet) that Afghanistan had to import 30 per cent of its food supply during the early 1990s. UNCTAD (1996) information suggests that since 1992 food production has begun to improve in certain areas, and this is confirmed by personal observation. The return of refugees, and investment by the UN and NGOs into inputs, irrigation-systems repair, flood protection, veterinary care, and reforestation, have helped substantially, particularly in the more fertile areas.

Poppy growing, for the production of heroin and opium, is a major element in the agricultural economy and the black economy. The main areas of production are the fertile Helmand Valley in the south, and Nangarhar in the east. Over 96 per cent of production is under Taliban control. The other main area of production, outside Taliban control, is Badakshan in the north-east, where worsening poverty led to increasing reliance on this crop. However the level of poppy production is carefully controlled by those managing the international heroin market, and is not open to all farmers. Opium and heroin production have increased dramatically during the years of conflict. Poppy production is estimated to have increased twelvefold between the early 1980s and mid-1990s, and the Taliban seem to have encouraged further expansion. Donini (1996a: 2) and UNDP (1993, ii. 28) estimated that by 1996, poppies were the country's main export crop, and that Afghanistan was responsible for some 40 per cent of world poppy production. Rubin (1997: 28) calculated that a 10 per cent tax on poppy production yielded US\$20–40 million a year. Following UN and international pressure, the Taliban have, from time to time, announced a ban on production, but there is little evidence of implementation. In 1998, the area under poppy cultivation increased by nearly 10 per cent, although production fell from 2,800 tonnes the previous year to 2,100 tonnes because of poor weather. The total value of opium poppy production in 1998, at farmgate prices at harvest time, was estimated at US\$69 million (*Afghanistan Outlook* 1999).

Heroin laboratories sprang up to capitalize on the large profits available from processing opium into heroin. The heroin is transported from Afghanistan to Europe through Pakistan, Iran, and Central Asia—and supplies some 80 per cent of European demand. However, only a small proportion of the revenue generated remains in Afghanistan.

7.2.2 Sectoral output: Industry

Before the war, Afghanistan had a rudimentary industrial base, which contributed 4 per cent to GDP in 1974–5 (EIU 1976: 28) rising to 9 per cent by 1980 (UNCTAD). The main *foci* were the processing of agricultural raw materials, cement, fertilizer, and artificial silk. Manufacturing seems to have increased in certain areas under the Soviets; this is supported by an estimated rise of 2.5 per cent a year in GDP from 1980 to 1985, despite poor agricultural performance. It deteriorated sharply after their departure. The steep fall in export earnings from natural gas and agriculture led to a cut in foreign exchange available for inputs. The UNDP (1993) estimates that industrial output fell 21 per cent between 1987 and 1991, stating that 'most manufacturing enterprises . . . have now ceased to operate or are producing well below capacity because of war damage and shortages of raw materials and spare parts' (i. 21). In the early 1990s, the German

Technical Cooperation Agency (GTZ) carried out a field study of textiles, dried fruit, fruit juice, and shoes, which reported drastically reduced output[11] and severe deterioration of the industrial sector (Taufiqi 1993, cited in UNDP 1993, iii. 177).

During the war, both domestic and foreign investment was negligible. The cities, where most industrial plant would have been located, suffered much destruction, and personal observation in Kabul confirmed that industry there had virtually vanished (BAAG 1997b). One industry, however, increased. The manufacture of weapons became an important industry during the war, often financed by outside donations. Much of this production was carried out in small workshops, but these were able to produce quite sophisticated weapons. Unfortunately, no data were available on the value of production or on how many persons worked in the industry.

7.2.3 *Sectoral output: Energy*

Before the war, Afghanistan's per capita energy consumption was among the world's lowest (EIU 1998: 65–8). The Soviets concentrated on developing sectors of benefit to them, including natural gas and defence. In 1967 they invested in a pipeline to transport gas to the USSR, which led to a marked increase in natural gas production. During the Soviet period, up to 85 per cent of gas was exported to the USSR. However, in the late 1980s the gas fields were closed and production fell by nearly 90 per cent. The tanker fleet and all pipelines to the USSR fell into ruin (UNDP 1993, i. 20). Production of coal—mined on a commercial scale before the war—was limited by the distance of the coalfields from the consuming centres and the underdeveloped state of infrastructure. When the Soviets left, production fell to an estimated 33 per cent of earlier output (UNDP 1993, iii. 55).

Energy consumption also declined. During the 1980s, UNDP estimates suggest a decline of nearly 10 per cent in per capita consumption, with sharper falls in the late 1990s. This is the result of scarce fuel supplies, the relatively high cost of fuel, and the increasing poverty of the Kabul population.

7.2.4 *Sectoral output: Utilities*

Basic utilities in urban areas suffered from military destruction and inadequate maintenance, as government resources dwindled or were redirected into military expenditure. As a result, cities had very restricted access to water and electricity, limited at best to a few hours each day in parts of the city. The electricity plant was damaged in 1990. This cut off the Kabul electricity supply for some years and led to an increase in the consumption of traditional fuels. The city came increasingly to depend on wood, coal, and petroleum-based products. Fuel supplies to the city were also deliberately blocked as part of the war strategy.

The absence of water supply systems in some cities forced people to use shallow wells, increasing the risk of contamination. The deterioration in the city sanitation and waste disposal systems led to a growing incidence of disease.

---

[11] Textile production fell 88 per cent; dried fruit 83 per cent; fruit juice 98 per cent; and shoe production 92 per cent.

7.2.5   Transport

Before the war, much foreign aid had been devoted to road building. The roads, however, deteriorated dramatically throughout the country as a result of poor mainten-ance, a lack of investment, and increased usage by heavy military vehicles. The poor quality of rural roads increased the difficulty and costs of transporting agricultural pro-duce to district markets, aggravating the food shortages and raising prices. One import-ant, adverse consequence was that the urban centres came to rely on food imported from Iran and Pakistan, while locally grown produce remained in the villages where it was grown. At the same time, efforts by relief agencies to move relief supplies into remote areas were seriously hampered by impassable roads.

The deterioration of the roads affected access to petroleum-based products needed for cooking and heating. Residents in remote areas in particular resorted to collecting wood and shrubs from the hillsides, which caused soil erosion and desertification.[12] Given these constraints, it is surprising to see how much trade continued to move along the main routes. On a visit to Kandahar in December 1995, Marsden observed con-siderable congestion as heavy lorries attempted to cross the city, weaving their way through deep ruts in the sand on what had once been a tarmacked highway.

7.2.6   Services

War tends to restructure economic incentives towards the informal sector and non-tradable activities, as discussed in Chapter 1, Volume I. In Afghanistan, there has been a clear shift from the formal to the informal in services as well as production, together with a move towards illegal and undesirable activities, such as poppy cultivation, arms production, drugs trading, and smuggling. This shift has negative implications for government revenue. These informal-sector activities are likely to be seriously under-estimated, or excluded altogether from any official estimates of GDP, trade, or other economic indicators, but they still make an important contribution to economic activity.

7.2.7   Banking and money

During the war, the population stopped relying on formal-sector, government-owned banks. The formal banking system collapsed when the Mujahedin came to power and was replaced by the money bazaar, which had traditionally been used to finance many transactions, including foreign trade.

With the collapse of the formal system, commercial operations and aid organizations had to rely on their own systems for financial transactions to move money around the country and provide security for their funds. Traders assisted with financial transactions between centres by arranging credit facilities with relatives and other contacts. The US$ was the basic currency used by the humanitarian agencies, while the Pakistani rupee became the major exchange currency in border areas within Afghanistan.

---

[12] UN *Statistical Year Book* (UNSYB) (1997) figures suggest that forest as a percentage of land fell from 3.1 to 2.1 per cent between 1990 and 1995, owing to its use as fuel and to timber sales to Pakistan that were main-tained over the war (Johnson 1998: 36).

An illegal activity that prospered was smuggling. Afghanistan had an agreement with Pakistan to allow goods destined for Afghanistan to travel from Karachi across Pakistan free of import tax. This agreement was abused by Afghan traders, who brought goods across Pakistan into Afghanistan only to smuggle them back into Pakistan, undercutting the Pakistani traders who had to pay import duty. Subsequently, in an attempt to stop this trade, the Pakistan government progressively reduced the number of items that could transit to Pakistan free of duty, and tightened customs control. Farmers interviewed in the Farah province mentioned widespread smuggling of luxury consumer goods across the Iranian border. There is no doubt that some traders became extremely wealthy from smuggling. This group had a vested interest in continuing the conflict.

7.3   Human Capital and Social Institutions

7.3.1   Human capital

In conflict, human capital is jeopardized by death, injury, migration, and the destruction of social infrastructure such as schools, clinics, and humanitarian government services. In Afghanistan the government made no attempt to offset the damage or maintain services, so the population had to fend for itself, with considerable support from external organizations.

The primary loss of human capital was the massive flight of people from Afghanistan and the displacement within the country. One-third of the population fled the country, and a further 3 million people were displaced internally. Frequently, as Marsden (1998: 14) describes, families would split, with some members moving to urban areas, some staying to work on the land, and others seeking work outside Afghanistan. In 1996, ICRC and Action Contre la Faim (ACF) surveys in Kabul concluded that 90 per cent of the populations sampled had moved at some point in the war. Sixty per cent of the ICRC sample had moved three or four times. A CARE survey of 934 widows in Kabul found that 80 per cent of them had been displaced from rural areas (BAAG 1997a: 14). Because these surveys were carried out in Kabul, where many displaced people sought refuge, they may overstate the degree of displacement nationally.

A major adverse effect was the departure of large numbers of skilled professionals, because of antipathy to those in power, and military activity. This exodus increased when the Mujahedin took over Kabul in 1992, and later, when the Taliban captured Herat in 1995. The closure of girls' schools and prohibition on the employment of women added to the determination of this group to leave.

Bars on female employment reduced the availability of human capital. Before the war, about 5 per cent of the female population was in paid employment. Paul (1997) and UNHCR (1997) estimates suggest that 70 per cent of schoolteachers and over 25 per cent of government employees were women. Under the Soviets, female education and employment rose markedly; for instance in 1988, women outnumbered male students at Kabul University (Moghadam 1994). The World Bank estimated female employment at 12 per cent between 1989 and 1994, but this decreased subsequently. A survey by Physicians for Human Rights (PHR) (1998) of 160 women in Kabul, found that 62 per cent had been employed before the Taliban take-over, compared to 20 per cent in 1998. The UN estimated that after the Taliban take-over, some 150,000 women were barred from working.

The conflict accelerated the process of urbanization. The population of all the major towns increased greatly, particularly when returning refugees opted to live in towns. At the same time many previous urban dwellers who could afford to leave emigrated. World Bank estimates suggest that urban areas expanded by some 3 per cent a year between 1980 and 1995—156 per cent overall. Attempts to attract professionals back to Afghanistan by various organizations met with a poor response. The few who returned encountered hostility, resentment, and suspicion. Inevitably, the war polarized people, and those living in exile risked being viewed as supporters of rival elements.

7.3.2 Social institutions

Stewart (1993) defines social institutions as the system of rules that governs society and relationships between people. These relationships encompass trust, a work ethic, and respect for property. Indeed, some theorists argue that secure property rights are the basis of economic development. War alters the prevailing set of social institutions in an economy by undermining trust, jeopardizing property rights, and legitimating illegal acts—such as harming people, or seizing property. Such activity has a corrosive effect on economic activity, as can be seen from the disintegration of markets, reduced production, and the vast exodus of people. As the erosion of societal norms is intrinsic to civil war, it is not possible for governments to prevent it; rather the people affected must themselves devise new ways of coping.

8   Impact of Conflict on the Macroeconomy

So what effect did these changes have at the macroeconomic level? While most areas of the economy declined throughout the period, the pattern and degree of erosion varied. Under the Soviets up to 1992, there were some positive results, including Soviet investment in manufacturing, natural gas, and the extraction industries, and benefits from aid, but agricultural output fell sharply. This was followed by a period of instability—which still continues—during which output fell in all sectors. Agriculture, always the first sector to pick up, showed signs of increased production before 1996, and since the Taliban take-over, it has continued to grow. In Afghanistan the adverse effects of war outlined in Chapter I, Volume I are clearly apparent; that is, lower exports and export earnings; lower imports; reduced investment and savings; falling government revenue and expenditure; higher budget deficits; and higher inflation. However, aggregate figures are scarce, often unofficial and contradictory. We relied on UNCTAD data, where available, as they seemed the most credible, and UNSYB data after 1991.

8.1   Impact on GDP 1980–97

Inevitably, the war had an adverse impact on GDP. UNCTAD statistics suggest that GDP fell by 20 per cent, nearly 2 per cent a year on average, over the decade 1980 to

1990. UNSYB estimated a fall of 7.4 per cent a year between 1990 and 1995 (which implies a fall of over one-third of the 1989–90 GDP level). It is suggested that most of this fall was made up in 1995, when GDP is estimated by UNSYB to have grown by 26 per cent. However, it probably fell in 1997 following renewed military activity and poor weather. Nepal's GDP, by comparison, is estimated to have grown by 4.6 per cent a year during the 1980s, and at nearly 5 per cent a year between 1990 and 1994. The LDCs grew at 2.1 per cent a year in the 1980s and 1.1 per cent a year in the early 1990s. Therefore between 1980 and 1994, Nepal's GDP grew by about two-thirds, the LDCs' GDP by nearly one-quarter, while Afghanistan's GDP shrank by half. It is reasonable to suggest that in the absence of war the Afghan economy would have grown at least in line with the LDCs, and perhaps as much as Nepal.

To sum up, the fall in GDP during the war had numerous causes, including:

- the extensive bombing of rural areas;
- a sharp fall in food production; and disruption of its distribution;
- the shift of war to urban areas and destruction of towns;
- the diversion of resources from physical or social investment to military use;
- the destruction of infrastructure, disruption of markets, and retreat to subsistence production;
- the exodus of people overseas, particularly the skilled, and educated;
- the fall in the labour force because of migration and the banning of women from employment;
- the diversion of men to soldiering;
- the high number of disabled;
- the reduction in inputs for agricultural production, and fall in exports and imports.

8.2   Impact on Trade

During the 1970s, the value of imports and exports increased about 20 per cent valued in US$. In the 1980s, under Soviet control, both the value and volume of exports fell over 70 per cent, mainly because of falling agricultural production, handicrafts, and after 1988, reduced natural gas production. The value of exports at end 1989 was US$235 million. The volume of imports increased dramatically to 1986 (by nearly three times), financed by Soviet aid. By 1990, imports had fallen back; they were only 47 per cent above the 1980 level, and valued at US$820 million. UNCTAD data show no clear trend for the composition of imports, but World Bank data show a large rise in arms imports with the ratio of arms to other imports rising from 55 per cent in 1985 to 310 per cent in 1991. The trade deficit increased substantially, from small surpluses immediately before the war. In 1990, it stood at US$649 million compared to US$69 million in 1980. These figures are set out in Table 2.3. Table 2.4 shows the changing composition of exports, notably the fall in agricultural exports. The increased share of exports taken by fuel and manufacturing masks the actual reduction of these in both value and volume terms. No estimates of illegal trading could be obtained, but these should not be overlooked, although much of the earnings from illicit trading went to people outside Afghanistan.

Table 2.3 Afghanistan: International trade, 1980–1993 (1980 = 100)

	1980	1982	1984	1986	1988	1990	1992	1993
Export volume	100	102.5	88.3	95.3	62.2	34.4	30.9	29.2
Export value (US$)	100	100.4	111.8	70.5	64.4	33.3	28.3	25.5
Import volume	100	193.5	289.2	275.3	158.1	147.3	108.3	116.5
Trade deficit, US$m.	−69	121	−417	−642	−278	−649	−500	−560
Trade deficit as % of exports	9.8	17.1	52.9	129.2	61.2	276.2	250	311.1

Sources: WBDI 1997 (cd-rom version); UNCTAD 1997; UNCTAD, *The Least Developed Countries* (various).

Table 2.4 Afghanistan: Changes in the composition of exports (% of total exports)

Year	Agriculture[a]	Fuels	Manufacturing[b]	Textiles	Unallocated
1980	46.0	33.1	14.8	22.2	6.1
1988	39.9	42.9	17.1	na	0.1
1992	28.2	47.6	23.7	na	na

[a] Includes categories 'all food items' and 'agricultural raw materials'.
[b] Includes handicrafts, mainly carpets, etc.

Sources: UNCTAD, *The Least Developed Countries* (various).

Table 2.5 Afghanistan: Arms imports as a percentage of all other imports

1985	1986	1987	1988	1990	1991
54.5	92.6	140.6	288.9	462.3	308.4

Source: WBDI 1997 (cd-rom version).

In Nepal, trade grew more rapidly. The value of exports in the 1980s grew just over 8 per cent a year, in marked contrast to the annual fall of 11 per cent in Afghanistan. The value of imports into Nepal grew at double the rate in Afghanistan in the 1980s, and from 1990 to 1994, it grew at 13 per cent a year compared to an annual fall of 2 per cent in Afghanistan.

8.3 Investment and Savings

In 1978, gross domestic investment accounted for 13 per cent of GDP and gross domestic savings for 10 per cent. No further data are available but all evidence suggests severe falls in both. In Nepal, investment accounted for 16 per cent of GDP in 1982, and this increased to 20 per cent a year to 1989 and 21 per cent between 1990 and 1994.

Prior to the war, the Afghan government devoted as much as 45 per cent of its expenditure to investment; this figure had fallen to 18 per cent by 1985 (EIU 1989: 70), and indirect evidence suggests a further substantial fall. There was virtually no private investment in the industrial sector during the conflict. Private investors were reluctant to build on land cleared of mines, even though the UN declared it safe. Later, foreign investors expressed some interest in exploiting the natural gas reserves and mineral deposits, but were waiting for a more peaceful and stable environment.

8.4   Foreign Exchange and Inflation

The contraction of foreign exchange and its diversion to purchasing military goods and weapons severely inhibited economic activity. Further, the growing trade deficit caused the real exchange rate to depreciate, increasing the debt burden. UNDP (1993) estimated that the currency depreciated nearly 3,000 per cent on the parallel market during the 1980s. In 1992 the formal currency market was abandoned. For two years the exchange rate remained stable, but from late 1994 to early 1997 it fell from Af 4,000 : US$1 to about Af 26,000 : US$1. From then it stabilized somewhat in areas at peace, such as in the south where the exchange rate was reported to be Af 22,000 : US$1 in early 1997 (FAO 1997, internet). In April 1999 Afghanistan Outlook quoted an exchange rate of Af 45,000 : US$1.

Turning to prices and inflation, UNDP estimates suggest that prices in Kabul rose nearly ten times (by 980 per cent) during the 1980s, and slightly more on food than other items. This was caused by inflationary deficit financing and a scarcity of many goods. Soviet efforts to control inflation with price controls, regularly injecting wheat into the market, and providing rations to civil servant families, did not prevent this inflation. We consider that the rise in prices may be understated for two reasons: first, because high weights were assigned to price-controlled and subsidized items, and second, because the price index focused on Kabul, which was largely free from fighting and scarcity during the 1980s, and benefited most from the government's anti-inflationary policy.

Inflation rose to very high levels during the 1990s. The government began to print money in 1987,[13] in order to sustain arms purchases. Anecdotal evidence in Rubin (1997: 32) indicates that food prices rose sharply (five- or even tenfold) at the end of the 1980s, accelerating further in the 1990s. For instance, World Bank data show the price of wheat increased by 37 per cent between 1988 and 1999; the price of bread in Kabul rose 400 per cent between January and April 1996; in April 1997, the price of flour rose 50 per cent (ICRC 1997, internet). From 1990 to 1993, the official Kabul inflation rate was over 150 per cent each year (EIU 1998: 65). No price index has been published since. Prices are estimated to have risen even faster in areas that were blockaded during the war (FAO 1997, internet).

8.5   Foreign Debt

During the 1960s and 1970s economic development was largely financed by foreign borrowing. Debt-servicing payments climbed from about 10 per cent of government

---

[13] The money supply grew nearly 37 per cent in 1989–90 (UNDP 1993, iii. 9).

spending in the late 1960s to 20 per cent in the mid–1970s. Almost half of all imports were also financed by borrowing from abroad. The foreign debt escalated during the war, from US$1.2 billion in 1980 to US$5.1 billion in 1990, and US$9.6 billion in 1993.

Afghanistan's debt in 1990 was over four times the value of Nepal's debt. The debt-service ratio was estimated at 8 per cent in 1980, rising to 41 per cent in 1991 (UNHTDS). Nepal's debt service also rose but less sharply, and much more foreign borrowing was devoted to productive investment. Until 1992, Afghanistan's borrowing was overwhelmingly from the USSR at concessional rates. From 1992, official aid decreased as the Soviet inflows ceased, and other donors insisted on some measure of peace as a condition for further funds. At that point, Afghanistan ceased all foreign debt servicing payments. The government then turned to borrowing from the domestic banks to finance the budget deficit, contributing to inflation and depreciation of the currency.

8.6 *Macroeconomic Impact: Conclusion*

The destruction wrought by the prolonged conflict and war was vast, as confirmed by all the indicators, and the economy shrank drastically. The deterioration was particularly severe during the post–Soviet period. Comparison with Nepal over the same period suggests that in the absence of conflict GDP might have been expected to grow by over 50 per cent with increases in manufacturing, investment and savings, and exports and imports.[14]

Afghanistan at present is best characterized as a number of microeconomies, dependent on some international trade, but particularly on developments in the black economy; that is, smuggling, opium, and timber, which expanded during the conflict. After the fall of the Soviet-backed government, Kabul, for example, suffered a dramatic fall in trade across the Salang Pass to the north as it was repeatedly fought over. Kandahar, after years of anarchy and large-scale destruction between 1992 and 1994, has become the entrepôt for trade moving from Central Asia through Herat. This includes the traffic in opium, heroin, timber, and smuggling. Following the capture by the Taliban in August 1998 of Mazar-I-Sharif, which had traded with Uzbekistan for many years, the border was closed. This caused a serious fall in economic activity.

9 Impact of the Conflict on the Mesoeconomy

In this section, we consider how military activity and government spending patterns shaped access to public entitlements—health, education, and water and sanitation services —and compare the situation in Afghanistan with that in Nepal and other LDCs. We trace the changes in public entitlements and explore the extent to which 'civic entitlements' compensated for a failing public sector.

---

[14] Nepal's manufacturing sector grew at an annual rate of 4 per cent between 1980 and 1990, and accounted for 9 per cent of GDP by 1994 (UNCTAD, various years).

9.1   Public Entitlements

Afghanistan's formal tax system, barely functional before the war in 1979, completely collapsed early in the war (EIU 1998: 64). Thereafter, government revenue was largely derived from taxes on trade.[15] Under the Soviets, the government gained substantial receipts from natural gas taxes, but these plummeted when exports were suspended in 1988. Revenues also fell sharply with reduced parastatal production and the transfer of property taxes to the municipalities (UNDP 1993, iii. 7). Ministry of Finance estimates suggest that total government revenue fell from 14 per cent of the National Material Product (NMP) in 1987–8 to 5 per cent two years later. When the Mujahedin took power, local warlords began taxing traders passing through the areas they controlled, and remitted little of this revenue to Kabul. When the Taliban took control, this practice was stopped, which won the approval of local traders. The Taliban reintroduced a formal tax collection system and have imposed three types of tax: a land tax, harvest tax, and an Islamic tax or tithe.

After the Soviet retreat, government expenditure fell sharply. Government also diverted spending from social and economic to military ends. At the same time, its capacity to provide services was severely eroded; indeed after 1992 the government largely disintegrated, and any governance was restricted to local control in Kabul and a few urban centres. The Taliban established a firmer hold on government, but failed to translate this strength into greater economic and social investment.

A skeletal government system remained. This ensures that staff, mostly, were paid—albeit at very low wages—and small resources were provided for the operation of services. The government's ability to provide services was minimal; UN (1998) referred to the 'total absence of any social services'. Figures on expenditure are scarce, but expenditure on agriculture, health, education, and water supply and sanitation fell to an extremely low level. Defence expenditure grew enormously, from less than 2 per cent of GDP in 1976 to nearly 10 per cent in 1985 according to IISS estimates.[16] UNDP (1993) estimates suggest that defence expenditure rose from about one-fifth to one-third of government expenditure between 1986–7 and 1991–2, while expenditure on education and health fell from 20 per cent to under 10 per cent. Rubin (1997) and Marsden (1998) suggest there is evidence to support the view that most resources continued to be diverted into waging war; Rubin (1997: 22) described Afghanistan as one of the most heavily armed countries in the world.

9.2   Civic Entitlements

The humanitarian agencies to some extent took on the role of local authorities in enabling some services to continue. They used their funds, both in Afghanistan and Pakistan, to rent buildings, purchase equipment and supplies, pay for transport, and employ staff. However, it has been suggested that the distribution of aid funds may

---

[15] However trade was taxed at unrealistic government-fixed exchange rates.

[16] These calculations rely on GDP estimates that are higher than those of the authors. Ministry of Finance statements of expenditure during the Soviet years do not seem to reflect actual spending.

Table 2.6 Afghanistan: Access to health care

	1978/79	1990/91	% change
Population/hospital ('000)	222.8	298.1	−33.80
Population/health centre ('000)	57.0	145.0	−154.39
Population/pharmacy ('000)	22.2	9.3	+58.11
Population/bed ('000)	3.0	1.6	+46.67
Population/doctor ('000)	11.9	4.6	+61.34
Population/nurse ('000)	35.2	7.1	+79.83

Source: UNDP 1993.

have distorted local power relations, allowing commanders to buy the support of the populace.

Insecurity and danger, including the looting of their offices, led both the UN and NGOs to withdraw staff from some regions. In March 1998, for example, UN agencies suspended operations in south-west Afghanistan citing government interference and harassment. In July 1998, the Taliban ordered all relief agencies in Kabul to move to a derelict compound, and closed down the offices of the 35 NGOs who refused to move. The UN and ICRC remained until August 1998, although UN international staff left for some months after the US bombing of an alleged base of the suspected terrorist, Osama bin Laden, and the subsequent murder of an Italian UN employee in Kabul. In March 1999, following Taliban assurances that they would be safe, with the exception of the US and UK agencies, the NGOs began to return (*Agence France-Presse*, 13 March 1999).

9.2.1 Health services
During the war, many health facilities were destroyed and medical personnel left the country. From 1992, the central government seriously neglected health spending. No official data are available, but indirect evidence is abundant. UNICEF (1998) states that the government financed none of the extended programme of immunization (EPI) vaccines in 1995–6, compared to an average of 20 per cent funding for LDCs. WHO estimated that in 1996, 70 per cent of the country's health-care system was wholly dependent on external assistance, which compensated to some extent (UN 1998).

The Soviets had established new health facilities in cities, although they were curative rather than preventive and reached a limited share of the population. Refugees living in Iran and Pakistan benefited from better health care than in Afghanistan, and possibly better than the care they would have received had there been no war. UNDP (1993) data on access to health are difficult to interpret, as Table 2.6 shows. Access to hospitals and health centres worsened as might be expected. For instance, 8 of Kabul's 14 hospitals closed between 1980 and 1993 (UNDP 1993: 29). However, the data suggest a greater number of pharmacies, nurses, beds, and doctors per head of population, which is difficult to reconcile with the scale of human flight and physical destruction.

Table 2.7   Afghanistan: EPI immunization rates, 1980–1996

	1980	1984–5	1987–8	1988–9	1990–4	1995–6	All LDCs, 1995–6
% financed by government	—	—	—	—	—	0	21
% children under 1 fully immunized:							
TB	8	11	27	38	44	47	78
DPT[a]	3	16	25	33	18	31	60
Polio	3	16	25	33	18	31	60
Measles	6	13	31	22	40	42	59
Pregnant women immunized vs. tetanus	3	4	6	20	6	37	48

[a] DPT includes diphtheria, whooping cough, and tetanus.

Source: UNICEF, *State of the World's Children* (various).

In rural Afghanistan, UN agencies and the NGOs delivered emergency aid, largely limited to caring for the war-wounded. As access to the rural areas improved after the Soviet departure, they worked to establish a network of curative and preventive services. In spite of partial coverage, the NGOs had a positive impact, particularly in the northern, eastern and western regions. Although beset by logistical problems, the coordination of NGOs' work is improved. They gave a high priority to EPI and mother and child health, with good results as shown in Table 2.7.

After 1996, NGO effectiveness in health-service provision improved, although it was somewhat undermined by a fall in funding for humanitarian programmes. Increased military activity from May 1997 jeopardized access in the north, while the Taliban, on gaining power, made it increasingly difficult for women to obtain health care for themselves and their children. For instance, for three months in 1997, women were prohibited from entering all but one poorly equipped hospital in Kabul. Restrictions were placed on the employment of Afghan women by NGOs, and female operating theatres were closed in all but two hospitals. When in 1998, Physicians for Human Rights (PHR) surveyed 160 women from Kabul (half living in Kabul and half recently migrated to Pakistan), they found a severe decline in the women's physical and mental well-being and noted the constraints to obtaining appropriate care.[17] Of 40 women interviewed in depth, 87 per cent reported a decrease in their access to health services, citing the following causes:

- economic hardship (61 per cent);
- absence of any female doctor (48 per cent);

[17] All PHR information was obtained from an internet press release on 5 August 1998 (http://www.reliefweb.int) and the *Journal of the American Medical Association* (JAMA) (http://www.ama-assn.org).

- restrictions on women's mobility (36 per cent);
- no chaperone available (27 per cent);
- hospitals refusing to provide care (21 per cent);
- not owning a *burka* (6 per cent).

In addition, 53 per cent of the women described occasions when they had been had been seriously ill and unable to seek medical care. Many said this was because they were frightened of being arrested or publicly beaten. Male Afghan doctors told the PHR that they could not carry out a proper examination of female patients because they were prohibited from touching them or looking at their bodies. One dentist reported that he had a lookout stand watch at the door when treating female patients. Apparently, Taliban guards checked on medical facilities assiduously, exacting heavy punishment for any transgression. WHO pressured the Taliban to allow the continued employment of female hospital staff, citing the alternative of the treatment of women by unrelated men. However, inside hospitals, segregation of staff made it difficult to deliver services efficiently, as nurses were unable to contact male physicians regarding medical issues. The Taliban's ban on medical and nursing training for women pointed to serious future problems for the provision of health care.

Other Taliban actions jeopardized women's health. For example, in 1996, they banned women from Kabul's 32 public bathhouses, the only places where many of them could bathe in hot water. As a result, health-care workers predicted an increase in gynaecological infections and scabies. They particularly feared a rise in uterine infection after childbirth, a major cause of maternal mortality. This ban also placed accompanying children at a greater risk of respiratory diseases (Rubin 1996). In addition, the wearing of the *burka* contributes to various health problems, including poor vision and hearing, skin rashes, headaches, asthma, alopecia, and depression.

9.2.2 *Water supply and sanitation*

Public health is of paramount importance in a conflict situation, as a lack of food and heat will reduce the population's resistance to disease and allow epidemics to develop. The absence of potable water, water-treatment services, and of public-waste collection can have potentially disastrous consequences. Communicable diseases became the leading cause of death in the country. It is estimated that in 1975, 6 per cent of the population had access to safe water, rising to 10 per cent in 1980, as shown in Table 2.8. By the late 1980s, the figure had risen to 23 per cent, but in the 1990s, it fell back to 12 per cent. At the same time, the rural–urban divide became more pronounced. The decline in access arising from damage to urban water systems was offset by NGO repair and improvement programmes, and the construction of new wells. Access in rural areas, which is much more restricted, should improve as a result of NGO programmes to repair wells and install handpumps.

Access to adequate sanitation facilities was minimal. The World Bank estimated it at 2 per cent in the mid-1980s, falling to 0.3 per cent in the late 1980s. The figure for 1990 to 1996 is given as 8 per cent, a marked improvement, although well below the 35 per cent figure for the LDCs. Solid-waste clearance had been neglected, but UN agencies and NGOs have undertaken clearance schemes in urban centres, often in

Table 2.8   Afghanistan: Access to water and sanitation

	1970+	1975+	1980	1985–87	1988–93	1990–6	LDCs, 1990–6
Population with access to safe water (%)							
Total	3	10	10	21	23	12	54
Urban	18	40	28	38	40	39[a]	78
Rural	1	5	8	17	19	5[a]	48
Sanitation access, total %				2[a]	0.3[a]	8[a]	35

[a] World Bank data.

Sources: UNICEF, *State of the World's Children*; WBDI 1997 (cd-rom version).

partnership with the municipalities and neighbourhood groups. Waste has been removed from the streets, drainage ditches cleared to allow water to move freely, wells have been chlorinated, and sewage removed.

9.2.3   Education

Education statistics are few. The World Bank estimates that only 1.4 per cent of GDP in the 1970s was devoted to education. UNESCO (1995) estimates that 13 per cent of central government expenditure was on education in 1980. This was not far below the average LDC figure of 16 per cent. UNDP data suggest the figure fell to 4 per cent in 1991–2.

Before the war, primary schools were accessible to half the population under twelve. Most provincial towns had a secondary school (EIU 1998: 66). UNDP (1993, i. 30) noted that while quality was low, the network 'serve(d) the needs of an elite minority of the population'. The Soviets built new schools, and emphasized adult literacy, particularly for women. Indeed in 1985, UNESCO praised their literacy efforts (Moghadam 1994). However, a 1991 study found that two-thirds of all schools had been damaged or destroyed, and by 1992 most of the educational infrastructure was said to have been destroyed (UNDP 1993, ii. 46). After 1992, many remaining schools were forced to close, and on coming to power, the Taliban closed Kabul's university. The university reopened in 1997, but women were barred from enrolling.

Both UNICEF and UNDP data show a fall in boys' participation rates during the 1980s, but rising rates in the early 1990s. In 1998, the rate for boys fell to 27 per cent from 63 per cent for the years 1990–5. Girls' participation, which rose for most of the period, fell from 32 per cent for the years 1990–5 to 4 per cent in 1998 according to World Bank data, given in Table 2.9. The rising girls' primary school participation rates reflects the priority given to female education by the Soviet-backed government of 1978–92, supported by resources allocated to teacher training by Pakistan-based NGOs. A matter of concern is the low participation rate of returning refugee children. The UNHCR (1999) reported that 82 per cent of school-age returnees were not attending

Table 2.9 Afghanistan: Gross primary school and secondary
school participation, 1960–1995

	1980–2	1986–8	1986–92	1990–5	1998/9[a]
Primary school participation (gross)[b]					
Boys (%)	54	27	32	63	27
Girls (%)	13	14	17	32	4
Secondary school participation (gross)					
Boys (%)	17	10	11	32	
Girls (%)	5	5	6	11	

[a] World Bank 1999.

[b] Gross participation is calculated based on the number of children at the level of schooling regardless of their age group divided by the population of that age.

Source: UNICEF, *State of the World's Children* (various).

Table 2.10 Afghanistan: Access to educational facilities

	1978/9	1990/1	% change
Participation rate (village and primary schools):			
Boys (%)	83.7	65.9	−17.8
Girls (%)	16.3	34.1	17.8
Students/primary school	269.4	1,067.8	74.8
Pupil : teacher	30.6	40.3	24.1

Source: UNDP 1993.

school, though many had done so in exile. The main reasons cited for this were economic hardship and Taliban prohibitions.

Western NGO involvement in education has been limited because of political and Islamic sensitivities. They generally limited their help to repairing or building school premises. The closure of girls' schools presented these agencies with a dilemma and they failed to reach a coordinated position by 1999. The UN agencies halted their education programmes in Taliban-controlled areas without girls' schools. The Islamic NGOs tried to negotiate a more moderate policy within an Islamic framework, with some limited success. An important element in this has been public support at the community level.

9.2.4 Comparison with Nepal

Social data for Nepal are scarce, but it appears that expenditure as a proportion of GDP remained broadly constant, increasing a little in terms of expenditure per head, in constrast to the falls already noted for Afghanistan.

Access to safe water increased sharply in Nepal from 11 per cent in 1981 to 48 per cent in 1995. School enrolment was traditionally high in Nepal. By 1992, virtually all children of primary school age had access to a primary school and 35 per cent of children of secondary school age were enrolled in school.

World Bank estimates show that 49 per cent of the population in Nepal had access to health care in 1995 compared 26 per cent in Afghanistan. Immunization rates (DPT) rose from 26 per cent in 1984 to 77 per cent in 1995, whereas they fell from 16 per cent to 12 per cent in Afghanistan.

Consequently, had Afghanistan followed the Nepal pattern, social services would have improved, but conflict largely prevented this from happening. Moreover, the situation worsened when Taliban restrictions on women were imposed. Aggregate data are not available for LDCs so no comparison was possible.

9.3   Conclusions on Social Sectors, Public and Civic Entitlements

Government spending on social services, never high, diminished considerably over the course of the war owing to military exigencies. The situation was made worse by the destruction of existing facilities and lack of government maintenance. NGOs helped to compensate for this void, and in areas where they were active, access to education and health facilities even improved. NGOs were able to provide little help to services dependent on public infrastructure, such as access to potable water and sanitation facilities. These remained low even by LDC standards.

10   Impact of the Conflict on the Microeconomy

In this section we consider the impact of war on the entitlements of individual households, drawing on statistical data where possible and Marsden's recent field research on the effects of conflict on different refugee communities. We examine shifts in the distribution of entitlements as a result of changes in government, and compare the fall in both market and public entitlements with the experience in Nepal.

Table 2.11 gives real estimates of GDP per capita between 1960 and 1992. No data are available between 1960 and 1988 but other economic evidence suggests GDP would have grown until the war began in 1979. Table 2.11 suggests GDP per head was about 10 per cent lower in 1991 than in 1960. Other quantitative indicators of well-being such as hyperinflation of food staples, a severe drop in average calorie intake, and rising rates of malnutrition echo this decline. Per capita calorie consumption fell from 2,186 in 1980 to 1,573 in 1992, before rising slightly to 1,670 in 1996. In the early 1980s, malnutrition affected 15 to 20 per cent of children under 5 (D'Souza 1984: 26). In 1994, a CARE study found growth-stunting (a key indicator of malnutrition) in nearly 50 per cent of children under 5, while UNICEF (1997) found that up to 35 per cent of children under 5 were affected by wasting.

UNICEF conducted a study of poverty in Afghanistan between 1977 and 1984, and estimated that 18 per cent of the urban population and 36 per cent of the rural

Table 2.11 Afghanistan: Real GDP per capita (Purchasing Power Parity), various years (US$)

	1960	1988	1989	1990	1991	1992
GDP per capita	775[a]	710	710	714	700	819[b]

[a] This figure is from UNHDR 1993. UNHDR 1991 gives a figure of US$670 but the later figure is used as presumably it was revised upward.

[b] This figure, given in UNHDR 1995, is from update of Penn World Tables using expanded set of international comparisons. The estimate may differ methodologically from those of previous years.

Sources: United Nations Development Programme, *Human Development Reports*, 1992, 1993, and 1995.

population were living below the poverty line. This compared well with average poverty levels in LDCs, which were 30 per cent for urban and 65 per cent for rural populations. Poverty has clearly increased in Afghanistan since 1984 in both rural and urban areas. In 1999, UNDPI stated that 'the proportion of the population living below the poverty line may be as high as 80 per cent'.

10.1   Kabul[18]

Anecdotal evidence suggests a high incidence of impoverishment in Kabul, where in 1996, 80 per cent of the population was alleged to be dependent on external assistance (UN 1996, internet). After January 1994, following heavy bombing, the population of Kabul fell from 2 million to less than 1 million as people fled to safer areas. Those who remained were according to the UN the 'poorest of the poor', and most had to borrow or beg even for basic necessities. Unemployment was widespread; WFP (1996) estimated that only 20 per cent of the population could find work, including the food-for-work programmes. A 1997 ICRC survey found that 80 per cent of the sample in Kabul suffered from some form of malnutrition (EIU 1997: 60), while an ACF study in Kabul of children under 5 found that 51 per cent were stunted (UNDPI 1999). The main problem was said to be very limited purchasing power rather than the lack of food per se.

The most destitute were Kabul's widow–headed households, where the head was unable to work owing to Taliban strictures (UN 1998), and households headed by the disabled and elderly. In 1997, the number of widows in Kabul was estimated at 38,000[19], with roughly 125,000 dependent children, while an estimated 15,000 families were headed by a disabled person. Eighty thousand people were believed to be in need of shelter (UN 1996a). Refugees who fled to Pakistan claimed that all who remained in Kabul were facing financial difficulty, and that a high proportion faced destitution.

[18] Because of military blockades and destruction of transport networks, Kabul is faring worse than other cities such as Kandahar and Herat through which most trade now passes (BAAG 1997a: 7). However, most studies were conducted in Kabul and it reveals, perhaps to a more severe extent, the changes cities have undergone in the 1990s.

[19] World Bank estimates that more than 300,000 women nationally were widowed.

Taliban restrictions on the population of Kabul had an impact on family survival. The climate of fear created by their enforcement hindered economic activity, and severely affected what had been a vibrant small-trading sector. This is not only because of the ban on female employment, but because men too were afraid to be out on the streets.

The search for income-earning opportunities puts people at risk in a war situation. In Kabul, periodic blockades of the city and other financial crises resulted in prices rising beyond the ability of much of the population to afford the basic essentials of food and fuel. In one incident, several men crossed the front line to obtain cheaper food supplies available on the other side, and most were killed. There were numerous examples of both adults and children going into areas they knew to be mined in their desperation to find wood for fuel.

Personal observation from 1995 onwards suggests increasing immiseration and new coping mechanisms. The most pronounced change was a drastic process of asset stripping among the poor. Street trade increased as people were forced to sell well-used personal possessions to ward off destitution. NGO studies (described in BAAG 1997a: 9–11) confirm this trend. For example, an Oxfam study of changes in the second-hand market notes a trend for assets of ever-declining value to be sold; indeed most stalls were selling goods of virtually no value, such as, a bent spoon, or half a *shalwar kamis*. An ICRC survey of 300 families in a hard-hit district found that 75 per cent of the families had sold more than one asset in the previous two to three months. A London School of Hygiene and Tropical Medicine study showed that 80 per cent of families were selling household goods to stay alive. Empty shops were visible everywhere, while any shops that remained had a limited turnover. Begging had become widespread, and indebtedness increased. The ICRC study found that 90 per cent of families sampled were in debt; nearly 70 per cent had borrowed from relatives, and another 25 per cent from neighbours. A CARE study found that 79 per cent of the 934 widows it was helping had loans of US$10 on average.

10.2   Refugees

In Afghanistan, in contrast to most war situations, the refugees were not the most vulnerable segments of the population. Rather, the evidence suggests that it was the better-off who had the resources to flee. They fled from insecurity, not because of destitution. Interviews with refugees reveal that their situation was insecure, but by and large, not desperate.

Most refugees in Iran and Pakistan seemed able to survive at an adequate level, as long as they were provided with certain entitlements in the form of rations, food subsidies, and access to water, health, and education. However, when these were withdrawn in September 1995 in Pakistan, and the Iranian government started to reduce these entitlements, refugees in both countries had difficulty maintaining their day-to-day existence, and many were forced to live at a marginal level of survival. Safety nets provided to vulnerable refugees in Pakistan, consisting of rations of edible oil, referral to vocational training, and income-generating projects, appeared to be inadequate. In Iran, the crackdown on migrant employment and services may have severe repercussions.

Most refugees were dependent on intermittent daily labouring to ensure the survival of their families. Older men faced particular discrimination as most jobs involved construction or casual labour. Those who appeared to survive best had acquired craft skills, such as carpet-weaving, before becoming refugees. Those who learnt new skills after becoming refugees showed mixed success. In the majority of refugee families, the women worked. However, most of the women interviewed indicated that this was in response to poverty rather than from choice, with the exception of the minority of professional women.

There appeared to be a correlation between how well off people had been in Afghanistan and their living standards as refugees in Iran. Although there were restrictions on the types of employment in which Afghans could engage, those who had previously enjoyed a reasonable level of income often brought savings with them, which helped to cushion them in difficult periods.

Interviews with refugees suggested that the extended family system of economic support appeared to have broken down, particularly in Iran, but also in the camps in Pakistan and even within Afghanistan. This seemed to stem primarily from the high levels of poverty. Both in rural and urban areas, the families that faced the greatest survival difficulties were those without any support from their extended family. Interviews in southern Afghanistan and the Farah province in the west suggested that widows no longer received the support that they might have received before the war. Families, therefore, resorted to various coping mechanisms, including selling personal belongings and relying on charity from other refugees (given on an ad hoc basis by individuals rather than through organized institutions). It was also common to borrow, often quite large sums of money, with little prospect of repayment. Some families relied, at least in part, on the labour of children as young as 5, while others placed their young children in orphanages. Some women worked as prostitutes while men begged.

Refugees indicated considerable reluctance to return to Afghanistan, mainly because of concern over security and employment. Many of those interviewed had come from urban areas and depended on being able to find labouring work. Other inhibiting factors were the high level of inflation and the knowledge that their relatives back in Afghanistan were unlikely to be able to help them. The absence of good education and medical facilities, particularly for girls, was another important deterrent to returning to Afghanistan.

10.2.1 *Returning refugees*

Most refugees returned to land they had previously occupied. Interviews with those who returned to their villages suggested that they were reasonably successful in restoring the agricultural economy—with a positive relationship between the provision of assistance by humanitarian agencies and the effectiveness of the reconstruction process. Farmers claimed that both the area cultivated and agricultural yields had decreased, except in districts with substantial inputs from humanitarian agencies. They added that increasing area cultivated and yields would require more irrigation. Refugees returning from Iran re-established themselves in the Farah province with reasonable success. None the less, poverty and population growth meant that a part of the population still needed to find work, illegally in Iran, and in Pakistan. Even in the three districts visited where agricultural production had returned to pre-war levels, a significant number of young people still went to Iran in search of work. This suggests that self-sufficiency may be hard to achieve. The departure of young persons slowed down reconstruction as the older people were less able to undertake heavy labouring. In southern Afghanistan the situation was somewhat different. Given reasonable growing conditions, the rural communities seemed able to survive economically with only minimal dependence on remittances from outside.

10.3   Women

Discrimination is reflected in a wide range of social indicators that relate to women. For instance, Afghanistan had the world's highest maternal mortality rate (MMR) at 1,700 per 100,000 births (UNICEF 1998). The literacy rate for women, at only 15 per cent in 1995, is one of the lowest in the world; this compares with 47 per cent for men (UNICEF 1998 and EIU 1997: 66). The problems facing women, particularly widows, as a result of Taliban edicts, have already been described. One result, however, is that widows who could not call upon the support of their extended family were, by and large, destitute and dependent on external relief. Of the reported 100 deaths from famine in the Hazarajat region in early 1997, most were women and children.

10.4   Health and Education

One might have expected an increase in disease and mortality as a result of the direct destruction and neglect of the public-health infrastructure. As the conflict moved from one area to another, the population shifted, often to urban areas. Overcrowding in cities created conditions rife for epidemics, while movements of displaced persons between communities allowed disease to spread easily. The breakdown of basic urban services heightened the risk of communicable diseases, while worsening nutrition levels and a lack of shelter also increased people's susceptibility to disease. Moreover new threats emerged such as cholera and chloroquine-resistant malaria. None the less, despite the war, some demographic and health-related indicators improved during the war years. The population increase remained high and life expectancy increased from 34 years in 1978 to 45 in 1996.

Most indicators suggest that maternal mortality worsened. UNICEF shows a rise from 600 in 1981 to 1,700 in the mid-1990s. Studies of child and infant mortality reveal a widespread variation in both levels and trends, which reflect changes over time and regional variation. UNICEF statistics suggest an overall decline, which, if true, could be the result of the attention given to mother and child health by aid agencies, and the determined efforts of the BBC Pashto and Persian Services to broadcast basic health messages.

In rural areas where NGOs were active, certain health indicators suggest considerable improvement. In Farah province, repatriated refugees attribute the increase in population to reduced infant mortality resulting from greater access to health clinics during the war when they were refugees, and in their villages when when they returned. In other rural areas and cities, there was a marked decline in access to health services. With the advent of the Taliban, and the bar on female access to health care, some worsening in female and child health must be expected. The PHR study cited earlier attempted to gauge the effects of the Taliban regime on women's health. Between 1996 and 1998 it found that over 70 per cent of the 160 women surveyed reported a decline in their physical well-being.

There is evidence of a high and in some cases rising incidence of disease. Leishmaniasis, for instance, rose from 14,000 cases in 1995 to 300,000 at the end of 1997 (WHO cited in BAAG 1997*a*: 10). Cholera, tuberculosis, polio, and acute respiratory infection (ARI) remained at high levels. Malaria was widespread. Diarrhoeal diseases accounted for over 40 per cent of mortality each year (UN 1998), while ARI is responsible for 25 per cent of all deaths of children under 5. Twelve thousand people died from tuberculosis each year, while there were an estimated 3 million cases of malaria in 1996, with pregnant women and young children most at risk.

Landmine injuries, drug abuse, and mental trauma can be directly attributed to the war. The statistics are by no means certain, but approximately 10 per cent of men are believed to have been involved in a landmine accident. By 1993, more than 40,000 people had been maimed or killed. In some regions the level of hospital admissions was up by over 20 per cent as a result of landmine-related injuries, while treating them added about 35 per cent to hospital costs (UN 1998). As areas accorded a low priority are unlikely to be cleared of mines, these casualties are likely to continue for decades. Nationally, it was estimated that up to two million Afghans were disabled, mainly from genetic causes, polio, or landmines (UN 1996*b*).

The incidence of mine injuries is estimated to have increased in Kabul under the Taliban. Rubin (1996) attributes this primarily to the closure of schools, including boys' schools, shut down because many of their teachers were women who were no longer allowed to work. Two other factors were the Taliban's ban on mine awareness training for women, and the return of security to some areas which made people feel it was safe to travel to previously inaccessible areas which were often mined (Rubin 1996: 5).

There is little firm information on drug abuse in Afghanistan. Opium has been widely used for a long period, and its use may be increasing. Observers recount how women in rural areas often take opium when pregnant and give it to their children to calm them. This practice can lead to learning disabilities and mental retardation. Anecdotal evidence suggests that heroin use is not substantial, although a 1992 USAID survey estimated that there may have been over 1 million heroin users (UNDP 1993, ii. 27). Ten to fifteen per cent of returning male refugees aged between 15 and 35 were believed to be heroin addicts. Evidence suggests that abuse increased among women and children. UNDCP is planning a new study of heroin use, meanwhile the USAID survey data should be treated with caution.

The war has caused severe trauma on the country's inhabitants and refugees. The PHR (1999) study found that 81 per cent of 160 women interviewed reported a decline in their mental health between 1996 and 1998. Moreover, 42 per cent were found to meet the diagnostic criteria for post-traumatic stress disorder, while 97 per cent exhibited major depression, 86 per cent showed significant symptoms of anxiety, and over 20 per cent indicated that they had suicidal thoughts either 'extremely' or 'quite' often. Nearly 85 per cent of these women reported that one or more family members had been killed during the war.

A 1997 UNICEF study in Kabul found that 90 per cent of over 300 children interviewed believed that they would die during the conflict, and that over 70 per cent of these children had experienced the death of a family member between 1992 and 1996; in 40 per cent of these cases the relative was a parent. Nearly all these children had witnessed acts of violence during the war; half had seen many people killed at once during an attack; and two-thirds had seen a dead body or body parts. Sixty per cent of the children admitted that they continued to be afraid, while 50 per cent cited fear as their strongest emotion. Nearly all were worried about their future safety and that of their families.

McLachland (1988) discussed the effects of the fall in living standards and increased incidence of bereavement on women. She noted the prevalence of psychosomatic symptoms among women and their reduced ability to work or even carry out normal domestic activities. Similarly, refugees interviewed in Pakistan often cited stress-related poor health as the reason for the inability of family members to work (BAAG 1996*b*).

We have already mentioned that Afghanistan has one of the highest illiteracy rates in the world, but there was evidence of some improvement among both males and females during the 1970s and 1980s. None the less, UNDP (1993, i. 31) states that the country 'is to all intents and purposes, functionally illiterate'.

10.5   Comparison with Nepal

Comparison with Nepal gives a mixed picture. Child mortality fell by about 50 per cent in both countries.[20] Maternal mortality fell sharply in Nepal—from 833 to 515 per 10,000 births—while most observers concur that in Afghanistan it rose sharply. Despite higher access to education in Nepal, the literacy rate appeared to be slightly higher in Afghanistan in the mid-1990s, but at 31 and 27 per cent for Afghanistan and Nepal respectively, it remained low in both countries. Comparative data for earlier years do not exist. Thus, it would appear that the health and literacy situation was not markedly worse in Afghanistan than Nepal, with the exception of maternal mortality, despite the hugely negative effects of the war on public services. It seems that within Afghanistan, the NGOs played an important role in maintaining entitlements despite severe challenges, while the massive movement of refugees and the relatively good provision they obtained in Pakistan and Iran provided a further safety net.

10.6   Security

A public entitlement less easy to quantify relates to the effects of insecurity and the breakdown of social cohesion. The war clearly eroded these entitlements for perhaps the majority of the population, particularly refugees. External involvement and aid were only been able to mitigate problems stemming from displacement.

---

[20] We use child mortality rather than infant mortality, which reflects the public health situation more directly, since other factors such as breast feeding may affect infant mortality.

A more concrete threat to security was the Taliban's physical punishment of those who violated their edicts. Women were particular targets because of the wide array of restrictions they face. A 1997 UNHCR report concluded that 'virtually all females (in Kabul) have been victims, or know someone who has suffered' while the 1998 PHR survey found that 69 per cent of women surveyed (also in Kabul) reported that they or a family member had been detained by Taliban officials. The PHR study noted that 68 per cent of respondents indicated 'extremely restricted social activities'.

Some refugees returned to areas in Afghanistan where they have family; others continued to work in exile but maintained close links with their families in Afghanistan. Yet others remained in exile, as a kind of underclass with an uncertain future. At a seminar in December 1995, a delegate spoke of the feeling of being uprooted and living in a foreign land in an uncertain state as antithetical to the sense of well-being gained from stability and cohesion.

11 Conclusions

In Afghanistan, the data though limited and unreliable, point to considerable economic decline because of conflict. The Soviets made some effort to bolster the economy and social welfare, but the attempt was short-lived. Subsequent governments made no attempt to protect the civilian population from the trauma of war. Microlevel indicators suggest a worsening of living standards since the start of the war. During the 1980s, the urban population was relatively privileged, but suffered most after the Soviet departure. Studies of refugees reveal that many endured a marginal level of existence. Those who returned to their communities were moderately successful at reconstructing their local economies. Those living in cities, particularly those in households headed by women or the disabled, faced extreme hardship.

None the less, despite widespread displacement and extreme military destruction, the population proved remarkably resilient. Market and public entitlements declined significantly, but civic entitlements compensated to some extent. There was an increase in malnutrition but no widespread starvation. UN and NGO activity allowed continued access to some schools and supported health-care facilities, in some regions even leading to an improvement in selected social indicators.

The advent of the Taliban in 1996, and their prohibitions relating to women and NGO activity, caused the situation regarding public and civil entitlements to deteriorate. However, as insecurity diminishes, revived economic activity should enhance market entitlements.

3

Mozambique: The Economic Effects of the War

TILMAN BRÜCK

1 Introduction: The Character of the War

Recent economic developments in Mozambique are frequently interpreted without adequate reference to the long period of war in the country. The effects of war are either ignored or misunderstood, being equated to the effects of an exogenous shock. Indeed, the IMF and the World Bank frequently call for adjustment policies, designed originally for peace economies, which are ineffective in a war-affected country. Aid agencies, on the other hand, treat war as an emergency, impacting on social welfare, and calling mainly for a short-term response on humanitarian grounds. Both positions neglect the long-term development implications of war. This chapter shows how the internal war in Mozambique caused microeconomic distortions and macroeconomic obstacles, and suggests how both the Mozambican government and donors might have responded to these challenges.

The Mozambican economy has suffered from internal war since 1964.[1] At first, war was shaped by the slow, partial successes of the left-wing Frelimo liberation army against the Portuguese colonial forces. The revolution in Portugal of April 1974 led to an ill-planned decolonization process, with much confusion and misunderstanding on both sides. There followed a brief period of relative peace and stability in the early years of independence, when a form of socialist economy was set up. Then an internal war, fuelled by regional, ideological, and local political differences, commenced in various parts of Mozambique with varying degrees of intensity. The impact was much stronger on the countryside than on the towns. After the Zimbabwean independence of 1980, which displaced former Rhodesian security forces into Mozambique, the war intensified and spread across the country. 1981 can be considered as the start of a new phase

I would like to thank Valpy FitzGerald, Frances Stewart, and a large number of people in Mozambique for their generous support and advice.

[1] See Newitt (1995) for an account of colonial Mozambican history and Hall and Young (1997) for more recent political events. Different perspectives on Mozambique's recent economic development include Abrahamsson and Nilsson (1995), Brochmann and Ofstad (1990), Brück (1996, 1997, and 1998), Brück, FitzGerald, and Grigsby (2000), Castel-Branco (1994), Cramer and Pontara (1998), Hanlon (1991 and 1996), Hermele (1988), International Monetary Fund (1998), UNDP (1998), and Wuyts (1996). The nature of the war in Mozambique is analysed in greater detail by Finnegan (1992), Geffray (1991), and Vines (1996).

of the conflict. In September 1984, after failing to join the Comecon, Mozambique joined the IMF and the World Bank. A programme of stabilization, structural adjustment, and trade liberalization was introduced, which reversed many of the former socialist policies. The war ended formally when a successful peace agreement between the Frelimo government and the Renamo rebels was signed in late 1992. The first multi-party elections were held in late 1994. Frelimo won both the presidential and parliamentary elections.

Internal wars may be viewed as fundamental disagreements between two or more groups within a nation involving competing claims over legal authority and political legitimacy. These wars are complex but not incomprehensible socio-economic events, which differ significantly from trade shocks and natural disasters (see FitzGerald, Chapter 2, Volume I). The economic effects of the internal war in Mozambique were shaped by the nature of the war aims, the methods of fighting adopted, and the war's perceived time horizon. Wars of destabilization aim to weaken an opponent politically rather than defeating it militarily. The methods used in such wars may involve one side using simple tools, while the defending opponent will resort to sophisticated weaponry as well. This inevitably leads to large-scale capital and technological destruction and to uncertainty. While at first war may be perceived as temporary, many wars turn into lengthy campaigns with an uncertain time horizon. If, after fighting starts, war is considered a quasi-permanent state, then agents' behaviour and expectations will quickly adjust to this situation.

The post-1975 war in Mozambique was an internal war of destabilization, with one side at first using very basic weapons and the other more conventional ones. The intention of the Renamo insurgency, and their initial Rhodesian and South African sponsors, led to a low-intensity destabilization war, waged to challenge the legitimacy and authority of the Frelimo government, rather than a full internal war aimed at taking over the administration of the country. This policy of destabilization through terror created much confusion, leading to a highly volatile situation in rural areas while the towns suffered from the attempts to rebut the rural attacks. This led to an uneasy stalemate for over ten years where the government was unable to protect the targets (mainly people and social infrastructure) except for those in core urban areas. The government opted for an expensive, high-technology strategy, unsuccessfully using its capital-intensive weaponry while Renamo pursued a low-technology labour-intensive strategy to achieve its military and political aims.

The general perception of the war was one of quasi-permanence. In fact, Mozambique had been at war for so many years that at the end of the war in 1992 only one tenth of the population had been economically active in the pre-war economy (Instituto Nacional de Estatística, 1997b). The end of the war was unexpected, and brought about by the end of the Cold War, the change of government in South Africa, as well as the internal economic situation and the financial exhaustion of both sides.

The remainder of this chapter will analyse key aspects of the war economy as well as the nature and the scale of the direct and indirect effects on the economy. The concluding paragraphs will discuss the policy implications of these findings.

Brück

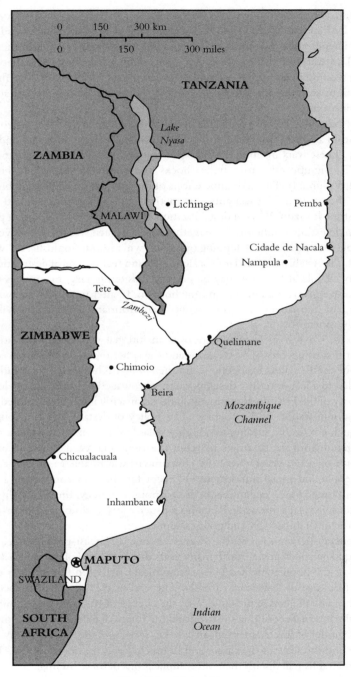

Map 3.1 Mozambique

2 Key Aspects of the War Economy

At the time of Independence, Mozambique's level of development was low even by African standards, despite the industrial growth induced by the Portuguese regime in the 1950s. Mozambique can be described as a poor agro-exporting country, dependent on and in need of investment and foreign aid. In 1970, GDP was estimated at US$1.25 billion, or US$132 per head (Ratilal 1990). Although this figure rose to US$196 in 1980, by 1990 GDP per head had fallen to US$115.

2.1 Domestic Capital and Investment

Capital and investment are the first and most obvious economic casualties of war. The characteristics of capital such as its visibility, mobility, divisibility and legality define how vulnerable particular capital is to war. Activities and sectors in turn are characterized by different degrees of war vulnerability. The agricultural sector in Mozambique, for instance, contained war vulnerable capital, particularly livestock and irrigation machinery. A war vulnerable sector will experience the equivalent of a cost shock since the erosion, destruction, and reallocation of its capital will decrease both the scale of activity in that sector, and in the overall economy. That is, a direct reduction in the capital stock used as an input into the production function will directly cause a reduction in the level of output equivalent to a move along the function towards the origin. For example, the Mozambique cashew factories in the countryside were frequently attacked and their assets destroyed (Cramer and Pontara, 1998; Ministry of Agriculture and Fisheries and World Bank 1998; Ministry of Industry, Trade and Tourism 1997; Strasberg, Mole, and Weber 1998; UNDP 1998). This stopped the processing of nuts and led to workers being made redundant. An indirect, transaction-cost effect as a result of market disorganization will cause the whole production function to shift downwards as the externality effects reduce the density of the market. Cashew traders, for instance, tried to continue buying nuts throughout the conflict, but as fewer farmers still collected nuts, they were forced to buy poorer quality nuts from poorly farmed trees. This meant that the traders had to work harder to purchase worse cashew nuts compared to pre-war times.

Holders of liquid capital will seek to reallocate their capital in order to optimize the portfolio in the light of the changed war circumstances. Many Asian traders moved their capital to neighbouring countries, the Gulf, or South Asia to avoid the impact of the war in rural Mozambique. On the other hand, some traders will actually experience an increase in trading profitability which will lead them to expand their activities. This applied to the import sector based in urban areas, especially after the liberalization of international trade and the increase in aid to Mozambique. War profiteers will also exploit temporary illegal profit opportunities—which may have high returns—providing an incentive to invest. Indeed, war profiteers (including arms traders or officers) are likely to have a high savings propensity to the extent that they view the war as temporary. General government policy will also influence incentives and risks, which affect the reallocation of capital and investment patterns.

War is thus likely to affect the adjustment coefficient of investment as well as the desired and current levels of capital,[2] particularly for war-vulnerable capital and in war-vulnerable sectors. That is, current capital is reduced through, for example, fighting while future capital may be reduced through long-term uncertainty and increased taxation.

2.2   Transaction Efficiency

Internal war in a developing country does not destroy global levels of technology, but reduces the local absorption of technology. In particular, war leads to significantly higher costs of market transactions, that is war reduces the transaction efficiency of the war economy (North 1990). War reduces the speed of adjustment through the nation-wide breakdown of markets, the individual firm's reduced ability to operate effectively, and by increasing uncertainty.

A long internal war in a developing country will have a major impact on transaction efficiency. A scorched-earth policy would have comparatively larger negative effects on technological absorption and transaction costs than a swift, stable, international war. Renamo pursued a scorched-earth policy in the rural areas hostile to its control. Its aim was to destabilize through deliberate random terror, and to cream off the rural surplus in order to finance its own war effort. However, this created an internally contradictory position in the longer run: Renamo acted myopically by destroying social capital and reducing the ability of the affected areas to produce output, therefore damaging its own source of war finance.[3]

If only private assets and no social capital are affected by war, a quick restoration of private-sector investment and output levels is possible after a war, making a post-war peace dividend feasible. Arguably, some sectors in Mozambique were less dependent on transactions and social institutions, and these were the first beneficiaries of post-war investment. These sectors included informal trading, the provision of imported consumer goods and some resource exploitation. However, if much social and private capital has been destroyed, private investment will not recover unless public investment and confidence accompany the return of peace. Low transaction efficiency in conjunction with high war uncertainty (see below) could lead to the destruction of the development capacity of large parts of the war economy. The destruction of confidence and of the capacity to absorb technology will be very hard to overcome, even in the long term.

2.3   Wartime Risk Attitudes

Risk, uncertainty, and expectations impact heavily on consumption and investment decisions. A situation of perfect certainty is one in which all future events can be correctly predicted by all economic agents, that is, perfect foresight exists. In reality,

---

[2] That is, for an investment (I_t) equation in terms of desired capital stock (K^*), existing capital stock (K_t) and the adjustment coefficient (λ) where the proportion of the required adjustment between desired and existing capital stock in the current year is determined by $I_t = \lambda(K^* - K_t)$.

[3] This is in contrast to the ongoing war in Angola where the government and the rebels maintain their financial resource bases through the wartime exploitation of off-shore oil and diamond deposits.

however, events are impossible to predict accurately. Risk represents the subjective probabilities that agents attach to the occurrence of future events. This means that microeconomic variables will not be deterministic, but have probability distributions of occurrence, which agents try to estimate based on their personal knowledge, experience, and expectation-generating mechanisms. In a war economy, this includes people's expectations of the time of and age at death. The major war risk in rural Mozambique was the random appearance of rebels, spreading terror and looting isolated villages. Farmers had to stand guard round the clock to be ready to flee the village as soon as rebels approached. Clearly this made the planning of agricultural production and the conduct of normal rural life extremely difficult.

An important question in this context is whether one would expect war to change people's attitude to risk. While such a change may seem likely, a more realistic approximation of risk behaviour is to consider an unchanged utility function across time, but to recognize that it is not people's attitudes but rather their actions that change as their circumstances deteriorate. That is, households approaching the survival threshold will not become more risk averse, but they will act differently in order to avoid a further deterioration of their situation. Each person has an inherent contingency plan for how to behave in the face of disaster. As the disaster draws closer, the pre-specified plan of action will be carried out, not a new plan.

If, for example, agents' survival probability is related to their consumption level but their utility function remains unchanged, their actions would focus ever more intensely on maintaining a minimum level of consumption as they approach the survival threshold. On the other hand, the population as a whole may exhibit various risk attitudes. For example, army recruits will not become more risk averse simply because they are fighting, but their personal attitude towards risk-taking will be determined by their personality from the start. Therefore, in this chapter it is assumed that the utility function will not be directly affected by war.

2.4 War Uncertainty

Uncertainty refers to the experience of a variety of risks in the whole economy. Expectations tend to be defined relative to some desired level of capital stock and may also influence the speed of adjustment of decision variables. The availability of information and functioning institutions will thus be crucial to coping with uncertainty at micro- and macrolevels of the economy. The expectation formation process itself may be damaged or affected by, for instance, a confusing war situation lacking clear battle lines or any victor, as was the case for many years in the Mozambican conflict.

War uncertainty is another extreme version of policy uncertainty. It is distinguished from other types of uncertainty by its near-perfect correlation of risks among households and its uninsurability. The source of much war uncertainty is the conflict over authority and legitimacy between two parties. The erosion of either authority or legitimacy increases war uncertainty. War uncertainty need not imply 'maximum' uncertainty, but rather a form of uncertainty related to fundamental state functions and actions. The imprecise nature of the start and end of wars means that both for agents affected and for research purposes it may be difficult to date wars in the economic sense. For most economic purposes, conflict lasts beyond the military campaign itself. Many current conflicts, for example in Angola, Sierra Leone, the Balkans, the former Soviet Union, or Iraq, persist with varying intensity over many years. The Mozambican internal war, however, ended quite suddenly and it became increasingly clear that the country had found a lasting peace settlement. In this case, the strong UN presence, high levels of aid, a successful demobilization and emerging democratic institutions helped to define a clear end to the war.

War uncertainty operates at both micro- and macrolevels of the economy. Capital, for instance, may be exposed to war destruction and dislocation at the micro level, through theft and violence (micro war uncertainty) and, at the macrolevel, through the abuse of state authority in a partisan way (macro war uncertainty). In addition, macro war uncertainty includes the use of the government fiscal machinery and economic regulation for war-related purposes, which inevitably reduces transaction efficiency.

For agents, war uncertainty will be more severely felt the less they are able to substitute for vulnerable assets or activities. The existence of vulnerability-reducing institutions, such as family, religious or ethnic networks and income diversification opportunities, reduce this exposure to war uncertainty, positively affecting people's welfare. In the coastal areas, for example, traditional fishing represented a less war-vulnerable activity and provided much needed nutrition, nutritional variation, and a source of income (Johnsen 1992; Tschirley and Weber 1994). The sharp reduction of remittances from South Africa, on the other hand, deprived many war-affected, rural households especially in southern Mozambique of an important and climate-independent source of earnings.

A basic consequence of war uncertainty is the large reduction of transaction efficiency. This in turn will reduce the size of the peace dividend and undermine confidence in the long-term viability of the economy. In addition, the reduction in confidence is likely to reduce the volume of asset transactions, except for the purpose of war-induced reallocation or war-profiteers' asset accumulation and profitability (as discussed in Keen Chapter 3, Volume I) with the consequence of reduced investment and productivity, fewer risk-reduction opportunities, and further reduced market density.

2.5   War and the Role of Government

The fact that many developing countries in conflict are also centrally controlled economies complicates the analysis, because it may not be clear whether distortions arise from state intervention or the conflict itself. On the one hand, socialist reforms often reinforce the effects of war, as by reducing the efficiency of the market they both have similar effects (Wuyts 1989). On the other hand, planning policies often are partially shaped by the experience of the war, so that a policy change is not entirely exogenous. This means that any formal economic analysis of an economy at war must avoid assumptions as to the free choice of individual consumption, investment, and output levels and specify clearly the constrained disequilibria which result (FitzGerald provides further discussion of this topic in Chapters 2 and 8, Volume I).

The more likely it is that the opponent's aim of assuming sole leadership will be achieved (or the more volatile the war perhaps as a proportion of domestic territory affected in a short time period), the more single-minded the government will become in pursuing its war policy. That is, the more threatened a government is the more it will regulate the economy to ensure its own victory. Indeed, wars typically cannot be won by deregulating domestic activity; military activity itself must be authoritarian and centralized (Milward 1970). Hence it was contradictory for the government and the donor community in Mozambique to attempt the transition from central planning to the free market while continuing the internal war.

2.6 Fiscal Deficit and Foreign Aid

2.6.1 Tax Revenue

The fiscal deficit is endogenously determined by warfare through its effects on tax revenue, government expenditure and foreign aid. Tax revenues depend particularly on the war experience of the population. A reduction in revenue may be counterbalanced to some extent through coercion, by an increase in tax rates or a broadening of the tax base. However, there could be decreasing tax returns due to tax evasion, which becomes easier to achieve successfully in times of internal war.

In a developing country like Mozambique, export agriculture is the easiest sector to tax, as it comprises a few readily recognizable units, such as multinational firms with offices in the capital and published annual accounts, large plantations and estates, obvious harvests and clear trading seasons, bulky export goods, and few exit transport channels, such as international ports. One would, therefore, expect the agricultural export sector to be particularly vulnerable to excessive war taxation. In fact, in Mozambique it was the import sector, utilizing mainly safe corridors, harbours, and airports, which was targeted for higher tax revenue. The share of import duties to total government revenue rose from 10 per cent in 1988 to 20 per cent at the end of the war in 1992; by 1995 it had fallen to 15 per cent (Comissão Nacional do Plano 1989, 1991, 1995; Instituto Nacional de Estatística 1997a).

2.6.2 Government Expenditure

Government expenditure will be affected by the nature of the war. The two sides may have different spending needs because of their different styles of waging war. The Renamo rebels did not aim to provide any consumption goods or social services in areas under their control. Instead, their main strategic aims were to reduce the government's tax revenues and its ability to deliver core services, and to raise non-financial resources from looting. In contrast, the government increased its regulation of the economy because it needed to raise further finance through taxation. Regulations such as production quotas, fixed prices, or contributions in kind gave the government further command over resources, but also increased market transaction costs. In addition, the government aimed to increase its spending in the urban social sectors to maintain its political support and credibility and to compensate for falling urban incomes.

2.6.3   Foreign Aid

Aid to a country may be increased or decreased in times of war, so it could have either a positive or negative affect on the fiscal deficit. Typically, investment or project-oriented aid will be reduced in line with a general reduction in investment but consumption and relief-oriented aid may be increased to lessen the negative human costs associated with war. Exogenous, donor-related political or administrative factors also determine aid flows to the recipient war-affected country. Such uncertainties surrounding the possible flow of aid are thus another factor contributing to the increased level of macro war uncertainty. Aid may either directly benefit the government (thus allowing increased government spending) or directly enter the private sector (increasing private capital stocks and consumption levels). In any case, foreign aid inflows will improve the balance-of-payments position but possibly increase uncertainty.

3   The Direct Economic Effects of War

In the next two sections, the arguments developed above are applied in more detail to the case of Mozambique. First, the direct effects of the internal war on various economic variables will be addressed. Then the macroeconomic implications of these direct war effects will be analysed by looking at the key variables—output, growth, consumption, welfare, and debt. Due to the poor quality of the data, changes in the war variables will be represented by various proxies.

3.1   Physical and Financial Capital

The destruction and erosion of immobile, and, therefore, war-vulnerable capital in rural areas is shown in Table 3.1. All forms of agriculture suffered severely from the two-thirds reduction in operational dams and plant nurseries as compared to the pre-war capital stock. The average destruction and erosion of all categories was 40 per cent. Assuming the war was at its worst during the 10 years prior to the peace agreement, this would imply an annual rate of war-related capital reduction of almost 4 per cent in addition to normal depreciation, leaving Mozambique with a net capital stock of near-zero by the end of this period because the new productive investment was so low.

The pre-war transport sector had been a large foreign exchange earner as goods were transported to the neighbouring states of Malawi, Zimbabwe, South Africa, and Swaziland. The railway system was a visually obvious target, and suffered a high level of destruction as a result. A total of 208 out of 222 units of rolling stock were lost or badly damaged between 1982 and 1989 (Comissão Nacional do Plano 1990; Stephens 1994; World Bank 1990).

The agricultural subsistence sector was better placed to adapt to the war than the agricultural export or manufacturing sectors because it depended on local purchases and sales, and local transport. Seeds benefited from being storable, easily concealed, and edible by their producers if necessary. Nevertheless, rebels burned fields, looted crops, destroyed tools, and killed cattle. Figure 3.1 illustrates how cattle production, a key

Table 3.1   Mozambique: War vulnerability of immobile capital, 1992

Immobile capital by sector	Number				Destruction (%)	Non-operational and destroyed (%)
	Operational	Non-operational	Destroyed	Total		
Agriculture:						
Irrigation systems	118	24	7	149	5	21
Dams	122	208	57	387	15	68
Seed production centres	13	9	0	22	0	41
Nurseries	38	19	4	61	7	38
Tick-cleansing tanks	70	299	40	509	8	67
Water supply:						
Wells	3,057	1,071	138	4,266	3	28
Holes	1,225	530	32	1,787	2	31
Fountains	484	205	11	700	2	31
Small water supply systems	96	84	29	209	14	54
Commercial buildings:						
Shops	6,664	1,318	2,381	10,363	23	36
Warehouses	369	8	40	417	10	12
Banks	144	6	4	154	3	6
Savings posts	54	31	0	85	0	36
Communication:						
Post offices	123	8	17	148	11	17
Rural post offices	49	90	13	152	9	68
Public administration:						
District admin.	117	33	42	192	22	39
Municipal admin.	99	83	120	302	40	67
Admin. residences	724	474	374	1,572	24	54
Average						39.7

Source: Comissão Nacional do Plano 1993*b*.

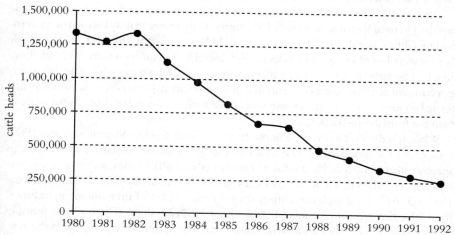

Figure 3.1   Cattle stock in Mozambique, 1980–1992

Source: Ministério da Agricultura 1994 (unpublished data).

Table 3.2 Mozambique: Foreign direct investment

Project status	Mid-1985 to mid-1993		Mid-1993 to mid-1994	
	US$ m.	% of total	US$ m.	% of total
Active/realized	165.6	26.8	40.0	9.0
Being implemented	62.8	10.2	217.1	49.0
Implementation not started	22.5	3.6	158.2	35.7
Cancelled/pending	366.5	59.4	27.6	6.2
Total approved	617.4	100	442.9	100

Source: Centro de Promoção de Investimento 1995 (unpublished data).

visible asset in subsistence agriculture, was strongly affected by war. Less than a fifth of the recorded 1980 cattle stock remained in 1992. Cattle were lost both through direct effects (rebels killing cattle to spread terror, to halt development, and to feed their troops) and indirect effects (lack of feed and veterinary care, short-term consumption needs of the population, and missing cattle markets to trade and replenish stock).

While the subsistence sector was more protected from the war by the nature of its activities, the countryside still endured a high war burden in terms of human costs. Many people were forced into extreme forms of self-reliance as the war destroyed all other forms of survival. Given the war situation, subsistence agriculture became an enforced alternative for previously better-off producers of cash crops, or a deliberate choice of survival activity for some farmers, and an unattainable means of survival for a large group of landless labourers and refugees.

One of the aims of destabilization was the destruction of nearly every concrete building in rural Renamo-controlled territories, which were mainly focused on government facilities. Local construction inputs could be obtained at little cost, so that simple houses were less of a target and so less war-vulnerable. Urban areas were quite safe from attack. The government sector, a major target, was always war-vulnerable, but many government activities were concentrated in the safer areas. Generally, one could say that formal sector activity was more war-vulnerable with the formal tradable sector more so than the formal non-tradable sector.

While it is difficult to measure domestic investment, foreign direct investment (FDI) is more readily quantifiable. The Mozambican government regulates FDI through an agency called Centro de Promoção de Investimento (CPI) for most sectors except minerals and commerce. Table 3.2 estimates annual FDI at about US$30 million during 1985–93. As it is difficult to confirm the implementation of investment applications, the CPI estimated actual annual FDI at about US$12 million (Centro de Promoção de Investimento 1995). This low value must have been due, at least partly, to the war. In comparison, in the immediate post-war period, mid-1993 to end-1994, US$443 million of FDI were approved by the CPI under new investment legislation.

Table 3.3 Mozambique: Destruction in the education sector

Year	Primary schools (Grades 1–5) closed or destroyed	
	Total no.	%
1983–7	2,655	45.1
1988	226	3.8
1989	238	4.0
1990	77	1.3
1991	206	3.5
Total	3,402	57.8
Total no. of primary schools in 1983	5,886	100.0

Source: Ministério da Educação 1994.

3.2 Human Capital

Human capital, that is the quantity and quality of labour available in the economy, also suffered erosion, destruction and reallocation. Table 3.3 shows the destruction and erosion of primary schools at an average annual rate of about 6 per cent for the years 1983–91. A similar destruction of hospitals and health posts occurred in rural areas (Cliff and Noormahomed 1988). The subsequent effect on the quality of human capital is not measurable although clearly evident.

Frequently, people subjected to hostilities became displaced either within their municipalities, within Mozambique or internationally. Table 3.4 indicates that war-induced population flows increased in the late 1980s. At the end of the war about a quarter of all domestic residents were displaced within Mozambique, and a further 10 per cent had become international refugees. An unknown number of Mozambicans (but over 20 per cent), although still living near their usual residence, had had their livelihoods destroyed by the war. These data suggest at least three things. First, the extent of the displacement of human capital in Mozambique was extreme, only comparable to a few other population movements following genocide in recent world history. Second, this vast migration must have been caused by extreme economic insecurity. And third, this level of migration will in turn have caused even greater uncertainty and increased transaction costs leading to increased claims on fiscal and aid resources.

Table 3.5 attempts to measure the impact of the war on children. It illustrates the psychological traumas and suffering experienced by children, and the crimes committed by war-affected children. These effects are likely to be more long-lived, at least in the minds of people, than any adverse economic shock or natural disaster of a similar magnitude and nearly every Mozambican will have been touched in similar ways by the war.

Table 3.4 Mozambique: Estimated total displaced, affected, and refugee populations

	Sept. 1986	Mid–1989	Oct. 1992
Affected	na	2,873,957	na
%	na	19	na
Displaced	na	1,689,492	3,728,000
%	na	11	26
Affected and displaced	3,482,626	4,563,449	na
%	25	30	na
Refugees	250,000	1,000,000	1,390,000
%	2	7	10
Displaced and refugees	na	2,689,492	5,118,000
%	na	18	36
Displaced, affected, and refugees	3,732,626	5,563,449	na
%	26	37	na
Total population	14,174,300	15,166,000	14,285,000
%	100	100	100

Notes: Affected persons are people whose homes or livelihoods have been destroyed but have not fled their general area of previous residence. Displaced persons are people who moved involuntarily within Mozambique. Data for refugees refer only to those persons living in neighbouring countries with 1986 and 1989 data restricted to Malawi, Zambia, and Zimbabwe.

Sources: Comissão Nacional do Plano 1987; International Organisation for Migration 1994; UNOHAC 1994; World Bank 1990.

Table 3.5 Mozambique: War experiences of children from war-affected areas

War experience	%
Witnessed physical abuse and/or torture	88
Witnessed killings	77
Served as porters for Renamo	75
Were abducted from their families	64
Witnessed rape or sexual abuse	63
Were physically abused or tortured	51
Witnessed family members killed	37
Were trained for combat	28
Admitted to being raped	16
Admitted to killing	9
Suffered permanent physical injury	7

Notes: Sample consisted of 504 children aged 6 to 15 years at the time of their war experiences, originating from 7 different provinces, all of whom had been resident in war-affected areas. Data collected between 1989 and 1990.

Source: Boothby, Uptom, and Sultan 1991.

Table 3.6 Mozambique: Commercial network for agricultural marketing

Commercial structure	No. of establishments nationally			% change, 1982–8
	1982	1985	1988	
Private shops	3,582	2,452	2,187	−39
Agricom fixed posts	235	150	62	−74
Other fixed posts	393	94	99	−75
All other structures	882	1,230	1,226	39
Total commercial structures	5,092	3,926	3,574	−30

Source: World Bank 1990.

3.3 Transaction Efficiency

The extent to which transaction efficiency was reduced by the war is very difficult to estimate. Possible proxies for this effect include domestic marketing activity and transport costs. Table 3.6 lists the net changes in numbers of operational units for various structures (buildings and some mobile marketing units). Warehouses, shops, and trading posts abandoned due to insecurity were eroded in value, or completely destroyed. The net loss for all structures in the period 1982–8 was approximately 30 per cent, suggesting a net annual loss rate of about 5 per cent. The destruction of the railway system, discussed above, was even greater.

Another proxy for transaction efficiency is the increase in distribution costs resulting from insecurity (requiring protection and reducing load factors due to coordination problems) and the reduced quality of transport infrastructure (reducing travel speeds, and increasing costs arising from more breakdowns on rough or mined roads). Figure 3.2 shows the distribution costs as a percentage of costs for four significant export and subsistence crops in 1989, under different security and transport scenarios. Distribution costs account for a larger share of total costs in export crops compared to domestic consumption crops. The potential savings from improved security are greater than the potential savings from transport infrastructure. For cashew, the most valuable food crop exported from Mozambique, distribution costs halve as one moves from war- to peacetime and improved transport infrastructure. Thus war imposed a tax on output which affected cash crops relatively more than other crops.

3.4 Uncertainty

During the course of the war, the Mozambican government built up its legitimacy and authority, and so was able to reduce war uncertainty over time. The government went through successive stages of war uncertainty from virtual chaos at independence to established authority soon afterwards, then to being the legitimate but threatened authority (by Renamo), and finally to becoming the recognized legitimate authority.

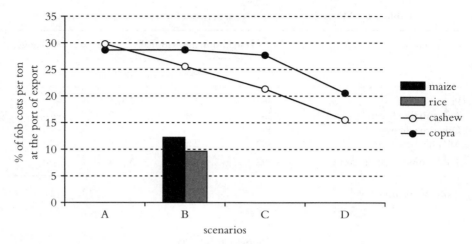

Scenario A: 1989 Mozambican situation with dedicated security force protection.
Scenario B: actual 1989 Mozambican situation.
Scenario C: same as B but with improved road transport infrastructure.
Scenario D: same as C but with improved maritime transport and security improvements
which would allow the elimination of military escorts (peace scenario).

Figure 3.2   Distribution costs in the Mozambican war economy
Source: World Bank 1989.

At the macrolevel, although state uncertainty declined during the course of the war, it
remained significant throughout this period. The main effects were on the reallocation
of capital and a loss of transaction efficiency. This was reflected in, for example, investment and population movements. Yet further macro war uncertainty was doubtless created by government spending as analysed below.

At the microlevel, a war of this type meant that civilians as well as soldiers faced
increased risks of mortality. Figure 3.3 compares national mortality rates (for all ages) to
war-induced mortality rates in several provinces over various years. While the national
mortality rate did not increase during the war years, directly war-affected people could
face mortality rates 3.5 to 7 times the national average (that is their probability of dying
increased up to sevenfold). This increased risk of dying radically affected people's
expectations, including their willingness to invest, and also their current behaviour—
possibly even more than capital losses. However, with peace, the risk of death rapidly
declines, whereas lost capital cannot be so easily replaced. Parallel with the increased
fear of death was the increased likelihood of famine, followed by the offsetting provision of humanitarian assistance. War, however, weakens the aid response to famine due
to increased transaction costs while famine itself may intensify the struggle to control
food resources.

Finally, landmines obviously increased the risk of mutilation (eroding human capital
in part) or death in Mozambique (Roberts and Williams 1995). Compared to the

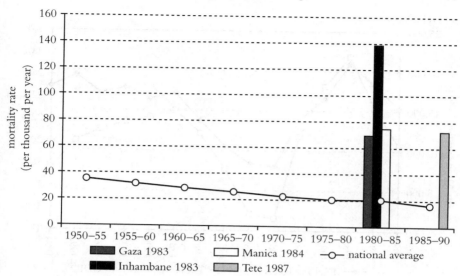

Figure 3.3   Mortality rates in war-affected areas of Mozambique compared
to the national average

Sources: Cliff and Noormahomed 1988; Comissão Nacional do Plano 1993*a*.

number of atrocities committed, the impact of mines is likely to be lower in numbers of fatal casualties during the war, particularly among people living in the areas that were being mined, as they could get to know the unsafe areas. Unfortunately, these mines will continue to destroy lives and keep the land useless for years after the ceasefire, extending the war uncertainty way beyond the end of the formal conflict. The largest negative impact of the mines in post-war Mozambique was in the slowdown and increased cost of reconstructing infrastructure and transport, rather than in the loss of value of rural agricultural land.

3.5   Public Finances

Three important aspects of public finance are tax revenue, government expenditure and the net fiscal deficit. Foreign aid may to some extent alleviate the fiscal constraint. Given the structure of the war in Mozambique, one would expect either declining tax revenues or increased tax rates, and an attempt to expand the tax base. In fact, the data presented in Figure 3.4a indicate that the real value of total tax revenues fell by half between 1981 and 1985 and by almost two thirds on a per capita basis.[4] Tax revenues rose with adjustment in 1985, possibly as a result of increased formal market activity (an implicit widening of the tax base) but they did not return to previous levels. Tax

---

[4] The data underlying Figures 3.4 and 3.5 are reproduced from Brück (1997), which is also available on http://www.qeh.ox.ac.uk/qehwps11.html. The values for 1994 in both figures are estimates. More recent data and events are analysed in Brück, FitzGerald, and Grigsby (2000).

a Level of tax revenue

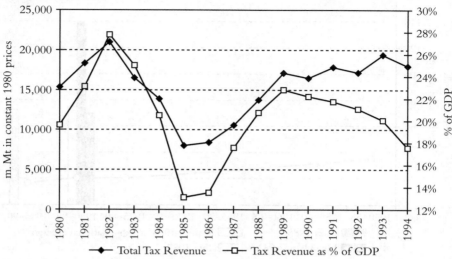

b Relative size of tax revenue

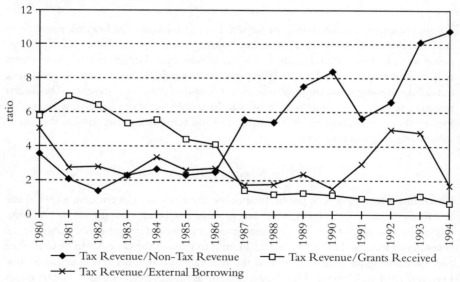

Figure 3.4   Fiscal indicators of the Mozambican war economy

Sources: Banco de Moçambique 1995; Comissão Nacional do Plano (various years); Ratilal 1990;
World Bank 1990 and 1992.

c Level of government spending

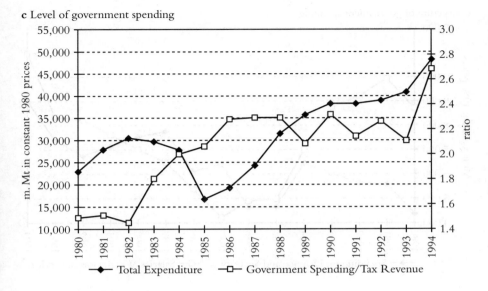

d Level of military spending

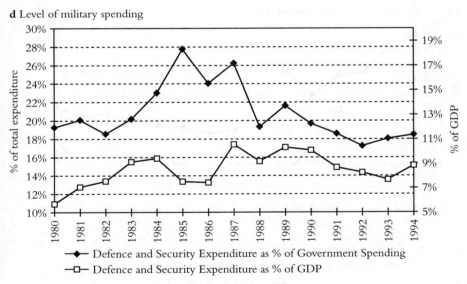

Figure 3.4 *(cont'd)*

e Structure of government spending

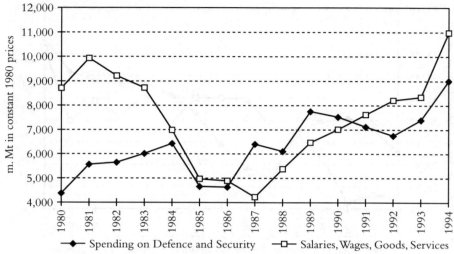

f Level of non-productive government spending

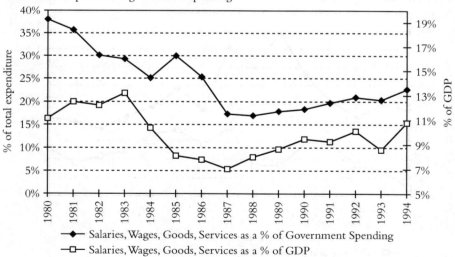

Figure 3.4 *(cont'd)*

g Level of government investment spending

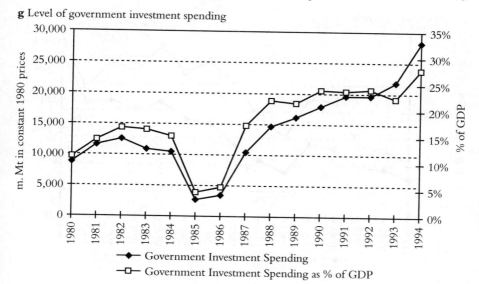

h Relative size of government investment spending

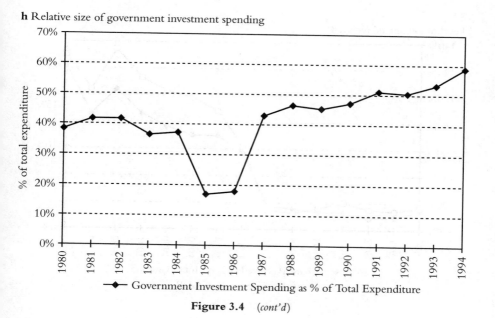

Figure 3.4 *(cont'd)*

i Level of budget deficit

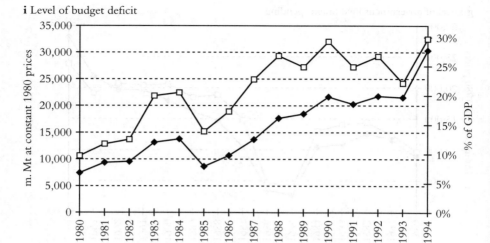

j Level of foreign aid received

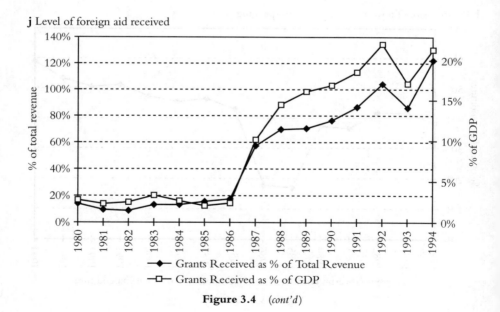

Figure 3.4   *(cont'd)*

k Structure of foreign aid received

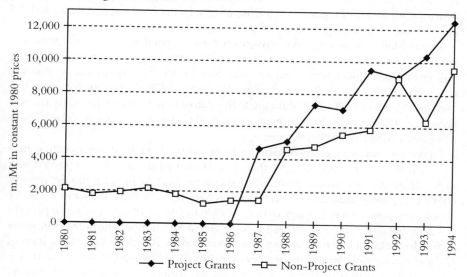

l Structure of budget deficit

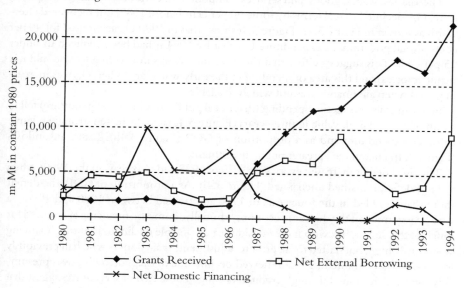

Figure 3.4 (cont'd)

revenue as a proportion of GDP declined again in the early 1990s, perhaps because the structural adjustment programmes only represented a once-off improvement, and did not yield any long-term growth in revenues.

Mozambique remains a donor-driven economy dependent on foreign grant aid. External aid has exceeded tax revenue in some recent years, as shown in Figure 3.4j. Following economic reforms, tax revenue rose in relative importance to non-tax revenue (Figure 3.4b). In the last six years of the war, 1987–92, the ratio for grants had averaged 16 per cent of GDP, showing their relative importance in financing the war economy. The relation of tax revenue to external borrowing was more volatile, both being determined by war conditions.

Figure 3.4c shows government spending from 1980 to 1994. Real government spending reached a low in 1985, but since then it has shown steady growth. For government expenditure (G) one would predict war spending (G_W) to increase during years of conflict. G_W more than doubled in real terms between 1980 and 1994 and it rose by almost nine points as a percentage of G from 1980 to 1985, and increased by 86 per cent as a share of GDP between 1980 and 1987 (Figure 3.4d). It should be noted that before 1980 Mozambican external security was threatened by Rhodesia so that the level of G_W was already high, while post-war levels included the high cost of demobilization— a peacetime cost of war. Yet G_W was volatile supporting the view that government spending contributed towards uncertainty in the economy either directly (through fighting) or indirectly (by raising demand or causing inflation).

The salaries, wages, goods, and services component of current government expenditure, G_H, declined in real terms by some 60 per cent before 1987, but recovered afterwards as shown in Figure 3.4e. Figure 3.4f shows that in 1980 G_H accounted for 40 per cent of total government expenditure but that by 1994 it had been reduced to under 25 per cent. This suggests either that the government was not willing to or could not maintain or expand this area of spending in the early war years (when G_W was increasing), and when aid finance was not widely available.

Economically productive spending (that is real public investment expenditure) fell to a fifth of its 1982 peak value in three years (Figure 3.4g) and decreased strongly relative to other expenditure and as a proportion of GDP (Figure 3.4h). Later, aid inflows (Figure 3.4j) encouraged greater public investment.

The fiscal deficit increased every year, except 1985 and two years in the 1990s when the real deficit remained unchanged (Figure 3.4i). As a proportion of GDP, the deficit more than doubled in the four years to 1984 and trebled between 1980 and 1990—a very heavy strain on the domestic economy. Initially, domestic financing accounted for much of the deficit, but with increased adjustment its role declined. External financing was initially high, but started to fall prior to adjustment, as aid donors who had previously lent money later granted it. The renewed decline in external borrowing was presumably supply-determined through credit-rationing. These two observations suggest that Mozambique was forced into structural adjustment as a result of the burden of war finance. With little Eastern bloc support forthcoming and finding it difficult to mobilize domestic resources, the government could not afford to self-finance both the war and development.

3.6   Foreign Aid

The move away from Eastern bloc support to Western aid facilitated a significant inflow of financial resources in support of the government. Grants increased from 2 to 3 per cent to about a fifth of GDP in the early 1990s (Figure 3.4j). In fact, grants were equivalent in value to government revenue between 1992 and 1994. Figure 3.4k compares grant aid for projects and non-projects. Both forms of grant have risen dramatically since 1986, although project grants have exceeded non-project grants, probably because of aid towards reconstruction programmes. Figure 3.4l shows the structure of the budget deficit including external financing, domestic financing, and grant aid. Since 1987, grant aid has far outweighed the other two components.

Although aid continued during the war, the timing and composition of grants suggest that foreign aid was determined by factors other than war, although since the end of hostilities, the economy has been aid-driven. In times of famine aid was delivered on humanitarian grounds or for general development purposes, but never explicitly to support the war effort. Aid in Mozambique should, perhaps, be seen as a variable independent of the war, though of huge importance in maintaining government expenditure patterns and levels. One might infer that international donors failed to use aid as a lever for ending the war in Mozambique.

4   The Indirect Economic Effects of War

The indirect effects of war arise from the direct effects discussed in the previous section. Per capita measures are used where appropriate. To enable comparison, data are expressed in constant 1980 prices using the GDP deflator. The quality of the macro data available for the period are exceptionally poor but certain broad trends in wartime behaviour can be observed quite clearly.

4.1   Output

GDP and global social product (GSP) are used as two proxy measures for output. Although calculated according to different methodologies, both series show similar patterns which allow comparisons over time. The data presented in Figures 3.5a–b show that both measures of output declined until 1986–7. While GSP per capita fell more steeply, both measures indicated a drastic decline of about 30–40 per cent in output in the late 1980s, following falling output of over a third during decolonization in the mid-1970s. The political shock of decolonization may have had long-term effects not so different from war (especially as a result of a reduction of human capital) although the increase in output during the period 1975–81 indicated that the shock had been at least partially overcome by the time the internal war intensified in the early 1980s. Decolonization would have had a once-off effect, which meant that expectations should adjust to the new regime. While it is not possible to quantify expectations, the expectation of an independence dividend in 1975 was probably more realistic than the expectation of a peace dividend in 1992.

The rise of measured output in the late 1980s indicated that the ongoing war was not the only relevant factor determining output in those years. Instead, the positive effects of the reform projects and the related inflow of aid allowed an expansion of output despite the continuous destruction of capital. The war effects became relatively less important as some war variables had a one-off effect. Uncertainty over lifespan, for instance, would have shifted up to a higher level for each war zone but would not typically increase thereafter. There was near-complete capital destruction in some areas, whereas the destruction of capital in other areas was offset by aid inflows, which prevented further falls in consumption. Arguably the productive capacity was not being maintained during the war. That is, increases in output were not achieved on a sustainable basis of domestically generated savings turned into investment but growth instead depended on an exogenously determined level of foreign aid inflows. This view of Mozambique 'living on a life-support machine of aid' during the war years is further supported by the above evidence on the level of aid supporting the fiscal deficit of the government.

4.2   Growth

War can be expected to reduce the long-term growth rate of the economy as a result of a reduction in capital, in transaction efficiency and an increase in uncertainty in the war economy. This result is unlike the effect of a natural disaster when one would expect an accelerated growth in the medium term. Testing this claim could be difficult as output growth is likely to fluctuate strongly and unlikely to show a clear long-term trend. Indeed, actual growth rates of GDP and GSP showed strong yearly fluctuations (Figure 3.5c). Yet the GDP series also showed a small trend. While practically all pre-1988 rates were below zero, most later values were near to or above zero growth. A possible interpretation is that the war initially reduced growth rates and then continued to dampen the hypothetical peacetime values although the economic liberalization helped improve growth. This supports the view that war damages the economy's growth potential beyond the period of the capital destruction and that growth may not pick up quickly (an output peace dividend) in the post-war period. Instead post-war policies must be designed to regenerate the sustainable growth potential (Brück, FitzGerald, and Grigsby 2000).

4.3   Consumption

Consumption can be expected to fall in a war economy as incomes decline. Real per head consumption declined for the first six years of the period as shown in Figure 3.5d, rose slightly for three years, but by 1994 had fallen to nearly half the 1980 value. Interestingly, government consumption, which initially fell relatively more than private consumption, responded to aid inflows and increased relatively more in the later years (Figure 3.5e).

Another interesting fact is highlighted by the relation of consumption to GDP (Figure 3.5f). Economic theory predicts that a shock-like, one-off reduction in capital will lead to a curtailment of consumption so that additional investment may rebuild the capital stock. Yet the prediction may not hold for the more complex case of a war as it will also reduce the ability of the economy to rebuild itself, hence further decreasing output. In fact, both consumption and output fell strongly in the first half of the 1980s but relatively speaking private consumption fell by less till 1987, thus maintaining a fairly constant share of private consumption to GDP. Only with the acceleration of structural adjustment from 1987 to 1989 did Mozambique experience a drastic fall of private consumption to GDP relative to the earlier war years as would be expected for most countries undergoing structural adjustment. This suggests that initial liberalization policies in a war economy may not have the same outcomes as in a peace economy due to the war-related reduction in the long-term growth rate in the economy.

In addition, the prospect of on-going warfare and corresponding capital destruction may have forced people into involuntary consumption before 1987. Alternatively, as mentioned above, people were so close to their survival threshold (note the falling output in the early 1980s) that their propensity to consume increased with declining incomes (Gersovitz 1983). Furthermore, the accumulation of a war-related budget deficit must impact on the long-term welfare of the population, although in the early 1980s some of the current population may not have amended their consumption pattern, and were maintaining relatively higher levels of consumption than output. In fact, higher discount rates in times of war further reduce the incentive to invest in the maintenance of future output. The high share of consumption will eventually lead to lower output, as the resources available for future growth will have been depleted.

After 1987, the faster growth of output could be either due to foreign aid or due to structural adjustment, or both. It is doubtful whether aid generally, and the composition of aid to Mozambique in particular, could have generated the growth in output witnessed after 1987. Aid certainly enabled a level of consumption to be maintained by some of the most threatened war and famine victims, and helped to sustain the level of public consumption from 1988 onwards. Structural adjustment probably increased the efficiency of resource use, encouraging non-consumption activities, and reversing the increase in the marginal propensity to consume with declining income discussed above. The rural sectors and rural population suffered substantially more from the war, whereas the urban sectors and population benefited from the market-oriented policy reforms. Thus, productivity gains in the late 1980s were achieved in the towns, while consumption in the countryside decreased. This illustrates the duality of the war economy in Mozambique where some productive sectors of the economy were less affected by the war. This introduced asymmetries into the development of the economic and political life of Mozambique. In the long term, this has led to post-war economic reconstruction in Mozambique primarily benefiting the urban, service-oriented sectors, while neglecting the rural areas, which has further reinforced wartime income inequalities.

In summary, total private consumption per capita decreased as a result of the war. However, consumption did not fall by as much as output until 1987 reflecting the behaviour of household consumption near the survival threshold. After 1987, reform-oriented and aid-financed policies assisted a recovery in incomes and consumption in the safer, mainly urban areas thus increasing rural–urban income inequalities beyond the end of the war.

4.4 Welfare

It is important to find measurable indicators of welfare. The one most commonly used is GDP per capita. This fell drastically as a consequence of war (Figure 3.5b). Social indicators such as malnutrition, infant mortality, and literacy rates provide more detailed indicators of welfare. The education sector suffered major capital losses (Table 3.3), mortality rates in war areas increased sharply (Figure 3.3), a large part of the population was displaced (Table 3.4), and many people, particularly children, were directly affected

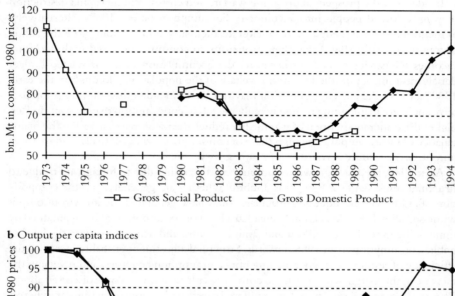

a Levels of total output

b Output per capita indices

Figure 3.5　Macroeconomic indicators of the Mozambican war economy

Sources: As Fig. 3.4.

c Change in output per capita

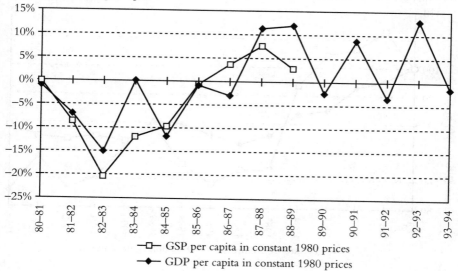

d Levels of consumption per capita

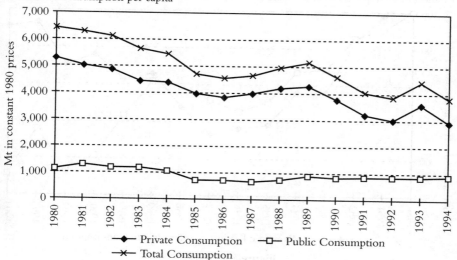

Figure 3.5 *(cont'd)*

e Output per capital indices

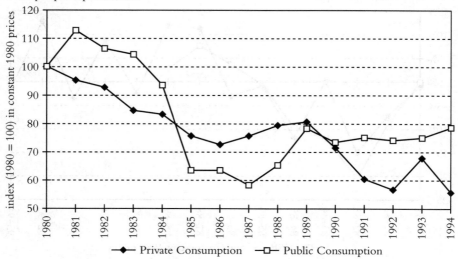

f Indices of GDP per capita and private consumption per capita

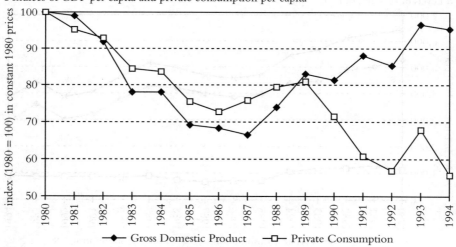

Figure 3.5   (*cont'd*)

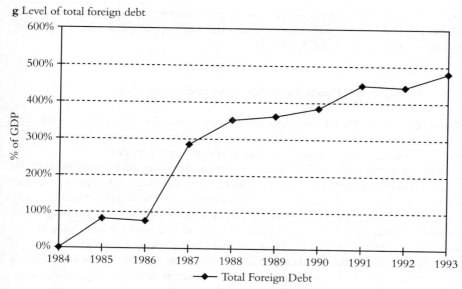

g Level of total foreign debt

Figure 3.5 (*cont'd*)

by the horrors of war (Table 3.5). Social indicators collected in the post-war period suggest that Mozambique had a human development index (HDI) of no more than 0.28 in 1995, the lowest HDI in southern Africa and lower than the HDI for sub-Saharan Africa of 0.39 (UNDP 1998).

The collection and measurement of reliable data, particularly under war conditions, and in a country where 95 per cent of the population are estimated to be poor, and over two-thirds considered to be absolutely poor (World Bank 1990) poses a severe problem. Indeed, poverty in this context implies an inability to collect and evaluate data, in the face of other, competing priorities. The lack of data on social variables can be considered as another cost of conflict. Yet all the evidence, even if anecdotal, points to a significant, widespread, and long-term decline in economic and social welfare as a result of the war.

4.5   Debt

Government debt may be expected to increase in times of war. Given the constraints on the domestic financial market (including its small size, undeveloped financial institutions, inflation, uncertainty, and lack of credibility), most government borrowing had to come from foreign sources. The total foreign debt stock increased continuously to 500 per cent of GDP after 1985, when the Mozambican government started to borrow from Western sources (Figure 3.5g). This is a reflection of the fiscal deficit accumulated over the war years, partly as a result of increased war expenditure and the government's reduced ability to generate domestic tax revenue. This enormous debt suggests that post-war economic reconstruction in Mozambique will be severely capital constrained and will not permit a significant increase in government social spending unless most wartime debt is forgiven soon after the end of the war, for example as part of the highly indebted, poor countries (HIPC) initiative.

5 Policy Considerations and Conclusions

The analysis of the Mozambican war and economy provides some useful insights into the economic effects of internal war on a very poor economy and how economic policy can alleviate the economic and development costs of conflict.

The war in Mozambique led to lower output and growth, both during the war and in the immediate post-war period. The conflict also had a significant negative impact on the capital stock and caused increased uncertainty, decreased transaction efficiency, an increased budget deficit, and increased government debt. The actual magnitudes of these variables were strongly influenced by other factors such as decolonization, government policy, and structural adjustment. In fact, the scale and the combination of the negative effects severely damaged the development capacity of the Mozambican economy and persisted beyond the end of the war, significantly delaying and diminishing the peace dividend.

Overall, war in Mozambique diminished the competitiveness of the economy and reduced the opportunities to communicate, negotiate, specialize, save, invest, produce, and trade. These effects distinguish war from a natural disaster or even from the experience of decolonization, where the basic functions of the economy are not challenged as severely or systematically. The very nature of the war in Mozambique with its aim of political destabilization had the most profound effect on the economy.

In addition, had the Mozambican peace agreement required a large-scale and Pareto-optimal distribution of post-war economic resources to reward the participants' peaceful behaviour, the slow growth in the immediate post-war period might have induced a return to fighting for economically less advantaged agents. Optimal post-war economic policy is thus also an important precondition for building long-term political stability.

While the war had overall negative effects on the macroeconomy, it also caused microeconomic distortions, which contributed to the structural distortion of the economy. Based on the war-vulnerability of capital, activities, and sectors, people reallocated their assets and activities, causing a shift either into safer urban, service-sector activities or absolute subsistence-sector activities. The rural and tradable sectors suffered greatly, while military-related, aid-supporting and aid-supported sectors benefited. Government strategy also changed endogenously as the need for war finance grew. The financial necessities of the war economy therefore stimulated the first ever transition from a socialist to a market economy.

Eventually even the end of the war was determined endogenously as the financial needs of both sides forced them to negotiate and agree a peace settlement. Yet donors for many years failed to use their influence in Mozambique to end the war before this point of financial and humanitarian exhaustion was reached. Foreign aid prolonged the conflict by freeing other tax receipts for the financing of the government war effort and by channelling resources, such as food aid, into the countryside where they encouraged the rebels to loot. Wartime aid policies ought to ensure that aid resources do not enable either side to extend the war. Given the government's need for additional financial resources, wartime donors had a powerful lever for helping to end the war earlier, which they failed to use. Instead aid donors preferred to distinguish between economic aid and political negotiations, when in fact these two factors are strongly related. Donors should have monitored the use of their funds more closely, predominantly financed humanitarian, institutional, and peace-building projects, and worked towards resolving the underlying political causes of the conflict. This would have ended the war earlier and would certainly have built a better foundation for post-war development.

Poor, smallholder farmers were so threatened by the war that their marginal propensity to consume increased with increasing adversity. During the war, inequality increased greatly between these and other war poor and the few war beneficiaries. Since the end of the war, the remaining holders of assets have been able to take advantage of emerging profit opportunities, dramatically worsening income inequality. It is not so much the total war-related loss of capital, but its unequal destruction and the increasing inequality of distribution which may prevent sustainable and equitable post-war economic development. Income inequality in Mozambique could thus be seen as one of the most enduring legacies of the war.

There has been a tendency in Mozambique to literally reconstruct the institutions and infrastructure that had existed before the war or even before Independence. Reconstruction should be less a physical exercise but instead build sustainable institutions aimed at fulfilling current development objectives. While these might require the rehabilitation of some colonial shops, roads, or plantations, frequently better alternatives more appropriate to the actual post-war economic situation of Mozambique could have been found.

Since Independence, considerable government attention and aid spending in Mozambique has focused on maintaining health and education services for the general population. These services had tended to be war-vulnerable in the rural areas, and probably contributed little to the maintenance of entitlements, or to the reduction of the high level of transaction inefficiency or uncertainty in the economy. Increasing efforts and funding need to be made towards constructing and maintaining institutional capacity by expanding civil, rather than social, expenditure. Measures might have been taken during the war to alleviate the negative effects of the conflict and to help prepare for post-war reconstruction. Institution-building policies could have included training, information gathering, administrative reform, and the strengthening of the law-making and judiciary systems. Although these measures are basically urban, public-service sector and aid-funded activities, they would have helped to bring about more rapid and equitable post-war growth. At the same time, these policies could have been complemented by consumption-oriented, short-term relief operations in the countryside to maintain the food entitlements of rural displaced people.

The most flawed policy in the post-war period arose from the belief that stabilization and structural adjustment would liberalize constrained markets and thus assist, for example, rural output and trade growth. Yet due to the type of war, its location and duration, as well as the years of socialist rural development, there was often no market to be liberalized and no supply response to be stimulated in the countryside. Instead, rural development should have been induced by building rural market institutions and facilitating emerging markets in the post-war period. This would have led to accelerated smallholder output growth, poverty alleviation, and export growth, which together would have helped to achieve the post-war macro objectives of the government (Brück, FitzGerald, and Grigsby 2000).

The reduction of the cashew export tax is a good example of how post-war policy failed to achieve its objective. The policy liberalization failed to elicit the expected rural supply response, because farmers were not yet ready to make peacetime, long-term investment decisions. Instead uncertainty, lack of knowledge, poor extension services, as well as imperfect trading arrangements prevented the farmers from increasing their cashew production as intended. Current policies in Mozambique should aim to accelerate agronomic research into cashew farming, disseminate this knowledge through extension services and support increasing competition among cashew traders to ensure a sustained and equitable distribution of the increased cashew export opportunities available to smallholders.

Post-war economic reconstruction in Mozambique has required large sums of money. Yet given the large war–debt burden and the already high levels of aid, debt forgiveness on a large scale was crucial. A strong case can be made for post-war members of the highly indebted and poor countries (HIPC) group to receive a larger debt suspension and final write-off to sustain their peace processes and to improve basic economic conditions especially for the poor. In addition, the nature of conditionality for post-conflict economies such as Mozambique should be different, placing greater emphasis on forward-looking policy conditions, on creating markets, and on building civil, legal, and judicial institutions. Indeed, government and donors in Mozambique will only be able to design policies that create sustainable and equitable development opportunities if they take into account the long-term legacies of Mozambique's war.

4

Mozambique: War, Economic Change, and Development in Manica Province, 1982–1992

MARK F. CHINGONO

1 Introduction

The political economy of Mozambique has been forged through the exigencies of warfare. Since 1964, when the independence war against the Portuguese began, the country has been a theatre of war. The lull following independence in 1975 was ended in 1976 by an undeclared war waged against Mozambique by the former settler government of Rhodesia.[1] In 1977, the Rhodesian Central Intelligence Organisation (CIO) created the Mozambique National Resistance (MNR or Renamo) as the 'fifth column' in its destabilization campaign against Mozambique.[2] At Zimbabwe's Independence in 1980 Renamo was adopted by South Africa and, subsequently, the movement graduated from being a mere Matsanga[3] outfit into a powerful force that later compelled the ruling Front for the Liberation of Mozambique (Frelimo) to back-track on many fundamental policy issues. Largely due to South African support and internal tensions, the war continued unabated until the signing of the Rome Peace Agreement in October 1992. This agreement paved the way for the elections held in October 1994 which returned Frelimo to power, albeit with a narrow margin. Since the elections, a fragile peace has held, characterized by fluidity and volatility. Economic reconstruction is now underway.

This chapter sets out to examine the relationship between war and the operation of the microeconomy. It focuses specifically on economic activity in Manica Province—the province where conflict lasted longest. The war is considered in terms of its economic impact and transformative potential with emphasis on the resilience and resourcefulness of displaced people in dealing with the problem of scarcity in a war situation. It is this

---

[1] This was in retaliation to Mozambique's adherence to the United Nations international sanctions against the illegal regime of Ian Smith which had unilaterally declared independence in 1965, and for Mozambique's provision of rear bases to Zimbabwean guerrillas.

[2] There are various contesting versions of exactly how Renamo came into being. The popular version is that it was created by the Rhodesian CIO and the Portuguese Special Force Units which fled Mozambique for Rhodesia at independence. The other version, which is common, at least in popular discourses in Manica Province, is that Renamo was founded by Frelimo defectors who later sought aid from Rhodesia and South Africa.

[3] Andre Matada Matsangaise was the first leader of the movement, hence the movement is popularly known as Matsanga.

resourcefulness that provided the dynamism for what is referred to here as the 'grass-roots war economy'. This spontaneous, informal, and ever-changing microeconomy accelerated the transformation of production relations from an economy of affection based on kin, lineage, and patronage into an aspiring capitalist economy.

Such resilience and resourcefulness point to an important observation. While it is possible to look at the interaction between war and economics in terms of its negative impacts, it can also be viewed as an historical process with many unexpected but far-reaching consequences for the country's political economy. In Mozambique, the years of war released latent entrepreneurial potential that catalysed economic change, especially through the grass-roots economy. Given the virtual collapse of the formal sector, the centrality of this alternative economy to the livelihoods of many displaced people cannot be overemphasized. The overriding concern of this exploration is, therefore, to understand the extent to which the grass-roots war economy provided a solution to some of Mozambique's wartime microeconomic problems and the extent to which it may also serve as a basis for post-war economic reconstruction.

The study is divided into six sections. Section 2 briefly looks at the structure and recent economic history of the country. Section 3 introduces the concept of a grass-roots war economy, and challenges the expectations that have been put forward about its nature. Section 4 considers the major events and factors that catalysed and shaped the grass-roots war economy in Mozambique. Section 5 then examines the range of economic and social behaviour which emerged in response to these factors; Section 6 considers the reconstruction issues in the light of this war economy, and Section 7 presents brief concluding thoughts.

2   The Structure of the Mozambican Economy

The Mozambican economy is largely agrarian and dependent on the export of raw materials for importing essential manufactured goods—mainly military hardware during the war. Just before independence, the country earned over half of its foreign exchange from the main agricultural exports crops, especially cashew nuts, cotton, citrus fruits, and copra. Other marketed agricultural produce was, and remains, crucial to feeding not only the towns but also many food-deficient rural areas (Mackintosh 1988). Maize and cassava are the main staple foods of the rural population and the country can potentially feed itself using the 3,000 plantations left by the Portuguese. In times of peace, 80 to 90 per cent of the working population would have been employed in rural agriculture, and before the conflict about 80 per cent of exports were agricultural products.

The country has considerable mineral resources, especially in the mines of the Zambezia province, which are mined for columbite, tantalite, beryl, mica, bismuth, and semi-precious stones (Saferworld 1994); gold is also found in Manica Province. The Manica reserves are officially estimated to be over 50 million tonnes, and in 1986 Lonrho[4]

_____

[4] Lonhro's farming and mining interests are quite extensive, which explains Tiny Rowland's (former Regional Director in Africa) personal involvement in the peace process.

negotiated an agreement to mine in the province. Potentially, tantalite exploitation is the country's most important mineral export. In times of peace, the country also has tourist potential with a ready market in South Africa. Vital to this tourist industry, Mozambique has the potential to earn large sums of foreign exchange from its rail and port infrastructure. The country has three good ports in Maputo, Nacala, and Beira, each providing access to world markets for neighbouring landlocked countries.

During the colonial era, the penetration of international capital in Southern Africa created a regional political economy in which Mozambique, like other countries of the region, became subordinated to serve the needs of capital accumulation in South Africa. Mozambique became a labour reserve for South Africa's mining industry as well as a market for South African produced commodities. From Manica Province, however, the majority of migrant workers went to Rhodesia and their remittances were a valuable source of demand and capital accumulation in the economy.

Revenues from port and rail services were not channelled into industrializing and developing Mozambique, but were drained away to finance the import of consumer durables and other consumer goods, mainly from Portugal. As a legacy of 500 years of Portuguese colonial domination, Mozambique became independent as one of the poorest countries in the world, with an average annual per capita income of US$117 in 1989 (Ratilal 1990) and with a structurally dependent and extremely vulnerable economy. Only at the beginning of the 1970s, were appreciable quantities of investment goods imported into the colony, which led to the emergence of an infant manufacturing industry. In Manica Province, these infant industries included a clothing factory Textafrika in Chimoio City, a timber factory at Ifloma plantation between Chimoio and the town of Manica, and a brewery and wine company in Manica town.

2.1   Recent Economic History

War and its needs have shaped the contemporary Mozambican economy. Frelimo's economic, social and political revolution of 1975–85 was conditioned by the needs of managing first, a crisis economy and later, a war economy. The independence war and the decolonization process entailed the total disruption of formal economic activity and losses in output. With a mass exodus of skilled personnel, capital flight, illegal exportation of plant equipment and deliberate sabotage by the departing Portuguese, recorded GDP fell by over 20 per cent between 1973 and 1975 (Ratilal 1990). The undeclared war with Rhodesia (mainly in Manica and Sofala provinces)—started when Mozambique closed its borders with Rhodesia in compliance with United Nations sanctions against the latter's unilateral declaration of independence—cost Mozambique about US$550 million by the time Rhodesia became independent Zimbabwe in 1980 (Ratilal 1990).

Faced with desertion, sabotage, and bad management of farms, factories, and shops in the early days of independence, the new government was obliged to intervene in order to avoid a complete collapse. At its Third Congress in 1977, with the aim of tackling the economic distortions and the social inequality inherited from colonialism, Frelimo adopted a development strategy based on central economic planning. In this model almost all economic policies and decisions were made in the context of a central state plan that set production targets and allocated financial and material resources. The role of the state in production was consolidated by the development of state farms, cooperativization of agriculture, and the promotion of heavy industry.

Threatened from within and without (by disaffected Mozambicans and their Rhodesian, and later South African, allies) defence of the revolution was dependent on the strength of the Mozambican army, which was ultimately dependent on the productive capacity of the economy. Without an army capable of resisting internal uprising or external aggression, the final conquest for freedom and independence could never take place. But a strong army was only viable at a high cost as arms and other necessary supplies had to be procured from abroad. These economic and politico-military considerations were coupled with a desire to meet the rising expectations of the people. The result was an ambitious development strategy dubbed the 'socialist big push'.

While the populist policies of the socialist big push were conspicuous for their investment drive, they generated resource requirements far in excess of the domestic capacity to save, and required financing through external credit, which increased indebtedness (Tibana 1994). Massive government intervention in an economy that was unable to respond to changing circumstances effectively meant that the socialist big push amounted to a shock of its own, with powerful implications for the behaviour of both private and public economic agents. It introduced absurdities into the consumption, savings, and investment patterns of the economy. For instance, price control resulted in falling production in rural areas, creating hoarding and shortages in the cities. In the agricultural sector in particular, centralized economic planning seems to have been the major cause of price distortions, and the consequent collapse of rural markets. By the late 1970s and early 1980s, the investment boom had led to fiscal and current account deficits; the net accumulation of public assets was very low relative to the resources manipulated through government revenues and spending policies (Tibana 1994). These distortions were amplified by the effect of fluctuations in world market prices, especially the steep rises in the price of oil, high interest rates, and variations in exchange rates during the early 1980s.

3   Concepts of the Grass-roots War Economy

Classic theorists on the effects of violence and conflict on the economy argued that, with a number of rival powers disputing violently for supremacy, the result, to quote Thucydides, is 'no commerce, and no safe communication', and as Hobbes wrote 'there [is] no place for industry; because the fruit thereof [is] uncertain'. Nef (1950) put it blatantly when he wrote 'war is inimical to progress'. Rimmer (1995) contrasts Africa with Western Europe, where the devastation of the Second World War was 'overshadowed by the effects on living standards of subsequent advances in science and technology, expansion in trade and accumulation in assets'. He concludes (p. 36):

No such positive side effects of the African wars are apparent. The results appear wholly negative. Societies and states have not been strengthened by conflict. Only the killing arts have been refined. Fanon's idea of renovating violence, that solely through the fire could true liberation be won, can have few adherents nowadays. Violence in Africa has begotten violence—not freedom, not dignity, not socialism, not nationhood.

Similarly neo-Marxist thinkers such as Hanlon (1984), Mittlemen (1988), Nilsson (1980) and Saul (1985) stressed the negative impact of externally engineered violence, and this led to the emergence of the 'destabilizationist paradigm'. Green, Saferworld (1994), and many other scholars writing on Mozambique, have commented on the destructiveness and negativity of violence; many more, for example Geffray (1991), Hoile (1989) and Hanlon (1984) have focused on the causes, and who is to blame for the conflict This analysis does not disagree with these authors, but instead, suggests that, on closer examination, the consequences of violent conflict are far more complex than the visible destruction. We suggest that it is important to shift the terms of the debate about conflict in a new direction, in order to illuminate the complex relationship between war and society.

This chapter focuses on relations between and among people, their economic and political engagement, and their changing relationship with the state. It stresses that the war gave rise to multiple unintended consequences with fundamental significance for post-war reconstruction and development. War and conflict are not always inimical to progress; on the contrary, in some specific circumstances, they accelerate change and development. The emergence of the grass-roots war economy in Manica Province is just one example of how war can be simultaneously destructive and constructive. Indeed war destroyed markets and commerce, but it also created new economic opportunities. These opportunities led to the emergence of a thriving grass-roots war economy, built on a precarious dialectic of constructive destruction.

Furthermore, even when the emergence of an alternative economy is acknowledged, the nature of that economy is often underestimated. Economic activities taking place outside the official system—known variously as the informal, underground, parallel, unrecorded, second, hidden, shadow, endogenous, irregular, alternative, unofficial, or black economy—exist alongside official ones in most countries in the world. The International Labour Organization (ILO), the agency that formalized the term 'informal economy', characterized it merely as a sector of the poor where the motive for entry into the sector is essentially survival rather than profit making (ILO/JASPA 1988).

The reality was different: despite the severe economic crisis and against formidable odds, the dispossessed took the initiative to provide for themselves what a weakened state could not, erecting, on the ruins of war, alternative economic and social relations. In Mozambique, the added dimension of war gave this economy distinct features— usually lacking, or less amplified in other countries where informal economies evolved gradually, under relatively peaceful conditions. Not all of those who participated in the grass-roots economy were poor, nor were their motives for entry merely to survive. Some people actually thrived and became wealthy. Corrupt bureaucrats and professionals used their office, influence, or contacts to acquire wealth through smuggling, fraudulent export, barter, speculation, bribery, and embezzlement, to invest in building houses, hotels, and restaurants, or in transport—the most rapidly expanding sectors in the economy. Similarly, some corrupt commercial elites, religious leaders, international agency personnel, soldiers and foreign troops, as well as international racketeers and their middlemen, were among those who gained substantial benefits, and, in many cases, became obscenely rich. It is in recognition of this uniqueness that the term 'grass-roots war economy' is used in preference to the others currently in vogue.

The concept of the grass-roots war economy is necessarily vague because it relates to a set of social relationships and processes, many of which lack precise definition. To start with, deciding which activities are grass-roots or what economic behaviour is caused by war must involve a certain amount of arbitrary demarcation. Similarly, the multiplicity of interacting variables poses difficulties in ascertaining analytical primacy of the variables in understanding the unfolding processes. Nevertheless, it appears to be the best concept for capturing the essence of the phenomenon under consideration: wartime economic activity at a microlevel. In this analysis, the grass-roots war economy will be defined loosely to mean that multitude of economic activities halfway between tradition and modernity that have sprung up unbidden among the dispossessed as they shift their ground from rural subsistence production into spontaneous micro-entrepreneurship in peri–urban slums. It is a production and exchange system based on adaptation and flexibility, enabling the war-weary community to deal with contingency and make basic choices for their survival and progress. The economy, run largely by self-taught 'barefoot entrepreneurs', arose through a process of voluntary and involuntary adaptation to new circumstance of uprootedness created by the war. It is the sum total of the diverse survival strategies adopted by the individuals who constitute this dynamic economy.

It is important to see the dispossessed's diverse survival strategies not simply as solutions to household survival or individual subsistence problems, but also as challenges both to the conventional wisdom on peasants' adaptability and to the development model based on state economic authoritarianism. Their activities in production and consumption have been the major force shaping the emerging socio-political arrangements, in particular the strengthening of civil society and the private sector vis-à-vis the state. In addition to shaping the course of the war itself, production, consumption, trade, and exchange, also played central roles in linking the polity to the socio-economic system.

3.1   Problems of Measurement: 'Tracing Statistical Fingerprints'

An evaluation of the interaction between war and economic change inevitably involves identifying factors and mechanisms responsible for the uneven distribution of the costs and benefits of war. These include: changes in the exchange ratios between basic and luxury commodities; changes in the proportions of total income received by different groups including those with the comparative advantage of violence; assessing the magnitude of direct physical destruction of infrastructure; and evaluating the indirect longer-term development costs. There were, of course, great difficulties in gathering accurate statistics on these matters.

Surprisingly, this difficulty was not nearly so great in the war period as it had been in the past because the IMF, World Bank, and other international agencies intervened in the economy to an unparalleled degree, making much more information available than before. Wartime macro data, however, are notoriously misleading. Cost-of-living indices in wartime may not give a true picture of what really happened for a number of reasons. First, in many cases, consumption patterns changed out of all recognition, either by households consuming less of normal foods, or dispensing with them altogether.[5] As such, any comparison of prices based on a pre-war system of weighting is not likely to be an accurate reflection of real changes in the cost of living. Second, and of central importance to this study, many commodities were obtained through barter exchange or at informal economy prices whereas the majority of indices reflect only officially controlled prices. On the whole, and precisely because unrecorded economic activity was much more common, it is probable that these official indices underestimate both the rise in the cost of living and the contribution of unrecorded economic transactions to the national GDP. Therefore, in order to get a more realistic picture of what was really happening to Mozambique's wartime economy, it is important to study the unofficial activity directly.

Measuring the magnitude of grass-roots economic activity is complicated. To start with, there are obvious difficulties in applying economic and statistical analysis to unrecorded economic activity such as consumption, savings, capital accumulation, and investment. Uncertainty and ambiguity among the economic actors about the ethical and long-term effects of their economic engagement and the processes they set in motion also meant many were not willing to divulge the sources and amount of their incomes. Furthermore, since these processes were governed by the probability and exigencies of the war, there were sudden large variations in prices and incomes, which mocked the idea of averages. In addition, prices were almost always negotiable on the spot—a crucial factor that distinguishes the informal economy from the official one. The frequent merging of the 'formal' with the 'informal', with goods and economic agents continuously crossing the boundaries between the two sectors, also creates considerable difficulties in ascertaining the magnitude of the grass-roots war economy's contribution to household income, national income, and GDP.

The traditional focus on the family household (nuclear or extended) as the main unit of analysis in understanding economic and social change is inadequate for capturing the essence of the 'transitions within transformation' unfolding in Manica Province. As a direct and indirect consequence of the war, the traditional family household unit was rapidly disintegrating and being replaced by multiple forms of cohabitation among people who found themselves thrown into similar predicaments by the war. Some households consisted only of women—daughters, mothers, aunts, and grandmothers—others only of young males separated from their families, living together, sharing food and income, and engaged in some kind of division of labour.

Focus on the individual is important because each person's experience of war is unique, and also leads us to an understanding of social relations within which these

---

[5] In some extreme cases, peasants in remote rural areas who had been cut off from the modern economy by the war had to survive on wild fruits and roots for food, and bark and leaves for clothes.

individuals stand. The point is that the individual economic actors are but the per-
sonifications of the whole economic and social relations that exist between them and,
in order to understand the whole it is useful to understand the parts. As we shall see,
the many individual survival strategies developed by the dispossessed involved new
wage and social relations of production—the producer related to others either in
production or via the market. Even 'self-employment', for instance, involved hiring
some labour, whether family or wage-labour. Yet many people were simultaneously
labourers working for a wage and capitalists employing wage labour. Thus, although
the focus is on individual survival strategies, it is important to bear in mind the dangers
of excessive individualization of what were and are, in reality, social relations of
production.

In view of these difficulties, this broad survey will be largely qualitative. The analysis
combines direct observation (made during March–October 1992) with secondary
data for assessing informal sector activity. With regard to the latter, the underlying
assumption is that macroeconomic indicators leave behind them 'statistical fingerprints'
which researchers can trace and interpret to build a picture. Such indirect techniques
include, for example, assessing changes in foreign currency demand within the grass-
roots war economy and examining the discrepancy with official statistics on expenditure and income. Using these techniques, which, of course, have their shortcomings,
shows, for example, that Mozambique's GDP during the period under consideration
must have been far higher, perhaps by 40 to 60 per cent higher than official figures
indicate.[6]

Finally, to some extent, the process of observation itself influenced findings but,
as Gribbin (1984) says of quantum mechanics 'nothing is real unless it is observed'.
Moreover, due to the obvious constraints of conducting research in a war situation, it
was not possible to follow the standard procedures of random selection strictly in select-
ing the case studies presented here. Thus the data presented below provide some indication of trends, rather than a definitive political economy of war in Manica Province.
The most enduring evidence that the grass-roots war economy did make a significant
invisible contribution to the economy is the fact that many Mozambicans still managed
to survive, and some even to thrive, in the face of national economic collapse.

4   Main Features of the Grass-roots War Economy

The grass-roots war economy emerged in response to a number of war-related factors
that both created new constraints and simultaneously opened up many opportunities.
Key factors included: the collapse of the formal economy; social displacement and
dispossession; loss of state control over law and the economy; restricted urban–rural
movement; and new channels for the distribution of goods.

---

[6] Detailed analysis of the proportion of the household basket of a small displaced community suggested that
40–50 per cent of these were procurred from the informal economy or through informal channels. A customs
official at the Machipanda border post thought smuggling accounted for about 60 per cent of the total volume of imported goods, and about 40 per cent of exported goods.

4.1 Collapse of the Formal Economy

The national economic cost of fighting the war was enormous. Although it represented only one set of 'shock events' that affected the operation of the grass-roots war economy, it was the most devastating. Throughout the 1980s defence expenditure averaged a staggering 38 per cent of total government expenditure, one of the highest rates in the world. About 70 per cent of this expenditure was on imports, which reduced the capacity to import non-war-related products and diverted scarce resources from national investment programmes. By 1992, Mozambique could be called a donor-driven economy; aid accounted for 50 per cent of the government budget, paid for over 75 per cent of imports and accounted for more than 70 per cent of the country's GDP. A year later the country had become the most aid-dependent nation in the world with a GDP per capita of less than US$100 (Saferworld 1994).

The war has been described as 'one of the most brutal holocausts against the human condition since World War II' (Saferworld 1994). Estimates of the costs of the conflict to the official economy vary enormously. The Minister of Commerce estimated that by 1989 the country had forgone some US$4.4 to 6 billion, whilst a 1989 UNICEF report put the losses in the region of US$15 billion, equivalent to four times the 1988 GDP (Saferworld 1994). Whatever the case, the point is that the war destroyed the country's productive capacity and amplified the problem of scarcity. This problem of scarcity was at the heart of the new economic behaviour of the actors in the microeconomy of Manica, and the ways in which they dealt with it had fundamental implications for the structure of economic organization, at that time and in the future.

Compounding this was the colossal loss in human capital (especially doctors, teachers, and engineers), which is probably the most valuable resource since it is much more difficult to replace than machinery. By 1986 100,000 people had been killed, 95 per cent of whom were civilians (Saferworld 1994). Nearly 1 million people were forced to take refuge in Malawi, Zambia, and Zimbabwe while another 6 million were internally displaced. The impact on productive activity was heavy. Mining of precious minerals such as tantalite had to be abandoned in the mid-1980s due to war. Similarly, by 1984, exploitation of the country's principal mineral deposits of an estimated 100 million tonnes of iron ore in Tete Province had ceased altogether. Frelimo development projects, schools, and clinics particularly in rural areas—were a prime target for Renamo. For example, by 1989 Renamo had destroyed 44 major economic units, including many sugar, cashew nut, and tea factories, as well as highly productive agricultural complexes such as the 120,000 hectare scheme in Manica Province (Ratilal 1990: 24). In addition, more than 1,120 rural shops and 1,300 vehicles were destroyed. The cumulative effect was to strangle the rural commercial network.

These factors combined to bring about a general deterioration in the official economy's capacity. Capital formation fell from 20 to 15 per cent of GDP in just two years, 1982–4, while recorded production also fell by about 23 per cent in the period 1981–3. Similarly, gross agricultural production fell by 23 per cent in that period, while industry and transport fell by 31 and 27 per cent respectively (Ratilal 1990: 29–30). By 1986 real GDP was just below 60 per cent of its level in 1980 (World Bank 1990), at a time when it had already fallen to 80 per cent of its 1975 level. Compounded by drought, there was an inevitable major food shortage throughout the country in the 1980s. The state sector, which was based on abandoned and destroyed farms, was not in a position to respond in terms of output—and this notwithstanding Frelimo's Fifth Congress declaration in 1989 to 'increase rapidly food production' (Frelimo 1989). Neither was the private sector able to make a significant contribution, for hitherto it had been starved of capital and often disregarded.

Not surprisingly, the government's options were severely limited when agricultural commodity production virtually ground to a halt due to the war. Marine export products—mainly prawns, shrimps, and fish—were the only sector relatively safe from the direct effects of war: there was, as a result, a tendency to over-exploit them to a point that threatened the long-term viability of the industry. The belated introduction of food rationing only fuelled the economic crisis as increased speculation and hoarding by both consumers and merchants led to further shortages and consequent price rises and inflation. By the end of the war the official economy of Mozambique was in a state of disaster and was considered to be one of the five poorest countries in the world (World Bank 1990). As with many other African countries exports could not keep up with imports, production lagged, industry barely functioned, scarcities were rife, the infrastructure had deteriorated drastically, wages were at starvation levels and nothing worked as it should. It was largely in response to this nationwide economic crisis that the people of Manica Province were forced to create a grass-roots war economy.

4.2   Social Displacement and Dispossession

Forced physical and social dislocation of the rural population was also a key cause of the emergence of the grass-roots economy on a much larger scale than had been the case hitherto, or was the case in relatively stable economies. Divorced from their traditional means of subsistence and violently displaced from their land, former agriculturalists were transformed into either wage labourers or barefoot entrepreneurs in urban areas where, unlike in the rural economies, the producer and consumer were no longer united in the same person.

Displacement on a mass scale in Manica Province began in the early 1980s. It was during that period, following South Africa's take-over of Renamo from the Rhodesian CIO upon Zimbabwe's independence in 1980, that haphazard banditry developed into full-scale civil war. Forced to flee for their lives, many people became refugees in neighbouring countries, especially Zimbabwe, while others managed to negotiate a dangerous survival in the rural areas. An unknown number joined the rebel army, and many more fled west to the relative security of towns such as, Chimoio, Gondola, and Manica and, after the 1990 partial ceasefire, into the Beira Corridor.

More than 250,000 out of an estimated total of 635,000 people were displaced in Manica Province. About 100,000 found relative security in the periphery of Chimoio City, which hitherto had accommodated only half that number. On arrival in Chimoio City, the first act that the dispossessed had to undertake was to find the means of providing for their basic needs. But this was 'another war', a war against hunger and certain death, fought differently by people with diverse social backgrounds. As one displaced man in Chimoio City put it: 'Hunger is more dangerous than war. You can run away from war, but not from hunger'. Finding a strategy for survival—a *manheira de ganhar*, as they call it—was the only option.

As fields were ravaged, entire villages destroyed, and survivors often compelled to flee to inaccessible, unproductive locations to avoid rebels, the operation of the rural economy was undermined and its productive capacity severely reduced. Accelerating this process of rural deterioration was the loss of the most productive members of the rural communities, young people who became the major combatants in both belligerent armies.

The majority of the displaced population lost a substantial proportion of their property on relocation. Since most were peasant farmers, their means of sustenance, tools, animals, land, and crops—were left behind as they fled for safety. Many families were split up, with some members trapped in rebel areas or murdered. In an attempt to check the overcrowding of the already crowded towns the government and NGOs did not distribute free food and clothes in the city. Thus on arrival in the urban accommodation centres the displaced people were forced to make use of personal and kinship ties to piece together their lives. Some brought previously acquired skills, and proven cultural resources to bear, such as, trust, loyalty, authority, and interdependence between kin and neighbours in the face of rapid change and uncertainty about the future.

4.3   New Formal and Informal Distribution Channels

While officially, there was no free emergency aid in the city, for this would have encouraged uncontrolled overcrowding, free food and clothes were distributed in the resettlement camps outside Chimoio City, such as Matsinye, or at district offices, which had become district forts. Emergency aid was normally delivered to such dangerous outposts under a military convoy; private entrepreneurs could also join in the protected convoy, but more often than not, they had to pay a reasonable bribe (protection charge) to the military chiefs in charge of such risky operations. Many dispossessed people complained that the emergency relief trucks left the city full, and returned half full; only half of emergency aid reached its destiny; the other half found its way to the shelves of the bureaucratic commercial elite.

The entrepreneurs in khaki, soldiers, especially the commandos who escorted convoys from Chimoio to Tete and the border with Malawi, made the most of this dangerous but profitable situation. During such long and dangerous operations, soldiers not only protected civilians and NGOs, but also engaged in what is euphemistically known as PRI (Individual Rehabilitation Programme—a corrupted version of PRE, the Economic Rehabilitation Programme), and bought sugar at the Malawi border for resale in Chimoio.[7] At the height of the war, foreign troops, especially from Zimbabwe, who could import goods without having to pay duty, had effectively become the main

---

[7] In fact, the author was arrested at one point for taking a photograph of commandos selling their booty from their truck in the city centre.

wholesale supplier for many shack-shop owners in Manica Province; in fact when this practice was stopped after the death of a Zimbabwean army officer who wanted to expose this racket, some shack shops in Chimoio collapsed over night.

Some NGOs, such as the Maforga Mission, defied government orders not to encourage the overcrowding of cities, by providing food, clothing, and training at their mission in Gondola City. The Mission and many other religious organizations were accused by other NGOs and government officials of using food aid as a bait for attracting converts. Employees of NGOs, apart from being the most highly paid social group, also had access to scarce commodities, which rather than consume, they often put on the informal market, thereby injecting more life into the grass-roots war economy.

4.4   *Loss of State Control of Law and the Economy*

Prior to the mid-1980s, state institutions had pervaded many aspects of life, and this was especially pronounced in the economic sphere where the state functioned as distributor of resources. The war marked a period of transition, which saw the state decline not only as an economic power but also as a keeper of law and order.

The state's loss of control over law and order and the rise in 'anarchy' generated psychological insecurity and fear, and brought to the fore people's basic survival instincts. Combined with the wide availability of arms received from Europe, this led to the adoption of extremely violent survival strategies. Piracy around the border areas and in the forests of Manica was a manifestation of the extent to which the culture of violence had permeated civil society. Similarly, the resurgence of aggressive and 'vicious market fundamentalism', based on crude exploitation of the destitute, reflected this merciless atmosphere. In a nutshell, by virtue of its violent disruption of the existing social order, war gave the grass-roots economy its violent and aggressive dimension. Often victims of violence reacted to violence by adopting violent survival strategies—what Wilson aptly calls 'cults of violence and counter-violence' (Wilson 1992).

4.5   *Restricted Urban–Rural Movement*

The fighting between government Frelimo troops and rebel Renamo soldiers severely restricted the movement of goods and people. Passing between areas controlled by the different armies was life threatening. The normal flow of commercial goods, traders, and commuters was greatly interrupted, causing localized shortages and strong price differentials across the no man's land between government and rebel-controlled areas.

4.6   *War Goods Distribution Channels*

The large-scale involvement of international aid agencies in the 'emergency rescue operation' as well as foreign troops influenced the character of the wartime economy in significant ways. These new economic actors brought both materials and goods—which found their way to, and revitalized, the market—and new values, which were actively reappropriated by the Mozambicans. The goods passed through new distribution channels which emerged during the war, based on connections and corruption, with many emergency relief goods failing to reach the intended beneficiaries, but instead forming the basis of a lucrative business for well-connected entrepreneurs.

4.7 Non-War-Related Factors

In addition to the events and conditions of war, a series of other factors worsened the conditions of the economy in crisis. These included the upheaval due to decolonization and a series of severe natural disasters such as the 1977–8 floods, and the 1981–3 and the 1991–2 droughts. Furthermore, swings in international commodity prices of major exports and imports also influenced the nature of the grass-roots war economy. The IMF and World Bank introduced structural adjustment policies in 1986–7 to liberalize the economy, legitimizing the acquisitive spirit, which had been suppressed under the socialist regime. As part of the measures, the state had to cut back its social-service provision and this entailed even more hardship, which in turn led to greater innovation for survival.

5 The Grass-roots Economic Response to War

In response to these aspects of war, the grass-roots economy saw the emergence of new forms of social and economic behaviour which were shaped by the constraints and opportunities described above. The key behavioural responses observed in the course of this study include: the proliferation of 'barefoot entrepreneurship'; changing household structures; exploitation of the urban–rural gap; new attitudes to risk; a boom in illegal activities; and the emergence of new social and economic transaction codes.

5.1 The Barefoot Entrepreneurs

War and displacement accelerated the transformation of peasants into barefoot traders by forcing them to become innovative and flexible, or face death by starvation. Mozambicans of different social backgrounds and positions reacted differently, adopting various individual and collective survival strategies, whose interaction constituted the dynamic of the grass-roots war economy. Economic motivation was related to their class position. For poor peasants-cum-capitalists, it was primarily survival. Owing partly to the diverse backgrounds of the economic actors, the economy was based on a hybridization of forms of economic organization, cooperation, and conflict, with the entrepreneurial ethic becoming increasingly entrenched.

The war-weary city of Chimoio hummed with economic activity. It was as if, as one research guide put it, 'every household had suddenly become entrepreneurial, with too many people struggling to sell the same commodities to fewer and fewer customers'. The competition that this created was fierce, minimizing profits for those stuck at this level of entrepreneurial activity. The markets in the peri-urban suburbs and the city centre bustled with trade. In the green zones on the edge of town, women, children, and men worked on the land growing vegetables and other crops for sale in the city. At home or in improvised workshops in the city men and boys worked with metal scrap and timber, producing household utensils and hardware such as pots, tables, doors and window frames. Similarly, women and girls worked at home making clay pots, mats, and clothes. Vendors and petty traders, selling all sorts of goods including cigarettes, vegetables, bread, maize meal, toothpaste, soap, clothes, and crafts spent stiflingly hot days walking around the city or sitting behind their market stalls hoping for customers.

Cooked foods—roasted nuts, cassava, and bread—as well as sweet beer were mostly prepared at home and sold at the market, on the main roads and in the city centre. While in neighbouring Zimbabwe women and children in urban areas spent long hours every morning queuing for bread,[8] their counterparts in Chimoio had difficulty in finding customers for the abundance of bread that they had made. Traditional opaque beer was also made and consumed at home. It became a major source of income for those who brewed it, as many people could not afford imported or commercially manufactured beer. The alienated turned to it as a way of drinking away their frustration and sadness— only to rediscover them when they became sober. Fast-food shacks made of bamboo, sack, and thatch, which sold hot tea, rice, and meat, became increasingly common although the hygienic standards were also low. This should not be surprising given that the vendors were mainly illiterate, starved of capital, and employed young children who were paid far less than adults.

Expensive white maize was brought into the city from rural areas, while the less desirable yellow food aid maize came from either wholesalers in town or through informal channels. Vegetables were either home-grown, usually on a collective basis in the so-called 'green zones' around the city, brought in from the few operating farms or, in the case of cabbage, imported (mainly smuggled) from Zimbabwe. Firewood was brought in from rural areas, or fetched from the ever-diminishing forests near the city, while bananas and sugar cane were mainly brought from the rural areas. The basic manufactured goods came either from Beira or were imported from Zimbabwe.

As more and more former rural dwellers became petty traders there was a spontaneous emergence of market places throughout the peri-urban slums. 'Sete de Abril' was one typical market at which peasant–cum–capitalists struggled to shape their livelihoods, which includes a broad cross-section of the activities of petty traders. The market was located about 2 to 3 km south-east of Chimoio near the junction joining the Beira–Machipanda road and the minor road leading to Macate, a locality 48 km south-east of the city. The market, situated in the largest *bairro* (suburb), was one of the busiest and largest spontaneous markets in Chimoio. It was divided into three main sections, which roughly corresponded to types of tradable commodities, economic status of the entrepreneurs, and income earned.

The smallest section of the market centre, comprised largely of newcomers to the city, concentrated on basic survival foods, including wild fruits, sugar cane, and cassava.

---

[8] Interestingly, denouncing the demonstrations by the Harare women for rises in the price of bread, the responsible minister advised the women to form their own cooperatives and make their own bread if they wanted the price to go down.

The 'barefoot entrepreneurs' at this section of the market were among the least privileged, merely eking out a living. The majority of men and women here were former peasants. As marginal entrepreneurs, they were also stratified with different levels of prosperity or poverty. Gender, class, and social status were interlinked. The women—approximately 45 per cent of all traders there—mainly sold agricultural produce including maize flour, vegetables, firewood, bread, bananas, sugar cane, salt, dried fish, and cooking oil; and the majority of them were aged between 13 and 18 years. The men, in contrast, sold manufactured commodities, which in relative terms tended to fetch more money.

Most of the oranges sold in this market, as in many other markets scattered throughout the city, came from a nearby citrus plantation. At the plantation, people were allocated a number of trees around which they worked, weeding grass in return for oranges. Since there were more people ready to work than was usually needed, the remuneration was low. Many people travelled up to 10 km from their homes to the plantation, and then worked six hours for just one sack of oranges. On resale in the city this would earn them 1500–2000Mt a day, which was insufficient for a decent meal in a city restaurant. But if this were done daily for a month, the earnings would exceed the minimum wage of 40,000Mt that, as noted earlier, was sufficient to feed a family of six for about a week. Those with contacts or who had the courage would steal oranges at night. But, as a 25-year-old woman who laboured for oranges pointed out, 'those who do not work sell their oranges cheaply, making it difficult for us to work and break even. Also those who get their oranges free of charge, through contacts at the citrus plantation, undermine us.' Not only did this create tension among the marginal traders themselves, but it also set in motion a process of social differentiation and stratification.

In order to get beyond this lowest level of entrepreneurship capital was needed, and many households made sacrifices in order to make that leap. As one barefoot trader selling wildlife meat put it idiomatically, 'In times like these, *mupfuri anodyira pasi*' (the ironsmith—who makes plates among other things—eats from the ground). In order to save some money to set up a more viable business enterprise, he and his family ate their *sadza* (staple maize-meal porridge) only with vegetables and not with the meat that he was selling.

Making this leap brought significant returns, enabling traders to hold stocks of manufactured and imported consumer goods such as soap, tinned fish, salt, sugar, and cooking oil. The second section of the Sete de Abril market housed this ever-expanding group of traders. Owning a stall there indicated relative success. All the small shops selling manufactured commodities such as matches, tobacco, and soft drinks from Beira or Zimbabwe were owned by men, most of whom were over 24 years. Young boys and girls, who were said to be less likely to be tempted to steal, manned these shack shops, while the owners concentrated on establishing networks of contacts to facilitate the procuring of goods. The goods were obtained through both legal and underhand tactics that, more often than not, included smuggling. Younger men provided the conduit facilitating the movement of goods between rural areas controlled by Renamo and Frelimo-controlled ones. Starting humbly like this, some traders were miraculously successful while many others barely managed to survive. Cases abound of individuals starting from nothing and graduating to some localized prominence. Some owners of large, established shops said that they had started with the savings made from running shack shops, which in turn they had set up by selling oranges.

The third section of the market represented, in relative terms, the upper tier grass-roots war economy consisting of stalls of second-hand clothes, popularly known as *calamidades*, Portuguese for 'emergency aid'. This section of the market in fact became the major destination for Zimbabwean buyers looking for clothes to resell at profits of up to 500 per cent in Zimbabwe. Zimbabwean dollars were not only accepted but were in great demand at this market. Commercial bureaucrats who had easy access to donated clothes employed most of the entrepreneurs there. These entrepreneurs were not just surviving but were actually getting rich. It was difficult to enter, but some of those who succeeded were said to have used their savings to open shops in town or purchase cars. The fact that some of the most successful enterprises there were owned by officials, with easy access to donated clothes, or by traders, especially Asians, who had shops and influential contacts, reveals the extent of interaction and complementarity between the formal and informal economies of a country in crisis.

Outside the market areas, entrepreneurs were active in production and services as well as trade. One example was Naftal Matos, well established as a self-trained welder in his locality, using a home-made blast furnace made of an old truck axle and a bicycle tyre rim and wood. He was serving almost the whole *bairro* in which he lived. In the early 1970s, Naftal had worked in Zimbabwe (then Rhodesia) as an unskilled assistant motor mechanic. When he came back after Mozambican independence in 1975, he settled in his rural home area as a farmer but when the rebels took control of this territory in the early 1980s, he was forced to work for them as a motorbike mechanic.

In 1991, he escaped to Chimoio with virtually nothing but his family and a few household utensils. On arrival, he joined hands with another newcomer, gathered some discarded metal pieces and began a welding business. When their business started to pickup, they had a disagreement, with counter-accusations of laziness and misuse of funds—this appeared not to be a rare occurrence—and Naftal set up his own business in his home. He was helped by his 12-year-old son who he said was not going to school, because the local school authorities wanted a huge some of money as a bribe to give him a place. Previous experience, as well as committed determination, were the crucial factors in the success of this man. He had not brought any material goods or valuables to start off with nor was he helped by kinsmen or relatives, but he managed to establish himself and gain respect and influence in his locality. There were many more examples of young men establishing themselves via technical innovations of this nature. One such self-trained radio technician was a young man who repaired, and even modified radios, using lemon juice as the cleaning liquid, firewood fire to melt the lead for welding together the radio wiring system, and sharpened wire as screwdrivers.

In summary, the Mozambicans in Manica Province seized and created opportunities for upward mobility. Yet not all the dispossessed were able to adapt to their new circumstances. Inevitably, this process produced tensions and alienation as some social groups gained substantial political and economic power while others lost it. It appears, that for many who fell by the wayside, the main constraint was a lack of initial capital to start off with. Many, because of the circumstances in which their uprootedness occurred, simply did not have the financial or the technological means to get off the ground. Lack of technical managerial skills meant that most entrepreneurs only managed to operate at a hand-to-mouth level—or worse still, their investments simply failed.

5.2 Changing Household Structures

Because so many young, active men had left their households to join the fighting on both sides, household structures were forced to undergo radical change. As household composition changed, earning power and economic responsibility shifted towards women and children.

Gender divisions were apparent in the grass-roots war economy, and largely determined the kind of 'acceptable' activity a person could engage in. This in turn determined one's earning power. These unwritten economic rules and codes of behaviour resulted from the historically specific structure of social relationships among economic actors within the Mozambican political economy. These rules were, however, not unchanging. Under economic pressure and over time, rigid definitions of what was acceptable were being challenged as more women ventured into areas that had hitherto been the preserve of men. Not only did women's trade increasingly become a primary source of household income, but it also gave them a greater degree of autonomy and independence, providing an impetus to the ongoing struggle to adjust the relative position of men and women. (For a detailed discussion of this process see Chingono (1996).)

Children also became more significant as economic actors. Indeed the ubiquity of child labour made it one of the most visible consequences of the war. School places were scarce. The destruction of schools by the war meant that only about 25 per cent of pupils eligible for primary school could get a place in Manica Province (Provincial Director of Planning, 1992, interview) and some parents found that they were required to pay a bribe. In Manica Province, many children were war orphans and many more were separated from their families by the war. Children, in general, seem to be one of the social groups most marginalized by the war. In response to this crisis, they engaged in diverse economic activities and adopted various strategies that met their current needs and helped establish links with kin and business contacts.

In Chimoio, Manica, and Gondola, and along the Beira Corridor, children as young as 7 years old were engaged in begging, selling cigarettes, and currency, working in small shops, and smuggling. Some ingeniously made wooden wheelbarrows or beautiful kerosene lamps and bird-shaped ashtrays with empty soft drink cans. Others learnt new survival skills, including building their own huts, running small enterprises and providing a multiplicity of services. It is not clear, however, whether this kind of child labour retarded their growth, reduced school attendance or hampered their studies, if at school.

Whether they were helping their parents or guardians or simply working for themselves, many children were responsible both for their own survival and that of others. Jorge Kanimambo, then a 17-year-old boy who lived with his sick mother in Chicacaule *aldeia* (resettlement camp) learnt survival skills at an early age. As his two brothers were both in the army, his father dead and mother ill, he shouldered all the responsibilities of running a household. For instance, according to him, after each of three rebel attacks, he and a friend with whom he had a reciprocal work relationship, had to rebuild their huts.

Another boy of the same age who also had to learn survival skills was Alberto, who had just escaped from a Matsanga attack in Dombe, leaving behind all his family. Like Jorge, he was building his own hut with the help of a new young friend who lived in the area with his parents. He was also selling thatch grass in order to get money for food. Younger children living with their parents made contributions to family income. All of the young children who dug with their bare hands for building stones and gravel to sell in Bairro Villa Nova said they gave the money to their parents to buy a bag of maize.

Other children, without rank or money, miserable and in rags, spent their lives loitering in the Machipanda border area, hoping for a good Samaritan to recognize their suffering and respond to their pleas for help. On crossing the border from the Zimbabwean side, the first depressing signs of an abnormal situation were the hopeful faces of visibly hungry children standing by or leaning on the border fence, their gaze fixed on incoming travellers. The children swarmed around travellers crossing the border like chickens waiting to be fed, and literally pulled at their luggage shouting: 'Please *tio* [uncle] let me carry it for you. Please *tio*, do you have [Zimbabwean] dollars for exchange?' or simply 'Can you please help me with money?' Small battles ensued as they fought amongst themselves to carry the travellers' luggage, or to get close enough to catch any coins travellers threw down. In some of these small fights, characterized by accusations and counter-accusations of lies, some even went on to say that only those whose parents were dead should be helped. Many of these children, mostly aged between 5 and 12 years, did not go to school and said they needed the money to buy food, to give to their parents, or to go to Zimbabwe.

This army of destitute children, as well as other suspect people (that is, those without the right papers), were frequently removed from the border area by officials, for allegedly pestering travellers. But this, like many other attempts by the weakened state to frustrate the dispossessed's attempts to survive, was not successful. In fact, some of the older children who managed to save a little money from carrying travellers' goods and selling money, ended up working in the Zimbabwean border city of Mutare as vendors selling eggs, cigarettes, and vegetables. Although they did not earn much from this kind of work, it was preferable to languishing in Mozambique: the hard Z$ currency earned provided start-up capital for a more lucrative activity, such as dealing in money, when they returned. This explains why, in spite of constant arrests and deportations to Mozambique by the Zimbabwean authorities, they still went back.

To sum up, while the traditional patriarchal family was weakened, the relationship between mothers and children was strengthened precisely because of their productive relationship. The children's contribution, apart from keeping them and their families alive and attaining some independence, contributed to the process of social differentiation and class formation. Children from elite and peasant backgrounds lived in totally different worlds: the privileged could easily cruise through life without having to learn to fend for themselves at an early age, unlike those from poor backgrounds.

5.3 Exploiting the Urban–Rural Gap

Urban–rural trade continued as many Mozambicans risked their lives daily by moving between Renamo- and government-controlled territories, buying and selling many different items, and exploiting the price differentials. Trucks and vans shuttled daily between the border town of Machipanda and Beira, then the 'peace corridor', packed to the brim with traders and their various goods as well as ordinary commuters. The Beira Corridor effectively became the economic lifeline of the central region.

Rural traders brought their agricultural produce to the city in order to buy basics such as salt, clothes, and soap for consumption as well as resale in the countryside. One 21-year-old man, Manuele Antonio, came from Macouya, a village further beyond Macate, deep in Renamo-controlled territory. Manuele was the oldest able-bodied man at home—his mother and father were ill and his two elder brothers had died in the army. Apparently believing that we were officials registering people for military call-up, he initially lied to us that he was 17 years old. He was selling 100 kg of white maize, which he had bought from local farmers in Macouya. He was also selling locally produced cassava and bananas to supplement his income. From his income he would buy soap, salt, and clothes for consumption as well as resale in the rural areas. The profits he made from selling agricultural produce were negligible, but the extreme scarcity of manufactured goods in rural areas ensured a significant margin of profit for those goods.

Central to the success of these traders' businesses were the dilapidated and unroadworthy trucks.[9] Most of these trucks were owned by urban-based commercial elites, working in the formal sector or in the state bureaucracy. Capitalizing on the crisis, these entrepreneurs did brisk business. More importantly, such ventures demonstrated the interconnection between the formal and informal economies, and how state elites actually facilitated rather than constrained the informal sector.

The drivers risked their lives driving trucks. A plausible explanation for why these men were prepared to take such risks, especially if one considers that they were poorly paid, seems to be the unprecedented opportunities—which they exploited to the full—of 'making quick money' by exploiting the price differentials between rural and urban areas. By trading in chicken and clothes, for instance, the drivers could accumulate a far larger profit in a much shorter period than any average entrepreneur. For example, a chicken costing roughly between 200 and 600Mt in the rural areas, would sell for 6,000–8,000Mt in the city, while a piece of cloth costing 1,000–2,000Mt would sell for more than 5,000Mt. As there were no tickets for payment of fares, the drivers and their assistants could easily pocket some of the revenue without detection by the owner. This seems partly to explain why the trucks were always packed to the brim with people, sacks, animals, chickens, and wood. In addition to this, by offering special privileges to some of their customers, the drivers not only gained influence and respect, but also important business contacts. Rural–urban trading was vital to the economy, and although rewarding, extremely risky.

---

[9] For fear of being arrested by the police for the road unworthiness of their trucks, most of the drivers never drove their trucks in the city, at least during the day.

5.4   The Environmental Impact

The war in Mozambique was not only fought by humans against humans, but also by humans against nature, and *vice versa*. As the section on, 'hunters and pirates' suggests, wildlife, in particular elephant, buffalo, and little game, were put at greater risk by the war; they were killed for food and money, and in a context of a breakdown of law and order, the killing was merciless and unregulated. Furthermore, the deeper people went into the bush, the higher was the risk of their getting killed, so people resorted to cutting down trees on the city perimeter, causing environmental degradation and deforestation. Most of the vegetables and other crops grown within the city or in green zones were grown along riverbanks. This caused so much soil erosion and consequent siltation that some of the small streams completely dried up. The dispossessed, denied alternative resources, will do almost anything to meet their immediate needs, regardless of laws or knowledge of the long-term effects on the environment. In the few safer rural areas, natural resources appear to have been exploited to an extent that undermined environmental sustainability. Avoiding this unintended consequence of specific survival strategies must be a major challenge facing policy-makers in the post-war reconstruction period.

5.5   New Attitudes to Risk

Rimmer (1995) remarked that political instability, insecurity, and outright conflict increased risks—and hence costs—so that transactions could not be completed profitably, or even at all in some trades. At the same time, however, it was precisely the presence of these risks that created the opportunity for large profits. The contrasting outcomes—on the one hand the threat of destitution and on the other the potential for rapid gain—led many people to engage in far more risky economic and social behaviour than they would have done in peacetime.

The story of Rosina Zacarias, a 30-year-old single mother of four, is typical of the hardships that forced people to take extraordinary risks. She claimed that she earned most of her meagre income 'little by little', by selling tomatoes and vegetables she grew in one of the many green zones of Dzembe. Her 9-year-old son helped her increase her income by selling firewood before and after school, which he too collected from Dzembe. Like many others in her situation, Rosina worked for far more than eight hours a day: preparing food for her children; walking to and from the fields carrying large bundles of firewood and vegetables on her head and back; working in the fields and selling her goods at the market. Daily she risked her life by going outside the city perimeter: although Dzembe is only 7 km south-east of Chimoio, the risk of being captured or murdered by the Renamo could never be ruled out. Before the partial ceasefire agreement of December 1990, Renamo attacks even within the city were quite frequent. Furthermore, her crops might be stolen—there was an increase in the number of people who earned their living by 'reaping where they did not sow'. Fetching wood, which was in great demand for cooking, heating, fencing, and building, from nearby bushes and forests was also fraught with danger, including the risk of amputation by anti-personnel mines or attack by wild animals.

In the orange groves, too, people engaged in theft instead of honest orange picking. During the drought of 1992, for those with the courage to steal oranges at night, the potential gain was high. For instance, from the sale of fifty bags someone could make enough savings to set up an average size mini-shop. As one militiaman who guarded the plantation divulged, dozens of women and children swamped into the plantation at midnight, filled their sacks and left. He said that when he asked them to stop most of the women would humbly reply: 'Shoot if you want. I have children to feed. I can't let them die while I look on'. He added that, knowing how painful hunger could be, he could not shoot at them, though this endangered his own job.

Truck drivers travelling between towns were also in danger of being killed by ambush or landmines in their long and dangerous trips through no man's land into rebel-controlled territory and back again. There were unconfirmed rumours that some of these drivers actually negotiated for their survival by making deals with the rebels, in which they would bring them urban manufactured goods in return for their safety. Sometimes they even acted as rebels' informers. As one driver put it, '*Kutofamba nekushinga nekuti urombo hunenge hwanyanya*' (it's suffering that gives us the courage to take risks).

Instead of taking physical risks, others chose to gamble financially. Three youths in the Sete de Abril market ran a gambling game called *rifa mundil*. They game was played by other youths as well as women with young children. The game involved throwing a dice with numbers corresponding to those written on the table. The clients placed bets of 100Mt (just enough to buy matches or a cigarette) on which number would come up. The winner took all the money except 100Mt, which went to the spinner of the dice. If no one won, the spinner took all. Despite the apparently low returns, youths spent the whole day hoping to win at the expense of others in this increasingly popular game. The elite also played *rifa mundil* in hotels and bars but for much higher stakes in an attempt to accumulate wealth rapidly.

Those successful in taking on the risks described above had a comparative advantage in their respective trades, which could easily be translated into a means for upward mobility within the anarchical war economy. A preparedness to take calculated risks, such as being arrested while stealing oranges or being captured by rebels or blown up by landmines, shaped the possibilities or constraints open to one: without 'having a go', the chances of success remained nil.

5.6   *Illegal Activities*

The most distinctive feature of the grass roots war economy—was semi-illegal, outright illegal and violent survival strategies of the scheming, greedy and cruel—those economic actors Keen (1995) identified as the beneficiaries of war. The collapse of state power and rise in anarchy offered the bureaucratic and commercial elite unprecedented opportunities for accumulating wealth. First, the state's incapacity to enforce labour laws, combined with the weakening of the labour movement, allowed these two groups to base their primitive accumulation of capital on the super-exploitation of labour. Most employed the poor who were desperate for cash in conditions that bordered on slavery. Others used their political position to accumulate wealth, mainly through

Table 4.1   Mozambique: Changes in grass-roots war economy exchange
rates in Manica Province

	March 1992	June 1992	October 1992
Currency	Mt	Mt	Mt
US$1	2,300	2,500	3,000
Z$1	300	500	650
SA Rand1	700	800	1,000

Sources: Author's observations.

underhand tactics, diverting public resources for personal gain and through bribery. This enabled rapid capital accumulation by those who became currency dealers, smugglers, pirates, corrupt officials, and abductors.

5.6.1   Currency dealers

Foreign currency peddlers, with their small bags full of Zimbabwean dollars, South African rands, American dollars and, as they put it, 'the debased and valueless Meticais' slung over their shoulders, spent their time hanging around the main stations of Chimoio, Manica, and Machipanda, waiting for clients. Most of those interviewed in Chimoio said they had started as petty traders with stalls at the main city market. Almost all of them still had these stalls but employed young boys to man them. Foreign currency dealers were central to enabling the activities of all the economic actors, especially importers and travellers, and to the integration of the Manica war economy into the global informal economy. They provided an essential service in a much more efficient way than the cumbersome bureaucratic red-tape procedures of the state-owned banks. If the currency required was available, the transaction just took a matter of seconds and the dealers were also ready to negotiate the exchange rate on the spot. In fact, the exchange rate was remarkably flexible in response to demand and supply and this gave the dealers an added advantage over the fixed official exchange rate. For example, within the six months from March to October 1992 the informal exchange rate had changed dramatically (Table 4.1). This compared with the more or less constant official exchange rate of US$1 to 1800Mt; Z$1 to 250Mt; and 1 SA Rand to 620Mt over this six-month period. The exchange rates varied between towns as well, with the Zimbabwean dollars completely valueless in Maputo, in significant demand in Beira, and in greatest demand in Chimoio, Manica, and at the Machipanda border post.

Although money-changing was a very lucrative economic activity, it was not only difficult to enter, as one had to have vital contacts in order to have a constant supply of hard currency (especially US dollars and South African Rands), but it was also vulnerable to external fluctuations. For example, in 1992 the effects of the devaluation of the Zimbabwean dollar were felt overnight in the Province and reverberated through to Beira, resulting in a simultaneous decline in the demand for US dollars and the supply of Zimbabwean dollars.

5.6.2   Smugglers, pirates, and border guides

Most of the basic manufactured commodities sold in the markets of Manica Province were imported from Zimbabwe—for example the sugar and bread consumed by the elites. But importing these goods was problematic. To start with, entry into Zimbabwe required a visa, but even a single entry cost more than two weeks' wages and so was prohibitive for the unsalaried. In addition, acquiring a visa involved other costs, such as travelling to the embassies or consulate and enduring bureaucratic red tape. Similarly, bribes were unaffordable for many unemployed people who intended to import and resell. In addition, not only was import duty too high, but on the Zimbabwean side there were severe restrictions on the quantity of certain scarce goods that could be exported. For example, when the export of bread and sugar started creating shortages and price hikes in Zimbabwe, the maximum number of loaves of bread that one was allowed to take was limited to two. These costs meant that those who managed to import through the proper official channels only made marginal profits. Consequently, many came up with ingenious smuggling strategies to beat the system.

Smuggling involved many risks, for not only was there a possibility of being arrested (and usually set free after being relieved of the goods by the hungry soldiers or police), but there was a greater danger from pirates who survived entirely on raiding and robbing smugglers. To counter police patrols, the smugglers cooperated with emergency taxi drivers, who had the advantage of speed and of whom they were major clients (as they charged for each bundle of smuggled goods carried). Using coded messages and whistles, they developed an intelligence network that ensured they were always a step ahead of the police. The insecurity caused by pirates, who lay in wait in the border jungles, had an interesting unintended consequence: the creation of employment for local youths as border guides and couriers, escorting and protecting smugglers against pirates, transporting the goods and keeping an eye on police movements.

Other traders and smugglers, not willing to risk arrest for illegal entry into Zimbabwe, met and exchanged their goods between the border posts of the two countries and returned to their respective countries. Many such traders made several trips each day, dumping their goods at the border before going back to get more. Judging by the number of trips that these traders were willing to make in a day, such activities were quite lucrative. Interestingly, the customs officials at the Machipanda border post turned a blind eye to hundreds of smugglers who daily jumped the border, during broad daylight, through bush paths less than a kilometre from the post.

Many of the smuggled goods ended up not only in the informal markets, but also on the shelves of established shops in Manica. In fact, some merchants in the formal economy relied entirely on smugglers or middlemen for certain scarce goods, which were difficult to import because of high import duties or quotas imposed by the Zimbabwean customs. Although there were cases of petty deception and cheating, what was remarkable was the level of cooperation and trust and the observation of unwritten codes of business conduct among these traders.

Smugglers and smuggling undoubtedly kept the grass-roots war economy moving. According to an officer at the Machipanda border post, more than 60 per cent of bread, beer, and sugar imported from Zimbabwe was unofficial trade. Smugglers also did brisk business: even after all costs, especially transport, were taken into account, importing and selling yielded profits of over 200 per cent. It was the final consumer who footed the bill, buying beer and bread in Chimoio for far more than double the prices at the border. Clearly, many of those involved in smuggling were certainly not just making ends meet, but were getting rich as well.

5.6.3   *Hunters, pirates and traffickers*

The increasing possibilities of making a quick profit by trafficking in items such as precious stones, minerals, rhino horns, and elephant tusks resulted in the growth of an underground army of hunters and pirates. Armed with guns or traditional weapons (bows and arrows) the hunters went deep into the forests, sometimes for weeks or months. In the jungle, their lives were endangered from all directions: government soldiers, Renamo rebels, wild animals, and 'hunters of hunters' or pirates. On contact with government forces in the bush these men were automatically arrested under suspicion of being bandits or informers—which usually some of them were as a price of not being harassed by the rebels—and were shot at if they tried to flee. In contact with the rebels, they were either captured and coerced into the rebel force or murdered if they tried to escape. The animals they hunted—elephant, rhino, and buffalo—are par-ticularly dangerous, especially when threatened. However, the most dangerous threat came from the army of professional 'hunters of hunters'.

This pirate army, unlike the rebels and government forces who only occasionally 'relieved' the hunters of the products of their labour, thrived solely on raiding and robbing the hunters. According to a police officer at the police station in Matsinye (literally meaning 'cruelty' in Shona), violent piracy was the most serious problem in the area. For example, within a period of two weeks in September 1992, the police officer reported that three hunters had been killed by pirates, one of whom was later brought to trial. The war was not only fought between government forces and the rebels: real battles were also fought between the pirates and hunters on the one hand, and between these two groups and the soldiers and rebels as well.

Yet it was not these men, daily risking their lives, who really benefited from this business. On the contrary, it was the 'big fish', the professional racketeers in their smart suits and expensive cars, not only from Mozambique but from countries as far north as Zaire, Nigeria, Sierra Leone, and Germany. Trafficking involved a number of actors, interwoven in an extensive worldwide network linking local dealers to international barons and, with respect to Renamo, to arms peddlers in the international informal arms market. It was alleged that some members of police, army, and foreign troops were also involved in trafficking, one reason why the state could not clamp down on this specific practice and illegal activity in general.

Local rumours abounded that some NGO and international agency personnel were also involved in this racketeering. In fact some government officials as well as ordinary citizens doubted the credibility of some NGOs which they saw as mere 'fronts' for siphoning off their wealth to Western countries. As a former employee of one such NGO said,

These people are intelligent crooks. They now know much more about this province than the Government does. For example, they have taken a satellite picture of the whole province and they know where all our minerals are located. They don't show us all their plans and the Director of PLANO (Planning Department) is stupid. He just follows what they tell him to do. You never know what they take with them when they go home.

These concerns, shared by many patriotic Mozambicans, though difficult to prove, cannot be dismissed as unfounded. The country's enormous mineral wealth, large natural gas deposits, and the increasing likelihood of offshore oil, have attracted the attention of mineral and energy-starved countries such as Italy, France, Japan, Germany, and more recently British Lonhro, which was extensively involved in the peace process.

In this context, Mozambicans can be forgiven for seeing their well-intentioned 'good Samaritans' as nothing more than opportunists in a crisis, interested only in profiting from the situation. If the above allegation were correct, then the actual beneficiaries were the jewellery firms in the West that got raw materials cheaply. The only local groups to benefit in a 'smart' way were the 'contacts' who acted as go-betweens between the labourers and the professional international racketeers. These groups, like the local employees of NGOs and international agencies, rose out of mass poverty to become the so called, 'new *assimilados*' (under colonialism, *assimilados* were those Africans deemed civilized by virtue of their education and wealth and hence accorded equal status to the Europeans).

Arms traffickers were another category of economic actors central to the institutionalization of violence in Mozambique. The arms trade not only fuelled the war but, as seen earlier, also gave another dimension to the grass-roots war economy as possession of arms provided people with access to local resources. In Mozambique, as in many other wars, the classic 'culprit' was the shady arms dealer, depicted as being 'without morals, [and] willing to sell to everybody and his enemy' (Brzoska 1995). As the arms dealers operated clandestinely in Mozambique, it was difficult to assess the extent of their activities and the size of their market. Part of this difficulty derived from the covert South African governmental activities of supplying the rebels with arms. Some underpaid government soldiers or policemen were also alleged to be involved in part-time arms dealing, for example by hiring out their weapons to armed robbers for a night or even selling them. Generally, it is a truism that buying and selling a gun in Mozambique was no big deal, but was a lucrative undertaking. With the end of the war this problem spilt over into neighbouring countries: some of the guns used in armed robberies in South Africa and Zimbabwe came from Mozambique.

5.6.4 Abductors

Slavery in Mozambique is not a thing of the past. In 1992, it was reported that a South African-based slave syndicate operating in the eastern Transvaal homeland of kaNgwane had abducted many young children from Maputo for sale in South Africa. In the central region a clandestine group of abductors was involved in similar activities. The slave traders enticed young children with false promises into crossing the border into Zimbabwe with them, and then sold them to white commercial farmers in the south-east of the country.

According to one former slave[10]-a 17-year-old boy at the time of the interview —who was abducted from Chimoio in 1986, the living and working conditions were appalling. They lived in barrack-like semicircular asbestos buildings with no windows; working from dawn to dusk with no pay, and barred from mixing with the local population. Rich peasant farmers, as well as urban petty traders, also employed cheap Mozambican labour in poor conditions. This reflects the increasing integration of the regional informal economies, and shows that it was not only Mozambicans who benefited from the effects of war.

5.7   Emerging Social and Economic Transaction Codes

The grass-roots war economy was in many respects more predictable and rational than the official one. Illegal and unrecorded trade was not haphazard but institutionalized, operating according to a system of rules known to all participants. Examples included the standardized values observed for barter transactions, the set rates for paying border guides, the terms set for clients, and the reciprocal obligations of personal ties. The trust and confidence inspired by personal relationships or a common cultural background provided the reliability and predictability that were lacking in the official economy. To some extent, therefore, the grass-roots war economy generated alternative economic institutions. Although for the individual actors involved, the new economic behaviour represented a pragmatic response to a crisis, overall their actions represented an institutional shift, and a challenge to the development strategy pursued by Frelimo since coming to power in 1975.

Moreover, the use of family bonds, kinship relations, and ethnic connections to get goods or other resources, practical help, or reduce costs, and ensure continued mutual trust and cooperation, was a common practice in the grass-roots war economy. This transformation of kin relations into capitalist ones, or their monetization was not unique to Mozambique. All over Africa, the poor have used the informal contracts kin and clan relations create as endogenous social security nets. As Jagganathan (1987) points out, such personal ties are 'social assets that create earning opportunities for the poor'.

These emergent economic forms contrast sharply with the pre-war situation in many rural communities, where products were destined for direct use by the community and not for exchange, and where production and organization were based on the 'economy of affection'. For subordinate social groups such as women and children, the collapse of the economic base of rural patriarchy and gerontocracy afforded them more freedom, and enabled them to engage in new economic activities, and enjoy the surplus. Similarly, the collapse of state power enabled social groups and movements to participate more effectively in the 'dialectic of control' and redefine the state–civil society relationship, expanding their political space. This transformation of the political economy seems to have cleared the way for capitalist development, a transition which Frelimo

---

[10] According to the boy, after escaping back into Mozambique, he had seen the man who had abducted him—by luring him into going for a fishing trip—with another man. It was not clear whether this other man was a potential victim or an accomplice. The case was reported to the police, who did not help.

had violently attempted to forestall with the slogan: 'kill capitalism when it is young like a crocodile' (Machel 1977).

In Manica Province, violence was both an integrative and disintegrative force; association and competition, cooperation and conflict coexisted in dynamic tension. For instance, the success and reliability of the grass-roots war economy was based on cooperation, trust, and a sense of community among its participants. Thus, as Fanon (1968) and Foch (1914) contend, in specific circumstances, wars can serve as a positive force in the development of social cohesion within groups—the dispossessed, in the case of Mozambique.

6 Issues of Post-war Reconstruction

Mozambique's grass-roots war economy, as with the informal economy in general, is the subject of much controversy. Some observers feel it holds considerable developmental potential, as an untapped resource of entrepreneurship which offers a solution to post-conflict reconstruction. Indeed optimists consider it an 'invisible revolution', or as the 'other path' to development (De Soto 1989). Others view it in a negative light as a mere haven for refuge at near-subsistence levels, inviting labour exploitation and class formation. Yet others, especially bureaucratic elites, have contemptuous disdain for the spontaneity of the informal economy as some of their remarks reveal: 'have you ever seen anything like this in the West? It is degrading and makes our cities dirty. All this will end after the war.' Such a diversity of views bears testimony to the ambiguities and contradictions of the grass-roots war economy; the reality is that these divergent views depict aspects of an extremely complex process, and reflect the ideological inclinations and assumptions of the individuals and institutions concerned.

Table 4.2 Mozambique: Key macroeconomic indicators 1976–1984
(annual percentage change)

Year	GDP (per capita)	Gross Investment	Exports	Imports
1976	−17.4	−3.7	−43.8	−20.4
1977	−1.6	−1.9	−32.1	−9.8
1978	−1.0	0.0	11.5	51.9
1979	−0.9	1.5	57.4	−0.4
1980	−2.0	93.2	−21.9	−5.8
1981	−6.3	0.0	−19.0	1.0
1982	−1.5	−52.5	−5.4	−2.9
1983	−18.1	−57.5	−49.5	−12.0
1984	−3.6	6.9	−44.0	−7.8
1985	−10.0	−19.6	−28.2	−9.9
1986	8.7	3.8	−23.0	43.0

Source: Tibana 1994.

We have seen that the grass-roots war economy provided a livelihood for many people, some of whom even got richer, and generated growth in certain sectors of the economy; to this extent it constitutes an 'invisible economic revolution'. No doubt there was widespread poverty in Mozambique, but the point is, that without the goods (primarily food) and opportunities provided by the grass-roots war economy, many more people would have starved to death. True, it was based on crude exploitation and social differentiation, and to this extent it may not represent the most desirable 'other path' to development. Certainly some aspects of the economy, like sex work, piracy, and slavery, were degrading, but not all activities were. Judging by the experience of other African countries and Mozambique's short post-war experience, the informal economy seems here to stay, and could even become the mainstay of the economy if the formal economy continues to falter.

Inevitably, such fundamental changes in economic behaviour and attitudes, wrought indirectly and directly by the war, had a strong impact on the organization of society, engendering shifts in the balance of power and political alliances at various levels. Significantly, the barefoot traders themselves indicated their wish to continue to be independent after the war, with some declaring that they would never work in bureaucracies or for anyone else.

This ethos of the emergent grass-roots war, though it undermined state control in some ways, did not challenge the existence of the state per se nor even the right of the state to intervene in the economy. Instead it seems the issue of contention was what form that state structure should take—who should be in control of it and, how, where, and when it should intervene in the economy.

In spite of the obvious advantages of informal economic activity to the survival of the state, the state remains the major obstacle to the expansion of this sector, in particular through restrictive legislation and bureaucratic requirements which stifle initiative. Flustered by the enormity of the problem, and unable to see elements of a solution, the Provincial Planning Department produced an endless list of priorities within priorities which were not only confusing, but bore little relevance to what was happening on the ground. Thus a fuller realization of the potential of the grass-roots war economy presupposes a reconceptualization of the role of the state in development; the state should create conditions conducive to economic innovation and enterprise, rather than stifle the development potential of the masses. Given the limited resources at the state's disposal, perhaps it makes sense for the state to streamline its responsibilities and concentrate on key areas such as the provision of infrastructure, education, health, and removal of bureaucratic rules that hamper economic activity. In other words, the state needs to redefine both its attitude towards informal economic activity, and its role in the economy, as well redirect its energies into critical areas and allow the micro-entrepreneurs to create markets where they have a valuable comparative advantage.

The most perplexing aspect of the grass-roots war economy was its diversity, in terms of both the range of its activities and the wealth of the entrepreneurs: while some barely managed to survive, others became very rich. This diversity in needs and survival strategies, which partly derives from the different social backgrounds of the participants, poses a serious dilemma for policy-makers in getting their priorities right.

Notwithstanding the obvious negative economic effects of war, the evidence of vigorous entrepreneurship, innovation, and the entrenchment of hard-working ethics, should leave no one in doubt that we have witnessed an unprecedented liberation of the potential of many Mozambicans. The war, by breaking asunder the fossilized structures of the old bureaucratic system, enabled the disinherited to take the initiative and demonstrate what they can do in the absence of state constraints. The war economy provided a functioning distribution system, which was so conspicuously lacking in the official economy. Were it not for the illicit trade and smuggling, Mozambique's people would have suffered even more acutely from lack of food and essential commodities. The challenge for post-peace reconstruction is, therefore, to create conditions conducive to the fullest realization of this potential, as well as to offer alternative opportunities for those engaged in counter-productive economic activities.

7 Conclusion

Whereas in many other countries the informal economy emerged alongside relatively well-established capitalist institutions, in Mozambique it arose within the context of a radical transition from a command economy to a free market one. Several key factors, described in Section 3, gave a 'quantum leap' effect to the emergence of the grass-roots war economy. War and displacement accelerated the transformation of peasants into barefoot entrepreneurs by forcing them to become innovative and flexible, or face death by starvation. The break up of state power removed obstacles to capital accumulation. The adoption of structural adjustment programmes in 1986–7 legitimated the acquisitive spirit, which hitherto had been condemned in the name of socialism, although dynamic elements of socialism were evident in the emergence of voluntary collectives and cooperatives. Large-scale intervention by international aid regimes not only injected money, goods and values into the system, but also led to the increasing integration of the Manica economy into the international economic system—both formal and informal. Not surprisingly the emergent grass-roots war economy was based on 'economic hybridization' with market relations adulterated by non-market ones, such as socialist and traditional 'economy of affection' ethics. In a striking similarity to the effects of slavery, the war generated economic and social processes, which offered opportunities to some. The war had fundamental implications for the evolution of the Mozambican political economy.

This analysis has attempted to provide a sociological interpretation of war and economic change, linking some events and details of the economic behaviour of real individuals to the structures within which they operated. Violence appears to have been the midwife of the emergence of a specific kind of capitalism, a hybrid arrangement, which has taken root mainly in trade rather than production. The war released the masses' latent entrepreneurial potential and forcibly entrenched entrepreneurial ethics. This has catalysed the process of capitalist expansion at a rapid pace, rare in normal circumstances. At a theoretical level, this development challenged populist approaches that emphasized the resistance of a communalistic traditional society and its concomitant 'moral economy' to market-related values. The supposedly conservative have become quasi-capitalists only constrained in their expansion by a lack of capital and technical know-how.

The main conclusion that can be drawn from these developments is, therefore, that war should not be considered purely in terms of disaster. Rather, it must be viewed in its dialectical relation to society as a social process capable of inducing simultaneous deconstruction and reconstruction, destroying some markets and creating others where none existed—ruining some people while making others very rich. The major mechanism responsible for the uneven distribution of the benefits and costs of war was the social position of the particular individuals within the economic structure and their personal experience of war. That social position determined the extent of vulnerability to, and capacity to cope with, the effects and opportunities of war.

5

Nicaragua: The Political Economy of Social Reform and Armed Conflict

VALPY FITZGERALD AND ARTURO GRIGSBY

1 Introduction

This chapter addresses the relationship between economic development, armed conflict, and social reform in Nicaragua under the Sandinista administration between 1979 and 1990.[1] This period saw a combination of ambitious reform based on land redistribution, universal social services, state investment, and income redistribution in a mixed open economy supported by aid donors on the one hand, and of increasing economic stress arising from externally supported insurgency, a trade embargo, fiscal strain, foreign exchange shortages, and rising inflation leading to electoral defeat on the other.

Two diametrically opposed views of this decade are possible. The first is that the model of social reform in a mixed economy was viable and that economic collapse was the direct—and intended—consequence of US pressure exercised for geopolitical reasons. The second is that poverty alleviation based on public expenditure is not consistent with a market economy, that military expenditure was largely a matter of state power rather than a real external threat, and that the economic collapse was the result of incompetent policy. In both these approaches the war is seen as an essentially exogenous shock to the economy.

In the first view, the war was part of a geopolitical strategy of the US government to contain revolutionary governments in the Third World by supporting and arming their political opponents—known as the doctrine of 'low intensity war'. This was international conflict which the Sandinistas could never win, in which the undermining of the Nicaraguan economy was an intrinsic part. In the second view, the insurgents were local phenomena and the costs enormously exaggerated by the Nicaraguan government for propaganda purposes. A more democratic government could have accommodated the opposition demands and need not have relied on military support from Cuba and the Soviet Union. The impact of the war only exacerbated what already were untenable economic policies.

[1] This chapter is based on a study for the Swedish International Development Agency, SIDA, reported in FitzGerald and Grigsby (1997); which also contains a complete statistical data base for 1975–95. Dr FitzGerald would also like to thank the MacArthur Foundation for support.

Map 5.1   Nicaragua

We argue in this chapter that neither of these views are in fact correct. There was a fundamental inconsistency in the Sandinista economic strategy; however, this inconsistency was not to be found in populist redistributive policies but rather in the model of state-centred accumulation. External pressure did have a drastic effect on exports and military expenditure; but this was largely compensated by high levels of external finance. Above all, we will suggest that the relationship between the war and the economy is highly complex, involving both the pressure of armed peasants for radical land distribution on the one hand and the enormous secondary cost of conflict in a small open economy on the other.

In order to address this complex inter-relationship, we attempt to answer three key questions:

- the way in which the direct and indirect economic consequences of conflict affected different social groups;
- how this economic impact was reduced (or increased) by government policies and the efforts of aid donors;
- the extent to which this economic impact in turn ameliorated (or worsened) the conflict itself.

After a brief outline of the social and economic features of the Somoza regime which led to the Sandinista revolution in 1979, Section 2 sets out the nature of the reform process initiated in the early 1980s. Section 3 examines the relationship between socio-political change in this period and the dynamics of the armed conflict which intensified with US support in the middle of the decade. The relationship between basic-needs provision, state investment, and macroeconomic stability is explored in more depth in Section 4. We then come to an assessment in Section 5 of the relationship between low-intensity war, socio-political stress and economic collapse in Nicaragua by the late 1980s. Section 6 turns to the end of the war, as the Sandinistas signed a peace treaty with the US-backed insurgents, and initiated a transition to orthodox policies of market liberalization and fiscal retrenchment, which were continued by the subsequent civilian government. Finally, some conclusions from the study are presented in Section 7.

2   The Transition from Predatory Capitalism to Mixed Economy

The model of economic development under the regime of the Somoza family (who had ruled Nicaragua for the previous 40 years) was characterized by rapid growth based on the expansion of agro-expert production and a highly unequal income distribution. The Nicaraguan economy grew at an average rate of 7 per cent annually during the 1960s and 5 per cent during the 1970s, well above the average for other middle-income developing countries (World Bank 1980).

Nicaragua's social indicators during this period were well below the average. Adult literacy was 57 per cent compared with 71 per cent for middle-income countries as a whole; while life expectancy averaged 55 years compared to 61 years for middle-income countries (World Bank 1980). These poor social indicators in a situation of rapid growth were due to a highly unequal income distribution as well as the lack of public investment in health and education. The richest 5 per cent of the economically active population received 28 per cent of national income, compared to 15 per cent for the bottom 50 per cent (Gibson 1987).

From the 1950s, economic expansion was largely due to the growth of export crops, particularly cotton, coffee, sugar cane, and livestock. Large landowners, who also dominated financial services and export marketing, expanded most rapidly in this model. Medium-sized commercial farmers also benefited, although they had to rely on the large landowners for access to export markets and bank credit. Small peasant farmers remained tied to food production—particularly maize and beans—and did not experience rising incomes; and so were forced to supply harvest labour to export farms. As a result, domestic food crop cultivation remained stagnant, while the acreage devoted to export agriculture increased from about a quarter to half of total land in production (Barraclough 1982).

Agro-export expansion generated acute social conflicts because of the eviction of peasants by capitalist farmers. The government partly alleviated these conflicts through colonization programmes in the under-populated Atlantic region. However, the policy of keeping real wages down by importing foodgrains contributed to the plight of peasant farmers. In fact, a weakened peasant economy was essential to agro-export expansion because it guaranteed a supply of cheap wage labour: a third of the seasonal workers were landless peasants who only had full-time work during the harvest season (CIERA 1984). Moreover, despite the rapid expansion of agro-exports and the beginning of an industrialization process based on food processing and farm inputs, the level of employment in productive sectors declined while that of the services sector increased as landless peasants migrated to the cities, particularly Managua. The proportion of the labour force employed in agriculture declined from 68 per cent in 1960 to 41 per cent in 1978, while that of the services sector—mainly petty commerce—increased from 23 per cent to 50 per cent during the same period (World Bank 1980).

This highly uneven pattern of economic growth was supported by macroeconomic policies that fully integrated the Nicaraguan economy into the international market while maintaining financial stability: the pegging of the national currency (Cordoba) to the US dollar, restriction of bank credit to deposited export income, and tight fiscal control based on low taxes and expenditure. The main purpose of monetary policy was to maintain the Central Bank's foreign reserves intact by limiting liquidity in periods of low export earnings; while the commercial banks provided working capital for the agro-export cycle by obtaining trade credits from purchasing countries such as the USA and Japan. Nicaragua's fiscal deficit never surpassed 5 per cent of GDP and never absorbed more than 10 per cent of domestic credit. Most public expenditure was financed by regressive indirect taxation, which accounted for 70 per cent of total revenue. Public investment was less than 15 per cent of total investment and was largely confined to building infrastructure for the agro-export sector; it was financed by long-term debt contracted from international development agencies.

This monetary system was also employed by the other Central American countries. The five central banks played a key role in the establishment of the Central American Monetary Stabilization Fund, the Central American Clearing House, and the Central American Bank for Economic Integration. These institutions constituted a virtual currency area linked to the US dollar and funded vital infrastructure provision for the region (FitzGerald and Croes 1988). These monetary and fiscal policies were maintained over three decades, and the exchange rate of the Cordoba remained unchanged at 7 Cordobas to the US dollar until 1978. This remarkable stability was also reflected in the relatively low inflation rate. Nicaragua's inflation rate during the 1970s was 11 per cent, compared to the average for middle-income developing countries of 13 per cent (World Bank 1980).

The failure to redistribute the benefits of economic growth was at the root of Nicaragua's social and political crisis in the late 1970s. The most important manifestation of this crisis was the growing strength of the Sandinista National Liberation Front

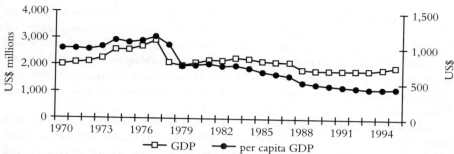

Figure 5.1   Nicaragua: Gross Domestic Product and GDP per capita
(at 1980 prices and exchange rate)
Source: Banco Central de Nicaragua.

(FSLN), which the Somoza government attempted to contain through increasing repression. Growing social and political discontent also provoked massive capital flight. The government response was to maintain financial stability by borrowing from international commercial banks: the external debt jumped from US$655 to 1,100 millions between 1977 and 1979. The government could not contain the economic or political crisis and had to devalue the Cordoba for the first time in three decades, shortly before the triumph of the Sandinista Revolution in July 1979.

The overthrow of the Somoza regime by a massive popular insurrection led by the FSLN in 1979 had significant human and economic costs. During the final military offensive from October 1977 to July 1979, 35,000 people died and about 10,000 people were wounded (over 5 per cent of the 1979 population); while a further 150,000 became internal or external refugees. In sum one-tenth of the Nicaraguan population became war victims. There were also significant economic costs: the destruction of capital stock and loss of inventories were estimated by the United Nations at US$381 million, equivalent to 18 per cent of 1980 GDP; during the same period total capital flight amounted to US$535 million, equivalent to a further 26 per cent of 1980 GDP (CEPAL 1981). The impact of this revolutionary conflict is clearly reflected in the 32 per cent fall in the GDP of Nicaragua in the last two years of the war, as Figure 5.1 illustrates.

The new Sandinista government sought to create an alternative to traditional capitalist development but also one which would differ significantly from orthodox definitions of socialist development. The main distinctive elements were first, in terms of development strategy, primacy was given to agricultural development and the exploitation of natural resources instead of rapid industrialization. Second, rather than a rapid and comprehensive extension of state ownership as in other socialist contexts, the policy was to combine different types of ownership and regulate rather than replace markets. Third, it maintained representative democratic institutions and competitive party politics, while at the time it sought to develop forms of popular participation in economic life, political decision making and state administration (MIPLAN 1980).

Agricultural development was seen as the key source of investible surplus through greater exports and as the basis for raising popular living standards through increased food supply. Industrial development was to be subordinated to agriculture, processing its products for export or producing wage goods while building up a capacity to supply inputs and even simple equipment. Popular living standards were expected to rise with the greater supply of wage goods, universal primary education and basic health care, better housing, and collective transport.

Full-scale nationalization did not take place because the revolution depended on a broad alliance across social classes and continued support from non-socialist countries. In addition, the Sandinista government was aware that large private agribusiness and manufacturers controlled much of the country's organizational and technical capacity. Small and medium producers and merchants were so widespread in both industry and agriculture that full-scale nationalization was not feasible politically and economically. None the less, the new government sought to expand the role of the state by converting the properties confiscated from Somoza and his allies into state enterprises. These included some 168 factories, making up 25 per cent of the country's industrial capacity, and 20 per cent of total farm land, including half of all farms of more than 350 hectares. The banking system, foreign trade, mining, fishing and forestry were also nationalized. State marketing boards were established for export and domestic crops, as well as large state commercial corporations for the distribution of imported machinery and inputs. An extensive state network of wholesale and retail stores was set up for the distribution of basic consumer goods. As a result, the public sector share in GDP rose from 15 per cent in 1978 to 37 per cent in 1980 (Gibson 1987; Ruccio 1987).

The other important structural transformation undertaken by the Sandinista government, more typical of socialist-oriented regimes in developing countries, was an economic strategy that attempted simultaneously to satisfy the basic needs of the population and to modernize the economy. 'Basic needs' meant the achievement of basic food security and the extension of social services, such as education, health, and housing. Government social policy aimed to guarantee free access to primary education and to basic health for the entire population. Modernization of agriculture and energy self-sufficiency would provide the basis for subsequent industrialization; and would involve intensive investment by state enterprises. The diversification of trade and financial links away from the USA towards other market economies, Latin America, and the CMEA socialist bloc was intended to be the geopolitical strategy of non-alignment (MIPLAN 1980).

The government sought to maintain macroeconomic stability in a dependent mixed economy through a process of supply management associated with the theories of the Polish economist Kalecki[2] rather than the demand management of Keynes macroeconomic policy (Gibson 1987). The reactivation of economic activity with stable prices was seen as a question of balanced investment financing, dependent in turn on the management of consumption. The essence of the Kaleckian approach is that in order to raise the rate of growth without inflation, and thus avoid a deteriorating income distribution,

---

[2] For a discussion of the relevance of Kaleckian theory to developing economies, see FitzGerald (1993).

the supply of necessary or basic needs goods and the taxation of non–necessary goods must both be increased (FitzGerald 1989).

Adopting this approach meant implementing a system of control of key prices: nominal wage rates, interest rates, fuel, and some foodstuffs, and above all the exchange rate. It was made possible by the state monopolization of banks, foreign trade, and wholesale trade. In effect, the state provided working capital and guaranteed support prices for each branch of production in agriculture and industry. Prices and credit facilities were to be set so as to motivate producers to maintain production without allowing excess profits. In this way, profit rates and savings were to be kept stable, and investment be financed out of bank deposits, state enterprise surpluses, and foreign aid (FitzGerald 1989).

Wage policy consisted in fixed nominal wages combined with the expansion of the *salario social* (social wage), which included a subsidy for the basic market basket of goods as well as improved, expanded, and free education and health services. In addition, the government strengthened the state role in the procurement and distribution of basic consumer goods to keep consumer prices down. Measures included the establishment of a centralized mechanism to procure foods, increased storage capacity, and secure channels for wholesale and retail distribution (Biondi-Mora 1990).

The impact of this structural transformation, and of the changes in economic and social policy, varied for different social strata. The expansion of the state and the basic-needs policy largely favoured public employees, industrial, and agricultural workers, and to a lesser extent, the urban informal sector. These groups became the backbone of popular support for the revolutionary government.

The peasants and the indigenous groups on the Atlantic Coast benefited from the expansion of health and education programmes, but were largely outside the distribution system for cheap consumer goods. Moreover, the conversion of confiscated lands into state farms and the nationalization of natural resources effectively excluded landless peasants in the mountains and indigenous groups of the Atlantic Coast from the substantial asset redistribution that took place immediately after the revolution. These two groups became the largest source of recruits to the counter-revolutionary forces. Although their profits were maintained, large and medium agricultural producers and manufacturers, and all commercial businesses, were severely affected by state intervention in both domestic markets and foreign trade, and government discrimination in the allocation of resources. These groups became the leaders of the political opposition to the government.

In contrast, wage and salary earners benefited from increased employment opportunities in both central government and state enterprises, as well as in the agricultural and the manufacturing sectors. A social wage and better working conditions helped to raise the living standards for these key groups (Biondi-Mora 1990; Castillo 1989). In addition, the government supported an accelerated process of unionization of the workforce. As a result, the number of unions and their membership rose sharply, from 133 unions with 27,000 members in 1978 to 1,099 unions with 130,000 members in 1984—40 per cent of the salaried labour force. The new strength of the trade union movement was reflected in the numerous collective contracts initiated with both state and private employers. Workers benefited from better working conditions and stores at the workplace that sold subsidized consumer goods. At the same time, the social security system was extended to the countryside, and for the first time, child-care facilities and health clinics were available to agricultural workers at their workplace.

The informal sector also benefited from subsidized consumer prices, transport subsidies, and expanded urban demand. The government allowed extensive urban land invasions, and often provided basic services to these new neighbourhoods, and legalized the ownership of these properties. Artisans organized into cooperatives benefited from access to credit and technical assistance, although they suffered from a shortage of inputs and priority allocation of foreign exchange to factories. Wholesale traders clearly resented state control of basic consumer goods. Initially, the government attempted to establish *tiendas populares* (popular stores) in every neighbourhood, but this generated resistance among retailers; so traditional *pulperías* (corner shops) were contracted to distribute rationed goods. As shortages occurred in the state-controlled markets, a parallel market developed even though petty traders outside the state network were harshly treated by state inspectors and the police.

The disruption of these informal trade networks not only affected urban traders, but also the traditional private agents engaged in urban/rural trade. They were displaced by new state agencies, which caused a breakdown of the rural marketing circuits, and led to a serious shortage of manufactured goods. This had an adverse effect on agricultural production. Rural traders were often influential members of their rural communities—rich peasants were involved in production, trade with the urban areas, and monopolized rural transport. These rich peasants became the backbone of logistical support for, and ideological leaders of, the Contras in rural communities.

None the less, most peasants also benefited from increased access to social services and to credit. The literacy campaign in 1980–1 and the adult education programme that followed were extended to some of the most isolated parts of the country. The literacy rate rose from 50 to 87 per cent. The number of peasant families that received credit tripled from 28,000 in 1978 to some 80,000—a quarter of all rural households—in 1984, and the vast majority of these households were organized into credit cooperatives (Enriquez and Spalding 1987).

However, the key socio-economic factor fuelling peasant discontent was the nature and pace of agrarian reform. The peasants had expected the landholdings of Somoza and his allies to be redistributed to them: their expectations were based on the explicit commitment to land reform of the Sandinista Front and its support for land appropriation, particularly in the last phase of the liberation war. Immediately after the July 1979 revolution, spontaneous peasant land invasions occurred throughout the country (Faune 1989). The Sandinista government changed its agrarian policy before the 1980–1 agricultural season started and decided to convert all confiscated land into state farms. Government officials and political cadres around the country were given the task of persuading landless peasants and agricultural workers to vacate the occupied land and promised permanent employment in the new state farms.

The state farms and the large private agricultural producers were seen as the centre of capital formation, modernization, and future growth: expropriation of state lands, formerly belonging to the Somoza faction, would put the state in a pivotal position to achieve this programme as it would directly control about half the large farms in the country without having to expropriate other large landowners. Indeed, the nationalization of banks and foreign trade would enable it to control remaining commercial farming indirectly. In addition, state control of credit and inputs could be used to encourage cooperativization among the peasants. The long-run strategic concept was to absorb all capitalist agriculture into state farms, and all small peasant farms into cooperatives.

Nevertheless, this approach was partially modified in 1983. Unprofitable state farms, together with some of the land expropriated from large private estates under the Agrarian Law of 1981, were given to landless peasant collectives. The new Agrarian Law gave the government legal authorization to expropriate idle, under-utilized, or rented land on estates of more then 500 *manzanas* in the Pacific region, and 1,000 *mazanas* elsewhere. In addition, distribution of state land to peasant farmers was accelerated in regions that were increasingly affected by the Contra war, as disaffected farmers had become the largest source of recruits to the insurgents. Thus, the number of peasant families in receipt of land rose from under 10,000 to more than 30,000, although this still only represented a quarter of the estimated number of landless peasants in the country (CIERA 1989).

The state-centred accumulation model also generated social and political discontent in the Atlantic Coast region. Large state corporations were created to manage the exploitation of the country's natural resources, particularly those on the Atlantic Coast that had formerly been controlled by North American corporations. Thus, the state acquired a virtual monopoly of large-scale gold and silver mining, forestry, and fishing. The government also set up a new regulatory institute for the environment and natural resources, which established two major forestry reserves along the Atlantic Coast. The underlying logic of Sandinista government policy was to integrate natural resources and the indigenous peoples of the Atlantic Coast into a Pacific Nicaraguan economy and society. It was hoped that large-scale state investment in infrastructure, combined with public management of the abundant natural resources of the Atlantic Coast, would lead to the modernization of the regional economies, and encourage the full integration of the indigenous peoples into Nicaraguan society. Not surprisingly, these groups rejected this approach, which completely ignored their historic claims to the Atlantic Coast's natural resources, and their right to preserve their ethnic identity.

As we have seen, the other key social group opposed to the Sandinista government was the business elite. Businessmen had been severely affected by a new round of expropriations, following the Agrarian Law in 1981. For instance, the Absentee Law gave legal authorization to the government to confiscate large commercial and industrial businesses whose owners had left the country; while the Decapitalization Law permitted similar action where capital flight was involved. In this way the state acquired the most important shopping centres in Managua, several large industrial plants, and about 60 per cent of the remaining large rural estates.

Commercial businesses were also adversely affected by the extensive state intervention in both domestic markets and foreign trade, particularly by restrictions of non-essential imports. In addition, the government used the confiscated businesses to set up its own chain of commercial stores with preferential access to scarce foreign exchange. Widespread shortages of non-essential consumption goods led to a growing parallel market based on smuggling. This meant that established private businesses were forced to compete against both the state enterprises and the informal sector. The business elite thus became the most active political opposition to the Sandinista government.

3   Socio-political Change and the Dynamics of War

The Nicaraguan business elite, which had opposed Somoza in 1979, initially formed part of the government with the FSLN, but became politically alienated as the centre of power shifted from the original Junta de Gobierno, the formal governing body after the revolution, to the Sandinista party directorate. Two prominent members of the business elite resigned from the five-member Junta de Gobierno in 1980, less than a year after its formation, when the Sandinista leadership sacked businessmen appointed to the Cabinet, and replaced them with party leaders. The original legislative body, the Consejo de Estado, was expanded to include representatives of Sandinista mass organizations.

This relationship deteriorated further when several months later, the president of the national agricultural producers' association (UPANIC) was killed by the Sandinista State Security while resisting arrest after joining an armed conspiracy. The Sandinista Front created a new agricultural producers organization (UNAG), with the purpose of undermining the leadership of the business elite among small- and medium-size agricultural producers, as well as preventing further erosion of its political support in the countryside. UPANIC had been particularly successful at organizing small- and medium-size coffee producers in the northern region of the country into credit and service cooperatives. For instance, the *Cooperativa Central de Cafetaleros de Matagalpa* grew to 7,000 members in 1980, and had dozens of local credit committees throughout the region. This 'traditional' cooperative movement, which had been supported both by the National Development Bank and by institutions affiliated to business associations before 1979, experienced a boom in membership among urban and rural merchants and private transport owners.

The first armed counter-revolutionary bands emerged in the Northern region, supported by these small- and medium-size coffee and cattle producers. These producers were afraid that state control of the rural economy would inevitably lead to the expropriation of their land. Some of the leaders of these bands were former Sandinista guerrillas, discontented because confiscated land had not been redistributed to landless peasants (Falla 1980 and 1981a). In addition, counter-revolutionary bands comprising members of the former National Guard were operating along the border with Honduras. Most of these insurgents came from the dry zone of the Northern region, one of the poorest areas of the country and a traditional source of army recruits under Somoza.

The Sandinista government responded to the emergence of armed counter-revolutionary bands with military and political action. Specialist military counter-insurgency units were formed from former guerillas to fight in the mountains, and the

Sandinista mass organization of small- and medium-size producers (UNAG) was used to strengthen political support in the countryside. These new military units inflicted heavy casualties on these bands and practically dismantled them. However in 1981, after the installation of the Reagan administration in Washington, the CIA regrouped the counter-revolutionary bands together with exiled National Guardsmen in Honduras to form the Nicaraguan Democratic Front (FDN), the so-called *Contras*. The FDN was armed and supported logistically by the US administration but manned by Nicaraguans.

The Sandinista Front attempted to maintain its political support in the countryside by creating a new organization of agricultural and cattle producers—the *Unión Nacional de Agricultores y Ganaderos* (UNAG). UNAG launched an extensive campaign to recruit the small- and medium-size producers, who either belonged to UPANIC organizations, or lived in areas that actively supported the first counter-revolutionary bands. The UNAG network extended throughout the country and was further strengthened by the affiliation of the large Sandinista cooperative movement, originally promoted by the Sandinista government and the Rural Workers Association (ATC). In addition, the government passed a new Cooperative Law, which established strict controls on the traditional cooperative movement and promoted those groups associated with the revolution.

The Sandinista Front attempted to integrate the indigenous groups along the Atlantic Coast region into these large Sandinista organizations, but failed disastrously. The government initially disbanded the existing indigenous organisation, *Alpromisu*, but had to accept the formation of a new ethnic organization along similar lines: *Misurasata*. Initially, *Misurasata* collaborated with the government to promote the literacy and health campaigns; a law was passed authorizing education in Spanish, English, and Miskito in the Indian and Creole communities. However, *Misurasata* demanded the recognition of indigenous property rights, including its natural resources, over a large part of the Atlantic Coast. The government rejected these claims, and fearful of a secessionist movement, arrested the *Misurasata* leaders. This led to open armed rebellion by *Misurasata*, whose leaders and several thousand followers fled to the Honduran Mosquitia. They had easy access to Honduras, because the Nicaraguan Miskitos regard the Honduran Mosquitia as part of the Miskito nation.

Misurasata allied itself to the FDN, also based in Honduras, and established their own military training camps with the help of the CIA and the Honduran military. From there they initiated a military offensive against Nicaraguan army posts along the Coco River, on the border between Nicaragua and Honduras. It appears that the aim of this offensive, the so-called 'Red Christmas' Plan of December 1981, was to provoke a Miskito uprising, seize some Nicaraguan territory, appeal for direct US military assistance and obtain international recognition for the formation of an independent state on the Atlantic coast. The government response was to forcibly relocate the Miskito communities of the Coco River: this military strategy prevented any territorial takeover by *Misurasata*, but had disastrous social and political consequences for both the Miskito people and the Sandinista Front.

Meanwhile, the recently formed FDN grew rapidly as a result of US government support and the rapidly deteriorating situation in the countryside. The Contras were better equipped and paid better than their Sandinista rivals, which helped their recruitment drive. In addition, peasant discontent with the Sandinista government increased when forced to sell grains and cash crops at low prices to state marketing companies. As these firms also failed to supply rural consumer goods and essential inputs such as tools and fertilizer, widespread shortages plagued the countryside. As a result, the FDN was able to triple its number of combatants from 4,500 in 1982 to 15,000 by the end of 1984 (Vergara, Castro, and Barry 1986).

The Contra forces were further strengthened by the emergence of a new counter-revolutionary movement, the Democratic Revolutionary Alliance (ARDE) led by a former Sandinista commander. This new organization operated along the border between Nicaragua and Costa Rica, where their leaders had fought during the liberation war against the Somoza regime at the end of the 1970s. ARDE was considerably smaller than the FDN (about 2,500 combatants at its height in 1983), but its political directorate included an ex-member of the first Junta de Gobierno and other prominent figures of the non-Somocista business group.

With the help of the CIA, the FDN acquired a considerable military capability with its own command structure and political directorate. The military structure included a regional command organized according to the geographical zones where the Contras had achieved a certain level of political support. Each regional command was in turn organized into highly mobile task forces, that operated mainly in the northern mountains ('peasant country') and in the North Atlantic region ('Miskito country'). In contrast to the troops and commanders, who were of humble origin, the political directorate was composed of large private businessmen and members of the traditional political parties. They were based in the USA and were in charge of the public relations of the Contra movement, and lobbying the US Congress for financial aid.

The Contra forces launched their first major military offensive in 1983 against the northern border towns of Jalapa, Somoto, and Ocotal, with the aim of provoking a massive anti-government uprising. They hoped to topple the Sandinista regime within a year or two. Initially, the Sandinista government responded with traditional counter-insurgency tactics: mobilizing a large volunteer militia force, known as the *Batallones de Infantería de Reserva*. These tactics included the forced resettlement of peasant families to large cooperatives away from areas of intense Contra activity. Civilian movement and the transport of food supplies were restricted, and police measures were taken against Contra collaborators. Land redistribution to landless rural workers and the formation of collectives was accelerated, particularly in the war zones and along the main rural roads. These collectives, which became the backbone of political support for the Sandinista government in the war zones, were subject to repeated Contra attacks, as were the state farms, health centres, and government agencies.

The Sandinista military strategists initially believed that the Contra offensive was a diversionary tactic to distract the Sandinista army from the primary US strategy—direct invasion by the US army. Indeed, this assessment appeared to be confirmed when USA invaded Grenada in 1983. Specialist CIA forces mined the main Nicaraguan ports and bombed Managua's international airport. Thus the government established a two-pronged defence strategy: to fight the Contras with militia troops, while the bulk of the professional army prepared to fight off a US invasion. The militia forces, mainly composed of industrial workers and students, received a basic military training but were poorly equipped and lacked discipline. While this strategy effectively prevented any further take-over of rural towns or permanent territorial control by Contra forces, it deepened the divide between the largely urban Sandinista forces and the rural population.

The formation of the armed wing of *Misurasata* and the FDN was part of a wider Washington strategy to overthrow the Sandinista regime, which the US government saw as a threat to its geopolitical interests in Central America in the context of the Cold War. The American government had hoped to create an Inter-American peace force, but this idea was rejected by Latin American countries. Instead, they supported the non-Sandinista members of the Nicaraguan government in an attempt to moderate the revolution. However, the US government obtained the collaboration of the Honduran military, which feared that the Nicaraguan revolution might spread to Honduras. The Reagan administration also claimed that the Sandinistas were supporting revolutionary activities in El Salvador as a justification for US intervention. The initial US reconstruction aid to Nicaragua, approved by Congress under Carter in 1980, was cancelled and Washington successfully pressured the IMF, the World Bank, and Inter-American Development Bank (IDB) to refuse any further loans to Nicaragua in 1983. In 1985 the USA imposed a trade embargo on Nicaragua in contravention of its bilateral treaty obligations and GATT rules.

The Reagan administration's policy towards Nicaragua was opposed by neighbouring Latin American countries, which wanted to see a negotiated solution. Mexico, Colombia, Venezuela, and Panama took the diplomatic initiative and formed the *Contadora* group, to resolve the conflict. Under strong pressure from NGOs, most Western European countries opposed US policy, supported the Latin American efforts towards negotiation, and continued to provide aid throughout the 1980s. Latin American countries and Western Europe, persuaded the USA to initiate direct negotiations with the Sandinista government, at the Manzanillo talks. However, in 1984, the USA abandoned these talks and called for the overthrow of the Sandinista government.

Egged on by the USA, the main opposition group, the *Coordinadora Democratica Nicaragüense*, led by an ex-member of the second Junta de Gobierno, boycotted the 1984 elections. Thus, the Sandinista Front easily defeated all other political parties, winning almost two-thirds of the national vote. None the less, the elections showed the FSLN to be politically weak in the countryside, particularly in war zones and where small- and medium-size producers predominated. In contrast, the FSLN did well in the urban areas and in those rural municipalities with a high concentration of agricultural workers (ENVIO 1985).

4 The Unfinished Reconstruction: Basic Needs, State Investment, and Macroeconomic Stability

The intensification of the Contra war had a considerable impact on the fragile recovery of the Nicaraguan economy that had occurred during the first half of the

1980s.[3] Domestic output failed to fully recover to the level of the mid-1970s; partly because of the heavy damage inflicted on productive capacity during the liberation war, and partly because of the structural change to the institutional framework of the Nicaraguan economy. In contrast, domestic demand was stimulated by income redistribution measures, expansionary credit policies, and the growing fiscal deficit. The resulting macroeconomic disequilibrium was at first financed by foreign concessional loans and donations, but later through 'forced savings' as household consumption was compressed.

During the first stage of economic reactivation in 1979–81, recovery was based on the expansion of both government expenditure and credit to agriculture, manufacturing, and commerce. The emphasis of government expenditure was on the provision of basic needs, in the form of subsidies to the consumer basket of goods, and the establishment of the national health and education systems. As a result, the fiscal budget in 1981 was nearly double that for 1977; while the proportion allocated to health, education, and housing rose from 20 to 29 per cent. Nevertheless, a large part of this expansion was self-financed, because fiscal revenues also doubled following improved tax collection—rising from 11 per cent of GDP in 1977 to 24 per cent in 1981. In addition, the tax structure was modified, giving greater weight to direct taxes while lowering import tariffs. The resulting fiscal deficit rose to 9 per cent of GDP in 1981, but was largely financed by exceptionally high levels of concessional loans and donations. Indeed, the stabilization role of relatively high levels of 'external savings' became a permanent feature of the Nicaraguan economy during the 1980s, averaging some 15 per cent of GDP each year.[4]

The government actively promoted domestic production by providing short-term and long-term loans at subsidized rates to large and small private manufacturing and commercial businesses, as well as to the newly created state enterprises. Domestic credit to production and service sectors rose from 30 per cent of GDP in the pre-liberation years to 55 per cent during the years 1980–4. Twenty-eight thousand peasants had received credit in 1978, three times that number in 1981 (Enriquez and Spalding 1987). These expansionary fiscal and credit policies led to the rapid recovery of private and public consumption and investment to its pre-liberation war levels. However, the effects of the civil war on industrial and agricultural production severely constrained domestic output. The hostilities caused a substantial contraction of industrial activity, following the destruction of factories and inventories, and the loss of managerial personnel. Agriculture was also affected, although less than industry. The main damage to agriculture was the slaughter of immature beef cattle and the smuggling of herds out of the country, which severely compromised the future of beef production.

The other major constraint on the recovery of domestic output was the reorganization of asset ownership discussed above, which hampered agricultural and industrial production and marketing. Fear of further land confiscation depressed investment and production by large private businesses, while the severe disruption of rural marketing

---

[3] The intensification of the war—measured in terms of economic and human losses—from 1983 onwards to its peak in 1987 is clear from Figures 5.7 and 5.8 discussed below.

[4] A trend which continued throughout the 1990s as well, causing a chronic problem of aid dependency.

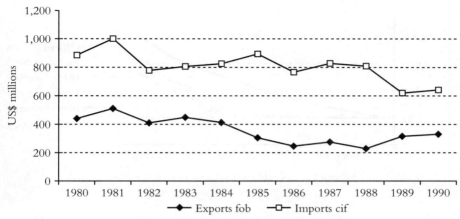

Figure 5.2 Nicaragua: External trade, 1980–1990

Source: As Fig. 5.1.

systems hindered peasant production. Meanwhile, the newly formed state enterprises were constrained by a lack of managerial and technical expertise, and capital to invest in the confiscated farms and factories. In particular, the key agro-export sector remained severely depressed because of producer uncertainty, combined with low world prices and an overvalued exchange rate. The marketing boards charged with the sales of the main export products operated a 'pool price system', which fixed an average price on the basis of the sale of each product to the different export markets at the existing fixed exchange rate. However, the revolutionary government inherited an overvalued exchange rate, and the rate of inflation was clearly incompatible with a fixed exchange rate (Ocampo 1991). As a result, domestic export prices remained depressed and producers lacked any incentive to improve production methods.

In contrast to the slow recovery of exports, the overvalued exchange rate, expansionary demand policies, and a plentiful supply of foreign aid fuelled the demand for imports. Import levels rose to new peaks for consumer goods, as well as inputs and capital goods, reflecting widespread shortages of consumer goods, spare parts and inputs following the liberation war. Not surprisingly, the propensity to import jumped from an average of 25 per cent of GDP in the pre-war liberation period to approximately 40 per cent of GDP in the 1980–1 period. This combination of an import boom with depressed exports deepened Nicaragua's external gap—to 25 per cent of GDP—as Figure 5.2 demonstrates. Increasingly, it became more important to obtain more aid rather than promote exports.

In 1982, the growing external trade gap forced the government to modify its economic policy. The price-pool system for exports was replaced by guaranteed prices, no longer linked to the exchange rate, and based on costs plus an agreed mark-up. The government created special bank certificates to allow exporters to recover a certain proportion of their income in US currency. At the same time, the government established different exchange rates for imported essential and non-essential goods, and imposed

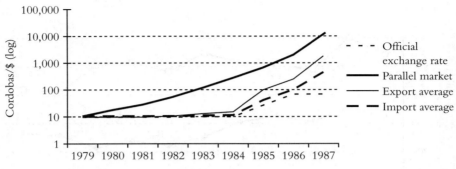

Figure 5.3   Nicaragua: Exchange rates, 1979–1987
Source: FitzGerald and Grigsby 1997.

quantitative import restrictions. Although these measures avoided the need to devalue the Cordoba—which was felt would trigger inflation without resolving foreign exchange shortages given the constraints on production—they resulted *de facto* in a multiple exchange-rate system as illustrated in Figure 5.3.

The Central Bank incurred large exchange-rate losses as export rates were much higher than import rates. This imbalance, which was equivalent to a growing fiscal subsidy for the private sector in general and consumers in particular, became a permanent characteristic of macroeconomic disequilibrium throughout the Sandinista period. The official exchange rate for imports was kept low in an attempt to reduce costs to the public sector and thus inflation; but the excess demand generated by growing public expenditure drove up the 'parallel rate' which was officially tolerated to encourage family remittances and finance non-essential imports by the private sector.

None the less, the new export incentives stimulated the agro-export sector, particularly cotton—although it did not return to the pre-revolution level. Coffee growers enjoyed a record harvest in 1982–3, which pushed production levels above the pre-war level, but this had more to do with increased access to credit by the large peasantry—who accounted for half of all coffee production—rather than to any export incentive. Small- and medium-size coffee growers had no access to these incentives which were designed to encourage large-scale private producers. The agro-export recovery, however, was largely nullified by a sharp deterioration in Nicaragua's external terms of trade, which worsened by 35 per cent during this period. Moreover, manufacturing exports to the Central American Common Market also fell as a result of the economic crisis in the region, and the subsequent breakdown of the integration scheme.

The other key aspect of agricultural modernization was the construction of large capital-intensive agro-industrial projects, aimed at promoting rapid technological change, improving Nicaragua's market position by exporting semi-processed products (rather than raw materials), and encouraging the rapid assimilation of imported capital goods into agriculture. The combination of increased mechanization and increased use of agricultural chemicals, together with the large capital-intensive projects, sharply increased the imports of inputs and capital goods for agriculture. Imports of agricultural chemicals rose by approximately 65 per cent, and capital goods, mostly tractors, more than doubled compared to imports in the 1970s (Spoor 1995). This modernization drive was underpinned by the availability of concessional loans and donations. Most of the imports of capital goods consisted of tractors, obtained with credit lines from the former Soviet Union, while significant donations of fertilizer were made by Western European countries. Nevertheless, herbicides and insecticides had to be obtained with short-term commercial credit in hard currencies.

The most important large capital-intensive project was a huge sugar mill, donated by Cuba; and although the costly irrigation equipment for the same project was obtained through a concessional loan from the Inter-American Development Bank, the construction of a large dam that was part of this project was fully financed from the national budget. This financing arrangement—with imported capital goods and imported equipment financed by foreign loans and donations, and local costs financed from the national budget—was applied to the whole public investment programme which tripled between 1981 and 1984, to reach 16 per cent of GDP.

In contrast to the price incentives for export crops, the government maintained low real farm prices for food products in order to keep consumer prices low for the urban population. Food consumer prices were actually frozen from 1980 to mid-1984. As mentioned above, the government tried to solve the food policy dilemma of low consumer prices and the need to stimulate production through producer prices by subsidizing the difference. But because of budgetary constraints real farm prices did not keep up with rising inflation. Consumer subsidies stimulated a higher demand for food, but the supply could not respond quickly enough. Supply was not only constrained by low prices, but also by food aid, the disarticulation of rural marketing systems due to the war and the state control of wholesaling, and the limited redistribution of land before 1984.

Food aid and imports were convenient in the short run for the national government, marketing boards and some state and private food-processing firms. Food aid provided a significant source of funding for the national budget, because it could be sold but did not have to be repaid. For the food procurement and distribution agency, ENABAS, the management of imported food was both simpler logistically (particularly to supply the towns) and, due to the overvalued exchange rate, more profitable than local procurement. Similarly, food-processing firms such as milk-pasteurising plants benefited from cheap and easy procurement of imported raw materials. Although food imports may have been justified immediately after the liberation war, basic food imports continued at more than triple the 1978 level until 1985 (Utting 1987). This meant that neither ENABAS nor the food-processing plants needed to promote production.

The displacement of the rural merchants by ENABAS caused a breakdown of the rural marketing channels and created shortages of basic manufactured goods in the countryside. Rural merchants had traditionally played a critical role, as they not only bought the marketed production of the peasants, but sold them basic manufactured consumer goods, inputs and basic tools. ENABAS initially tried, but failed, to replace these merchants as the main purchasers of the peasants' basic grains production. As a result, the countryside was plagued by shortages, and the price of manufactured goods rose sharply. In addition, despite rising market prices, the government failed to raise guaranteed procurement prices, so that the peasants were actually subsidizing urban food consumption. Hence, the terms of trade for rural producers declined, resulting in a further disincentive to increase peasant production. This was clearly reflected in the downward trend of maize production (the peasants' most important food product) despite the significant expansion of rural credit.

In addition, ENABAS marketing policy discriminated against the less accessible regions. For example, the largest proportion of corn marketed by ENABAS was bought from the Pacific coast, but the majority of the nation's corn is produced in the north (Spoor, 1995). This meant that ENABAS purchased very little from distant areas while private marketing was severely restricted. This was true not only for corn but also non-irrigated rice. ENABAS also had easy access to donated wheat, which the urban population substituted for corn tortillas when it was cheaper. This had the unintended consequence of substituting imported wheat for domestically produced corn. As for beans, consumers rejected the replacement of the local variety of beans (*frijoles rojos*) by imported beans. Thus, ENABAS was eventually obliged to purchase beans in the remote production zones; this led to bean production experiencing a modest recovery from pre-1979 (Spoor 1995).

Meanwhile, large-scale private and state-farm production of rice and sorghum flourished. These producers were favoured by the heavy investment in new machinery and cheap imported inputs, as well as energy subsidies for irrigation. The government permitted the large-scale private producers to set up their own marketing organization, COARSA. The cultivation of sorghum had several advantages over that of cotton, and partially replaced it in the Pacific plains. It was easier to cultivate, less affected by climatic variations, and it benefited from high subsidies for inputs and machinery. It was also highly mechanized, which was an advantage in the face of powerful trade unions. Demand for sorghum grew rapidly as a result of the government policy of promoting poultry as a substitute for beef, the traditional animal protein food. Poultry and eggs replaced beef in the national diet, after the loss of cattle to indiscriminate slaughter and smuggling to neighbouring countries during the liberation war. Furthermore government policy aimed to export the remaining beef production.

The decimation of the national herd also affected milk production; in the short run the government substituted national production with imported milk. At the same time, it was developing large-scale milk production projects such as Chiltepe, with Canadian and Cuban government aid. This policy totally neglected the small- and medium-size producers who had been the primary suppliers of the nation's milk until 1978. The Contingent Plan for Basic Grains, which promoted the production of corn in the Pacific plains, in a rotational system with cotton, under a massive irrigation scheme using the waters of Lake Nicaragua, undermined the smaller growers. The overall strategy was to replace small- and medium-size peasant production of basic national food products by large-scale state production. Intensification of production, rather than land redistribution, was seen as the solution for domestic food production. In 1984, when the Minister of Agriculture announced a halt to further land reform (Ortega 1990) only 9 per cent of the total arable land had been redistributed to 31,000 families, little more than a quarter of the estimated number of poor landless peasants (Utting 1987).

None the less, severe food shortages emerged as the state network attempted to respond to the greatly increased food demand from the army, at a time when food imports faced increasing restrictions and domestic production remained sluggish. The state distribution network was unable to meet demand at controlled prices, and many people were forced to turn to parallel suppliers at much higher prices. This two-tier pricing system created large price differentials between official producers' prices and market prices, which provided incentives for peasants to sell to private traders and attracted thousands of people to the informal sector, including public employees and workers. Small city merchants[5] made huge profits from speculation with food products, while the state-regulated distribution network was plagued by petty corruption.

Nevertheless, although price controls in the market place were virtually impossible to implement, the government did ensure that a large proportion of products sold in 'secure outlets' could be bought cheaply. In addition, public employees as well as workers from state and some private enterprises enjoyed subsidized meals in the workplace. Social programmes assisted certain sectors of the population by donating a specific quantity of food products to nutritionally vulnerable groups. Per capita consumption was above pre-liberation war levels in 1984, although below the level achieved in 1980–2 when food imports flooded the country (Utting 1987).

Popular living standards also improved as a result of the expansion of public health and education, despite a substantial fall in average per capita incomes after the liberation war. The expansion of the health network and preventive health campaigns succeeded in reducing infant and maternal mortality, while specifically targeted nutritional pro-grammes successfully reduced malnutrition. As Figure 5.5 indicates, this was obtained by a considerable increase in the numbers of medical personnel; the emphasis being placed on the use of paramedics and midwives in preventive health based on small local clinics rather than capital-intensive curative care in hospitals. None the less, the enormous increase in medical consultations—which rose from 1.9 million in 1975 to 5.0 million in 1980, and 5.7 million in 1985—also created growing pressure on supplies of drugs (largely imported with aid funds) and demand for hospital treatment. The numbers of X-rays, laboratory tests, and surgical operations all doubled during this period. The most striking consequence was the sharp decline in the infant mortality rate, which fell from 97 per thousand live births in 1977 to 70 in 1985, and continued down to 62 in 1989.

Immediately after gaining power, the Sandinista government launched a very suc-cessful literacy campaign—the *Cruzada Nacional de Alfabetización*—which reduced the illiteracy rate from 50 per cent in 1978 to 12 per cent in 1981. This was followed by a determined effort to ensure universal primary education and to raise the coverage of secondary education—an effort that was also successful as Figure 5.5 indicates. In fact out of a total population of 3.27 millions in 1985, some 0.75 millions were enrolled in

---

[5] Popularly known as *burguesía de delantal* (the 'apron bourgeoisie') after the market women's customary attire.

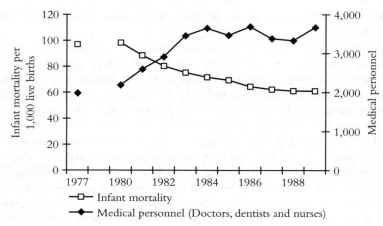

Figure 5.4   Nicaragua: Health indicators, 1997–1989
Source: Ministario de Salud.

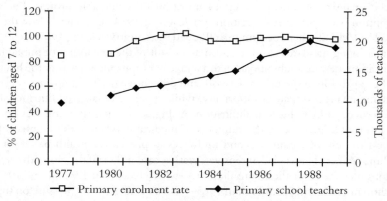

Figure 5.5   Nicaragua: Education indicators, 1977–1989
Source: Ministario de Education.

the education system—an achievement which also reflects the age structure of Nicaragua. The number of primary schools was doubled between 1977 and 1984, and the number of teachers increased by one-half, allowing the expansion of pupils to be accompanied by a reduction in average class sizes. Progress on the quality of secondary education was limited by the lack of books and other teaching materials; while the opening of universities to all secondary graduates and ex-combatants had a predictable effect of lowering academic standards. As in the case of health, the expansion of primary education as a form of basic-needs provision, and thus real income redistribution, increased the social demand for further services which the state was unable to provide. The result was deteriorating standards which were aggravated by the effects of conflict—both the targeting

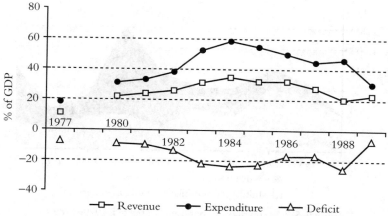

Figure 5.6 Nicaragua: Fiscal indicators, 1977–1989
Source: As Fig. 5.1.

of schools (and teachers) by the Contra and the military mobilization of young men by the government.

As the war intensified in the mid-1980s the contradiction between, on the one hand, maintaining the basic-needs policy, increasing military defence expenditure and investing in projects and, on the other hand, declining foreign aid, the failure of production to fully recover to pre-liberation war levels and the increasing economic damages caused by the war, became unsustainable. The government attempted to solve this dilemma by increasing fiscal revenues, but failed to prevent the fiscal deficit from rising. Tax revenues rose through a combination of better tax collection and higher taxation of property and non-essential consumption. As a result, fiscal revenues increased sharply from an average of 12 per cent of GDP in the pre-liberation war period 1974–8 to 35 per cent GDP in 1984. Nicaragua had one of the highest levels of taxation in Latin America.

Nevertheless, government expenditure grew faster than tax revenues, particularly after 1983, because of a sharp increase in defence spending and the initiation of the state agro-industrial projects. Expenditure rose from 20 to 57 per cent of GDP in 1975 and 1984, respectively, resulting in a huge fiscal deficit equal to 22 per cent of GDP—as Figure 5.6 indicates. Within this total, the fastest growing category was—as might be expected—defence expenditure, which by the mid-1980s was running at some US$300 million a year, equivalent to 15 per cent of GDP. This fiscal deficit could not be financed from foreign aid which started to decline. Instead, it was financed by recourse to the Central Bank: domestic credit to the government expanded at an average of 91 per cent per year and doubled nearly every year between 1981 and 1984.

During the first half of the 1980s, foreign aid had come predominantly from 'Western' sources, particularly Western Europe and Latin America. However, pressure from Washington reduced this support: as Figure 5.7 indicates, in 1984 foreign aid shifted towards 'Eastern' sources—primarily the socialist countries grouped in the CMEA. Three-quarters of total aid from 1984 to 1988 came from the latter source. Until 1984,

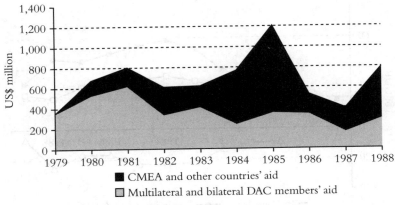

Figure 5.7   Nicaragua: Foreign aid contracted, 1979–1989
Source: As Fig. 5.1.

the government had received loans from multilateral and Western bilateral sources, and lines of credit (tied to the import of specific products) from socialist countries. After 1984, multilateral funding virtually ceased, and Western bilateral aid shifted to lines of credit. In addition, Nicaragua received petroleum on credit from Venezuela and Mexico, but this ceased after 1984 when Nicaragua failed to repay its accumulated debts; from 1985 the (then) Soviet Union became the country's only fuel supplier.[6]

The flexibility of funds declined significantly due to these shifts in foreign aid, which was almost all tied to specific imports. The shift to socialist aid sources also resulted in a decline in product quality, and the need to adapt to different technology. In both cases, aid dependency resulted in the importing of whatever goods were offered, independently of their consistency with household consumption patterns or existing technology and skills.

Besides declining cash aid to finance the fiscal deficit, there were two other important sources of monetary expansion. First, as already mentioned, credit expanded substantially to the productive and service sectors at subsidized interest rates. This did not encourage financial discipline, and bad debts reached one-third of the total outstanding banking credit at the end of 1984. Moreover, the government also condoned the massive debt accumulated by state enterprises as well as that of both large and small producers of basic grains. As a result, the solvency of the banking system was threatened, and had to be periodically refinanced by the Central Bank. These Central Bank losses, combined with the losses from the operation of the multiple-exchange system discussed above, could only be financed by monetary emission as there was no domestic bond market.

The combination of a huge fiscal deficit, the erosion of capital in the banking system, and exchange-rate losses caused a substantial expansion of the money supply and pushed inflation well above previous levels. The rate of inflation measured by the consumer

---

[6] Ironically, this oil was refined by the Exxon refinery which had not been nationalized.

price index (CPI) rose from an average of 6 per cent a year during 1976–8 to 20 per cent per year during 1980–2, to an average of 70 per cent per year during 1983–4. In addition, these high inflation rates resulted in the widespread 'dollarization' of the economy reflecting the government's increasing loss of control over the private economy. Thus, the average official exchange rate was only a minimal fraction of the black–market rate, generating significant price distortions throughout the economy and fuelling speculation as indicated by Figure 5.3.

The effect of this inflationary spiral on income distribution was inevitably negative, the burden of reduced consumption falling mainly on those households in the peasant and urban informal sector who were not directly protected by the state or with access to real assets. This problem had been recognized by policy-makers from the start of the Sandinista administration:

If inflation occurs because of a fiscal deficit caused by a lack of legitimate taxation, this is in fact equivalent to an illegitimate tax on the poor.   (MIPLAN 1980: 129; authors' translation)

5   Low-intensity War, Socio-political Stress, and Economic Collapse

The failure of the Contras to achieve a rapid victory over the Sandinistas led to a reorganization of the Contra forces and a shift to a strategy of low-intensity war in 1984–5. The main purpose was the political delegitimization of the Nicaraguan government and the promotion of economic chaos. Part of this strategy was the CIA effort to unify the Contra forces under one umbrella organization, the *Resistencia Nicarguense* (Nicaraguan Resistance). The RN was organized on similar lines to the FDN, with a political directorate composed of even more prominent and prestigious members of the traditional political parties and business sector—including fewer former Somocistas, and including representatives of ethnic groups such as the Miskito. For Washington, this group represented the future government of Nicaragua. On the economic front, as we have seen above, the USA imposed a trade embargo in May 1985 and increased pressure on its allies to reduce their support for the Sandinistas.

The sharp deterioration of the Nicaraguan economy, a lack of flexibility of foreign aid and the intensification of the Contra war prompted the Sandinista government to modify its political and military strategy, as well as its agrarian and economic policies. The Sandinista army sought to regain the military initiative in 1984 by recruiting and organizing thousands of conscripts into specialist forces that could overwhelm the Contra forces. Recruitment of new conscripts began in 1985 under the law of military service that had been passed in late 1983. These Light Infantry Brigades (BLI) included both young men and women trained to be the new backbone of the army. BLI conscripts, often students, were better educated than the former reserve infantry battalions, very well disciplined and better trained in their treatment of rural people. At the same time, the government shifted the emphasis of its agrarian reform to land redistribution to the peasantry instead of expanding state farms. It also stressed food production over exports, substantially reduced subsidies for urban popular consumption, and improved the rural terms of trade.

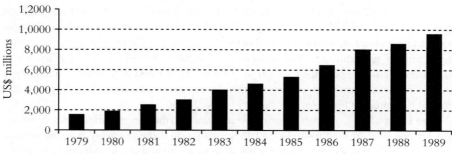

Figure 5.8 Nicaragua: Outstanding debt, 1979–1989
Source: As Fig. 5.1.

The last major insurgent incursion took place in September 1985. Contra forces tried to take La Trinidad in the interior of the country; the attack was a failure and the RN forces were wiped out. From then on, the Sandinista army took the offensive, defeating the Contra forces in the field and attacking their border bases; although their logistic support across the Honduran border supported by US forces could not be attacked. By 1987, the Sandinista army could legitimately claim to have achieved 'strategic victory' as the RN no longer occupied Nicaraguan territory although they continued cross-border incursions for a further three years. As Figure 5.8 shows, the peak of the war in terms of human losses was 1987, after which the overall level declined and the balance shifted towards Contra losses as opposed to Nicaraguan civilian victims.

In spite of the Reagan administration's ongoing commitment to a 'military' solution to the war, the Central American presidents pressed for a political solution to a war which was bankrupting the whole region. In 1987, backed by neighbouring Latin American governments in the Contadora Group and the European Community, the five presidents signed the Esquipulas Accord. This peace agreement established the conditions for a negotiated solution to the conflict, and negotiations began between the *Ejercito Popular Sandinista* (EPS) and the RN—effectively between Managua and Washington.

The years 1985 to 1987 were thus those of the most intense fighting, greatest damage, greatest number of casualties, and highest military expenditure. Over half of the government budget was spent on the war effort, rising from 8 per cent of GDP in 1981 to 19 per cent in 1985. The average level of economic damage sustained during this period (1985–7) was approximately equal to the country's GDP. These damages were mainly of two types: first, the direct effect of conflict in the field—including buildings and infrastructure destroyed, inventories and cattle stolen, and crops abandoned—at replacement cost; and second, the net loss to the economy from the trade embargo and the denial of multilateral credits—estimated as the increase in transport and credit costs involved in using alternative suppliers.[7]

---

[7] For more details, see FitzGerald and Grigsby (1997). The data was collected monthly by the Nicaraguan government on the basis of field reports, and checked by the United Nations for publication in the annual CEPAL report on the Nicaraguan economy (see FitzGerald 1987). Using the standard CEPAL macroeconomic model for Latin American economies, calibrated for Nicaragua, it was also possible to calculate the overall output loss due to the foreign exchange shortages arising from the above two categories (see Di Addario 1997).

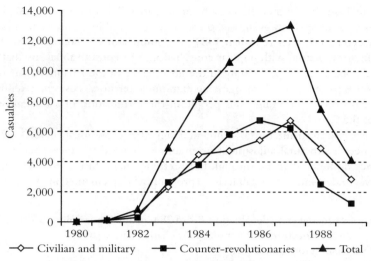

Figure 5.9 Nicaragua: Human losses from war, 1980–1989
Source: FitzGerald and Grigsby 1997.

At the same time that the EPS shifted onto the offensive, the government modified its agrarian policies in an attempt to recover peasant support. This new stage of agrarian reform had two elements: first, increased land distribution—in the two years 1985 and 1986, a further 30,000 families benefited from land distribution (more than in the five previous years). Second, the conditions for receiving land were made more flexible as peasants were no longer required to work in collectives. Third, the government reduced the limit on farm size subject to expropriation, in order to increase the supply of land for redistribution without affecting state farms—30 per cent of all land expropriation took place in 1986 (Spalding 1994). However, in spite of these modifications, agrarian reform was still limited in its social impact, affecting some 15 per cent of the country's arable land, and benefiting less than half of the official estimate of landless peasants. In addition, the state farms were still the favoured sector in terms of resource allocation.

Improvements were also made to the rural marketing system. Grain purchasing prices were increased substantially, and wholesale trade was partially deregulated to allow the free movement of goods within—albeit not between—regions (Spoor 1995; Utting 1992). The supply of peasant consumer goods as well as tools and other inputs improved due to changes in ENABAS policy as the purchaser of grain and seller of supplies to peasants. In addition, a comprehensive network of rural peasant stores was launched by UNAG with the support of the Swedish government. Hence the terms of trade and power shifted in favour of the peasantry as a result of better production prices, and a better supply of consumer goods, producer inputs, and tools.

The Sandinista government also sought to win back support from the indigenous groups. In 1985, the government began negotiations with the indigenous leader Brooklyn Rivera in order to organize the return of the Miskito, who had been forcibly resettled in Tasba Pri, to their Rio Coco communities. The government also declared an amnesty for indigenous groups who had been involved in Contra activities: 2,000 people accepted this offer (Gurdian 1989). A commission was established in 1986 to discuss the formulation, with popular consultation, of a constitutional law that would allow a certain degree of autonomy in the governance of the Atlantic Coast regions. This law was passed in 1987, recognizing communal territory, customary tenure, and the participation of the indigenous people in the formulation of a natural resource policy for the Coast.

On the economic front, the government designed an economic plan for 1987 which was in effect a structural adjustment programme designed to correct relative prices and reduce domestic demand through fiscal retrenchment (SPP 1987). This new approach was underpinned by a stabilization programme implemented in 1986, including (Pizarro 1987):

- a major exchange-rate devaluation (from 28 Cordobas per dollar to 70);
- the gradual unification of the multiple exchange-rate system;
- a credit ceiling for bank loans;
- higher nominal interest rates for the productive and service sectors;
- the elimination of subsidies for basic consumer products;
- the reduction and rationalization of state investment, and
- a freeze on government current spending.

The underlying logic of these adjustments was to keep inflation within manageable levels, and to provide resources for military expenditure by reducing civilian expenditure. The government decided that it could no longer supply basic consumption goods to the entire population, instead a system of providing basic needs by the state on a regional basis was set up. These basic needs were now only distributed through military posts and at workplaces, limiting access to subsidized food to soldiers and employees.

Nevertheless, the impact of the war on both domestic output and government expenditure, and the inconsistent application of the adjustment package worsened rather than lessened Nicaragua's macroeconomic disequilibrium. Domestic output shifted downwards to a new 'plateau' in the second half of the 1980s (see Figure 5.1), as a result of war damage to the country's productive capacity, labour shortages, inadequate supply of inputs, and the US commercial embargo. In addition, the government adjustment measures failed to restrain the sharp increase in military expenditure, while long-term investment projects and subsidized support prices for export production created inflationary pressure which reduced fiscal revenues, and nullified the effect of the credit limits and interest-rate increases, fuelling domestic demand expansion. Tax revenues fell from 30 per cent of GDP in 1984 to 21 per cent of GDP in 1987, and the fiscal deficit rose to 18 per cent of GDP (see Figure 5.6). Continued monetary emission and the loosening of controls led to a process of hyperinflation: the GDP deflator, which had stood at 100 in 1980 and 201 in 1984, reached 2,051 in 1986 and 12,777 in 1987; requiring a re-denomination of the currency in 1988 which had little effect—in 1989 the new deflator rose a further 50 times. The trade deficit widened to 30 per cent of the GDP, financed mainly by import credit lines from the former socialist countries (see Figure 5.7).

Agriculture was the productive sector most affected by the war, because thousands of peasants were displaced from the fertile agricultural and cattle-producing regions, that became war zones. Some fled to neighbouring countries, others to Nicaraguan cities, while many were resettled in other parts of the country. Agro-exports, in particular, collapsed. Cotton production declined by almost half compared to 1984, as the large-scale private producers had either abandoned the country because of the war, or switched to producing sorghum because of more attractive prices. Cotton also faced significant labour shortages and a relative scarcity of the inputs traditionally supplied by US firms. Coffee declined principally because the bulk of production was located in what were now war zones; it dropped to half its 1983 levels. Sugar and beef were primarily affected by the closure of the US market. Coffee prices were not subsidized, so producers increasingly diverted their sales to the parallel domestic market.

Domestic agricultural production increased but not enough to offset the fall in agro-exports. The government gave priority to food products for domestic consumption in order to guarantee an adequate supply for the army and the rest of the population. Food production benefited from the acceleration of land redistribution to the landless peasants from private landowners, who fled the country, and from the attempt to rationalize state-farm landholdings. It also benefited from the partial deregulation of the basic grains market. In addition, the state farms expanded the irrigated areas for basic-grains production, and poultry production benefited from the cotton-growers switching into sorghum for feed.

The manufacturing sector was oriented towards war needs, particularly the production of food, clothing, shoes, construction materials, and metalwork, but contracted slightly due to the lack of an adequate supply of inputs, and the complete switch of supply lines to meet the needs of socialist countries. The contraction of agricultural and industrial output together with the expansion of domestic demand led to an increase in both relative and absolute terms of the informal sector and encouraged rural migration to the cities. Managua, the capital, doubled its population between 1978 and 1987.

Meanwhile, the application of the government adjustment package reduced civilian expenditure by more than half, while military expenditure rose to 18 per cent of the GDP in 1987 and absorbed half of the government budget. Civilian spending cuts were made by freezing the wages of public employees and cutting public investment in roads and social services. Central government spending was cut by half in real terms compared to 1984. None the less, expenditure on core social services was maintained, and the improvement in social indicators in literacy, infant mortality, school enrolment, and life expectancy were largely preserved until 1987.

The implementation of large-scale agro-industrial projects, however, was not affected by these austerity measures, which led to a significant expansion in long-term credit from the state investment bank (*Fondo Nicaragüense de Inversiones*), which in turn relied mainly on the Central Bank for funding. The implicit deficit due to unfinanced public investment was equivalent to about 10 per cent of GDP in this period (FitzGerald 1989). The continuation of these projects, started before the war and often of limited economic merit except in the longer term, was completely unjustified under wartime conditions. These projects generated a shortage of construction materials and were carried out at the expense of maintaining existing productive capacity.

Further, the government's attempt to unify the exchange rate for exports failed because of an initial substantial increase in the support price for coffee and cotton. As a result, the implicit exchange rate for these products was five times that of other exports, leading to a breakdown of the system and chaos. In addition, exporters received part of the price in US$. The underlying logic of this policy, was to keep the large private and state agro-export production from total collapse. Thus, the gap between the implicit exchange rate for exports and the official exchange rate for imports widened considerably. The average exchange rate for exports in 1987 was ten times the average exchange rate for imports (see Figure 5.3) and consequently, Central Bank exchange–rate losses increased to 7 per cent of the GDP (Grigsby 1987). Expenditure on large-scale investment projects, combined with exchange–rate losses, was equal to the fiscal deficit (17 per cent of the GDP), implying an extraordinary actual deficit of one third of GDP. Almost all of this was financed by domestic money creation by the Central Bank. Not surprisingly, by the end of 1987, the country suffered from hyperinflation which had a critical effect upon the Sandinista's electoral defeat in 1990.

There has been heated debate as to whether an alternative set of policies could have avoided the collapse of the Nicaraguan economy in the second half of the 1980s under the Sandinista government. The two most important critiques of Sandinista economic policies—from the 'orthodox' and 'progressive' viewpoints—agree on two issues. First, the economic packages of 1986–7 were inconsistently applied. Planned fiscal adjustment measures were mainly implemented, but exchange-rate adjustments and credit restrictions were not. Second, there were considerable lags between the need for a policy and its implementation, so that adjustments were often made too late, which worsened economic disequilibrium. The lack of consistent macroeconomic management could partly be explained by the Sandinistas' unwillingness to establish clear and strong authority over the economy and to delegate any authority to the Central Bank or Finance Minister, particularly over the level of military expenditure. Hence, inflationary pressures were built into the political system.

Orthodox critics argued, additionally, that there were two fundamental errors in the 'basic-needs' approach. First, the Sandinistas' attempt to redistribute income and implement the 'state-centred accumulation model' was in direct contradiction to reality, in so far as a significant portion of the economy was still in the hands of large private producers (Medal 1988). And, having challenged property rights through confiscation, the government was unable to restore the confidence of the private sector, in fact passing additional laws after initial confiscation, such as the Absentee Law, only exacerbated the problem. The second fundamental error was the government's excessive economic intervention, 'the strong preference for intricate government intervention rather than traditional orthodox macroeconomic management' (Ocampo 1991).

The progressive critics—advocates of the Kaleckian 'basic-needs' approach—disagreed. Regarding the first 'error', they argued that the private sector was heterogeneous and that a large portion did cooperate, however reluctantly, with the Sandinistas: also, the treatment of the private sector by the Sandinistas was not so different from that of the Somoza government and, therefore, was not a fundamental source of new discontent. With regard to state economic intervention, the basic-needs advocates argued that price intervention was needed to ensure redistribution, particularly to control luxury consumption in favour of basic needs (Utting 1992). Furthermore, it would have been important to isolate Nicaragua from external shocks, in order to implement a national development strategy in favour of the popular sector (Gibson 1987).

What both of these perspectives failed to appreciate was the role of the peasantry in the economy. The orthodox argument that the key structural error was the policy towards the private sector is wrong, not only because of the progressive counterarguments above, but more fundamentally because of the significant weight of the peasants and medium-size producers in the economy. The large private sector that was supposedly so important was only critical in cotton, precisely the export that collapsed; its importance has thus been exaggerated. Moreover, the orthodox critics failed to recognize that the implementation of orthodox macroeconomic management basically implied adopting the same pre-revolutionary macroeconomic policy and management that guaranteed private accumulation irrespective of income redistribution: this ignored the popular character of the revolution itself.

The fundamental problem was the Sandinista government's emphasis on a state-centred development model, namely the nationalization of confiscated lands and natural resources, to the exclusion of landless peasants and indigenous groups (FitzGerald 1989). Land confiscated from Somoza should have been redistributed to the peasantry, while the bulk of confiscated agro-industrial and manufacturing enterprises could have remained in state hands; this would have given the Sandinistas sufficient control. In addition, greater land redistribution to the landless would have given the new government a more solid social support base in the countryside, and might even have generated fewer conflicts with the large private sector, which itself was disturbed by the seemingly endless nationalization of private farms.[8] Moreover, as discussed, the ill-conceived state-led modernization of the agricultural sector—including both green revolution technology and large state agro-industrial projects—was a destabilizing factor.

As for state intervention in domestic markets, orthodox critics were largely correct in concluding that this was excessive. It was wrong to de-link entirely from world market prices for exports and imports, not only because of the exchange-rate losses but also because the subsidizing of input prices favoured inefficient production methods, and discriminated against those who used foreign exchange most efficiently—that is, the peasants.

Moreover, the nationalization of rural/urban trade and distribution channels was misguided, because the state was incapable of replacing the private merchants and market mechanisms given the predominantly small-scale character of production and commerce. Instead, the public enterprises should have played a stabilizing role in both food production and consumption, regulating food prices to maintain a certain price range; this would not only have avoided the substantial subsidies to cover the losses of

---

[8] See also the discussion in Chapter 2 of Volume I of this study, where alternative approaches to 'paying for the war' are discussed.

these enterprises but also generated more political support in the countryside. In addition, it was misguided to rely on imports and donations to satisfy basic-needs consumption, instead of adopting a policy to encourage increased domestic food production.

6   The End of the War?

Following democratic elections, the Chamorro administration came to power in 1990. Its policy of rapid privatization and dismantling of the welfare system reduced the fiscal deficit and stabilized the currency, but it did not stimulate economic output and led to widespread unemployment and increased poverty. Aid dependency continued, but none of the underlying problems of the economy were tackled, in part because of the empowerment of workers and peasants prevented any return of the private sector to the Somoza system.

The first post-war phase had in fact already begun in 1988 with the declaration of a unilateral ceasefire by the Sandinista government. This comprised two stages; first, a failed application of an orthodox package of economic stabilization measures by the Sandinista government, and its subsequent abandonment during the transition to the new Chamorro administration in 1990. The second stage from 1991 to 1996 included the introduction of a successful stabilization package backed by multilateral institutions and foreign donors, which finally eliminated hyperinflation, although it did not restore the trade balance or resolve the debt problem.

The strategic defeat of the counter-revolutionary forces did not stop them from inflicting significant economic and political damage on the country, with continued US support. At the same time, as the Nicaraguan economy was spinning out of control, the socialist bloc—the primary source of foreign aid for the Sandinistas—was experiencing its own serious internal difficulties. These factors lay behind the government's decision to seek an internationally backed peace agreement in 1986.

The Esquipulas Accord between Nicaragua and the other Central American countries guaranteed that Nicaragua would no longer support revolutionary movements in Guatemala and El Salvador, and logistical support for the Contras by Honduras and Costa Rica would end. The Sandinistas also agreed to restore freedom of expression and full political liberties, that had been suspended during the war, and bring forward the date for the next national elections. These provisions favoured the opposition political parties with links to the political parties in power in the other Central American nations. The Esquipulas Accord was, in some ways, a continuation of the Contadora process, in that it was an initiative that came from Latin Americans themselves.

The Nicaraguan government hoped that these international accords would cut off the Contras' primary lifeline. Shortly after the signing of the Esquipulas Accord in August 1987, the Sandinistas began a parallel process of direct negotiations with the Contra forces themselves. The Sopoa accord, signed in March 1988, established the first ceasefire agreement and included mechanisms for Contra disarmament and an amnesty if a peace accord were signed. The Sandinistas hoped that this would lead to a resumption of relations with the USA.

The Sandinistas also tried to strengthen or re-establish economic and political ties with Western nations and multilateral funding agencies. The fundamental goal was to stop the economic deterioration and begin reconstruction. In order to restore the government's financial control of the economy it needed to cement its alliance with the large private sector, in order to boost the export sector.

Though the Sandinistas did re-establish negotiations with the IMF and other multilateral agencies, the government's orthodox packages were undertaken without multilateral funding, although some aid was obtained from Western Europe following the Stockholm Conference. Three rescue packages were launched in 1988–9, one maintained price controls for basic consumer products and wage controls; the next two abandoned price and wage controls, re-establishing market mechanisms. The first two packages were primarily directed at realigning relative prices, while the third was fundamentally anti-inflationary. All three included massive devaluations; attempts to cut the fiscal deficit—though only the third was successful; and attempts to eliminate credit subsidies, which all three failed to do to differing degrees.

The first of these packages was implemented in February 1988. The distinctive element was monetary reform: the population was given three days in which to exchange their 'old' Cordobas for *Córdobas Nuevos* at the rate of 1,000 to 1. This led to an initial 20 per cent reduction in the money in circulation, curbed the market speculation in foreign currency, and impoverished the Contra forces who held large cash deposits (Gutiérrez 1989). Of the three sources of monetary emissions, however, only exchange losses were cut significantly, through the unification of the official exchange rates. Since the average official exchange rate for imports was substantially lower than for exports, unification implied much higher input prices for exporters. In addition, the government decreed a wage adjustment of 650 per cent. The level of the new unified rate was still overvalued, as reflected in the considerable gap remaining between the black-market and new official rate.

However, the fiscal deficit was not reduced and no mechanism adopted for adjusting the nominal exchange rate so as to keep the real exchange rate at a competitive level. The 1988 plan included a reduction in the fiscal deficit to 10 per cent of GDP, but the government failed to reach this goal—the result was actually 26 per cent. It did not cut the defence budget, social spending, or central government spending, perhaps because of the incipient and fragile nature of the peace process, and because sectoral priorities had not changed. Domestic credit continued to be a source of monetary expansion: long-term credit to large-scale state agro-industrial projects was unchanged. Although a credit ceiling was imposed and interest rates were raised, inflation eroded any fiscal benefit.

The second package, in June 1988, liberalized the majority of prices and wages, with the exception of petrol, public transport, and central government salaries. The government partially indexed interest rates to inflation and, in practice, established a crawling peg mechanism for ongoing devaluation. This time the gap between the black-market and official rate was significantly reduced. This package also cut central government expenditure, and reduced the number of public employees. Real public-sector wages fell, although food subsidies partly offset the effect. Nevertheless, the government failed to reduce the fiscal deficit mainly because of Hurricane Joan, in October 1988, which caused damage estimated at US$840 million (CEPAL 1988). The combination of repeated devaluation and unrestricted demand increased inflation, already at hyper-inflationary levels.

With annual inflation running at 33,000 per cent in 1988, severe cuts were made in the national budget of January 1989. Some 21,000 military employees and central government personnel were laid off (ENVIO 1992). The budgets of health and education, defence, public investment, and the central government were cut by more than half of those of 1988, reducing government expenditure from 46 per cent of GDP in 1988 to 30 per cent in 1989 (see Figure 5.6). The fiscal deficit at last fell from over 25 per cent of GDP to 7 per cent. Inflation was reduced, as well as the gap between the black-market and official exchange rates.

Domestic credit remained as the main source of monetary creation. The amount of credit was cut, credit ceilings were lowered, and interest rates were fully indexed to inflation. Nevertheless, there was strong opposition to these policies from all productive sectors. The government's initial response was to confiscate the properties of the leaders of the coffee-growers who led the political opposition. Negotiations in April, in particular with the large private sector, resulted in the re-establishment of subsidized credit and highly favourable debt restructuring for cotton and food producers. Moreover, state trading companies continued to be bailed out rather than being restructured.

These three economic packages were costly in terms of production, employment, and living standards. The accumulated drop in GDP in 1988 and 1989 was 14 per cent (see Figure 5.1). Industrial output fell by one-third because of the severe contraction of the domestic market. Agricultural production fell by 10 per cent, mainly in the large-scale agriculture sector following the removal of subsidies to inputs and machinery, and the reduction of credit subsidies, particularly for cotton, rice, and sorghum. In contrast, peasant agricultural output increased, particularly of basic grains, because of the delayed impact of land reform, the relative pacification of former war zones, and the deregulation of the basic-grains trade. Peasant agriculture is also significantly less dependent on credit and imported inputs. Sizeable government layoffs led to an upsurge of informal economic activity. Food consumption levels fell dramatically during 1988–9. Average per capita calories and protein intake fell to just 1,591 calories and 37 grams: this was 14 per cent and 26 per cent below the minimum recommended levels (Utting 1992).

In the February 1990 elections, the Sandinistas were narrowly defeated by a coalition of centre-right parties grouped in the *Unión Nacional Opositora* (UNO) backed by the USA. Violeta Chamorro became president and under the new Chamorro administration, the US trade embargo was lifted, aid was restored, a peace accord was finally signed with the Contras, and the demilitarization of the country began. About 100,000 soldiers from both armies returned to civilian life. Nevertheless, this massive reduction in the size of the military forces, and the absorption of former soldiers proved difficult. Most were given some land, but no other explicit financial support. Programmes to provide credit for basic grains were poorly coordinated and lacked a long-term goal. In addition, hardly any of this credit was repaid, so that few received any support beyond the first year, and many were forced to sell their land. Landless, many turned to criminal activities as a way of life.

A successful stabilization plan was finally launched in 1991. The key factor in its success was the substantial foreign-aid backing, which made it possible to anchor the exchange rate, following the 400 per cent 'maxi-devaluation'. The heterodox element in this plan was the inclusion of price controls of basic consumer goods, public services, and public transportation. Prices were controlled primarily through the massive import of foodstuffs, and the use of a state distribution network. After about one year, the anchored exchange rate was followed by a crawling peg mechanism which increased the dollarization of the economy.

With this stabilization plan, the fiscal deficit was eliminated so that for the first time since before the revolution the government had a surplus on central government operations. This was accomplished by offering a 'conversion plan' to public employees (which was accepted by 11,500 civil servants, about 12 per cent of the total), failing to adjust public-sector salaries for inflation, and a sharp cut in military spending. Because debt-service payments were made out of fiscal revenues, Central Bank credit to the government became negative. At the same time, the deficit of the nationalized banking system was eliminated, and private banks were allowed to operate. The new private banks attracted significant deposits, and the country's financial savings expanded rapidly. These banks lent little money, however, preferring lower risk investment abroad, particularly in the USA. Indeed, the only sector to attract new investment was trade.

Nevertheless, the external trade gap increased from 32 to 45 per cent of GDP between 1990 and 1996, as a result of an aid-financed consumer import boom, combined with the slow recovery of exports. Imports, particularly luxury consumer goods, grew as a result of cuts in tariffs from an average 80 to 10 per cent, and the combination of this trade liberalization with abundant foreign aid. Between 1991 and 1995 foreign aid represented on average 30 per cent of GDP; of which one-third was tied and two-thirds were allocated in cash. Over half this cash aid, however, went to debt payments as part of the successful renegotiation of the debt (Neira and Renzi 1996). Renegotiation implied only partial debt forgiveness; the majority of the agreement comprised long-term restructuring at concessional interest rates. Hence, paradoxically, by the mid-1990s Nicaragua was paying more in debt service than before, as the renegotiation was only valid if payments continued (Dumazert 1987).

The USA financed the stabilization plan initially. Once inflation was under control, the multilateral agencies took over, and the USA withdrew, letting other nations, particularly Taiwan and other South-East Asian countries, offer industrial aid while Western Europe maintained its aid to rural and social development projects. None the less, the social costs of these changes were high. Cuts in state spending resulted in a significant reduction in the social wage, as the population now had to pay again for health services, and education. The proportion of households living in extreme poverty increased from 30 to 38 per cent between 1990 and 1996 (Neira and Renzi 1996). Increasing poverty and unemployment forced thousands of Nicaraguans to migrate to the USA and neighbouring Central American countries. Poor and lower middle-class households became increasingly dependent on foreign remittances, mostly from the USA: one-third of Managua households received remittances from abroad, and the proportion was even higher in smaller cities like Leon and Bluefields. There has also been

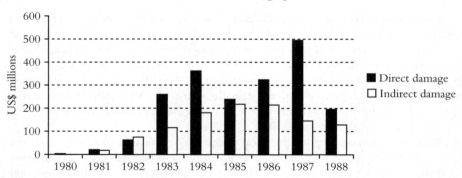

Figure 5.10   Nicaragua: Economic damage from war, 1980–1988

(*Note*:   Direct damage includes production losses and destruction of infrastructure, etc.;
'indirect' damage includes costs of trade embargo and loss of concessional credits.)

massive seasonal migration to Costa Rica to work on the banana and other plantations, or in construction. It is estimated that about 200,000 Nicaraguan workers were
working illegally in Costa Rica in the early 1990s—that is, about one-fifth of the workforce. In addition, there was a sharp increase in rural and urban delinquency, including
drug trafficking.

In summary, post-war reconstruction was characterized by a highly exclusionary
pattern of economic rehabilitation. Monetary stabilization remained fragile because it
was highly dependent on foreign aid, which began to decline in the mid-1990s. New
concessional financing from the IMF would imply greater fiscal contraction, which
would worsen the negative income distribution effects. Nicaragua seemed to be trapped
in a 'low-equilibrium growth trap', generated by low expectations of future economic
development which further depress private investment and increase social tension.

7   Conclusions: The Economic and Social Costs of Conflict in Nicaragua

We have argued in this chapter that the relationship between war and the economy
cannot be reduced to a simple causality in one or other direction. The Sandinista strategy of transition to socialism based on state-centred accumulation generated grass-roots
political and armed opposition as a reaction to the agricultural modernization project,
which included the conversion of the land holdings of Somoza and his associates into
state farms instead of redistribution to landless peasants. In addition, the state-control
model undermined the basic needs project that the Sandinistas claimed to be promoting.
Both were initially financed by an exceptional influx of foreign aid; but as aid diminished
and war losses increased, instead of transferring resources from non-essential to basic-
needs consumption, the model gradually led to the transfer of resources to the state itself.

We have seen how conflicting interpretations of the relation between war and the
economy dominated the debate on Sandinista Nicaragua. Orthodox critics argued that
the reform strategy was economically untenable, and that war only speeded the inevitable

return to conventional economic policies; while radical critics argued that external aggression was the cause of economic collapse—and, indeed, this was the objective of the 'low-intensity conflict' strategy of the US administration in Central America. In contrast, we have tried to show that the war and the economy were inextricably linked.

The form of agrarian modernization adopted under Somoza in the 1960s and 1970s led to social inequality and popular insecurity, creating the conditions for political rupture and armed insurrection. The 1979 revolution had high costs in terms of human life and economic destruction, although the disruption of internal and external commercial and financial networks probably had more significant consequences in the longer term. The main changes in property relations, trading systems, income distribution and social provisioning that were carried out during the first half of the 1980s responded in part to popular demands for welfare improvements and in part to a vision of economic modernization.

Our analysis of the social groups which benefited from, or opposed, these reforms identified the strategic position of landless peasants, who were frustrated both by the decision not to break up large private landholdings, and by the breakdown of traditional trading exchange between the rural and urban sectors. As the complex relationship between the economy, society, and conflict unfolded, producers and workers formed alliances with the revolutionary government or opposed them, and economic policy became the victim of—and a contributor to—the war itself. The Sandinista government during the period 1980–4 attempted to raise production by extending rural credit and undertaking a massive public investment programme on the one hand, while controlling the distribution of basic goods and importation of many foodstuffs on the other. The macroeconomic implications of this strategy, however, undermined the distribution objectives through inflation and led to a loss of control of the economy due to conflict with the resource requirements of the military effort itself.

Economic imbalance worsened as the external constraint tightened and military expenditure grew after 1984. The government responded by attempting to stabilize the situation, and changing agrarian policy; the former action was largely unsuccessful, while the latter policy though correct in content, came too late. The underlying problem was not so much one of economic management, but rather neglect of the peasants and over-reliance on aid, while (successfully) pursuing counter-insurgency operations. This is what undermined the economic strategy, rather than the populist economic policies or the cost of the war itself.

The effect of conflict on policy-making capacity was critical. During the armed conflict itself, the level of economic losses and the external constraints severely reduced room for manoeuvre. Policy priority was short-term resource acquisition rather than longer-term economic development. After the armed conflict, the inherited debt and the continued state of uncertainty about the balance of power at all levels of society limited economic policy to monetary stabilization and a certain degree of liberalization, rather than a planned economic reconstruction programme involving a recovery of export capacity and the reduction of poverty.[9]

---

[9] See Bruck, FitzGerald, and Grigsby (2000).

Deliberate pressure from Washington directly contributed to the high economic cost of conflict as the judgement of the International Court of Justice in 1986 against the USA explicitly recognized.[10] These costs were composed of two parts:

• First, the direct costs of wartime destruction by the insurgents. These cumulative costs totalled some US$2 billion between 1980 and 1988—equivalent to one year's GDP or a quarter of the foreign debt. The cost of 62,000 victims on both sides, half of whom were killed—nearly 1 per cent of the population—has no economic equivalent.

• Second, the losses to the economy arising from the US trade embargo imposed from 1983 to 1990, and the effective blocking of loans from international financial institutions, at a combined cost of US$1 billion. To this could be added the 'multiplier' effect of lost foreign exchange on levels of domestic production, in which case the total cost might reach US$ 5 billion.[11]

The conflict also had long-term consequences which remained after the democratic elections of 1990 and the transition to a market economy. The most striking 'inheritance' was the accumulation of external debt—totalling nearly US$6.7 billions in 1990 —nearly four times the level of GDP. This enormous debt burden was generated by sustained balance of payments deficits financed by official loans provided by friendly governments. It is difficult to say how much of this was caused by conflict and how much by poor economic management; but on the conventional criterion that to be sustainable[12] the level of debt should not exceed twice GDP, at least US$3 billion of the debt was 'extraordinary' and clearly only lent due to the conflict situation.

The private sector experienced a high degree of uncertainty during the 1980s, which continued well into the 1990s. This affected different groups in distinct ways. Multinational corporations maintained a cautious attitude with minimal investment. Small producers invested when there was a modicum of security and access to resources— particularly in land and foreign exchange. Large- and medium-size domestic firms, however, have invested very little over the past twenty years; they confined their activities to financial and commercial activities which promised rapid gains and high cash liquidity. When the low rate of private productive investment and the high level of destruction are taken into account, it is not surprising that Nicaraguan GDP in 1995 was at the same level as 1971, and per capita incomes well below that of 1960, even after five years of peace.

Finally, and in the long run most important, the level of distrust built up between the social actors, the weakening of institutions, the break-up of families, the increasing levels of poverty and marginalization, and the loss of linkages with the external world, all contributed to a marked decline of the effectiveness of Nicaraguan institutions. This remains the most serious obstacle to the resumption of economic development and the reduction of poverty.

[10] See International Court of Justice *Case Concerning Military and Paramilitary Activities in and Against Nicaragua (Nicaragua v. The United States of America): Judgement of The International Court of Justice* (General List No. 70) The Hague, 27 June 1986.

[11] In 1989 these were presented to the International Court of Justice by the Government of Nicaragua in pursuance of the obligation on the USA to pay damages in the 1986 judgement. However, in 1991 the new government abandoned the claim as a condition for renewal of US aid.

[12] This is the criterion applied by the World Bank or the 'HIPC' debt reduction initiative, for which Nicaragua was only considered to be eligible in 1999.

6

Sierra Leone: War and its Functions

DAVID KEEN

1 Introduction

The civil war in Sierra Leone can be seen as a fairly conventional, long-running battle between 'two sides'—the government and the rebels—each seeking to defeat the other. According to a rather simplistic, but widely held view, the rebels have been trying to overthrow the government and the government has been trying to defeat the rebels. A number of parties—including the UN, the local press, and many international aid agencies and foreign journalists—adopted and used this model of war when discussing the conflict in Sierra Leone.

A brief account of the war along these lines would go something like this:

The rebel Revolutionary United Front pushed into Sierra Leone with Liberian support and advanced through southern and eastern Sierra Leone in the first half of 1991 only to be pushed back by government forces (with the aid of Guinean and Nigerian troops) in the course of the second half of 1991 and subsequently in 1992. After that, the war reached a stalemate. The rebels scored periodic successes only to be repeatedly pushed back by government troops. Civilians were caught in the crossfire. There was major displacement and human suffering. Finally, in 1996, both sides came to a tentative ceasefire agreement.

Viewing war as analogous to sport—a contest between two more-or-less disciplined teams with each seeking to win—can provide at least a starting point in an attempt to understand the conflict in Sierra Leone. However, it suffers from a number of drawbacks. Part of the purpose of this analysis is to explore the limitations of such an approach to the study of conflict.

We also take issue with another (contrasting) set of discussions. Some of the more obvious shortcomings in the 'sporting' model of war have, unfortunately, prompted a number of observers, both inside and outside Sierra Leone, to go to the other extreme. According to these observers, the war in Sierra Leone, far from being an orderly contest, represents a kind of anarchy, an orgy of mindless violence. Liberal commentators and aid agencies in particular have emphasized the economic destruction and human suffering the war has wrought. Journalists have highlighted the apparent incoherence of the rebels' political programme, and they have been joined by human rights campaigners in emphasizing the 'inhuman' atrocities committed by a variety of parties in the conflict. In an extremely influential article, Sierra Leone was held up as the archetypal case of a country descending into chaos, with primitive instincts seen as rushing in to fill the vacuum left by a collapsing state and a deepening Malthusian crisis (Kaplan 1994).

Map 6.1   Sierra Leone

Closely linked with the common portrayal of war as chaotic and irrational has been a tendency, both in relation to Sierra Leone and other war-affected countries, to dissociate violence from peacetime economic and political processes. Frequently, war has been seen not only as irrational but as exogenous, something superimposed on society rather than emerging from relationships within society, a sudden break from peacetime rather than a product of peacetime processes. Outside agencies have often spoken of the need to rebuild the Sierra Leonean economy after the disruption of war, without apparently wondering whether the nature of this economy might not have generated the war in the first place. Meanwhile, Sierra Leonean officials and journalists often portrayed the violence as a kind of alien madness descending on a once peaceful society, a belligerent strain of virus from neighbouring Liberia that spread to Sierra Leone and infected its people. Richards (1995: 37) mentions the idea, common in some quarters of Sierra Leone, that young warriors were drugged with rebel 'medicine' for which there was no antidote.

It appears that some observers began by assuming that conflict would be characterized by a certain set of norms, codes, and goals (that is that people should fight to win, that war is 'a continuation of politics by other means', that civilians should be exempt from conflict, and so on). Then, when the conflict deviated from what it was 'supposed to be', these observers concluded that the conflict was simply 'anarchy'. Meanwhile, even in the face of growing evidence to the contrary, other observers (including many in United Nations organizations) continued to speak—often for self-interested or, at the very least, bureaucratic reasons—as if the conflict were simply a fight between 'the government' and 'the rebels'. This attitude has been very damaging.

Rather than assume a particular set of goals (and, perhaps, diagnosing 'chaos' when these goals seem to be absent), I attempt to explain the conflict in Sierra Leone by analysing the actions and goals of those orchestrating and carrying out acts of violence. This includes not only rebel violence but more particularly the largely neglected area of government violence. This chapter emphasizes the importance of local and individual goals during the conflict, and stresses the need to look at the process by which civilians became fighters. It argues that much of what appears to be 'mindless violence' is actually, in some sense, rational. Indeed, while analysts often discuss the *causes* of violence, this chapter emphasizes its *functions*. The approach adopted here is to look at the details of violence, quoting from participants and observers, rather than assuming we know what war is and then seeking to find the 'causes', or historical antecedents, of an apparently self-explanatory phenomenon. The war in Sierra Leone has been a particularly organized kind of chaos, a particularly rational kind of madness. The war meant not simply the collapse of a system, but the creation of a different kind of system. The near collapse of the government's ability to maintain economic activity (starting well before war and worsened by war) did not mean there was no economic activity. A powerful war economy emerged in Sierra Leone, based not simply on random looting but on often well-organized expropriation and exploitation of material resources of civilians, leading to different economic systems in different areas. Armed groups exploiting the war economy evolved relationships with a number of economic actors, including indigenous traders, multinationals, aid agencies and, not least, their alleged adversaries.

2 Uneven Development

Even under colonial rule, a pattern of economic development based on the extraction of largely unprocessed raw materials had combined with widespread corruption among Sierra Leonean politicians and traditional chiefs to create deep pools of resentment among those excluded from this system of profit and power. Towards the end of colonial rule, and during the early years of independence, efforts were made to rationalize the Sierra Leonean economy, to reduce the extent of illegal economic activity, to increase the tax revenue from primary product exports, and to use the proceeds for developing the country's infrastructure and social services. These efforts met with some, limited success.

During the 1970s and 1980s, the formal institutions of the Sierra Leonean state again started losing control of the economy (and even losing the capacity to raise revenue). Privatization schemes advocated by the World Bank and the IMF tended to encourage the farming out of trading operations to businessmen (often multinationals and local Lebanese traders) or to their political allies (Reno 1995; Sesay 1993; Zack-Williams 1995). This created a series of private monopolies rather than realizing the aim of the international financial institutions: an efficient, competitive market. An expanding illegal sector—with government officials turning a blind eye to, and often participating in, smuggling—seriously reduced the state revenues from diamonds and other primary products in the 1980s. According to senior informants inside the diamond industry, diamond smuggling reached around US$300 million every year, and probably increased as the conflict progressed.

President Siaka Stevens, who dominated Sierra Leonean politics in the 1970s and early 1980s, built up his own fortune and those of his key political allies, notably a small group of Lebanese, by acquiring for himself and them a key role in these monopolistic private concerns, using government control over import/export licences and the allocation of foreign exchange to favour his own clients. As a result of Stevens' economic reforms, an increasing proportion of diamond production was smuggled out of Sierra Leone without ever passing through government hands. Further, when it came to assessing export taxes, diamonds that did pass through government hands were typically severely undervalued. This undervaluation was carried out by the Government Diamond Office, which was managed and part-owned by Jamil Mohammed, the most important Lebanese trader and a close associate of Stevens. This arrangement benefited both government officials and private export companies at the expense of the Sierra Leonean treasury. In real terms, by 1985–6 domestic revenue collection had plummeted to just 18 per cent of the levels in 1977–8. The creation of private monopolies compounded the existing resentment at Sierra Leone's uneven development. Among the most disgruntled groups were those excluded from trading in the reserves of diamonds.

Meanwhile, generous external credit allowed the government to continue to use state resources to win political support, even as revenue sources were transferred into private hands. In effect, Stevens was using his own private access to finance to build highly personalized networks of support outside of the state system. By the early 1980s, Stevens' non-budgeted discretionary spending (financed in part by Lebanese banks) had reached more than 60 per cent of operating budgets, with development spending falling to only 3 per cent of the overall budget by 1984. Payments to chiefs out of the development budget were correspondingly reduced. This helped Stevens to reduce the independence of the local chiefs, and to bring economic activity 'more directly' under his control. To this end, Stevens also centralized decisions over the issuing of licences, appointed chiefs to the National Diamond Mining Corporation, and relied increasingly on Lebanese traders to arrange diamond digging and selling at local level. Where chiefs from the southern-based SLPP party could not be successfully incorporated into Stevens' system of profit and power, they were replaced by nominees from Stevens' own All People's Congress party.

At the same time, as rice production failed to keep pace with population increases, Stevens used food aid to cement his political power base. However, whilst a few privileged groups had special access to political patronage, most people had to rely on the oligopolistic and inflationary 'free market', especially for the staple food, rice. Commercial imports were controlled by a handful of Lebanese families, who profited from this control at the expense of the consumer. Inflation accelerated when, as part of a package of structural adjustment, a major IMF-sponsored devaluation of the Sierra Leonean currency, the Leone, saw it fall in value from 50 pence (sterling) in 1978 to just over one penny in April 1987.

Despite abundant mineral wealth and fertile soils, Sierra Leone remained one of the poorest countries in the world. Geographically uneven patterns of development and service provision (notably, poor water supplies) maintained an astonishingly low life-expectancy in the south of the country—as late as 1987, it was reported to be 21 years at birth. Meanwhile, the already fragile education system throughout Sierra Leone was further damaged by public spending cuts and rapid inflation following the forced devaluation of the currency. As state revenues collapsed, the state was unable to suppress discontent.

In 1985 Stevens' appointed successor, President Momoh, inherited a major financial crisis. To attract IMF support, he had to approve harsh austerity measures, including a drastic reduction in petrol and food subsidies. Momoh tried forcibly to recapture the diamond trade for the state, by concentrating the diamond industry in the hands of a few foreign firms. However, this constituted a major threat to hundreds of smaller-scale Lebanese and politician mining operations, employing tens of thousands of Sierra Leoneans, and Momoh lacked sufficient local clout to enforce the new edicts. Nevertheless, he was able to weaken the Lebanese hold on the diamond industry, and diggers and mine operators, threatened by Momoh's initiatives, provided a fertile environment for the rebels, often dealing directly with the rebels as the war progressed.

3 Rebellion and its Function

Conflict in Liberia spilled over into Sierra Leone in March 1991. The incursion into Sierra Leone was sponsored by Charles Taylor, who was angry at Sierra Leone being used as an air base for the ECOMOG forces operating against his forces in Liberia. These forces effectively prevented Taylor from taking the Liberian capital of Monrovia. He also had a second motive: namely to tie up ECOMOG troops (including Sierra Leonean troops) who would otherwise have been deployed against him in Liberia. Certainly, Nigeria and Guinea, perhaps appreciating Sierra Leone's vulnerability, agreed to send troops to Sierra Leone to assist Charles Taylor.

The small band of armed men who moved into Sierra Leone from Liberia called themselves the Revolutionary United Front (RUF). They included some NPFL military personnel, some mercenaries from Burkina Faso, and some Sierra Leoneans who had earlier fought with the NPFL and who appeared to be under the leadership of a former photographer called Foday Sankoh. Initially at least, the RUF got arms from Libya, Burkina Faso, and Côte d'Ivoire, using the same supply network as Taylor (*Africa Confidential*, 3 Feb. 1995). One point of attack for the RUF was the town of Koindu, in the north of Kailahun district; another was at the Mano river bridge in Pujehun district, on the road from Monrovia (Richards 1995: 147). The group that attacked at Koindu progressed as far as Daru in southern Kailahun, where it was halted by Guinean and Sierra Leonean government troops; the group that attacked at Mano river bridge progressed as far as Sumbuya. By July 1991, RUF forces had, for the most part, retreated to the southern and eastern fringes of the country (CRS 1995: 36). After the NPRC coup of 1992 the group that was halted at Daru attacked the diamond-rich district of Kono, and took control of Kono in October 1992.

The RUF tended to portray itself as seeking major political change at national level. As its name implies it had a revolutionary agenda. For its part, particularly in the early days of the RUF rebellion, Freetown tended to portray the RUF as a foreign-inspired movement, largely unrelated to the aspirations of ordinary Sierra Leoneans. Meanwhile, the international media tended to portray the conflict as a struggle for control over the state of some kind of mindless violence. This tended to deflect attention from the way in which the RUF managed to become a vehicle for a wide variety of Sierra Leonean groups, with different local and individual goals. Paradoxically, as we shall see in Section 5, the groups using the RUF for their own local goals included elements of the Sierra Leonean military itself. Participation in, and support for, the RUF served a number of political functions at local level, as well as a range of economic, psychological, and security functions.

Strikingly, the first aim of those fighting has not necessarily been to win the war. Indeed, in order to understand both the rebellion in Sierra Leone and the rather strange governmental response to this rebellion, it is necessary to set aside this idea that war is only about winning, and the closely related idea that civil war is about gaining, or retaining, control of the state. The RUF has a kind of political ideology, albeit one that remains confusing for most Sierra Leoneans. Richards (1995: 135 and 157) noted the influence of Libyan revolutionary populism, as Libya offered a refuge for dissident students from both Sierra Leone and Liberia. Richards also suggested that the RUF, by presenting the rebellion as an uprising by the Mende ethnic group, was trying to provoke some form of retaliation by the Sierra Leonean government against that group. Richards argued, that it was hoped that this would secure widespread Mende support for the RUF, in the same way as the Liberian government's retaliation against the Gio and Mano had prompted widespread support for the rebel NPFL. The RUF's claim to be a political movement is given some support by the fact that RUF spokesmen repeatedly condemned government corruption, and the grave shortcomings in the provision of health and educational services. Some kind of radical political ideology also seems to have been implied in the RUF's practice, notably in the early phase of the incursion, of executing local merchants, government officers, and some chiefs (Richards 1995: 139). That the RUF rebels were often far from indiscriminate in their use of violence was emphasized by one farmer from Pujehun district; who told me that:

They (the RUF) were only brutal to those they thought were a threat—if you looked intelligent, a post office worker, a bank clerk, a policeman. But those people left. The government people left.

In line with this interpretation, a doctor from Bo district said:

[In 1991] the rebels looked for prominent people—businessmen and politicians—and killed them and destroyed their homes. We thought the rebels were out to break the government's back with such activities.

Despite this discriminatory violence and hints of a political ideology, there was widespread cynicism in Sierra Leone about the real aims of the rebels. Richards noted the bemusement of Mende villagers in the face of Burkinabe revolutionaries lecturing them in French. One teenage boy talking of a rebel attack near Pujehun town expressed the scepticism of many when he said:

They called themselves freedom fighters. They were burning houses, but I did not see looting. They were aged 15 to 30. They said they had come to free us from the APC. We just felt they were rebels.

The widespread confusion over the real aims of the RUF was later encapsulated by a satirical columnist writing under the pseudonym 'PEEP' in the newspaper *For Di People* (5 June 1995):

One question that PEEP has always found interesting is 'What is the RUF fighting for?' And PEEP never agreed with the common answer . . . 'nothing', so he sat down to think of a list of reasons for the mayhem, burning and looting the rebels have imposed on Sierra Leone . . . Could it be because Foday Sankoh feels there is not enough mint in the new improved black DIAMINT? Does he want the old MALTINA bottles back? Is the RUF angry about the new one-way-only traffic flow on Kissy Road and Fourah Bay Road?

Richards stressed the limited appeal of the RUF's anti-mercantile and anti-governmental ideology. Contrary to attempts to demonize them, traders (many of whom were Mandingo) were often reasonably well integrated into local Mende communities, and government officials, often seen as poorly paid victims, rather than perpetrators, of government abuse.

The numerical weakness of the original rebel groups needs to be emphasized. Nevertheless, the RUF did achieve a major disruption and displacement of Sierra Leonean society. It did this, partly by taking advantage of local grievances and the frustrated desires inside Sierra Leone; many groups who had been marginalized in some way at the local (or sometimes national) level found that the rebellion provided them with a means of achieving some form of redress against, or revenge for, their grievances. This is not to say that these groups 'joined' the RUF, in the sense that they took orders from the RUF leadership or subscribed to RUF ideology; many rebellions including the Sierra Leone rebellion, have drawn strength from a loose and shifting coalition between ideologues and those with more pressing, immediate and self-interested goals.

3.1   Economic Functions

While most analysts stressed the strategic objective of Charles Taylor when explaining how war spilled over from Liberia into Sierra Leone, the economic motivation of the incursion has been overlooked. One motive was a simple desire for loot. Richards (1995: 163) noted that the Burkinabe contingent used warfare as 'a new and more violent form of target migration, with looted stereo sets, motorbikes and cars substituting for the radios and bicycles of earlier times'. Conscripted youngsters spent much of their time 'headloading' stolen property for the mercenaries, whose bonuses were said to be small. The Sierra Leonean rebels, on the other hand, preferred to loot cash and food to goods, as consumer durables were seen as difficult to carry and difficult to dispose of. One aspect of the economic motivation for the incursion that has received little attention was the dispute between NPFL rebels and Sierra Leonean soldiers and police. One Sierra Leonean who spent his time between Pujehun town and Freetown recalled:

Liberian soldiers would loot in Liberia (televisions, generators and so on), and bring them over, even as far as Freetown. They would give to our soldiers for them to sell. The Liberians cannot sell them themselves. The soldiers were supposed to give things in return—money or sometimes monkeys, which are not so favoured in Sierra Leone.

A young Liberian working at the Mano river bridge when the Taylor rebels entered Sierra Leone remembered the tensions which resulted from the failure by Sierra Leonean police and soldiers to pay for the looted goods they had already received:

We had some security—police, army. The Taylor rebels brought TVs, videos, cars, electrical goods, loot from Liberia and gave it to the head of police for him to sell to Freetown and Kenema and give them money. After he sold these materials, he would not carry the money back, and made excuses. I was at Bo-Ngella. So the rebels used to come to Sierra Leone frequently to make contact with the police and army and go back. Rebels would come in as far as Kenema, come in freely, usually without getting money, so they got annoyed. I used to go and sell clothes at the bridge in Bo-Ngella, Mano river bridge. The rebels used to tell the army in joking fun that they will one day come for their money in Sierra Leone. So in doing that, rumours began to go around that they will attack the area. So we used to overlook what they were saying. We were drinking beer all together. So one morning the Taylor rebels attacked at Bo-Ngella. We ran away to Zimni, 27 miles away.

The involvement of Sierra Leonean officials in the Liberian war economy proved to be a precursor of their involvement in the Sierra Leonean war economy. Further, the collaboration of Sierra Leonean soldiers with NPRC fighters, originally for economic purposes, led to government soldiers' collaboration with RUF fighters to exploit Sierra Leonean civilians. In addition to the benefits of looting, siding with the rebels provided significant economic benefits—notably through participation in an emerging trading network (particularly in diamonds) that was based on Charles Taylor's concept of a 'Greater Liberia'. This provided an alternative to the tightly controlled networks of patronage and trade based on Freetown. Traders who had been marginalized by Momoh's reforms (mostly Lebanese) were particularly receptive to this alternative outlet. The fact that the diamond-rich district of Kono proved a major focus of rebel activity underlines the importance of the economic motivation among the rebels.

A further source of support for the rebels were chiefly families who had been excluded, for one reason or another, from the economic and status benefits of local office, and who exploited the rebels' violence against their own rivals for the chieftaincy. This kind of rivalry was given an extra edge by a feeling in the south that some chiefs were no more than corrupt APC appointees, installed by Stevens as part of his drive to gain control over the institution of chieftaincy. During the rebellion, attempts were made to turn the violence of government soldiers against rival chiefly families.

A widespread perception in Sierra Leone that wealth had been achieved through corrupt practices—a perception that, as we saw in Section 2, had considerable validity—constituted another significant factor in the rebellion, lending a degree of legitimacy to violence and robbery that might otherwise have been seen as wholly immoral and unacceptable. This was nowhere more evident than in the economically vital rutile mining area, where resentment at Creo and expatriate privileges prompted considerable employee and ex-employee support for the attacks on the installations in January 1995.

3.2 Psychological Functions

Although war is often been portrayed as damaging to the mind (and with good reason), it also provides positive mental stimulus, such as excitement, status, and a kind of psychological release. This came through clearly in informants' accounts.

Richards has emphasized the importance of Rambo and other violent Western role models for Sierra Leonean youth. He suggests that,

Rambo is a hero figure not far removed from the violent, amoral, forest-going trickster of Mende tradition, Musa Wo . . . Teenage and pre-teenage rebels took part in massacres attired as if acting out scenes in a Rambo or Bruce Lee film.

This theme was also emphasized by my informants. They stressed, in addition, that paying homage to western cultural heroes costs money, money which could sometimes only be obtained by violence. Thus, one teacher with a long experience of teaching in Bo said:

Before the conflict, the percentage of literate was so low. In the bigger towns, the dancing, type of dress, the Americanization, the Michael Jackson thing, prevailed in the towns very quickly, and then mostly boys became interested in that type of life—not so interested in education. The Rambo type of thing, thrillers, the boys will know almost anything about Rambo. The country is invaded by Western things. They can know Western cassettes by heart, but they cannot go to school. Money became the watchword . . . Children are interested in this kind of Western lifestyle, but they can't afford it. They must buy the T-shirt with the photo of Rambo, Mike Tyson, Bob Marley . . . Perhaps the child can't pass exams, and then he starts perambulating. Attackers found it very easy to recruit people, other boys. Most of the lazy children will find it more interesting to live that way than to go to school.

Richards has suggested that conflict often allowed young people to express qualities of inventiveness and daring that found few outlets in peacetime. Although some people have emphasized that such arguments may glorify violence, it seemed important to explore the possible psychological functions of acts of terror. Quite apart from the emulation of Western role models it appears that acts of terror often served a purpose in allowing those who had been made to feel 'small' to feel big and powerful. One aid agency official who had been working in Kenema district explained:

Southern Kenema people said the first people in the rebellion were a mixture of Burkinabe, Liberians and Temne. They obviously had been trained and seemed to have some kind of programme. The second wave, about a week later, was their own brothers who'd been in Liberia and came back with guns and said 'Now I have power.' They were often coming back to make havoc in the towns they came from.

First-hand accounts of rebel atrocities suggest that some young men were interested in inflicting not only violence but also some kind of humiliation. This could include attempts to compel 'approval' of, or indifference towards, atrocities from the relatives of those directly abused, as if the rebels were staging a bizarre drama with a script that made them look like 'big men'. One teenage boy recounted a rebel attack south of Koribundu:

We decided to go to our grandfather's place. When we got there, the rebels came. My grandfather was killed by the rebels in front of the house. They put him in front of the house. They gathered his wives, and they shot him. They asked the wives to laugh.

One young man from Kailahun district recounted his experience of a rebel attack—another horrific incident culminating in 'forced laughter':

These five men asked us whether there are government troops in the village. We said no. So they said we should all take off our shirts. We did. My younger brother was wearing a shoe boot, so they said he was a soldier. I denied it. So the armed men said we were trying to hide the government troops. I told them my brother was not a soldier. So they said I was covering for a government soldier, and in due course they will kill me. But I begged for mercy, so they never killed me. So they called up my younger brother and laid him on a long table in front of everyone and cut his throat and killed him. They asked me to clap and laugh. Having no power, I just did what they told me.

A wide range of informants spoke of the widespread anger among Sierra Leonean youth, particularly males, at their perceived low status in a society offering them few opportunities to advance or to perform a meaningful role. One local worker with Catholic Relief Services spelt out the link between poor educational facilities and rebellion. Again, his account hints strongly at a perceived danger of humiliation among young people, and a sense that the threat of being laughed at could be turned on its head:

The educational system has increased rebel and soldier numbers. A lot drop out of school early, and these do not have fair job opportunities and having gone to school, they do not want to go back to their villages and till the land. They feel they are a little too enlightened to go back and till the soil! They feel their friends will laugh at them, and say you are still farming even though you went off to school. They saw that being a rebel you can loot at will, then you have a sway over your former master, who used to lord it over you, or the others who might have laughed. You might as well go to the bush and become a rebel. There is no master there. You are master of yourself . . . In my time, there were no celebrations at time of exams. Now they make elaborate parties and the children feel big and then when the results come, they have all failed. They cannot get jobs. They cannot go back to school.

One Western aid worker took up a similar theme:

Before the war, there was a run-down of the system. A lot of the youths had dropped out of the school system, or were still in but not very interested . . . By fighting, you get a lot of money and excitement and see the country. You're going from being nothing in a village to being Rambo.

One experienced worker with the aid agency Children Associated with the War reported on the relatives' reaction when boy soldiers returned home:

Often, (the families) said the children had got out of hand even before the war, and it was difficult to control them. The children had sometimes taken to the life of war—drugs, looting—before the war . . . Some had never been to school. Some were drop-outs from school . . . Around 60 per cent have not been to school, about 40 per cent dropped out.

Abuses inside schools also appear to have played a role in generating a powerful anger in some quarters. One former teacher recalled his own time at school, and linked his experiences with the conflict:

Some teachers used inhuman punishments on us, and the authorities never took them to task. One master would make us roll in prickly plants till we were pierced all over our bodies. Some children were made to stare at the sun. Others were beaten in a vicious way. This has made a lot of anger. The rebels targeted five teachers at Moyamba. You need punishments done with love, and corporal punishment as a last resort.

3.3   Security Functions

Many youths were coerced into joining the rebels. And some youths considered it safer to join the rebels than risk being accused by government forces of being a rebel. When government forces gained control of a town or village from the rebels, youths could easily be accused of sympathizing with the rebels, which might lead to their execution. Separation from parents could be a powerful impetus to recruitment, as Children Associated with the War staff emphasized:

Some children had already become drop-outs and were no longer in the care of their parents. When the rebel war came, most felt it was at least an opportunity to get a base other than their parents. Some who were in the rebel area saw their parents killed or missing. Everybody tried to save themselves. There was no security.

4   Abuse by Government Troops

A key reason for the rapid advance of the rebels in the first half of 1991 was the minimal resistance they faced from Sierra Leonean government forces. One farmer from Pujehun district said:

The RUF boys had two-way walkie-talkies. News of the easy advance was passed on. They said, 'Come, there's no resistance. The APC is nothing.' Another group entered Pujehun at Sulima, hearing the word . . . Until the rebels came to the town of Pujehun and then Koribundu, the government did nothing.

There was no government military base in Pujehun district, and the rebels were able easily to take Sulima.

Fear of a military coup had encouraged the government to keep its own army small in size and short of arms and ammunition, and it was paramilitary forces belonging to the ruling All People's Congress (APC) that provided the only possibility of serious resistance. These forces were also in retreat, however.

Poor conditions and lack of military support for government soldiers at the war front played an important role in precipitating a military coup by junior military officers in April 1992. Many hoped that the fall of the APC government would take the sting out of the rebellion, since the RUF had always justified its rebellion as a stand against 'APC corruption'. A further source of optimism was the pledge by the new NPRC government to bring the war to a speedy conclusion. Neither hope proved well founded.

For most ordinary Sierra Leoneans, the NPRC's failure to suppress the increasingly brutal RUF was a major blow. Worse still was the involvement—limited but increasing—of Sierra Leonean government forces in abuses against civilians. These abuses dramatically increased the levels of suffering and displacement among Sierra Leoneans. Even excluding refugees, roughly half the country's population had been internally displaced by late 1995.

First, under President Momoh and then increasingly under the new head of state Captain Julius Strasser, successive governments in Freetown sought to expand the Sierra Leonean army with a view, it appeared, to defeating the rebels. The army was rapidly expanded from around 3,000 to some 14,000. However, most of those recruited were little more than street boys (many of them from Freetown). They received very little training—anything from three weeks to nothing at all. And they received very little pay. This pattern of recruitment, training, and remuneration for government soldiers created conditions in which the exploitation of civilians (and, often, the avoidance of fighting) became likely. Indeed, sending this kind of ragtag army into resource-rich areas to do battle with the rebels proved a recipe for disaster.

Since many of the army's new recruits were from Freetown and northern Sierra Leone, they lacked social ties with the Mende who predominate in southern and eastern Sierra Leone. This appears to have facilitated the abuse and exploitation of civilians in these areas. It is true that many Mende were recruited into the army. It is true, also, that most Sierra Leoneans are profoundly aware of the danger that Liberian-style ethnic conflict can be encouraged by giving too much weight to ethnicity as a factor in conflict. Nevertheless many Mende point out that it is the Mende who have suffered the worst abuses and exploitation in the war. Many Mende perceive a northern bias in the army dating back to the APC.

Many of the boys who joined this ragtag army might easily, under slightly different circumstances, have joined the rebels. Joining the army, like joining the rebels, offered the prospect of access to cash and material goods. In addition, many youths perceived (probably correctly) that joining one armed party or another would make them less vulnerable to violence and exploitation. One boy from Pujehun district recalled how he came to join the army:

We went to our village. I was there with my father and mother and brothers and sisters. The rebels came there and attacked us and we were separated. I was on my own. I tried to find my way to [village near Pujehun town]. I arrived there. It was because of the war. I went to the town chief. I was with the town chief for three months. This was 1992, the rainy season. I was working for the chief, doing farming. It was too bad. I was thinking about my parents. I thought they had killed them all. [In the village] they didn't take care of me. Food was difficult. Sometimes I would go to the gate and join the soldiers to sleep there. I decided—because I have not yet seen my parents and I don't know anyone in the place—to join the military force. I was still looking for my parents. The town where we were living, the house was burned. My uncle was killed, and parents disarranged. I didn't have food to eat, clothes to wear. It was the only thing to do. They [the soldiers] told me to join and I will be able to see my parents. They will take me round the villages.

Mirroring the practice among the rebels, drugs were given to army recruits. One aid worker with extensive experience working with displaced people and former fighters said: 'Drugs are given as part of the ration—in the government army and by the rebels. There's cannabis in peacetime, and cocaine when there's fighting to be done. And people lick gunpowder.' This was confirmed by boys I spoke to. One said: 'You could open a bullet and eat gunpowder. I tried gunpowder. It made me feel brave. It was only once in a while.'

Another unstable element in the forces at the disposal of the government were the ULIMO (United Liberation Movement for Democracy in Liberia) irregulars. These were Liberians (mostly from the Krahn ethnic group) who had suffered at the hands of Taylor's forces, and who were seeking, as at least part of their agenda, to reverse the expansion of Taylor's influence in Liberia and Sierra Leone. ULIMO forces acquired a reputation for brutality. From early 1993, they were also increasingly drawn into looting, that is, following an economic agenda rather than concentrating exclusively on the political agenda of suppressing the rebellion.

A further source of recruits for the government forces were Sierra Leonean youths who had fled to Liberia when the army and ULIMO pushed back the initial incursion. Signed up in a camp for the displaced in Monrovia, these youths were apparently never put on the army payroll. One Pujehun farmer commented: 'Those were the new breed of rebels.'

As civilians found themselves increasingly abused not just by RUF rebels but by government forces (notably the ULIMO irregulars), groups of traditional hunters—known as kamajors—took over the role of community self-protection. By the beginning of 1993, the principal remaining rebel stronghold in Pujehun district appeared to be the chieftain of Sorro Gbema in the extreme south of the country. Traditional hunters got together to try to flush out the rebels. Although this action might have appeared consistent with a counter-insurgency strategy, the initiative actually led to major tensions between the kamajors and the army.

The loss of the diamond-rich district of Kono to rebel forces in October 1992 was an economic disaster for the government. Retaking it was a priority. Despite the range of unstable elements being drawn into the government forces, the Sierra Leonean army—with significant assistance from foreign troops—recaptured the diamond-rich district of Kono from the rebels in February–March 1993. This was an important turning point in the war.

Senior NPRC officials were implicated in illegal diamond trading, using the proceeds both to purchase arms and 'line their own pockets'. It was also clear that certain privileged elements of the military—notably the Tiger battalion that played a key role in the April 1992 coup—used the seat of government in Freetown for personal enrichment. For example, they had a degree of access to international aid. The NPRC's claim to be leading a crusade against APC corruption was revealed as a sham. In these circumstances, it proved difficult to prevent poorly paid and poorly trained government soldiers from lining their own pockets at the expense of civilians. Since the NPRC coup had put the military in charge, military officials were able to abuse civilians and engage in illegal economic activities with a high degree of impunity. Senior officers were to lecture junior soldiers on discipline; in any case senior officers were unlikely to want to draw attention to or rein in activities in which they themselves were implicated.

Having regained Kono, government forces were able to extend their control over most of the country. By the end of 1993 the rebel RUF had been largely dislodged from the areas of the south and east previously under its control (Amnesty International, September 1995). Many felt that the war was effectively over. However, government soldiers, finding that they were able to profit from diamond mining in particular, realised that their continued presence in resource-rich areas like Kono depended on continued conflict. An end to the war would have meant an end to a lucrative business. As one experienced French aid worker put it:

At the end of 1993, there was a lull in fighting. We started rehabilitation work. With the lull, a lot of the soldiers based in Kono saw diamond areas (often for the first time, since people don't travel much)—also in Tongo. 'We could get rich', they thought. 'We have to justify our presence here, and the way of doing this is to stage ambushes etc.'—so that they can stay in the area and continue mining. This is why Kono is a no-civilian area for so long, and why Tongo is a no-civilian area. Young guys [in the army] saw their bosses making a profit, and they thought 'Why can't we?' It's becoming ugly, very ugly.

Partly to consolidate military access to resources and partly in response to civil defence initiatives that threatened the army's control, a policy of evacuating civilians was adopted in many areas, notably Kailahun district and Pujehun district. A senior Sierra Leonean aid worker commented:

At the end of 1993, chiefs were asking for the military to get out of their district and asking for the government to give them arms and training so they could defend themselves. But the military didn't like it, so they trampled on that . . . At the time, the top people in the army in the north thought you'd be arming the Mende.

After December 1993, one senior Sierra Leonean professional dealing with the displaced in Bo nopted that:

People who had returned to Kailahun and Pujehun were being chased away by soldiers that they had lived with and knew very well, with threats of death if they reported the identity of their tormentors to authorities.

One teenage boy, having originally fled from rebel attacks on Pujehun town and surrounding villages to the village of Nomorfaama, recalled:

On the 25th December 1993, the rebels sent a letter saying they were going to attack Nomorfaama. After they wrote this letter, the government soldiers left Nomorfaama, and went to Kenema. The civilians stayed. When the rebels came to Nomorfaama, they took the ammunition and arms because there was no soldier in the town. It is strange that the soldiers would leave their ammunition in the town when they left. We were blaming the man in charge of the government soldiers in that area. We were saying he must have an idea why he's doing that. Maybe he wanted the rebels to come there. I don't know why.

Aid workers received information that the whole of Pujehun district was being evacuated by the army, with a huge camp for displaced people created at Gondama, near to the town of Bo. The Senior District Officer in Bo told me in 1995:

We've been asking the government to assist our local boys with shotguns, so people can protect their lives and property. We haven't got a good response . . . Last year (1994), the government thinks chiefs have the intention of using their guns against them. People think it's an upcountry war, and they're just insensitive . . . After the chiefs' conference, the war took a dramatic turn. Everybody's been chased out of his chiefdom—as if to say 'You're being punished'. Before that, the chiefdom headquarter towns were much safer. Almost every chiefdom headquarter now is attacked.

According to my informants, the government's abandonment of arms at Nomorfaama was part of a pattern of cooperation between the RUF and sections of the Sierra Leonean military. Government forces would leave their arms and ammunition for the rebels in a designated town. The rebels would pick up the arms and extract loot, mostly in the form of cash, from the townspeople, and then themselves retreat. At this point, the government forces would reoccupy the town and engage in their own looting, usually of property (which, as noted, the rebels found hard to dispose of).

A boy soldier remembered his experiences in the government army at this time:

Some soldiers were looking for rebels. When they attacked, they met rebels. When the civilians moved, whatever was in the town they [the soldiers] own it—money, rice, radios. If the younger ones do stealing, the older ones will take it from you. I took something once. They took it from me straightaway.

In the absence of effective government protection, many civilians looked to the Nigerian and Guinean troops for protection, although it is alleged that the Sierra Leonean government deliberately withdrew even this protection. One resident of Gondama camp told me:

I was here in the December 1994 attack (on Gondama camp). In November, we got a letter stating the rebels were coming to visit us. There was a festive occasion in Bo, they called on the security to go and be in Bo for the celebrations. We said on no account should they withdraw the contingent here for a celebration. At that time, there was a serious threat within the area that the rebels were coming in their hundreds. We hold the authorities responsible. We had only six Nigerians here left, so they could not confront these guys. The attackers were around 50—about 30 in combat gear and 20 in civilian clothes.

Four months later, just before the April 1995 'rebel' attack on Kono district, foreign troops stationed in Kono were removed.

Despite attempts to punish civilians for organizing their own defence, more civil defence organizations were formed and strengthened in many towns, including Bo, Kenema, Makeni, and Koindu. Many people in Sierra Leone advocated civil defence committees, organized around traditional chiefdoms, progressively taking over responsibility from government troops for defending rural areas. If the major threat to civilians at this stage had really been the RUF, then the government might have been expected to support such initiatives, but rarely did.

Eyewitness reports confirm that when rebels attacked the town of Bo in December 1994, prompting resistance from the Bo civil defence, government forces turned their fire on the civil defence. One woman from Koidu describes the importance of the civil defence organization there:

The population that was in Kono, they relied on the civil defence. It was really organized, about 3–4,000 people with shotguns. Every home was subscribing—1,000 leones a week. The civilians were really happy about the civil defence. People even volunteered to donate more than the 1,000 leones. The chiefs were very happy, and the civilians. That's why the civilians didn't flee—because they relied on the civil defence.

In the face of this resistance, the army used the threat of a rebel attack to exploit resources and civilians in the area, and to oppose the civil defence organization which had tried to impose limits on the army's exploitation. The same woman recalled:

We were having threatening remarks from our own people, that they will see that the rebels will enter in Kono. And even the civil defence at checkpoints were threatened by our own people, the army, destroying the checkpoints of the civil defence. One of my friends was at a checkpoint. One of the youths was wounded by one of the lieutenants, who cut across his fingers. The army said they will allow the rebels in. The people were not allowing them [the army] to mine. They were saying the soldiers shouldn't be involved in mining. So now they started threatening people because they were not involved. Some were involved. Some of the bosses were. The junior ones weren't. The whole army was told not to mine, but being a boss I can do anything.

An elderly woman who said she returned to Koidu from Freetown in April 1994 to look after her small business, stressed the conflict between the army and civilians (including the civil defence):

When we came back to Koidu, soldiers were harassing civilians, removing valuables. They wait for you to extract gravel, and then drive you off and take the diamonds . . . When they sent the new CO [commanding officer] in charge, they made sure he could control the soldiers. But there was no way the soldiers would stop mining. They were mining all the productive areas, but the harassment of civilians stopped. There were no complaints that soldiers were taking the productive areas. Everyone was afraid, and there was no one to complain to. The mines engineers were afraid of the soldiers. The civil defence do their best. Every house gives some 1,000 leones per month. Villagers were paying, the whole of Kono district. It was compulsory—if you don't pay, you go to court. They were raising a lot of money. The civil defence people were working well, doing their best, but they found that when they used to go to the war front to fight with soldiers, the soldiers would turn and kill them. Even then, they still summoned up courage to fight since they knew the people relied on them. There was a time when we had a meeting. All agreed they would prefer using foreign troops, Guinean troops, Nigerian troops, and the army was very bitter about that.

Meanwhile, government soldiers were participating in attacks on the economically critical bauxite and rutile mining areas in the south-west of the country.

An eyewitness to the 'rebel' attack on the Sieromco bauxite mining area in January 1995 reported that many of the 'rebels' were recognizable as soldiers who had previously arrived by helicopter to safeguard the site amidst reports that rebels were in the vicinity. Gunfire at the site had actually begun at the soldiers headquarters. Some government soldiers also appear to have played a role in subsequent attacks on the nearby rutile mines. Some soldiers appeared to back the rebels, or even behave like rebels, in protest at their exclusion from the lion's share of the loot and international aid. As one Sierra Leonean with good contacts in the military put it:

It's a covert mutiny. The view is: 'We went in support of you and you are not looking after us. We still face the same lack of welfare, boots, medicines, food, and human care and contact. We cannot even meet with you now.' Armed youths who attacked Njala University in January 1995 left a letter saying they had been part of the group overthrowing the APC and that they were disillusioned with the NPRC for departing from its stated good intentions.

A further destabilizing factor was the continuing allegiance held by many government soldiers to disgruntled politicians of the previous APC government. These soldiers often owed their jobs to these politicians. These politicians' houses were sometimes spared when gunmen selectively burned a village.

The 'rebel' attack on Kono in April 1995, was preceded not only by a withdrawal of foreign troops from the area but also by the 'disappearance' of significant numbers of government troops based at Ngaya, near Koidu. An eyewitness said that, having retreated to a village near to Koidu, she was hoping that the government soldiers would flush out the rebels. However, she saw soldiers joining groups of rebels and running with them. The soldiers even took off their uniforms. When government soldiers entered Koidu—in new uniforms, with new arms and a lot of ammunition—she saw them noting down the locations of houses, which were later burned. Other witnesses reported government soldiers looting in Koidu, and washing gravel to find diamonds. When reinforcements arrived from Makeni on April 29, they too joined in the looting. Soldiers shouted threats at the civilian population, complaining that people had been willing to 'carry' for the rebels, but were now unwilling to do the same for the soldiers. On 23 May, Koidu town was attacked once more—this time apparently by 'proper' RUF rebels in conjunction with about 60 government soldiers, mostly young officers. In addition to looting and illegal diamond-mining, soldiers also made money by 'taxing' trade and production—virtually the exacting of 'protection' money. Aid officials, diplomats, and diamond traders all spoke privately of how some traders had arrangements with the military so that they would not be attacked. Arrangements between traders and soldiers were encouraged by the fact that soldiers needed to sell their looted goods and the diamonds they had mined or stolen. Further, soldiers would often take a cut of the profits when rice was transported from Freetown to towns like Bo and Kenema, where prices had rocketed because of the large concentrations of displaced people and the inability of many people to farm. Thus, soldiers were benefiting from price movements which the soldiers' violence had, in large part, caused.

Another salient feature of the war economy was soldiers' involvement in the harvesting, sale and 'taxation' of valuable agricultural produce such as cocoa and coffee. People ejected from Kailahun and Pujehun districts saw the army's involvement in agricultural production as a major reason for their forcible displacement. Although cocoa and coffee could be harvested with minimal labour inputs, the quality of crops suffered as a result. When civilians suggested to government soldiers that they would be better off cooperating with civilian labour, rather than ejecting civilians completely, in some areas soldiers were willing to retain a limited labour force.

4 Aid and Silence

Donor pressure on the NPRC undoubtedly helped bring about elections in Sierra Leone. In combination with protests from Sierra Leonean peace organizations, donor pressure was particularly important, in early 1996, when elements of the military were clearly trying to sabotage the election process. British support for the election process was especially significant. Nevertheless, the pattern of international intervention (and non-intervention) in the face of Sierra Leone's catastrophe tended to prolong and deepen the suffering in important respects. Most importantly, the international community failed to speak out openly about government abuses, notably in the period 1993–5. Amnesty International and the US Committee for Refugees produced important and informative reports. But the silence within the UN was, for the most part, deafening. A World Food Programme representative encapsulated an unhelpful approach when he said: 'The government says it wants peace, but the rebels refuse. So how can you link aid to peace?' This line of reasoning accepted the NPRC propaganda at face value, and ignored the government's major role in human-rights abuses. One priest with many years' experience in Sierra Leone summed up many people's frustration with the UN when he said, 'UNICEF are talking about iodised salt when the whole place is burning.'

Britain and France in particular failed to evolve a joint position on the related conflicts in Sierra Leone and Liberia, and even European Community officials were privately critical of this. France's influence with Taylor, Côte d'Ivoire, and Burkina Faso could have been used to much better effect. Noting a widespread disappointment with Britain's role, one senior Sierra Leonean transport official said in July 1995: 'We feel very badly let down . . . If Britain said openly we are not happy with the situation here, people here will be dancing in the streets.'

The INEC electoral commission also took a weak position on government army abuses. When I asked the head of INEC, James Jonah, why there was no firmer action to control errant officers, he replied: 'But people criticize the NPRC for dismissing people. You have a long list of people they have dismissed. Yet people are still not satisfied.' It is now widely accepted that only a very small proportion of those guilty of negligence or abuse were brought to trial. The opportunities for donor pressure on human-rights issues were considerable. Yet public statements were conspicuous by their absence, and any private pressures were largely ineffectual. Increased aid and creditor support during the war actually helped maintain the government in Freetown as a kind of enclave economy. The government, failing to fund its own army (except indirectly through tolerating looting and illegal mining), was able to avoid printing large quantities of money and, almost bizarrely, to keep inflation under control. This, in turn, helped ensure continued flows of external finance as the NPRC maintained its image of financial orthodoxy.

One of the reasons why the war, for a while, did not have a disastrous impact on government finances or inflation was that key sectors of production, notably diamonds (as we saw in Section 2), had already fallen outside the realm where they could be taxed before the war began. One of the effects of donor support for the NPRC government appears to have been to allow the government to avoid the necessity of bringing diamond production under the control of the treasury; instead, NPRC officials were able to continue, and deepen, the Sierra Leonean tradition of using the country's precious mineral resources for private gain.

With Freetown being maintained as an enclave economy, journalists and officials from abroad and at home were to a large extent shielded from a proper awareness of the devastation upcountry. As one priest put it, 'The EC is providing the electricity and roads. They're making the government look good. It's a sham. And then the government forces are just beating up on everyone.' The concentration of aid in Freetown may have been a factor encouraging many traditional chiefs to go to Freetown and set up a council of Paramount Chiefs, in turn encouraging some to neglect the immediate protection of their people upcountry.

The concentration on humanitarian aid at the expense of addressing deeper causes of suffering in Sierra Leone appears to have been damaging in another respect. Those Sierra Leoneans who served as intermediaries between the displaced and the aid agencies could, potentially, have played an invaluable political role in lobbying both the government and international actors to address the root causes of displacement. These intermediaries included Paramount Chiefs and a range of educated groups, notably teachers. However, these intermediaries were often able to benefit personally (both materially and in terms of influence) from international aid that was frequently poorly targeted. In this sense, they acquired a vested interest in continued suffering as well as an interest in keeping quiet on topics that might jeopardize (in the eyes of the government) their status as 'respectable' representatives of the displaced. Even the churches were often able to use aid distributions, to boost their influence and reward their followers.

One Catholic official summed up the relationship between aid and what he saw as a culture of excessive deference in Sierra Leone, a widespread desire to say what might be pleasing and lucrative rather than what might be an accurate depiction of reality:

The aid business is a way of life. It's an income. It's keeping the country going . . . There's a division of things in the NPRC: 'We'll make use of the diamonds. You live off the aid in Freetown.' There's a vested interest in keeping the chaos going, and attracting the aid. Some white people fall into the trap of being a provider. It doesn't help at all. It carries on this sycophancy, this false world, this use of language that is going nowhere.

With Freetown having been preserved from experiencing or even perceiving the devastation elsewhere in Sierra Leone, many did not treat the war with sufficient seriousness. The Creole community in Freetown, many of whom had never ventured outside the city and had no relatives upcountry, were widely seen as insufficiently concerned with the devastation beyond the capital. And just as international silence tended to discourage protests within Sierra Leone, the reverse was also true. In June 1995, a columnist in the *Weekend Spark* observed perceptively:

Remember, our once beautiful towns of Yele, Yonibana, Rotifunk, Yormandu, Tombodu, Koindu and so many others have been reduced to charred ruins. Yet still, most of us in the city [Freetown] shed only crocodile tears and express no heart-felt remorse by trying to save our nation. What do we then expect of the international community? Since we seem to be down-playing the seriousness of the destruction of human life and property, even though the international community through embassies is quite privy to the reality on the ground, they also adopt the same lukewarm attitude towards our national tragedy. At a funeral no one can attempt to weep more than the chief mourner.   (commentary by Koyie Mansaray, *Weekend Spark*, 30 June 1995)

In Sierra Leone, silence and violence were blood brothers.

5   Conclusion

Although war is typically portrayed as destroying incomes, harming the body, and damaging the mind, participation in war can also enhance incomes, protect the body, and excite the mind. We need to understand not just what war can do *to* people, but also what war can do *for* them. Without this, there may be little chance of engineering a lasting peace. Recognizing the rationality of violence, on the other hand, offers important opportunities for policies that will address some of the roots of violence. The economic and psychological functions of violence for youths attracted both to the rebels and government army underline the relevance of policy conclusions drawn by Richards (1995: 164) in his study of Sierra Leone:

The antidote to the further spread in Africa of violence based on the enrolment of disaffected youth will require particular attention to be given to those factors likely to engender the confidence of the younger generation in the structures of state and civil society. The recent experience of Liberia and Sierra Leone suggests that fashionable concern with forest conservation and human rights will mean nothing unless the international community is prepared to renew its enthusiasm for those old and unfashionable concerns, education and employment.

The violence in Sierra Leone cannot be adequately characterized as a 'rebel war', though this has been the preferred term of the government, the largely pliant press, and the UN. Nor was it legitimate to treat the crisis as simply a 'food emergency'. As with the Oklahoma bombing, there was an attempt to locate the source of violence *outside* of society, whereas in fact violence was nurtured within the society.

By September 1996, Sierra Leone had a democratically elected government and seemed poised on the brink of a peace settlement. However, unless serious attempts are made to resolve the underdevelopment and neglect of state institutions (notably education) that lie at the heart of the country's conflict, even a formal peace agreement with RUF leader Foday Sankoh will be unlikely to last. His followers in the bush are already voicing a sense of unease that they may be abandoned, just as the young supporters of the NPRC coup came to feel abandoned by their leadership before embarking on widespread abuse of civilians. Alarmingly, the whereabouts and conditions of the vastly expanded Sierra Leonean army remained unclear. The temptation to engage in attacks on civilians and then blame the 'rebels' (with whom no formal peace agreement has yet been signed) remains a powerful one.

Although a degree of order has been restored to the diamond districts in particular by the South Africa-based mercenary company, Executive Outcomes, there are widespread fears that the price for this order will be the extraction of diamonds on terms that are favourable to Executive Outcomes and associated foreign companies like Branch Energy (registered in the Isle of Man). Since the extraction of minerals without substantial benefit for ordinary Sierra Leoneans has been at the heart of the resentment that fuelled the country's war, this appears to be a dangerous development. There is also a danger that protection for civilians will only be taken seriously in areas with sufficient mineral resources to attract mercenaries and multinationals.

Attempts at demobilization that do not simultaneously address the reasons why youths were mobilized in the first place will be doomed to failure in the long term. As with humanitarian aid, there is a danger that demobilization schemes will be unthinkingly superimposed on a set of political and economic problems, without considering how these underlying problems might be addressed. Rehabilitation will need to go beyond the recreation of the political economy that itself engendered the conflict. Close attention to the priorities of young people in particular will be needed in order to offer the kinds of roles in rehabilitation work that capture the imagination and restore a sense of self-worth.

Meanwhile, the creation of accountable security institutions—perhaps some combination of a reformed army (emphasizing local recruitment), a reformed police force, and expanded civil defence forces—will be critically important. A delicate path will have to be forged between ridding the government and military of those who orchestrated abuses, and driving them into the renewed orchestration of abuses as a result of their possible exclusion from the trappings of power. Perhaps most helpful of all would be a more open and honest discussion, within and outside Sierra Leone, of who has been doing what to whom, and why.

7

Sri Lanka: Civil Strife, Civil Society, and the State 1983–1995

MEGHAN O'SULLIVAN

1 Introduction

Efforts to understand the complex relationship between war and economic change, or development, often focus on the mechanisms through which war inflicts costs. In contrast, this chapter looks beyond the destructive elements of conflict to examine the transforming effects of conflict. Like other changes in economic incentives, war does not arrest all economic transactions, but alters the environment in which they take place. Some economic processes viable in peacetime are no longer profitable or even possible in a war context because conflict changes the parameters of the market place. However, for the very same reason that some opportunities are destroyed, others are created. By examining changes at both the macroeconomic and household level, this chapter seeks to explore the ways in which people and organizations have altered their behaviour in order to cope with the changing realities of war.

A macro analysis of a country at war would demonstrate the transforming effects of conflict by revealing the varied trends behind the anticipated decline in production. Given the change in incentives created by the war, certain sectors may be predictably more afflicted, while others may prosper, even though the net outcome may be a decline in GDP. At the household level, we generally associate conflict situations with increased poverty and deteriorating physical conditions. Often, the reasons for this adverse situation are evident. However, as we are resolved to look at war not simply as a destructive force, we recognize that conflict must change peoples' strategies for survival, not simply render the old ones ineffective. Identifying such transformations will

I am grateful for the help and information provided by many people whom I interviewed including Mr K. Ponnampalam, former Jaffna Government Agent; Mr Varadakumar of the Tamil Information Centre; Ms R. Sebastian, journalist; Mr A. Arudpragasam, former head of the LTTE Industrial Development Organisation; Ms M. Dharmadasa of the American Embassy as well as others from Jaffna Teaching Hospital, Eastern University, University Grants Commission, Commissioner of Essential Services Offices, various political parties and NGOs, militant groups, and private individuals wishing to remain unnamed. Without the assistance of these people, it would have been impossible to piece together the picture presented in Section five. Moreover, I am indebted to Frances Stewart and Nandini Gooptu, as well as others at Queen Elizabeth House, Oxford, for their advice and support. Finally, I would like to thank the Beit Fund for Commonwealth History, Brasenose College, the Norman Chester Fund, and the Graduate Studies Committee for financial support.

better enable us to formulate policies most likely to limit the costs of war and, where possible, to encourage continued development even during periods of conflict.

After analysing war-inflicted change at the macrolevel, this chapter will focus on the impact of war at the household level—and therefore on human welfare—by using a modified entitlements approach. Sen (1981) first wrote of market entitlements, the income secured by direct production which is used to purchase commodities. Stewart (1985), in developing the basic-needs literature, added to Sen's framework by introducing the concept of public entitlements—services such as education, health care, and food rations normally associated with government responsibility. This sum of purchasing power from private incomes earned on the market plus social benefits from public provisioning is referred to as household entitlements, the loss of which obviously leads to human costs and suffering. This chapter will maintain this framework with the addition of the concept of civic entitlements, the assistance provided to the population by non-governmental institutions to supplement market and public entitlements. Public and civic entitlements, although dealt with separately, together comprise non-market entitlements. War, in influencing macro and meso situations, alters the way in which people procure both market and non-market entitlements. Of course, the most tragic case would be when people failed to secure these entitlements at all. However, as this is rarely the case, the most important questions become how do people change their economic behaviour in order to maintain market entitlements? What new structures arise to meet human needs and deliver non-market entitlements as old structures fail?

An investigation of war and development would be incomplete without one further analytical category. Development costs are those caused by destruction of existing capital (physical as well as social), diminishing new investment, and destruction or reduction of human resources. These costs can be shaped by the macro and meso situations, such as when the need for funds to enlarge the army provokes the termination of a public works project. Yet, at the same time, development costs—such as the disintegration of trust—can likewise shape the macro and meso environments to the extent that they erode the basis for many economic transactions and the development of institutions. During wartime, with the destruction of institutions and the shortened time horizons for building reputations and economic relationships that insecurity brings, opportunistic behaviour can become more profitable. In these conditions, a society can move from 'a trust equilibrium' to 'an opportunistic equilibrium'.[1] Needless to say, this bodes badly for society and the economy.[2]

This chapter uses the framework developed above to examine the experience of Sri Lanka, a country long engulfed in violent conflict. Although this study incorporates both quantitative and qualitative information, the usual problems of the counterfactual prevail. Comparing the situation in Sri Lanka before the conflict and over the war years has limitations as 'non-conflict' effects from Sri Lanka's changing economic circumstances are incorporated in the trends, making it difficult to separate out the effects of

---

[1] Collier (1995), in seeing institutions as essential in lowering transaction costs, also links a breakdown in social capital to the economic costs of war.

[2] Stewart (1995) finds that organizations which function on what she terms a 'trust/reciprocity mode' of operation instead of a 'market' or 'hierarchical' mode are the ones achieving the greatest successes.

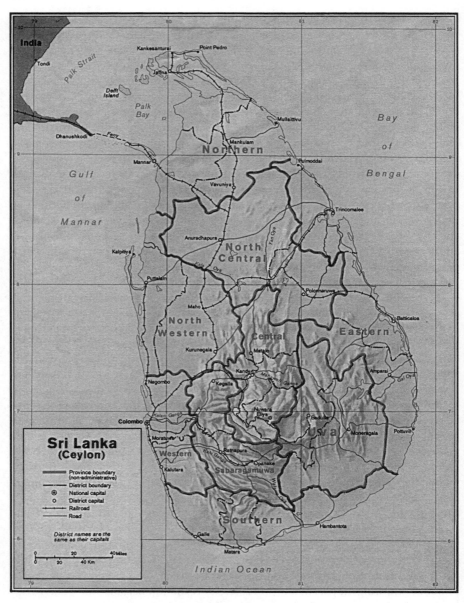

Map 7.1   Sri Lanka

war. Comparing Sri Lanka to other countries in the region can illuminate how Sri Lanka may have fared had it not been faced with conflict, but, again, one must be conscious of the many specific elements that affect country developments. Still, by looking at absolute changes, inter-country comparisons, and changes in trends, we hope to obtain an indication of the impact of the war on Sri Lanka.

The chapter will identify notable ways in which Sri Lanka's experience has departed from conventional expectations about countries undergoing war. These departures may be better interpreted when certain qualifications are made about the war in Sri Lanka. The war, while unquestionably damaging the economy in some respects, has not led to a termination of growth. Another distinguishing feature of the Sri Lankan war is its relative geographic concentration: the violence has been largely confined to the northeast.[3] This reality influenced our expectations and shaped the framework employed. While the fighting has not disrupted daily life in the southwest directly, we still examine the impact of the conflict on this region. Although one might not expect to see in the southwest the severity of economic dislocation and human suffering present in the war regions, in this chapter we anticipate that the conflict will nevertheless shape the functioning of the market and of public and civic entitlements in the more peaceful regions, although through the less direct mechanisms expounded on later. Consideration of the war zone (the northeast) separately from the area outside military activities (the southwest) is also warranted because the collection of information used in formulating 'national' human indicators has almost without exception excluded households from the northeast since the mid-1980s. Even within the area of military activities, there is a need to distinguish between regions. The relative ethnic homogeneity of the north, as well as the mode of warfare employed there, separates it from the east. These differences have seriously affected the opportunities for securing entitlements in the two areas, making it essential to analyse each region individually and dictating the structure of this chapter.

2   Overview of the Sri Lankan Conflict

Since independence in 1948, the relationship between Sri Lanka's two main ethnic groups, the Sinhalese (74 per cent of the population) and the Sri Lankan Tamils (12 per cent), has been marred by ethnic tension, sometimes flaring up into race riots and more recently, into civil war. Strains between the communities can be traced to legislation favouring the Sinhalese in linguistic, economic, and political spheres. The subsequent alienation of the Tamils from the state eventually led their main political representatives, the Tamil United Liberation Front (TULF), to advocate a separate Tamil state in the Northern and Eastern Provinces in 1976.

Earlier educational reforms discriminating against the Tamils and a stagnating economy had ensured that by the late 1970s, a large number of Tamil youths were both

[3] The exception to this is the years 1987–9 when the Janatha Vimukthi Peramuna (JVP) insurgency terrorized the south. For the most part, this chapter will be limited to assessing the impact of the conflict between the government and the Liberation Tigers of Tamil Eelam.

Table 7.1　Ethnic composition of the population of Sri Lanka, 1981

Group	% of total
Sinhalese	74.0
Sri Lankan Tamil	12.6
Indian Tamil	5.5
Muslims	7.4
Moors	7.1
Malays	0.3
Others	0.5
TOTAL	100.0

Note: Unlike other communities in Sri Lanka, the Muslims consider their religion the primary determinant of their identity. However, despite identifying themselves with a religious marker, they are essentially considered to be an 'ethnic' group in Sri Lanka. This categorization reflects the dominance of ethnicity in Sri Lankan politics.

Source: Department of Census and Statistics (1986), *Census of Population and Housing 1981*, Colombo: Department of Census and Statistics.

estranged from the state and unemployed. Unsurprisingly, they proved to be easy targets for the recruiters of militant separatist groups like the Liberation Tigers of Tamil Eelam (LTTE),[4] particularly as the TULF's peaceful techniques proved largely ineffective in establishing a satisfactory measure of devolution for Tamil areas. This disaffection, coupled with an increasingly repressive army presence in Tamil areas, erupted into violence in July 1983 with the killing of 13 Sinhalese soldiers in Jaffna in the Northern Province. This event triggered week-long, island-wide, anti-Tamil riots leaving hundreds of Tamils dead and tens of thousands homeless.

Despite sporadic negotiations, violence, which eventually brought government forces into full conflict with Tamil militant groups, has continued to wrack the island until the present day. A peace accord between the Sri Lankan and Indian governments as well as many Tamil militant groups (although not the LTTE) was signed in 1987. Yet it only brought more violence to the island, both in the form of sustained fighting between the LTTE and the Indian Peace Keeping Force (IPKF) as well as an uprising led by a radical left wing Sinhalese organization, the Janatha Vimukti Peramuna (JVP), opposing Indian involvement.

After the IPKF departed from Sri Lanka in June 1990, something of a stalemate developed. The LTTE maintained exclusive control over much of the Northern Province, including Jaffna city, running a *de facto* state there. The government was unable or unwilling to challenge this, and its response was limited to occasional shelling and an economic blockade of the Jaffna peninsula. Although the early 1990s were marred by assassinations of prominent national political figures, the violence remained mostly confined to the northeast.

---

[4] At the time, the LTTE was called the New Tamil Tigers.

This situation changed shortly after the People's Alliance came to power in the 1994 elections on a platform calling for peace. Shortly after the new government was formed, a ceasefire was negotiated, only to be broken by the LTTE several months after its commencement. Soon afterwards, a series of government offensives in late 1995 and throughout 1996 dramatically altered the ground situation. By the end of 1996, the government had regained control of most of the Jaffna peninsula and substantial portions of the Northern Province for the first time in many years. The following years, from 1997 until 2000, saw a series of battles between the government and LTTE, one of the most prolonged and perhaps most strategically important being the ultimately failing effort by the government to gain control of the road connecting Jaffna to the rest of the island. Although the LTTE offered tough resistance in some areas, it was forced to relocate to parts of the Northern Province in the mainland (the Wanni)[5] and the Eastern Province for the late part of the 1990s. However, as the year 2000 unfolded, the LTTE began to make substantial forays into government-held territory in the north, once again threatening the government's control of Jaffna.

The Sri Lankan government has supplemented this military activity with efforts to formulate proposals intended to give the northeast greater autonomy; however, these initiatives have been bogged down in political rivalries and constitutional impediments. While the significance of these recent military and political occurrences is critical to any resolution of the conflict, this chapter is concerned with the situation in the northeast up until November 1995, that is, before the LTTE's control of Jaffna was challenged successfully. Examining this era is by no means a moot exercise now that many of the structures described are, for the time being, non-functional. By understanding the situation before the changes of the past years, we are better placed to predict and to mitigate the costs of the current fighting.

3   Macro Impact

The basic supposition that strife damages the growth of countries at war is borne out by the experience of many conflict-torn countries examined in this volume. As illustrated in Table 7.2, Uganda, Mozambique, and Ethiopia all endured significant slowdowns in GDP growth during the years each country was at war. In contrast, the statistics for Sri Lanka indicate that its economy, rather than contracting during the period of war, actually grew, on average, faster than in the pre-war period. Of course, comparisons must be made with caution given the different structures of the economies in Table 7.2, changes in international environment over time and, importantly, the varying policy regimes of each country and in each period. Even given these considerations, the experience of Sri Lanka clearly differs dramatically from that of other countries at war. Even more surprisingly, in terms of growth, the performance of Sri Lanka compares favourably with other developing countries not at war. Similarly, in terms of GNP per

---

[5] The Wanni is a term which refers to most of the combined northern districts of Mullaitivu, Kilinochchi, Vavuniya, and Mannar. See Section five.

Table 7.2   GDP growth rates in conflict countries: annual percentage change

	Pre-war	War	Difference
Sri Lanka	3.2	4.4	1.2
Uganda	4.8	−0.5	−5.3
Mozambique	5.3	−1.6	−6.9
Ethiopia	3.6	1.0	−2.6

Notes: 1. Sri Lanka: pre-war period 1970–82; war 1983–98; the war in Sri Lanka is still very much unresolved. Therefore, these statistics are used not because the war was ended in 1998, but as the most recent figures available. 2. Uganda: pre-war period 1967–71, war 1971–86. 3. Mozambique: pre-war period 1970–4, war 1976–92. 4. Ethiopia: pre-war period 1963–81, war 1981–91.

Sources: IMF, *International Financial Statistics Yearbook* and World Bank, *World Tables*; Collier 1995.

Table 7.3   Non-war comparisons

	GNP per capita 1995 (US$)	GDP average annual growth (% 1965–80)	GDP average annual growth (% 1980–90)	GDP average annual growth (% 1990–5)
Sri Lanka[a]	700	4.0	4.2	4.8
South Asia[b]	350	3.7	5.7	4.6
Low-income economies	430	4.8	6.0	6.8
Low-middle-income economies	1,670	5.5	2.3	−1.5
Middle-income economies	2,390	6.2	1.9	0.1

[a] Sri Lanka is considered a low-income economy by the World Bank.
[b] South Asia includes Bangladesh, Bhutan, India, Myanmar, Nepal, Pakistan, and Sri Lanka.

Sources: World Bank, *World Development Report*, 1992, 1997.

capita, Sri Lanka's income per capita is close to double the South Asian average as well as significantly exceeding the average of its counterpart low-income economies.

A closer look at Sri Lanka's growth rates over the period of conflict does indicate some considerable fluctuations which correspond with episodes of violence on the island. In particular, the years of the JVP rebellion, from 1987 to 1989, saw a marked decline in growth as is indicated by Figure 7.1. Overall, the period from the onset of the conflict with Tamil groups in 1983 to the suppression of the JVP in 1989—when annual growth averaged 3.7 per cent—was one of the slowest periods of growth in the post-independence history of the country. These trends suggest that Sri Lanka did not entirely escape the dampening effects of conflict, but simply managed to mitigate them better than other countries at war. Despite these qualifications, it is still interesting to consider how Sri Lanka's unusual performance has been possible. What are the conditions that have kept Sri Lanka's growth positive, if not consistently robust, at the

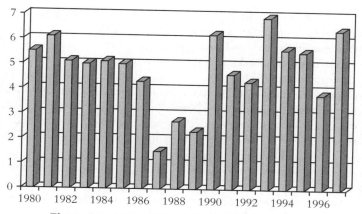

Figure 7.1   Sri Lanka's annual GDP growth rates (%)
Sources: Central Bank of Sri Lanka (various years), *Annual Reports*.

same time two civil conflicts persisted? An examination of the most common causes of macroeconomic dislocation in war economies—mainly physical production disruptions, uncertainty, and macroeconomic imbalances—may answer our queries about the country's unusual growth performance during wartime.

3.1   Physical Production Disruptions

The impact of war on a country's production is largely shaped by the geographic area affected directly by war activities and the distribution of productive assets in that country. As mentioned earlier, for the most part, the war between the government and the Tamil rebels has been geographically limited to the Northern and Eastern Provinces which together comprise 28 per cent of the land area of Sri Lanka.[6] Therefore, we would expect production disruptions to reflect the structure of the economy in those two provinces.

Conditions in the Northern Province have never been particularly favourable to agriculture and, consequently, those searching for employment often needed to look beyond the agricultural sector. In fact, the limitations on cultivation in the Jaffna peninsula have been used to explain the traditional Tamil emphasis on education undertaken in the hopes of securing a job in the public sector and the subsequent steady flow of Tamils seeking employment outside the Northern Province. For those remaining in the north, the main options for employment were in small-scale trade, minor food-crop production, fishing, or one of the state industries established there in the decades after independence.[7]

---

[6] These two provinces were merged under the Indo-Lanka Accord of 1987.
[7] These industries are the Paranthan chemical factory (only 1 on the island), the Kankesanthurai cement factory (1 of 3 island factories), the saltern at Elephant Pass (1 of many), the mineral sands factory at Pulmoddai (only 1 on the island), and 1 of the 2 island's flour mills.

The economy of the Eastern Province, in contrast, is heavily dependent on agriculture. Island-wide, agriculture accounts for 26 per cent of GNP and almost half of employment. Plantation crops and paddy production each account for slightly more than a quarter of this total. The Eastern Province is responsible for close to a quarter of the paddy acreage cultivated in Sri Lanka and for nearly the same percentage of the total paddy production. Fishing also accounts for much of the east's contribution to national income: the combined fish catch of the Northern and Eastern Provinces in the past has equalled 40 per cent of the country's total. As in the north, some small trade and state run industries—such as the only paper factory in Sri Lanka and one of the three sugar factories—have boosted non-agricultural income.

As expected, government statistics indicate production losses in the sectors to which the north and east made the greatest economic contributions. Statistics from regional industries point to severe production disruptions. Paranthan Chemicals in the north was producing only 12 per cent of its annual average tonnage in 1985 before temporarily closing in 1986.[8] Similarly, the cement plant at Kankesanturai, after operating at near capacity between 1979 and 1981, reported a loss of Rs. 227 million (approximately $US9 million) in 1984 after operating at only a quarter capacity (Central Bank of Sri Lanka, various years). Production at sugar factories in the northeast declined steadily throughout the 1980s, averaging 58 per cent of 1982 levels throughout 1987–90. Statistics do not exist on smaller, local industries in the Northern Province. However, the majority of them were choked to closure either by the government embargo on material goods allowed into the north or due to the collapse of the larger industries (particularly fishing) for which they had provided complementary services.[9] The fishing industry has been seriously hampered by bans imposed by the Sri Lankan army on fishing along the north-eastern coast since October 1984.[10] The fish catch, after modest increases in the early 1980s, dropped by a quarter in 1985, remained at low levels for the following years, and still had not reached 1983 levels of production by 1992. More explicitly, the percentage of the national fish catch provided by the northeast dropped by over half and remained at low levels into the 1990s.[11]

Agricultural statistics also indicate losses in production caused by the ethnic conflict. As examined in later sections, these shortfalls can be attributed to production disruptions from fighting and fear of cultivating—as many paddy workers were killed while in their fields—as well as to damaged irrigation and infrastructure. Decreases in paddy production during the 1985–8 period alone cannot signal a war-related phenomenon when the poor harvests of 1986 and 1988 and the drought in 1987 are taken into account. Yet, when paddy production by district is examined, the impact of the war is evident. Total paddy production for Sri Lanka was almost identical at 2.5 million tonnes for both the 1982–3 and 1987–8 cultivation years. Yet production in war-torn districts

---

[8] Paranthan Chemicals produced an annual average of 4,630 metric tons of chemicals between 1979 and 1981, yet produced only 548 metric tons in 1985.

[9] For more information about local industries, see the last section of the chapter.

[10] These bans forbid all forms of sea fishing in the north (although many fishermen are said to risk their lives in order to fish at night) and outlaw night fishing in the east.

[11] In 1981, the northeast provided 57% of the nation's fish. In 1987, the northeast contributed only 23%.

Table 7.4 Sri Lanka: Paddy production (tonnes) 1982/3 and 1987/8

District	Total 1982/3	Total 1987/8	% change
Jaffna	94,147	15,898	−83
Mullaitivu	38,162	14,584	−62
Mannar	64,889	44,836	−31
Trincomalee	119,395	57,188	−52
Batticaloa	152,736	42,687	−72

Source: Central Bank of Sri Lanka, *Annual Report on the Economy*, 1983 and 1988.

Table 7.5 Sri Lanka: Paddy purchased under the guaranteed price scheme 1982/3 and 1987/8 (tonnes)

District	1982/3	1987/8
Jaffna	5,181	16
Mullaitivu	9,632	—
Mannar	8,062	85
Trincomalee	36,662	3,913
Batticaloa	29,415	—

Source: As Table 7.4.

of the Northern and Eastern Provinces show dramatic declines (Tables 7.4 and 7.5).[12] Major decreases in the amount of paddy purchased by the Paddy Marketing Board (PMB) under the Guaranteed Price Scheme over this same time period most likely suggest production disruptions, and at the very least signal marketing and transportation problems in the northeast region.[13] Production of minor food crops such as maize, chillies, red onions, and sorghum—the entirety of which was grown in the northeast, particularly in Jaffna—also slowed significantly over the 1980s.

While the traditional economic activities of the northeast have been seriously disrupted due to the conflict, the impact of these economic disturbances on the national economy has not been dramatic[14] due to the distribution of the island's productive assets. A sectoral breakdown of Sri Lanka's GDP demonstrates that in the pre-war period (1978–83), non-export agriculture[15] and fishing—the two sectors in which the

[12] Several districts in the deep south—the heart of the JVP insurrection—such as Matara and Hambantota, also suffered serious production losses during 1987–9.

[13] This decrease in paddy purchased by the government does not necessarily reflect a decline in production, but certainly a reluctance to sell produce to the government in a situation of uncertainty.

[14] The Ministry of Shipping, Ports, Relief and Rehabilitation estimated that damage to agriculture, fisheries, irrigation, and industry in the northeast averaged approximately US$10m. a year (Ministry of Shipping, Ports, Relief and Rehabilitation 1994).

[15] Virtually the entirety of Sri Lanka's export plantation products (tea, rubber, coconuts) is grown outside the northeast.

northeast makes its prime contribution to the national economy—accounted for not quite 15 per cent of GDP (World Bank 1995: 30). Of this percentage, the northeast's share is just a portion; before the conflict, the northeast contributed approximately 40 per cent of national fish production and 30 per cent of agricultural production to GDP. In fact, despite the losses incurred in these sectors in the northeast, non-export agriculture and fishing expanded to 18.5 per cent of GDP during the war period.[16] Industry,[17] export agriculture, and services—sectors which are almost exclusively concentrated outside the northeast—comprised the remaining five-sixths of GDP. Not only was the bulk of economic activity centred outside the war zone—a distribution pre-dating the war[18]—but two of these sectors, industry and services, were the fastest growing ones.[19]

3.2 Uncertainty

Many of the obvious ways in which warfare influences economic activity—such as through the destruction of infrastructure, the displacement of people and workforces, and the disruption of utilities—is reflected in our previous examination of physical production disruptions. However, given the concentration of economic assets in the southwest and the concentration of violence outside these areas, we would anticipate that economic disruption, and its root war-related causes, would be minimal in the southwest. While this expectation has some validity, it ignores the potentially large impact that uncertainty might have on all regions of the economy, whether suffering the direct effects of violence or not. Unquestionably, war, and the uncertainty it brings with it, results in a general loss of confidence and a reluctance to invest. Although it is impossible to quantify the amount of investment that was lost as a result of the Sri Lankan conflict, anecdotal evidence suggests that many foreign investors shied away from Sri Lanka once it became embroiled in domestic conflict and violence. Even some firms, such as Motorola and the Harris Corporation, which had already made substantial and irrecoverable investments in Sri Lanka, curtailed their investment in the wake of the 1983 violence (Athukorala 1995). The net cost of the loss of this investment would far exceed the amount directly invested, as this investment spurred growth in exports, jobs, and government revenue.

In addition to these losses in investment, we would expect that the uncertainty perpetuated by the conflict damages the economy by destroying *social capital*—the nebulous product of institutions of the state and civil society (see Coleman 1990 and

[16] This development is better understood when the attempts to make agriculture more productive throughout the rest of the island are considered. By far the most notable of these efforts was the undertaking of the Mahaweli irrigation scheme intended to provided irrigated land to 70,000 landless households.

[17] While the industries in the northeast were hit hard by the war, they account for a very small percentage of total industry.

[18] Despite the presence of these industries, the northeast has remained much less developed than the rest of the country on an industrial level. Many Tamil leaders have accused the government of intentionally keeping the northeast underdeveloped and channelling resources elsewhere. See Manogaran (1987).

[19] Industry and services grew at an average rate of 4.2% and 7.2% respectively from 1978 to 1983 compared with agriculture which grew at a still substantial 4.1%. Central Bank of Sri Lanka, *Annual Reports* (various years).

Table 7.6   Sectoral composition of Sri Lanka's GDP at constant factor prices (% of GDP)

	1970	1975	1979	1982	1986	1989
Agriculture, forestry, and fishing	28.3	25.7	25.0	26.4	25.5	22.7
Mining and quarrying	0.7	2.6	3.5	2.4	2.3	2.9
Manufacture	16.7	15.1	14.4	14.4	15.7	16.8
Construction	5.6	4.3	5.2	8.4	7.2	7.0
Electricity, gas, and water	0.8	0.8	1.0	1.2	1.2	1.3
Transport, storage, and communications	9.5	10.0	9.3	11.3	11.7	11.4
Wholesale and retail trade	19.2	19.3	19.2	20.8	20.9	21.0
Banking, insurance, and real estate	1.2	1.8	1.9	3.9	4.5	5.1
Ownership of dwellings	3.0	3.1	2.8	3.4	3.1	3.0
Public administration	3.9	4.9	4.9	3.1	4.6	5.0
Services (n.e.s)	11.1	12.4	12.9	4.9	3.7	3.7
GDP total	100.0	100.0	100.0	100.0	100.0	100.0

Source: Central Bank of Sri Lanka, *Annual Report on the Economy* (various years).

Putnam 1993). Normally, these institutions constrain opportunistic behaviour, and by doing so, reduce the costs of conducting transactions in society.[20] The weakening of society's institutions, when coupled with an increasingly insecure environment, undermines normal economic activity. At the same time, such a scenario often opens doors for activity that is both illegal and immoral, escalating the costs of war to society and individuals.

While it is difficult to determine whether this breakdown of social capital has occurred in any particular society, we can hypothesize what the structure of an economy suffering this sort of collapse would look like (Collier 1995: 5–8). We might expect a decline in production in sectors that were the most transaction intensive, such as those which involve both the purchase of inputs and the marketing of output. Formal manufacturing would be one such sector. Similarly, assets that are both visible and mobile are the most precarious, making asset-intensive sectors unattractive in wartime. Again, manufacturing would be a good example of an asset-intensive activity. Sectors that are transaction–producing, such as transport, trade, financial services, or asset–providing, such as construction, would also be insecure. Lastly, we can predict that investment, particularly in transaction-intensive sectors and in visible and mobile assets, would dwindle.

Clearly, the composition of Sri Lanka's GDP, as shown in Table 7.6, and the change in it over the war period beginning in 1983, do not confirm our expectations. Formal manufacturing, an activity predicted to be the most vulnerable, substantially increased its contribution to GDP over this period. Other transaction-intensive sectors—transport, storage, and communications, wholesale and retail trade; and banking, insurance, and real estate—also showed particularly strong growth. Construction declined moderately,

[20] See North and other new institutional economists for more on how institutions reduce transaction costs.

reflecting a cutback in the government infrastructure programme more than anything else. Sectors that were deemed relatively less vulnerable to the influence of war, such as agriculture, actually accounted for less of GDP after a decade of conflict than before the war period.

Since we assume that there is some validity to our framework for predicting production shifts between sectors, we are again left with the task of explaining Sri Lanka's deviation. Production in the aforementioned sectors was expected to decline because social capital and the institutions that create and enhance it break down in wartime, contributing to transaction costs and greater risks of immobile and visible assets. As Sri Lanka's productive patterns did not reflect such a decline, we must explore the possibility that institutions in Sri Lanka were resilient during wartime.

To begin with, it is important to distinguish between institutions of liberal democracy and institutions of government. Sri Lanka's institutions of government, instead of collapsing as many governments experiencing a civil threat have, actually underwent a period of self-empowerment that occurred, not coincidentally, at the same time that civil unrest was intensifying. This empowerment was achieved partially at the expense of the institutions of liberal democracy. The party in power took advantage of its more than two-thirds majority in parliament to manipulate the constitution. Numerous amendments were made and the provision of a referendum was used to extend the life of parliament in the absence of scheduled elections. Presidential and parliamentary elections held in the late 1980s were conducted under intimidation from both state and anti-state forces. The public service, autonomous at independence, was increasingly used as an instrument of the party in power.

While institutions of liberal democracy came under stress, the increasingly authoritarian government was better able to pursue its agenda which contained a strong economic component. The United National Party that came into office in 1977 promptly initiated a stabilization and liberalization programme under the guidance of the international financial institutions. As the civil conflict, beginning in 1983, sent one set of incentives to the market place, the extremely powerful government sent another.

The changes in the sectoral composition of GDP over the period of the war are better interpreted in light of the government's economic programme implemented virtually during the same period. This economic plan, particularly in the early years, was dominated by a large public investment programme centred around the construction of a massive irrigation project, called the Mahaweli scheme, and a public-housing programme. This agenda explains the rise in investment and construction in the late 1970s and the first half of the 1980s. Similarly, the surge in the trade-related component of GDP can be explained by the trade liberalization and promotion measures undertaken by the government which included the development of a strong new government institution aimed at reducing transaction costs in the trading sector, the Export Development Board.[21] With the need to address macroeconomic imbalances becoming imperative in

---

[21] The Export Development Board's activities included many export promotion programmes such as credit schemes to exporters for export-related investment, duty rebate schemes, and export awards. Its activities were financed by the Treasury and by receipts from particular trade duties.

the 1980s (see Section 3.3), the government scaled back public investment. This would explain not only the relative drop in investment, but also the decline in construction. The levelling off of trade activities at about 21 per cent of GDP probably masks two opposing trends: a slowdown in import activity caused by the curtailment of the government's investment programme[22] and a flourishing of new export trade resulting from the introduction of new liberalization reforms in 1990. Moreover, the fluctuations in foreign direct investment, while in some respects a reaction to civil unrest,[23] also clearly reflect government policy. In 1990, the government began reversing its policy of heavily regulating foreign direct investment. It formulated a package of tax incentives and generous depreciation allowances, as well as decreasing the transaction costs of investment by having a Board of Investment handle all aspects of foreign investment negotiation. These policy changes clearly contributed to the post-1990 surge in foreign investment.

Undeniably, the effects of the dramatic policy changes instituted by the new government are thrown in with the effects of the war. Certainly, the war inhibited the efforts of the government to proceed with the liberalization process in the fashion it would have preferred (see Kelegama 1997). While it is impossible to disentangle entirely the influence of conflict from that of policy, on the basis of both economic evidence and knowledge of the government's empowerment, one can infer that the influence of the policy regime more than offset the influence of the war on the economy *outside the northeast* from the 1980s to 1995. We predicted that the war would harm the economy by making economic transactions more costly and economic relations less predictable. However, the strengthening of the government and its institutions (even when done at the expense of the institutions of liberal democracy), the government's avowed commitment to economic reform, and the support of the international community for the policy proved dominant. In the battle of competing incentives stemming from war and policy change, economic policy appeared to be the more influential.

3.3 *Macroeconomic Imbalances and Development Costs*

Two mechanisms through which one might expect the war to have an impact on the macroeconomic situation are foreign-exchange constraints and government budget deficits. As in the case of uncertainty, an examination of both must seek to separate the influence of war from that of other occurrences.

One of the most obvious ways a war influences foreign-exchange earnings is by hampering a country's export sector. Yet, unlike other foreign-exchange constrained economies at war, Sri Lanka's exports did not plummet during the conflict.[24] Although the

---

[22] Moreover, by the late 1980s, export activity had been dampened because the benefits of the initial devaluation had been eaten away by the appreciation of the exchange rate caused by inflows of foreign capital. See White and Wignaraja (1992).

[23] The surge in FDI beginning in 1990 closely, although not perfectly, coincides with the end of an insurrection led by the JVP—a rural southern-based Sinhalese group which destabilized the southwest for much of the 1987–90 period. In 1990, the government forces finally eradicated the threat, although at a great cost to people's lives and civil liberties.

[24] Nevertheless, in the absence of conflict, greater investment levels would have led to higher exports.

Table 7.7   Sri Lanka: Percentage of total value of exports

	Plantation exports	Industrial exports	Plantation and industrial exports
1978	73	15	88
1983	52	35	87
1988	37	48	85
1991	27	60	87

Source: Derived from *Annual Report on the Economy* (various years).

composition of export earnings changed significantly over the war period (Table 7.7), both the plantation products[25] that dominated export earnings up until the mid-1980s and the industrial exports[26] that later overtook them as Sri Lanka's greatest export earners, were concentrated outside the war area and therefore were relatively isolated from production disruptions. In fact, even after several years of an industrial policy aimed at promoting industrial activities in rural areas, by 1994 only 23 per cent of industries registered under the Ministry of Industrial Development were located outside the Colombo area in the Western Province (Central Bank of Sri Lanka, *Annual Report 1994*: 64).

While total exports declined in absolute value in the mid-1980s, this decline was far more a reflection of poor international tea prices than of decreased tea production.[27] Nevertheless, the conflict did influence export earnings in more indirect ways than disrupting production. For example, the 1985 LTTE threat to poison tea exports was certainly partially responsible for the decline in world prices for Sri Lankan tea in the 1980s. In 1985, the price of Sri Lankan tea was almost exactly equivalent to the average world tea price. Yet by 1986, the Sri Lankan price had dropped by 25 per cent, compared with a world price drop (reflecting Sri Lanka's prices as well) of 16.7 per cent (Sri Lanka Tea Board, Tea Brokers Association of London).

In contrast to the indirect impact of the war on export earnings, hostilities had a profound direct effect on earnings (and consequently employment) generated by the tourism industry in Sri Lanka. After growing by more than 20 per cent per annum between 1978 and 1982, tourism earnings began to drop abruptly after the widely

[25] This was despite the fact that the vast majority of the plantation workers are ethnically Indian Tamil, descendants of those brought by the British from India to work on the estates in the colonial period. But far from being a seat of Tamil opposition, the Indian Tamils have generally supported the UNP after the new constitution it pushed through in 1978 which ensured the Indian Tamils a comparable place in society with other ethnic groups. As relatively recent arrivals to the island, Indian Tamils were hitherto regarded as 'second-class citizens' and were deprived of the vote and equal citizenship.

[26] The rapid growth of the textile and garment industry has been concentrated in the southwest region. This is partially because it is in the Colombo area that Biyagama and Katunayake (the two Export Processing Zones) are located. Furthermore, as much of the investment in this industry is recent, both foreign and domestic investors have limited themselves to the relatively stable southwestern region of the country.

[27] In 1986, Sri Lankan tea was commanding the lowest price in the world resulting in a decline in the value of tea exports of 23% from the previous year. Statistics indicate that tea production showed an upward trend throughout the 1980s despite declining export values.

publicized nationwide ethnic riots in 1983.[28] After declining to 50 per cent of the total number of 1982 visitors in the late 1980s, arrivals began to increase, until 1996, when visitors to Sri Lanka again plummeted by 25 per cent after the bombing of the Central Bank and a commuter train in Colombo. Even if we assume that a very modest pace of growth in tourism would have occurred in the absence of war, the gap between 'counterfactual' foreign earnings from tourism and actual earnings is significant. Assuming that the number of tourist arrivals would have continued to grow at between 5 and 7 per cent from 1982, Kelegama, Tiruchelvam, and Manikawasakar (1995: 20) estimated that the average annual loss to Sri Lanka's tourist industry due to the conflict ranged between US$200 million and US$300 million. This annual loss nearly equals the entire foreign exchange earnings brought in by tea exports in 1982, when tea was the largest export earner.

The conflict also influenced foreign exchange availability by affecting the composition of imports. At times, the government was forced to increase imports of rice due to fluctuations in paddy production. Increased imports of military equipment also consumed foreign exchange resources. A significant rise in remittances from Sri Lankan workers in the Middle East helped finance the new war-related demands as well as the huge imports of capital goods required by the large public-investment programme and the increases in imports anticipated in the wake of liberalization measures. Nevertheless, the country was forced increasingly to rely on foreign savings, swelling the current account deficit.[29] However, these current account difficulties did not initially translate into balance of payment problems or an unwieldy debt burden[30] because of the financial support of the international community. Not only was the sheer volume of aid very large, making Sri Lanka one of the most heavily aided countries in the world, but close to three-quarters of the aid was disbursed on a grant or long-term loan basis (World Bank 1994).

Throughout the 1980s and 1990s, Sri Lanka struggled with large fiscal deficits, aggravated by, although not always entirely due to, the war effort. In the early years of the government's ambitious infrastructure programme before the strife began, government expenditure rose rapidly as revenue declined.[31] Inflation, encouraged by government commercial borrowing as well as import price rises, rose to 26 per cent in 1980. Realizing the economy's position was unsustainable, the government introduced austerity measures[32]

---

[28] Although the unrest has been primarily geographically limited since this time and tourists continue to be generally safe travelling throughout the majority of the island, the general reputation of Sri Lanka abroad is that it is a country experiencing a bloody civil war. This is in part due to the press coverage given to the LTTE and their 'suicide bombers' as well as to a concerted campaign on the part of LTTE operations abroad to dissuade visitors from going to Sri Lanka. Recognizing this, the government hired an American public relations firm to devise a campaign aimed at boosting Sri Lanka's international image as a tourist destination.

[29] The current account deficit averaged 9% of GDP from 1985 to 1989. (World Bank 1994.)

[30] Concern over the debt, while not large by developing country standards, mounted in the 1990s.

[31] Government expenditure rose rapidly to 49% of GDP in 1980 from 43% in the previous year. Revenue declined mostly in response to policy measures which lowered duties paid on exports. (World Bank 1994.)

[32] These measures included a reduction in public investment from 18.3% of GDP in 1980 to 14.6% and 16.7% in 1981 and 1982 respectively. These cuts in capital expenditure largely protected the huge Mahaweli project and the public-sector housing programme at the expense of other development project costs which were cut by 32%. (World Bank 1994.)

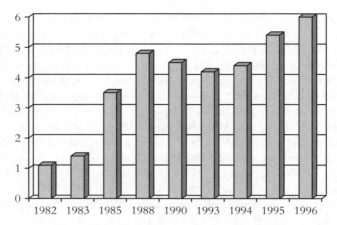

Figure 7.2   Defence expenditures as % of GDP

Sources: Central Bank of Sri Lanka (various years), *Review of the Economy* and *Annual Reports*.

in the early 1980s which could account for a slowdown in growth even apart from the ethnic violence which began in 1983. Although the government reined in the budget deficit considerably, the deficit began to rise again in 1984, this time spurred by increases in defence expenditure (Figure 7.2). The increase in defence and public order expenditure accounted for 40 per cent of the total increase in government expenditure in 1985; in 1987, defence and public order expenditure increased more than three times the rate of the aggregate increase in government expenditure. Military procurement efforts, in late 1995 and 1996 contributed to fiscal deficits near 10 per cent of GDP. Not only should the costs of the war be measured in terms of a bloated deficit which encouraged inflation and scaled back growth, but the war also necessitated large budgetary transfers to public corporations in the northeast, the area of conflict.[33]

In order to increase military expenditures as well as to preserve expenditure on social services,[34] the government adopted a dual strategy. First, the government imposed a defence levy on the population in the mid 1990s, essentially, a tax for the explicit purpose of waging the war. Second, the government chose to decrease absorption by forcing declines in certain types of public investment.[35] In actuality, this trade-off had been occurring since 1986, when expenditure on economic services, which constitutes expenditure on the maintenance and promotion of large development projects, began to decline. Amounting to 14.8 per cent of GDP in 1982, this category of government spending decreased to 9.3 per cent in 1987, and dropped even lower in subsequent years (see Table 7.8). This reduction in economic services was responsible for a decline in

---

[33] Eighty-two per cent of the total budgetary transfers to public corporations during 1987 went to the Sri Lanka Sugar Corporation in the northeast. Central Bank of Sri Lanka, *Annual Report*, 1987.

[34] Decreases in capital expenditures were undertaken not only to protect military expenditures, but also to maintain expenditures in social services. This is examined in the subsequent section.

[35] The government also began to privatize small and medium-size firms, initiated some tax reforms, and continued to liberalize the external payments system. See World Bank (1995), 32–6.

Table 7.8 Sri Lanka: Government expenditure on economic
affairs and services (G_{es}) as a % of GDP

	1982	1983	1984	1985	1986	1987	1988	1989	1990	1991	1992	1993	1994	1995
G_{es}	14.8	12.7	12.6	11.4	11.4	9.3	7.8	7.6	5.3	6.1	4.6	5.6	4.4	5.0

Source: Derived from IMF, *Government Finance Statistics Yearbook* (various years) and IMF *International Financial Statistics* (various years).

capital accumulation and, subsequently, constituted a developmental cost for Sri Lanka. Elsewhere, an estimate of the development costs of the war brought about by the decline in government expenditure on economic services has been attempted using a crowding in model of investment (O'Sullivan 1994). The loss in investment from the first stage of the war, 1983–9, was then translated into a loss in output totalling Rs. 15.6 billion which, at the 1985 exchange rate, was equivalent to US$576 million.[36] This exercise demonstrates the large impact that a seemingly small concession—a decline in government expenditure on economic services—can have on a war economy.

4 Household Impact: Human Welfare Outside the War Region (the Southwest)

This section considers the impact of the war on human welfare outside the war zone using the 'national' statistics available to gauge household well-being in the southwest. As mentioned earlier, these statistics, although ostensibly referring to the country as a whole, rarely incorporated data collected in the northeast after the advent of the conflict. For this reason, we can use 'national' statistics as a good proxy for 'southwestern' statistics. As shown in Tables 7.9 to 7.10, human indicators corresponding to the situation in Sri Lanka's southwest defy expectation by comparing favourably with other countries at war (as well as with other Asian countries and with the averages for all low-income, low-middle income, and middle-income economies). This is true both in terms of the absolute levels of the indicators as well as their trends. For example, both in terms of health and education, Sri Lanka matched the best efforts of two Asian countries, the Philippines and Malaysia, which began the 1970s with levels of human development similar to Sri Lanka's.[37] Moreover, during the period examined Sri Lanka has consistently shown improvement from its own pre-war levels, as a look at income

---

[36] This is not intended to represent the total cost of the war. Samarasinghe estimates that the destruction of capital and lost output as a result of the war from the 1983–8 period is upwards of Rs. 145,000 million or 13% of total GDP during that time.

[37] These statements must be qualified by noting that Sri Lanka actually experienced an absolute decline in the average calories per capita between 1985 and 1990. This is a result of a cutback in the policy of food subsidies instituted in the late 1970s as part of the initial adjustment programme. Instead of direct rice rations, the government distributed coupons to households that were judged to be most in need. The value of these coupons remained nominally constant in the face of high inflation throughout the 1980s, explaining, at least in some part, the decline in average calories consumed. (Edirisinghe 1987.)

Table 7.9 Human indicators of countries at war

Indicator	Sri Lanka				Afghanistan				Ethiopia			
	1975	1985	1991	1997	1975	1985	1991	1997	1980	1985	1990	1997
Life Expectancy*	65/69[a]	69/73[b]	69/74[c]	71/75	40/40[a]	41/42[b]	43/44[f]	45/46	40/44	43/46[b]	44/47	42/44
Infant Mortality Rate†	41[a]	23[b]	19[c]	14	183[a]	170[b]	160[f]	151	155	132[b]	124	107
Adult Literacy Rate (%)*	90/76	92/82	93/85[c]	94/88	25/4	35/8	40/11[c]	48/18	28/11	32/15	36/20	41/29
Gross Primary School Enrolment Ratio (%)*	81/74	104/101	109/106	110/108[d]	44/8	27/13	34/19	64/32[c]	48/27	45/30	39/26	48/27[c]
Gross Secondary School Enrolment Ratio (%)*	47/49	60/66	70/77	72/78[e]	13/2	11/5	18/9	32/11[c]	12/7	15/10	16/13	13/10[c]

Indicator	Mozambique				Uganda			
	1980	1985	1990	1997	1980	1985	1990	1997
Life Expectancy*	42/46	42/45[b]	42/45	44/47	48/49	48/49[b]	46/47	43/42
Infant Mortality Rate†	145	136[b]	150	135	116	116[b]	104	99
Adult Literacy Rate (%)*	44/12	44/14	49/18	57/25	60/31	65/37	69/43	75/53
Gross Primary School Enrolment Ratio (%)*	109/81[g]	99/76	77/57	70/50[e]	56/43	82/67[h]	83/66	81/68[e]
Gross Secondary School Enrolment Ratio (%)*	8/3	10/5	10/6	9/6[e]	7/3	13/7	17/10	15/9[e]

* Male/Female.
† Refers to deaths per 1,000 live births.
[a] 1977, not 1975.
[b] 1987, not 1985.
[c] 1990, not 1991.
[d] 1996, not 1997.
[e] 1995, not 1997.
[f] 1992, not 1991.
[g] 1981, not 1980.
[h] 1986, not 1985.

Source: World Bank (1999), *World Development Indicators CD-ROM.*

Table 7.10 Human indicators of Sri Lanka compared with other Asian countries

Indicator	Sri Lanka				Malaysia				Philippines			
	1975	1985	1991	1997	1975	1985	1990	1997	1975	1985	1990	1997
Life Expectancy*	65/69[a]	69/73[b]	69/74[c]	71/75	64/67[a]	68/72[b]	68/73	70/75	58/62[a]	62/66[b]	64/67	67/70
Infant Mortality Rate†	41[a]	23[b]	19[c]	14	34[a]	17[b]	16	11	108[a]	45[b]	42	35
Adult Literacy Rate (%)*	90/76	92/82	93/85[c]	94/88	76/55	84/69	87/75	90/81	88/85	92/90	93/92	95/94
Gross Primary School Enrolment Ratio (%)*	81/74	104/101	109/106	110/108[d]	92/89	101/100	94/94	101/103[d]	na	108/107	115/110[f]	109/100[g]
Gross Secondary School Enrolment Ratio (%)*	47/49	60/66	70/77	72/78[c]	46/38	53/53	55/58	57/65[d]	na	64/65	74/73[f]	77/78[d]

Indicator	India				Nepal			
	1975	1985	1990	1997	1975	1985	1990	1997
Life Expectancy*	53/52[a]	58/58[b]	59/60	62/64	47/45[a]	53/51[b]	54/53	58/57
Infant Mortality Rate†	129[a]	97	80	71	142[a]	109[b]	101	83
Adult Literacy Rate (%)*	52/21	59/29	62/37	67/39	34/5	43/10	48/14	56/21
Gross Primary School Enrolment Ratio (%)*	94/62	111/80	110/84	109/90[d]	86/16	108/50	132/81	127/90[b]
Gross Secondary School Enrolment Ratio (%)*	36/16	48/26	55/53	59/39[d]	23/4	38/12	46/20	50/25[i]

* Male/Female.
† Refers to deaths per 1,000 births.
[a] 1977, not 1975.
[b] 1987, not 1985.
[c] 1990, not 1991.
[d] 1996, not 1997.
[e] 1995, not 1997.
[f] 1989, not 1990.
[g] 1993, not 1997.
[h] 1994, not 1997.
[i] 1992, not 1997.

Source: World Bank 1999, *World Development Indicators CD-ROM*.

Table 7.11   Income poverty in Sri Lanka*

Measure	1985–6	1990–1
Reference poverty line: Rs. 471 per person per month		
Headcount index	27.33	22.36
Poverty gap index	6.54	4.82
Squared poverty gap index	2.31	1.62
Reference poverty line: Rs. 565 per person per month		
Headcount index	40.60	35.34
Poverty gap index	11.09	8.80
Squared poverty gap index	4.30	3.20

Notes: The headcount index measures the incidence of poverty; the poverty gap index measures the 'depth' of poverty; the squared poverty gap index measures the 'severity' of poverty. See n. 38.

   * Data exclude the Northern and Eastern provinces.

Source: World Bank (1995), *Sri Lanka Poverty Assessment*: 7.

poverty in the country confirms. Table 7.11 reveals that not only the *incidence* of poverty in Sri Lanka, but also the *depth* and *severity*[38] of it, decreased considerably from 1985–6 to 1990–1 despite the pressures of the war. Understandably, one wonders how Sri Lanka was not only able to maintain high human indicators outside the war zone, but also to improve them during wartime. The following analysis examines how household entitlements, and therefore human welfare, were maintained in the face of conflict.

4.1   Market Entitlements

In order for the stagnation in private consumption between 1985 and 1990 (Table 7.12) to be compatible with the notable declines in income poverty, a significant redistribution of wealth must have occurred during this period. Nationwide Gini coefficients —improving from 0.32 in 1985–6 to 0.30 in 1990–1—confirm this.[39] Moreover, a sectoral analysis revealed that the decline in the incidence of poverty was attributable largely to diminishing poverty in the rural sector. Rural poverty decreased following a rise in consumption together with a notable decrease in inequality. In contrast, the urban sector experienced an absolute decline in consumption and relatively little redistribution—bringing about an increase in urban poverty over the same period (World Bank 1995).

   [38] The incidence of poverty is the proportion of those people living beneath the poverty line in terms of straightforward consumption statistics; the depth of poverty accounts for how far people are from the poverty line; the severity of poverty refers to an indicator which gives greater weight to the poor the further away their consumption is from the poverty line.
   [39] Incidentally, these Gini coefficients are on par with other South Asian countries and generally compare favourably to other developing countries.

Table 7.12 Real annual growth of private consumption and GDP per capita (%)

	Consumption per capita (CPI deflator)	Consumption per capita (GDP deflator)
1953–65	0.6	0.4
1965–70	4.0	5.3
1970–7	7.4	2.6
1977–85	5.3	4.6
1985–90	0.0	1.4
1990–3	1.7	2.3

Source: World Bank (1995), *Sri Lanka Poverty Assessment*: 5.

Growth in consumption in rural areas during these years seems consistent with available information about agricultural wages and employment (World Bank 1995: 10). Yet reasons for improved distribution of rural consumption require more detailed analysis.[40] Certainly one possibility is the influence of government programmes, most notably Janasaviya, a scheme involving cash transfers to households in the hope that they would redirect some expenditure into training or entrepreneurial activities, thereby allowing families to 'exit poverty'. Whether Janasaviya achieved its aims is a matter for debate and further study.[41] However, for the purpose of explaining why distribution of rural consumption became more equitable from 1985–6 to 1990–1, Janasaviya holds some clues. Although the programme only started in 1989, by December 1990, it is possible that over 11 per cent of rural households,[42] the poorest ones at that, were receiving cash benefits of Rs. 1,458 (approximately three times the poverty line for individuals) per household per month. This would have had a notable impact on the distribution of consumption, leading to a lessening of rural poverty.

Market entitlements in the 1990–3 period are harder to analyse given the lack of data. Nevertheless, established growth in consumption levels was most likely accompanied by a more equitable distribution of consumption given that growth was driven by labour-intensive industries (World Bank 1995: 11). A large percentage of these new employment opportunities were in garment manufacturing, a sector which flourished partly as a result of liberalization measures, but also because of active government encouragement. In particular, the government-promoted 200 Garment Factory Programme

[40] The World Bank suggests that the new patterns of distribution may have to do with the breakdown of private transfers or with a changing propensity to save. (World Bank 1995: 10.)

[41] Mr Susil Sirivardana, former commissioner of the Janasaviya programme, points out the wide coverage of the scheme, the creation of private assets and personal savings, and communities sense of self-sufficiency when speaking of the successes of Janasaviya. (S. Sirivardana, interview by author, Sri Lanka, November 1995). On the other hand, the World Bank is less confident about the results of the programme. (World Bank 1995: 71–3.)

[42] By the end of 1990, Janasaviya was disbursing cash grants to over 230,000 of the poorest households (or 8 per cent of the total) in the southwest. As poverty in Sri Lankan is largely a rural phenomenon, we can assume these households were disproportionately rural.

(GFP) helped support job creation in this sector. Intended to bring industrialization and employment opportunities to rural areas,[43] the 200 GFP offered numerous incentives, including guaranteed garment export quotas, to those who opened new garment factories providing employment to more than 500 workers. The attractiveness of the incentive package varied inversely with the remoteness of the factory location.[44] While there has been some controversy over the 200 GFP's impact on the viability of the manufacturing sector given the anticipated phasing out of export quotas (see Kelegama 1994), the effect of this programme on employment is undeniable. In its first year, from 1992 to 1993, the number of employees in the garment sector increased by almost 50 per cent from 159,400 to 230,000 (Kelegama 1994: 18). This type of government-sponsored employment creation seems certain to have decreased poverty further during the 1990–3 period.

4.2   Public Entitlements

Although Sri Lanka's historical commitment to universal access to health and education services must be considered when assessing current human indicators, the country's impressive performance over this period suggests that public entitlements were pre-served in areas outside the war zone throughout the period of social turbulence. An examination of government expenditure indicated that while other countries at war were forced to curtail their spending on health and education services, Sri Lanka main-tained health and social expenditure during the wartime period under consideration here in excess of pre-war levels (Table 7.13).[45] The increasing proportion of GDP devoted to public social spending represents absolute expenditure increases in outlays given the positive growth rate of real GDP over the war years.

How did Sri Lanka maintain these expenditure levels in the face of war? The answer partly lies in Sri Lanka's increasing GDP together with an increasing ratio of revenue to GDP, which sustained revenue significantly above pre-war 1982 levels. Still, this cannot account fully for the increase in social expenditures as defence and public order expenditures soared, averaging close to 4.5 per cent of GDP in the first half of the 1990s (compared to 1.0 per cent in 1982). A rising deficit forced the government to cut spend-ing in the late 1980s and 1990s. However, while the government chose to preserve increases in defence and public order spending, it also sought to protect spending on health, education, social security and welfare. Additional resources to maintain these priorities were freed up by a decline in government expenditure on economic services as discussed earlier.

---

[43] The emphasis on rural areas is a response to the unemployed youth unrest that lay behind the 1987–90 JVP insurrection.

[44] This incentive structure was created to encourage the opening of factories in the more remote areas where unemployment was more acute.

[45] It should be noted that expenditure on public entitlements, particularly in welfare spending (reflective of spending on food rations) suffered significant reductions with the initiation of the liberalization and adjust-ment programmes in the late 1970s. So while government expenditure in many areas rose from pre-war (1982) levels, in many cases it still reflects a cutback from levels in the mid-1970s.

Table 7.13 Sri Lanka: Government expenditure as percentage of GDP

Year	Health	Education	Social security welfare	Defence	Public order	Defence and public order	Economic services	Housing
1982	1.17	2.95	3.63	0.49	0.48	0.97	14.8	na
1986	1.25	2.80	2.94	2.42	1.00	3.42	11.4	0.57
1989	1.84	3.03	3.88	1.82	1.48	3.30	7.6	0.44
1990	1.53	2.78	3.73	2.69	2.05	4.74	5.3	0.29
1993	1.41	2.81	4.25	3.08	1.07	4.15	5.6	0.22
1995[a]	1.66	2.85	5.11	4.12	1.10	5.22	5.0	0.58

[a] Provisional.

Sources: Derived from IMF *Government Finance Statistics Yearbook* (various years), and IMF *International Financial Statistics* (various years).

While aggregate expenditure on health and education confirms that Sri Lanka protected spending on public entitlements, the composition of spending in these sectors reveals how efficiently and equitably this expenditure was distributed. In the case of education, we find expenditure was increasingly concentrated in the primary and secondary sectors over the war period;[46] spending on university education as a percentage of total educational expenditure declined steadily throughout the war period. A further breakdown of expenditure on university education illustrates that recurrent university spending was maintained or increased while capital expenditure was severely cut (University Grants Commission, various years). So while overall education spending was channelled towards maintaining the universal free primary and secondary education that generated high literacy rates and average years of schooling across socio-economic levels, it was done so at a longer-term cost for development.

Of course, achievements in education have spillover benefits for public health. The combination of well-educated mothers, Sri Lanka's network of easily accessible health institutions, and the wide dissemination of information through the media has kept the country's mortality rates low. Yet, recent evidence pointing to little improvement in the incidence of morbidity from preventable diseases possibly reflects a poor allocation of resources within the health sector throughout the war period (World Bank 1995: 57). Instead of focusing spending on preventive health care and primary-level facilities, Sri Lanka's health budget during the 1980s exhibited contrary trends. While capital health expenditure has not been neglected, it has been overwhelmingly concentrated in the higher-level sectors. Other expenditure choices—such as cutbacks in government spending on housing—may also have negative implications for public health.

[46] The World Bank argues for even greater efficiency in educational expenditure in Sri Lanka, criticizing the allocation of funds for university education—although decreasing as a percentage of expenditure on total education—for rising too quickly (given that overall education expenditure is rising). (World Bank 1995: 52–3.)

4.3 Civic Entitlements

The role of non-governmental organizations (NGOs) and informal networks in sustaining household entitlements is also significant despite widespread government involvement.[47] It is estimated that close to 30,000 NGOs operate in Sri Lanka. Many of these are community level groups, approximately 300 are domestic NGOs claiming multiple branches nationwide, and dozens more are branches of international institutions (World Bank 1995: 129). Sometimes an NGO works with the government to complement public entitlements as was the case with a joint government/UNICEF/WHO immunization programme. Despite the poor allocation of government expenditure within the health sector, this programme enabled the country to make impressive progress in one of the most important areas of preventive health care during the period that the civil conflict intensified. Most often, domestic NGOs work independently of the government to supplement market and public entitlements by providing functions ranging from financial services to maternal health care.

While the involvement of NGOs in the southwest is significant, they are not the only civil institutions supplementing household entitlements. Like many other Asian societies, the family network is an invaluable support structure in Sri Lanka, and there is evidence that this support is both substantial and widespread. In fact, it was estimated that in the mid-1980s, 87 per cent of unemployed males and 96 per cent of unemployed females were supported by their families, often for long periods of time (Department of Census and Statistics, 1988). Similarly, poor households whose heads are disabled, elderly, or widowed would not be able to survive on government transfers to the destitute poor alone as these transfers would only raise household income to one-tenth of the poverty line (World Bank 1995: 71). Clearly, these households must have additional ways of boosting their entitlements, most likely through the support of relatives.

5 Household Impact: Human Welfare inside the War Zone

Evaluating human welfare inside the war zone is clearly a more challenging task than assessing welfare in peaceful areas. Less information is available and it is harder to verify; human indicators that do exist are less reliable; informal mechanisms are more important in stabilizing society. Despite these difficulties, it is possible to establish how people's private economic activities have altered and providers of non-market entitlements have changed.

Although the region of military activity in Sri Lanka is the northeast, the situation in the Northern Province differs significantly from that in the Eastern Province.[48] Within the Northern Province, a distinction must be made between the Jaffna district and the Wanni, a term which, loosely defined, refers to most of the combined Northern districts of Mullaitivu, Kilinochchi, Vavuniya, and Mannar. Control of the Wanni has

---

[47] See Van Brabant (1997a) for a history of NGOs in Sri Lanka.
[48] Districts in the Northern Province include: Jaffna District, Vavuniya, Kilinochchi, and Mannar. Districts in the Eastern Province include: Ampara, Trincomalee, Batticaloa. The two provinces were joined under the treaty with India in 1987.

often been split, with the government claiming influence over Vavuniya town and points south, as well as some isolated strongholds, and the LTTE dominating much of the jungle and northern towns.[49] In contrast, large parts of Jaffna District had been almost exclusively under the control of the LTTE from 1990 until November 1995. Because of this, beginning in 1990, the government used its armed forces to blockade Jaffna from the rest of the island.[50] Not only were virtually all connections with the rest of the country severed, but there were strict limitations on the type of commodities—from fuel to umbrellas—allowed into the district (Tamil Information Centre 1993: 21). In contrast, the Eastern Province, for much of the war period, was not under exclusive command of either the government or LTTE forces. While some war-induced shortages were not uncommon, no official blockade of the east existed at any time. Naturally, these varying ground situations influenced the areas' respective economic situations and households' ability to maintain their entitlements. For this reason, the different regions must be examined separately. Given that the majority of the population of the Northern Province resided in Jaffna district before the recent government offensives, our look at the north will be confined to Jaffna, with occasional references to the Wanni.

5.1   *The Northern Province: Jaffna District*

Although there are some significant discrepancies among sources reporting human indicators for Jaffna, we can often use government figures and Tamil estimates to define the probable limits within which the reality lies. In this way, it is possible to get an approximation of the infant mortality rate (IMR) in Jaffna. While Jaffna had by far the lowest rate of Sri Lanka's 24 districts in the 1970s, it began to increase slowly with the onset of conflict in the mid-1980s, and more dramatically in the 1990s after the blockade became effective. Estimates for 1993 vary from 33 to 41 deaths per 1,000 live births (Sivarajah 1994: 41, tables 9–11). Nevertheless, if we take the higher estimate, which is almost double Jaffna's IMR of 1974, it still compares favourably to other countries at war, and even to other Asian and developing countries in general.

Statistics on immunization coverage by district allow us to examine the absolute levels and trends in vaccination rates in the Northern Province (Table 7.14). In 1990, immunization coverage in this area was close to national averages, yet by 1994 there was a significant decline in the rates for Jaffna, which both doctors and NGO workers agreed was probably a reflection of how the statistics were collected, rather than a significant decrease in coverage.[51] Yet, even if we reject this interpretation and contend

---

[49] Continuous battles have frequently changed the military landscape since 1995, after which these characterizations are not as accurate.

[50] While the embargo was officially imposed in August 1991, Tamil sources claim it was effectively imposed in 1990.

[51] As the rates are based on the number of births in the district, a declining rate in Jaffna could reflect the reality that more people in the surrounding areas of the north are coming to Jaffna to deliver their children. This is likely as health facilities in Jaffna have been maintained in comparison with many facilities in other parts of the Northern Province. This interpretation would be consistent with the dramatic increases in immunization coverage in the rest of the north (Vavuniya) as well as serving to explain decline in the percentage of those vaccinated in Colombo.

Table 7.14   Immunization coverage by district, 1990 and 1994
(percentage of one-year-old children and pregnant women immunized)

District	B. C. G. vaccine		Diphtheria pertussis and tetanus vaccine		Oral polio vaccine		Measles vaccine		Pregnant women immunized with tetanus toxoid vaccine	
	1990	1994	1990	1994	1990	1994	1990	1994	1990	1994
Colombo	103	68	84	61	84	65	72	57	53	49
Northern Province:										
Jaffna	86	77	81	66	81	65	78	64	59	66
Vavuniya	29	95	32	84	30	79	26	73	22	62
Eastern Province:										
Batticaloa	50	92	34	88	34	88	34	70	19	94
Ampara	25	58	23	64	23	65	20	60	15	41
Trincomalee	84	115	59	106	56	106	56	112	58	137
Sri Lanka	84	86	86	88	86	88	80	84	58	79

Note: Jaffna includes Kilinochchi district. Vavuniya includes Mannar and Mullaitivu districts. For some districts, the immunization coverage is over 100%. This discrepancy is caused by population movements between districts which may cause the number of children immunized in one district to be greater than the actual number of births in that district.

Source: Ministry of Finance, Planning, Ethnic Affairs and National Integration and the UNICEF (1995), *Progress Towards Mid-Decade Goals in Sri Lanka*: 51.

that the trend was downward in Jaffna, absolutely, vaccination statistics suggest that the level of coverage was still more comprehensive in Jaffna than in Colombo.

Undergraduate university admissions statistics are the most revealing of the human indicators regarding education. Tamils in Jaffna have long placed an emphasis on education. The historical success of the Tamils in attaining university places on merit, and the subsequent legislation introduced to curtail their admittance, have been issues of conflict between the Sinhalese and the Tamils for decades. Today, we can look at the success of students in the north in securing university places *on merit* as a reflection of the quality of primary and secondary education in the district (Table 7.15).[52] In the Jaffna district, while 30 per cent of all students nationwide admitted under the merit quota were from Jaffna in 1982 (despite the fact that Jaffna pupils only comprised 6 per cent of the nation's total students), this number had dropped to 15 per cent by 1991–2. Yet even with this decline, students entering university in 1991–2 on merit were three times as likely to be from Jaffna as mere district/student ratios would suggest. Moreover, next to Colombo, Jaffna remained the district with by far the largest number of merit entrances (University Grants Commission, various years).

[52] The Sri Lankan system of university admissions involves three components: a district quota which is linked to the district's population as a percentage of national population, a merit quota which absorbs the students exhibiting the best performance regardless of their district of origin, and a disadvantaged quota which makes special provisions for students coming from districts that are regarded as having inferior educational facilities. Given these three categories of admission, the merit entrances are the best reflection of the performance of the students and, therefore, of the quality of their schools.

Table 7.15 University entrants from Jaffna District

	1982–3	% Sri Lankan Total 1982–3	1988–9	% Sri Lankan Total 1988–9	1992	% Sri Lankan Total 1991–2
Total number	647	12.7	452	8.8	963	12.2
University students admitted by merit from Jaffna	419	30.0	270	18.1	586	15.1
Number of university students admitted by district quota from Jaffna	228	6.2	182	5.0	377	9.4
Percentage of Sri Lanka's high school students from Jaffna		6.0		5.1		5.1

Source: University Grants Commission (various years), *Statistics on Higher Education in Sri Lanka*.

Unquestionably, the situation suggested by human indicators for the early 1990s, while certainly worse than the high standards enjoyed in Jaffna in the 1970s and early 1980s, remained far superior to that found in other war zones. Although the trends of indicators in the Northern Province were downward, in many cases their absolute level, remarkably, was comparable to indicators for the nation overall. Not to belittle the deterioration that occurred or to suggest that the suffering there has not been significant,[53] the question still arises, 'Why are these figures not worse'? Their maintenance, even at deteriorated levels, indicates that the decline in human welfare was somehow mitigated. How was this the case in a situation of war and economic blockade? The following sections, by exploring what happened to entitlements, sheds light on this question.

5.1.1 *Market entitlements*

Due to the war, many Jaffna residents who were formerly gainfully employed lost their primary source of income. The vast majority of Jaffna's 65,000 cultivators were forced to abandon their fields once the economic embargo took effect (Tamil Information Centre 1993: 5). Although the army did occupy some agricultural areas, the main reason for the dramatic reduction in the area cultivated was the lack of fuel for irrigating,[54] ploughing, harvesting, and transporting crops. Essential fertilizers used in the rest of the island were not available to the Jaffna farmer because of the ban on chemicals. Similarly, the district's fishermen, estimated to support 25,000 families at one time, lost their livelihood when the implementation of a security zone prohibited fishing.

---

[53] The Medical Institute of Tamils (1994) estimates that as of 1994 in Jaffna alone close to 8,000 civilians have been killed and 2,600 maimed for life. This number represents deaths before the governments wresting of Jaffna from the LTTE in 1995/6 and the nearly continuous fighting that followed. This human misery is compounded by large numbers of semi-permanent refugees: in Jaffna there were recently estimated to be over 250,000 displaced people living with friends and family or in 'welfare centres' even before the resurgence of fighting displaced thousands upon thousands more.

[54] Very little land in Jaffna is cultivable without some sort of man-made irrigation system. Most water pumps in Jaffna were electrically operated.

Although some continued to fish illegally, many fishing families were forced to live in welfare centres (Manickavasagar 1994: 12).

The economic blockade, by banning or placing strict limits on the entrance of building materials, fuel, vehicles, and all sorts of machinery into Jaffna, caused countless small factories and workshops to shut, rendering more than 11,000 skilled workers unemployed (ibid). Not only did large state industries suffer, but local industries that complemented fishing and agriculture ground to a halt. The blockade meant that all but the most well–connected traders were put out of business. Professionals, who used to comprise 10 per cent of Jaffna's population, figured highly among those who left the district for abroad or other parts of Sri Lanka.

In the face of the destruction of long–standing employment opportunities, some residents of Jaffna maintained important sources of income while others developed entirely new ones. Surprisingly, even when Jaffna remained firmly under LTTE control, the Sri Lankan central government was still the major employer and most important source of income in the Jaffna district. The government paid the monthly tax-free wages[55] of approximately 5,200 teachers and close to 1,000 people working at Jaffna Teaching Hospital as well as paying pensions to over 18,000 Jaffna pensioners (Hodson 1995). The total amount of government wages, salaries, and pensions paid to people in LTTE controlled areas in the Northern Province was said to equal Rs. 753 million in 1992 (US$15 million), with 80 per cent of this going to the Jaffna district.[56] Furthermore, the Ceylon Electricity Board and Sri Lanka Telecom continued to pay their former employees, although for years there was neither electricity or telecom-munications in Jaffna. In 1993 alone, these two organizations reportedly paid 317 people in Jaffna a total of Rs. 15 million (US$300,000) (Ceylon Electricity Board, Sri Lanka Telecom).

The LTTE itself became an important source of employment, not only for armed combatants, but to many others in 'non–military' positions.[57] Besides payments made to families of the LTTE, the LTTE paid salaries to its own civil service workers who staffed courts, police stations, health posts, and administration offices. Specialized LTTE organizations, beyond providing employment themselves, opened new avenues to earn income. The most prominent example of such an organization is the Tamil Eelam Economic Development Organization (TEEDO), the economic wing of the LTTE. Said to have had a budget of Rs. 250 million (approximately US$50 million) collected from Tamil expatriates, TEEDO is reported to have employed 1,500 paid workers and

[55] Ironically, while the government did not tax the wages it disbursed in Jaffna, the LTTE did tax these people.

[56] Estimates made from reports from the Education Ministry, Pensions Department, Ministry of Health, Government of Sri Lanka Budget Estimates.

[57] One of the main source of funds used by the LTTE to pay employees and run programmes is contribu-tions from abroad. Foreign Minister Laksham Kadirgamar said that he had been informed that as much as US$3–4m. was being raised by the LTTE in Canada a month while £250,000 were collected a month in Britain (Reuters News Service, courtesy of SLNet, 14 June 1996). The LTTE also relied heavily on taxes of all kinds (dowry taxes, sales taxes, transportation taxes) as well as transfers from India. The United States State Department (1995) reported indications that some Tamil communities have been involved in narcotics smuggling, possibly adding to LTTE coffers.

6,000 volunteers (Srishnamugarajah 1994: 10). The Industrial Development Organization, the arm of TEEDO charged with 'formulating industrial policy for Eelam', played a role in developing new industries and in supplying raw materials to remaining industries.[58] Through TEEDO, the LTTE encouraged the diversification of crops and the invention of technologies to overcome supply shortages.[59]

Unquestionably, remittances from abroad and transfers from other parts of Sri Lanka constituted an invaluable source of income for Jaffna residents. Sri Lankan banks played a significant role in moving these remittances, although they are unwilling to provide information on the extent of the inflows. The Tamil Information Centre in London estimated that there were approximately 400,000 Tamils living abroad (with close to half living in India), and surmised that the majority sent some sort of remittances back to Jaffna. Although it is impossible to appraise the value of these inflows, some sources have estimated that they could reach tens of millions of US dollars each year.

Several Tamil sources estimated that the majority of families in Jaffna city had some form of income from government transfers, LTTE salaries or handouts, and/or remittances. Even so, there were many without a direct share of one of these resources or some other form of direct employment (such as in services). Nevertheless, while the war made many more conventional professions redundant, it created opportunities in the informal economy which enabled some to make a living. The blockade created shortages, allowing some to profit from smuggling and hawking goods. Others stayed alive by charging commissions for services such as waiting in queues and cashing salary checks or by collecting fees for typing letters to the government demanding compensation.[60] Still more gained from the lack of fuel which forced people to rely on alternative modes of transportation.

In assessing market entitlements, it is important not only to examine sources of income, but also to establish whether goods—particularly food—were available for purchase. Trade between Jaffna and the rest of the country began to suffer in the mid-1980s due to increased risks of transporting stock (Seabright 1986), but was virtually halted after the imposition of the government blockade. As most internal industrial and agricultural production was also suspended, food and other consumer commodities became scarce.

However, after the government imposed the blockade, it provided the Northern Province with shipments of food and essential items under the guidance of the Commissioner of Essential Services. While humanitarian concerns surely played some part in the motivation behind this massive relief effort to meet people's basic needs, the operation was also a concerted effort to win and maintain a modicum of credibility with the Tamil people. Moreover, international politics undoubtedly influenced the government's

---

[58] These industries include sweets and soft drinks manufacturing, natural curation of leather, and salt pans. (A. Arudpragasam, former head of the LTTE Industrial Development Organisation, interview by author, Sri Lanka, October 1995). Interestingly, Mr Arudpragasam reported constant battles with the military wing of LTTE over resources.

[59] Some of these inventions include radios which could be operated by sewing machines and vehicles which run on kerosene and vegetable oil.

[60] Reuters, courtesy of SLNet, June 1996.

domestic policy. India, as it claims a large Tamil population itself, has long been entan-
gled in Sri Lankan politics, either directly or indirectly. From providing safe havens and
military training bases in south India for Sri Lankan Tamil militants to sending an Indian
Peacekeeping Force to the island from 1987–90, India has been an important actor in Sri
Lanka's conflict. Although state-sponsored Indian intervention declined dramatically
after the assassination of Rajiv Gandhi—commonly attributed to the LTTE—calls
across the Palk Strait to mitigate the suffering of Tamils in Sri Lanka have been taken
seriously by the Sri Lankan government.

   Whatever the motivation behind its actions, the government has remained unique
in its commitment to prop up the entitlements of people living in enemy-controlled
territory. It aimed to achieve this by supplying shipments of rice, sugar, milk powder,
kerosene, and some agricultural inputs to multipurpose cooperatives (MPCs) in the
north. Displaced people were supplied with coupons which allowed them to secure
free rations at the MPCs while the rest of the population was allowed to purchase the
items at a price equivalent to the Colombo price plus shipping costs. The government
claimed to supply around 65 per cent of the food requirement for Jaffna through these
channels. In 1993, the government maintained that in Jaffna alone it supplied over
Rs. 700 million (US$15 million) in essential items. In addition to direct government
supplies, the Commissioner of Essential Services authorized boats to carry shipments
for private traders to Jaffna. The market value of food and other goods supplied by these
traders in 1993 was over Rs. 800 million (US$17 million).[61]

   There are several important things to note about this transfer of commodities from
the government and sanctioned private traders to LTTE areas. First, the scarcity of
essential goods in the north caused primarily by the economic blockade opened up
opportunities for enormous profit to anyone engaged in trading with the north. Allega-
tions of corruption involving government officials and army officers overseeing the
shipment of these goods were rampant, although difficult to confirm. Second, delays in
the shipments were inevitable. The Tamil Information Centre, given information by
the Jaffna Citizens Committee, claimed that much of the food sent by the government
did not reach the north, particularly in times of major conflict between the LTTE and
the army. Lastly, these shipments run by the government greatly benefited the LTTE.
The Tigers were said to demand one-third of every private shipment landing in Jaffna,
although it is unclear whether they were paying a nominal price for the goods or considering their appropriation a tax. Also, the MPCs in Jaffna, although not under direct
LTTE control, were heavily influenced by the organization. The LTTE was able to
direct the disbursement of food as well as to buy food directly from the MPCs to use
for their cadres or for resale later. Beyond the obvious benefits of having access to food
supplies, the government's relief programme released the LTTE from the obligation of
fully providing for the population under its control. Although, in relinquishing much
of this effort to the government, the LTTE forwent some opportunities to solidify support, the government relief programme allowed the LTTE to focus its efforts on fighting the war.

---

[61] Commissioner of Essential Services.

In addition to government efforts, the LTTE played an important role in maintaining the availability of commodities in Jaffna through its smuggling networks. It is said that any item banned by the blockade could be secured through the LTTE, although often at an exorbitant price. An estimated two-thirds of the supply of rice to the Jaffna peninsula came from the other districts in the north and was controlled by the LTTE. Other items were smuggled in from the rest of the country at night. Moreover, supplies from south India reportedly continued to play a large role in providing LTTE areas with food, fuel, and even medicine. While the support from India was on a grand scale in the 1980s, even after its decline in the 1990s, certain groups and individuals in India continued to provide key resources and links to the outside world to the militants in Sri Lanka. The extent of the LTTE's involvement in controlling supplies could be seen in 1995 when difficulties between the LTTE, the central government, and International Committee of the Red Cross prevented the shipment of food to the north for several months. Despite the absence of government supplies, the price of rice remained close to Rs. 30 per kilo, compared to Rs. 17 in Colombo (Hodson 1995: 5). The LTTE was also heavily involved in distributing supplies. In doing so, it influenced the distribution of wealth by engaging in discretionary pricing of food. Better-off families often paid steep prices for food while the poor, and families of LTTE cadre, would receive food at no cost.

5.1.2 *Public entitlements*

Government educational institutions in the north came under serious stress, particularly due to lack of facilities. The Tamil Information Centre estimates that as many as 79 of the original 561 primary and secondary schools in Jaffna district were damaged by the fighting and another 100 were occupied by the army at some point in the last decade (Tamil Information Centre 1993: 11). Shortages of school supplies and the lack of electricity decreased student productivity. The University of Jaffna suffered even more severe problems with facilities: blockade restrictions on computers, chemicals, electrical equipment, printing paper, and similar equipment hampered teaching as well as halting research efforts. Given this situation, it was difficult for the university to retain academic staff, adding to the cycle of underutilization.

Certainly, educational standards suffered under such strains, a grievous occurrence for a people who greatly value education. Yet, it is remarkable that these government institutions continued to function at all in an area almost entirely under the domination of a group against whom the government was waging a long, bloody war. As of August 1995, 186,000 primary and secondary students were enrolled in 485 government schools in Jaffna (Hodson 1995: 6). Moreover, the government annually made provision for Jaffna school students to take the Sri Lankan equivalent of the A-level exams.[62] Although the physical facilities of schools were poor, a higher percentage of teachers in Jaffna had either teacher training or university qualifications than in any other district in Sri Lanka outside the Western Province (Colombo area). At the tertiary level, the

---

[62] Although the government does make these arrangements, the Tamil Information Centre complains that exams are often disrupted. (Tamil Information Centre 1993: 11.)

government continued to fund the University of Jaffna and its 2,500 students (although expenditure was primarily recurrent) despite the increasing influence of the LTTE on the institution. (University Grants Commission, various years). Officials from the University Grants Commission in Colombo asserted that the standards of university education were maintained by relying on external examiners, although privately some northeastern academics admitted that this process was open to political manipulation.

The strains on public health and government health institutions resulting from the war were even more severe than in the education sector. The impact of the economic blockade on public health can be seen directly in some instances. The mortality rate rose due to the increasing incidence of malaria (a reflection of bans on mosquito-killing sprays) and the lack of antibiotics and rabies vaccines. Shortages of psychiatric drugs, anaesthetics, painkillers, oxygen, medical equipment, and generators were acute. Staff vacancies at Jaffna Teaching Hospital were estimated in 1995 to be close to 40 per cent and concentrated in the more skilled levels; whereas in the mid-1980s there were six surgeons, in 1995 there was only one. These constraints, coupled with significant war-related increases in health care needs—both physical and psychiatric—obstructed health practitioners from effectively treating those requiring medical attention.[63]

Still, the continuation of government health services in Tiger-held territory was impressive. The main health facility in the Northern Province, the Jaffna Teaching Hospital, functioned almost continuously throughout the period of investigation with the support of government funds, although at a very basic level. While the condition of health institutions in Jaffna were unsatisfactory by any standard and government expenditure on medical supplies for Jaffna Hospital was significantly below that of other government teaching hospitals nationwide, the continued application of some government resources enabled a dedicated staff to maintain at least a basic structure of health services during the time in question.

5.1.3 Civic entitlements

Certainly, the government was surprisingly involved in maintaining both the market and public entitlements of those living in LTTE-controlled Jaffna, beyond what we would expect to find in a war situation. Nevertheless, continued government involvement cannot explain fully the sustenance of household entitlements relative to other war zones. The importance of civil institutions in Jaffna rose after the onset of the conflict. While the role of the family was considered earlier, this section will concentrate on three types of civic institutions—international NGOs, independent local organizations, and LTTE-affiliated organizations—which became essential in bolstering dwindling household entitlements in Jaffna.

In the first half of the 1990s the international NGOs working in Jaffna played several critical roles in easing the hardships associated with war. Perhaps most importantly, they

---

[63] Despite an increase in the number of operations performed in Jaffna Teaching Hospital by 40% between 1982 and 1993, the number of oxygen cylinders provided by government declined to just 9% of what was supplied in 1982. The need for psychiatric care has similarly increased dramatically. Sanitation problems have increased both the need for preventive health care and the incidence of morbidity. (Kanagaratnam 1994: 81–3.)

facilitated relief efforts. Generally, this meant administering and supplying welfare centres where many of the displaced live.[64] Yet the ICRC claimed a much broader role, going beyond their usual activities, by escorting essential supplies to Jaffna and maintaining a protection zone around Jaffna Teaching Hospital. Additionally, international NGOs complemented the government services, particularly in the health sphere. Médecins Sans Frontières ran a small hospital in Point Pedro staffed with international surgeons while other NGOs facilitated the delivery of emergency medical supplies to remote areas. Lastly, international NGOs took the initiative in areas where the government lacked either the resources or the ability to implement basic needs programmes. For instance, Save The Children ran schemes to train midwives and health workers while UNICEF concentrated its efforts on improving sanitation supplies and providing school equipment.

The second type of NGO heavily involved in Jaffna was the independent local organization—groups organized by citizens of Jaffna with no formal affiliation to any international NGO, the government, or the LTTE, although often reliant on expatriate or foreign funds and the tacit approval of the LTTE to operate in Jaffna. The focus of these groups was understandably much narrower yet, together, their activities spanned many areas to provide specific services to the disadvantaged of Jaffna. For instance, many groups, such as the Mental Health Society, worked with those suffering psychological trauma. Others helped people to augment their market entitlements through training from income generation projects. Organizations such as the Centre for Women and Development sought to bolster public entitlements by complementing basic health care services with education programmes for women. Some organizations' activities were more research oriented, developing general educational projects and researching the effects of war.

LTTE-affiliated organizations were the last type of non-governmental groups influential in promoting household entitlements in the north. Just as the LTTE played a significant role in maintaining people's market entitlements, it was heavily involved in relief, rehabilitation, and development. Most of this work was done through the Tamil Rehabilitation Organization (TRO), a group respected by many international relief organizations. Expenditure statements from the TRO reveal an annual budget over Rs. 50 million (US$1 million), about 30 per cent of which was said to come from Tamils living abroad.[65] One-third of these resources was channelled towards displaced people and an additional third was devoted to families who had lost their breadwinner in the war. The remaining third was allotted to projects in one of seven areas: education, health and nutrition, housing, agriculture, income generation, rehabilitation, and general community development (*Information Bulletin*, Tamil Rehabilitation Organization, June 1994). Specific programmes included: LTTE feeding centres which distributed

---

[64] The number of those living in welfare centres fluctuates greatly, mostly depending on military operations. The Medical Institute of Tamils (1994) estimated 38,000 lived in such centres in 1993; the UN Humanitarian adviser, on a visit to Jaffna in the summer of 1995 estimated 16,000. Government offensives of the late 1990s have displaced anywhere from 200,000 to 500,000 additional people in the north since the end of 1995. (See US Committee for Refugees 1997).

[65] The rest of this budget was amassed through taxation of the population, smuggling of goods, and, some allege, trafficking in drugs.

milk and nutritional supplements to over 2,000 pregnant women and small children; a Self-Employment Fund which granted loans for productive purposes to close to 5,000 families in its first year; and the Child Rehabilitation Programme which oversaw initiatives including orphanages, foster parent schemes, and the running of 74 pre-schools district-wide (*Future Quarterly Newsletter*, Tamil Rehabilitation Organization). The LTTE even tried to address doctor shortages in the district through the creation of its own medical school.[66]

While LTTE programmes helped at least a segment of the Jaffna population augment household entitlements, the LTTE also stabilized life in a war zone by making Jaffna a 'crime-free society'. While government institutions that previously used to enforce law, contracts, and disputes no longer operated in Jaffna while it was under LTTE control, the LTTE provided a new set of its own institutions—a fully functioning judicial and police system independent of the LTTE combat forces—to do the same jobs. Although there is no question that this order was built on a foundation of fear, opportunistic behaviour reflective of a breakdown of institutions which might be expected in many countries at war certainly would not have been tolerated in Jaffna. In this environment, many types of civil institutions were able to operate,[67] providing an important support network for the destitute and suffering.

5.2   The Eastern Province

Prominent Tamil politicians have long claimed the Eastern Province as part of the Tamil homeland, although many Sinhalese and Muslims contest the claim that this area was traditionally an area of exclusive Tamil habitation (see de Silva 1995). Regardless of the historical accuracy behind the development of the concept of a Tamil homeland, the LTTE has consistently regarded the Eastern Province an inalienable part of Tamil Eelam. This is despite the fact that the area, in contrast to Jaffna,[68] is ethnically mixed, being the home to substantial communities from Sri Lanka's Tamil, Muslim, and Sinhalese populations.[69]

This demographic situation, and the 1987 agreement with India that promised a referendum in the Eastern Province to determine whether the area should be joined with the north, opened the way for extremely divisive patterns of warfare in the east. The actions of both the LTTE and the Sri Lankan forces intentionally pitted the commun-

---

[66] The LTTE reportedly began their own medical school as a reaction to the very low percentages (10%) of doctors staying in the northeast after being educated at Jaffna Teaching Hospital.

[67] An exception is local organizations that would be critical of LTTE rule. While the southwest of Sri Lanka had a large number of human rights/advocacy groups critical of the government, similar organizations would not be permitted by the LTTE in Jaffna.

[68] Jaffna is virtually homogeneously populated by Tamils. Formerly, there was a small but important Muslim trading community living in Jaffna town, but in 1990, the LTTE evicted all Muslims from Jaffna by force.

[69] According to the last census (1981), 40.9% of the Eastern Province is Sri Lankan Tamil, 32.5% Muslim, 24.9% Sinhalese, and the remainder Indian Tamil. The bulk of this substantial Sinhalese population was settled in the east as part of a government colonization programme aimed at distributing land to the landless from the (Sinhalese-dominated) wet zone. Despite this stated objective, there was a political motive to dilute the Tamil populations of the east with Sinhalese colonies, a policy that became one of the roots of Tamil discontent.

ities living there against one another. The LTTE is generally held responsible for the massacre of hundreds of Muslims in 1990 and 1992—an attempt to drive the Muslim population out of the east. For its part, the government contributed to violence between communities both in its provision of arms to small groups (called 'homeguards') of Muslims and Sinhalese and in its use of Muslims in identifying Tamils associated with the LTTE. Largely as a result of these tactics, violence in the east was not limited to fighting between the security forces and the LTTE, but also involved clashes between the Tamil and Muslim populations. While the problems suffered by the people of the north were largely due to the economic blockade during the period under consideration, people in the east endured repeated massacres, round-ups, disappearances, and identifications. Perhaps because of the divergent allegiances of the people in the Eastern Province, the area was not entirely under the control of the LTTE or the Sri Lankan forces. While the security forces for the most part controlled the urban areas, many rural areas switched between LTTE and government control for years.[70]

Reliable human indicators for the east are even more scarce than for the north. Available regional indicators on maternal mortality, immunization rates, and educational performance suggested that the east remained at a lower level of development than most areas of Sri Lanka, including the north. Yet, in contrast to the north, it appears that in many cases, the indicators improved. Nevertheless, it should be noted that the few statistics that exist are believed to mask severe discrepancies between urban and rural areas. Many NGO workers and doctors believe that remote rural areas, which repeatedly passed from LTTE to government control and back again, suffered the most. Some even maintain that the east actually fared worse than the north (Ratneswaran 1995). Despite our inability to assess human welfare in the east definitively, it is possible to address some important questions. To what extent was the struggle to maintain household entitlements in the east similar to what happened in the north? What sorts of new economic patterns and civil institutions evolved in response to changed realities?

5.2.1 Market entitlements

As mentioned earlier, the pre-conflict economy of the Eastern Province was much more dominated by agriculture than that of Jaffna. Although no recent statistics exist, it is estimated that the vast majority of those employed worked in agriculture; the fishing sector was the next largest employer. Small traders catered to local needs but the large retailers and exporters of the southwest were generally absent from eastern towns.

Like Jaffna, agricultural production in the east was disrupted as is suggested by dramatic drops in paddy production and the virtual elimination of paddy purchased by the government (Central Bank of Sri Lanka, various years). Yet, while agriculture in Jaffna was disrupted primarily due to a lack of fuel, in the east the problem was one of insecurity and fear of cultivation. Most paddy fields in the province lie in the less populated rural areas where the LTTE was most active. Moreover, many Muslim-owned paddy lands lie in Tamil areas and vice versa. Throughout the late 1980s and early 1990s, people from all communities in the Eastern Province were frequently killed or

---

[70] This is particularly true in Trincomalee, and to a lesser extent, in Batticaloa.

abducted while tending to their fields (*Daily News*, Colombo, 10 Apr. 1985; 7 Jan. 1988; 1 Aug. 1990; 11 Sept. 1992). At times, Muslim farmers who were allowed to cultivate were reportedly forced to pay the LTTE for this right (*Daily News*, Colombo, 11 Sept. 1992; 14 Mar. 1993). Muslims often sought government security forces to safeguard them as they worked in the fields, while Tamils requested the protection of the LTTE to do the same. Reportedly, paddy lands were appropriated, livestock killed, and harvests destroyed by both security forces and the LTTE. As a result of these difficulties, some estimate as much as half of the paddy land in the east remained uncultivated during the worst years in the 1990s (*Sunday Island*, Colombo, 8 Nov. 1992).

Barriers to agricultural production were not confined to the paddy fields. In one district, the army required licences to prove ownership of fields before they were harvested (*Sunday Island*, Colombo, 8 Nov. 1992). Moreover, both the army and the LTTE often demanded portions of the harvest, with government soldiers frequently extracting a share at checkpoints (Srishnamugarajah 1994: 8–9). With all these impediments to securing their livelihood, farmers were often forced to enter welfare centres in order to survive.

Trade in Jaffna was disrupted largely because of the government-imposed blockade which isolated the peninsula. In contrast, disruption of trade in the east reflected the insecure situation of the area. Numerous army checkpoints—as many as 14 in a 50-mile stretch, requiring passengers to dismount and display their packages—complicated efforts to bring goods to markets not only in terms of time, but in the bribes that were often necessary to obtain army clearance. Hostility between communities also constrained travel. Until mid-1993, Muslims reportedly could only travel three days a week with security escorts to the towns (Srishnamugarajah 1994). Tamils could not travel through Muslim villages or in Muslim vehicles and *vice versa*, creating a real impediment to free movement as Muslim and Tamil villages often border one another in the east. Economic activity was further dampened after massacres of Muslims forced many of the traditional money lenders, who often were Muslims, to flee their homes (*Sunday Island*, Colombo, 8 Nov. 1992). Nevertheless, while the net effect of the conflict on trade was undoubtedly negative, there is evidence of some new patterns of trade. As Muslims and Tamils avoided travelling to areas where the other community was dominant, Muslim traders brought goods to the edges of Muslim areas and Tamils set up service shops on the borders of Tamil villages, as if in recognition that the two communities were economically interdependent.

In the midst of this breakdown of much income-earning activity, the government continued to pay the salaries of almost 14,000 teachers and medical workers and the pensions of over 10,000 pensioners, a transfer which equalled Rs. 565 million in 1992 (approximately US$11 million).[71] The fertility of eastern land, in contrast to the aridity of the north, meant that the potential for serious food shortages was much less than in the north. Nevertheless, the government provided substantial amounts of food relief to the large displaced population from the east.[72]

---

[71] Estimates made from reports from the Education Ministry, Pensions Department, Ministry of Health, Government of Sri Lanka Budget Estimates.

[72] Approximately Rs. 270m. worth of food was delivered to the east in 1993.

5.2.2 Public entitlements

As in the north, the government worked to maintain the educational institutions in the east, funding 830 schools there and one university, the Eastern University in Batticaloa (Ministry of Education and Higher Education, 1993: 6). Yet in contrast to Jaffna where the lack of facilities was one of the major factors impeding education, the schools and university in the Eastern Province suffered more from numerous disruptions reflecting the ongoing violence between the government, the LTTE, and various communities in the east. Massacres and round-ups often led to population shifts as people fled out of fear or desperation. Although much of this displacement was temporary, it was often on a large scale, requiring many school buildings to house the dislocated. For instance, the Eastern University was closed for the last six months of 1990 as refugees sought protection there. Schools located in rural areas, where almost two-thirds of the children in the east study, often suffered high absentee rates, both of students and teachers who were frequently afraid to attend school. One reason for this was that the LTTE was known forcibly to recruit from schools; similarly security forces at times searched schools and took students into custody.

Almost as a reflection of the society it was supposed to serve, higher education in the east became ethnically polarized. After 1985–6, no Sinhalese students were allocated places at the Eastern University, and from 1990–1 until 1995, Muslim students were transferred to other universities, leading many of them to fail their degrees.[73] In 1982, Eastern University (then Batticaloa College) was 17 per cent Sinhala, 60 per cent Tamil, and 23 per cent Muslim. In 1991–2, it was 97 per cent Tamil (University Grants Commission, various years). To make tensions worse, the poor school education in the east meant that the Eastern University was incapable of filling its 'merit places' with easterners,[74] so it had to accept northern students who could not be accommodated at the University of Jaffna. This not only skewed ethnic ratios further, but effectively channelled resources intended for eastern education to other regions.

While some of the inadequacy of eastern education was in part an effect of war disturbances, it also remained a reflection of educational institutions historically less-developed than the rest of the island. According to the 1981 census, literacy rates in the eastern districts were the lowest in the country, falling considerably below all northern districts. Moreover, the east had many fewer schools equipped to teach A-level classes (particularly in the sciences) than other regions and had the highest percentage of untrained teachers in the island. Clearly, the war worsened a situation already in need of improvement: schools will not be upgraded and more qualified teachers will not be attracted to the east while the war persists.

The government also maintained health institutions in the east during the conflict but, like the schools and university, their effectiveness was compromised by the nature

[73] Reportedly, the percentage of those passing their degrees fell from 75% to approximately 50% in 1991, 1992, and 1993.

[74] Only students from the Eastern Province would be willing to attend Eastern University due to the security situation there and the relatively undeveloped facilities. Because of these reasons, students with the best connections—often the 'merit' students—transferred elsewhere. This damaged the university by not only keeping bright students away, but because funding for the university was partially based on the number of students in attendance.

of the war in the east as well as their initially low levels of development. Personnel and facilities remained as limited as they had been for decades. The east ranks among the lowest regions in the country in terms of beds and doctors per 1,000 people and the percentage of specialist positions filled (Natchinarkinian 1994: 15–18). This led one NGO worker in Batticaloa to claim that, 'The government is unable even to provide for normal health needs' (Srishnamugarajah 1994: 8). However, the relative availability of medicines and equipment in the east meant that both doctors and facilities there were more productively utilized than in the north.

As we have seen, tensions impeded travel, making it difficult for many to reach health facilities, particularly in times of crisis. Others avoided health facilities because of their close proximity to army camps. The Department of Community Medicine at the University of Jaffna estimated almost half of Batticaloa's health facilities, and a quarter of those in Trincomalee and Amparai, were not in use for this reason (Natchinarkinian 1994: 24). While the Jaffna Teaching Hospital treated any unarmed person—government soldier, Tiger, or civilian—in need of medical care, eastern health institutions were not always bastions of impartiality. Stories about the army or the LTTE taking prisoners from hospitals were widespread, and it was not uncommon to hear narratives about a Tamil or Muslim being refused medical assistance from a practitioner of the other community during the worst periods of violence.

5.2.3   Civic entitlements

The number of NGOs and the assistance they collectively provided was far less significant in the east than in the north. The situation in the Eastern Province varied from district to district with Batticaloa having relatively more NGOs functioning than Trincomalee or Amparai.[75] Those operating concentrated primarily on relief work targeting the displaced populations; very few were involved in development and rehabilitation work despite the clear need to supplement government health and education facilities, and to develop income-earning skills of the population. While some international NGOs functioned in the east, their involvement was less comprehensive than in the north. A number of national organizations also worked in the east, many of them with communal affiliations. Local organizations also cropped up, although not anywhere on the scale of the north, yet they remained poorly funded and organized in many cases. Lastly, the LTTE organizations, which played a substantial role in augmenting household entitlements in the north, were unable to function as effectively in the east because of the dominance of the security forces and the volatility of the ground situation there.

Several factors helped to explain the absence of a major rejuvenation of institutions of civil society and alternative structures in the east, compared to the situation in Jaffna. First, it must be noted that the east was historically the least-developed region of the country (outside the plantation area). The east's low literacy rates and standards of

---

[75] It is estimated that about 20 NGOs operate in Batticaloa, a handful in Trincomalee, and perhaps only a few in Amparai. (Srishnamugarajah 1994).

education and its highly patron–client based political culture contrasted greatly with the well-developed civil society of the north. While this environment would not necessarily be expected to breed large numbers of civil institutions, it also did not produce many easterners qualified to obtain jobs abroad. Consequently, the majority of those emigrating out of Sri Lanka have their roots in the north. Given the ties of the expatriate Tamil community, it is not surprising that international concern and international NGO activity focused on the north, not the east. Furthermore, the lack of easterners abroad inhibited the development of expatriate networks to fund local eastern organizations or to pressure international organizations into doing so.

Perhaps the greatest impediment to the growth of NGOs in the east was the way the war was fought there. By pitting citizens of the east against one another, and by involving frequent battles between the security forces and the LTTE in many areas, the war bred deep distrust, fear, and suspicion among different segments of the communities. In short, there was a breakdown in social capital. The sort of organizations this climate gave rise to were not the institutions of a civil society dedicated to helping people cope with the hardships of poverty and war. Rather, it encouraged militant organizations, gangs, and 'homeguards' which were only accountable to their leader, or at best, their village or community. Moreover, the frequent fluctuations of many rural areas between army and LTTE control not only hampered the growth of these institutions, but, where they did develop, constrained their ability to function properly.

6 Conclusion

The experience of Sri Lanka undoubtedly holds some surprises for those familiar with economies at war. As we have seen, Sri Lanka has managed to sustain positive (though varying) levels of growth throughout the years of civil conflict. As illuminated in the macro section, this positive growth does not suggest that Sri Lanka's conflict did not exact a substantial economic cost on the country. On the contrary, the cumulative impact of production disruptions, lost investment, unwieldy macroeconomic imbalances resulting from war-related expenditures, and the opportunity costs of military outlays was substantial. While this chapter has not sought to minimize the macroeconomic costs of the conflict in Sri Lanka, it has sought to take a different perspective, examining why these macroeconomic costs were not even greater. Similarly, in looking at household entitlements, this chapter has noted how Sri Lanka did so well to improve household entitlements (and by implication, human welfare) outside the war area, and to limit damage to entitlements within the region of military activities. Mindful of the specific circumstances surrounding every country at war, can we come to any broad conclusions from Sri Lanka's experience?

Clearly, the actions of the government played a significant role in maintaining household entitlements, to different degrees, both outside and inside the war zone. In the region outside military activities, the government influenced market entitlements through its promotion of manufacturing, as well as government cash transfers through programmes like Janasaviya.[76] Public entitlements were maintained by devoting steady proportions of government expenditure to education and health. In the war-torn northeast, the government tactics at first glance seemed contradictory. By blockading the north, the government obviously increased the human costs of the war. Yet, the extensive relief programme of the government—aimed at propping up market entitlements and maintaining basic public ones—was clearly an effort to control these human costs, even at the expense of aiding the LTTE indirectly. These seemingly conflicting objectives are understandable when we consider the political implications behind government expenditure. By buttressing household entitlements of Jaffna citizens, the central government was underlining their status as citizens of Sri Lanka, not Tamil Eelam. If the government were to let the Tamil people in the north waste away behind the blockade it imposed, some feel that international pressure—from India in particular—could threaten the government's autonomy. Moreover, such a government-induced crisis would completely invalidate the claims of the government to be at war with the LTTE not the Tamil people, and would further jeopardize the already precarious position of the moderate Tamil political leadership which has developed a complex interrelationship with Sinhalese governments.[77]

Of course, government involvement at this level both in the southwest and the northeast necessitated large and increasing social expenditure in the face of simultaneously rising defence expenditure. Even bearing in mind Sri Lanka's continued positive growth, so unusual for a country at war, we can uncover lessons relevant even for countries with differing macro situations. First, the experience of Sri Lanka demonstrates that liberalization and adjustment programmes are not necessarily incompatible with war. Nevertheless, it is equally clear that such programmes, if intended for countries at war, must embody a different set of objectives than the conventional sort. There should be more of a focus on liberalization and deregulation measures, and less of an emphasis on decreasing government absorption because, plainly, the preservation of social spending is especially needed in wartime. While a combination of these measures may be problematic, for a country that gleans much of its government revenue through trade taxes, such imbalances could be evened out with foreign aid. The market should not be allowed exclusively to determine the allocation of resources during wartime, but there is a role for the government to encourage the placement of resources in labour-intensive industries that will provide broad-based growth and boost market entitlements for the poor.[78]

Second, in maintaining social expenditures, Sri Lanka did incur longer-term development costs through decreased capital accumulation. This willingness to sacrifice capital expenditure was exhibited not only in the choice of the government to allocate spending *among* sectors, but also *within* sectors. This decline in capital accumulation will

---

[76] Although not discussed in detail here, the government's investment projects also sustained market entitlements by providing employment while simultaneously increasing the productivity of particular industries, notably agriculture.

[77] For example, the current People's Alliance government has relied on the support it receives in parliament from the TULF members of parliament as well as other Tamil groups turned political parties.

[78] This does not need to be done through state corporations, but can simply involve certain government programmes directing private investment—such as the 200 Garment Factory Programme in Sri Lanka.

continue to hamper the growth of the economy even after the conflict has been resolved. Of course, wherever possible, spending on development should be maintained throughout the war years, although its form should be altered to reflect the realities of the war. Nevertheless, given that the government was forced to cut back on capital formation (and forgo some longer-term development) in order to fund social spending (and prevent further human costs), we should ask whether this was a good trade-off. While the government's choice is not surprising in the light of Sri Lanka's history as a welfare state, it is also a politically astute decision. Since long-term growth is reliant on a healthy and well-educated workforce as much as it is on capital formation accrued through expenditure on economic services,[79] cutbacks in social expenditure —a form of capital expenditure in human resources—would also have resulted in development costs in the long term.

Moreover, the experience of Sri Lanka clearly indicates that robust governmental institutions—by overpowering war-created uncertainty, by enabling the government to prop up citizens' market and public entitlements, and by providing a stable environment which allows civil institutions to flourish—are critical in mitigating the costs of the conflict. Therefore, prioritizing government expenditure in a way which minimizes the stress on government institutions is wise. Clearly this may mean preserving household entitlements, whose losses are felt immediately and can encourage dissatisfaction with the government, prolong instability, and weaken institutions, at the expense of long-term capital formation as Sri Lanka did. Sri Lanka's case demonstrates that, if liberalization and adjustment programmes are structured to take into consideration these sorts of priorities, their implementation during wartime could benefit a war-torn country by buttressing government institutions and signalling the support of international financial institutions. Simply in serving these functions in Sri Lanka, the economic reform programme contributed to the island's positive growth during wartime.

Inevitably, such conclusions leave us grappling with the uncomfortable possibility that Sri Lanka's experience suggests that all government empowerment—even that which comes at the expense of liberal democracy—can be justified during wartime as the only way in which entitlements can be safeguarded. Undoubtedly, the government's self-empowerment in Sri Lanka held grave costs, not least the tens of thousands who died or disappeared during the JVP rebellion, and such costs would need to be carefully examined before suggesting such a conclusion. Yet, such a conclusion would overlook other important lessons from this case study. In particular, it would fail to recognize that Sri Lanka's experience signals that entitlements can be maintained even in the absence of a strong *state* framework.

The concepts of social capital and civil institutions (sometimes called networks of civic engagement—see Putnam (1993) and Coleman (1990)) are generally associated with good governance, institutional effectiveness, and even economic performance. However, results from this study indicate that they are equally influential in mitigating the costs of war. While this could be easily foreseen, most people would predict that conflict necessarily depletes social capital and weakens civil institutions, rendering the

---

[79] See the New Growth Theory literature such as that written by Lucas (1988) or Barro (1990).

discovery of their role in minimizing war costs of little practical value. What makes the Sri Lankan case of importance is that it demonstrates that social capital and civil institutions can be maintained and can even flourish during conflict, even in the absence of any significant state presence. On first impression, these observations could be seen as a triumph for those advocating that civil society blossoms where the state recedes.[80] However, a comparison of the situation in Jaffna with that in the east suggests otherwise.

In Jaffna, social capital and civic institutions were critical components of society's coping strategies. In the east, this was clearly not the case. Acknowledging the differences between the regions noted earlier, can we say what determines the generation or deterioration of such factors in areas of conflict? To begin with, the mode of warfare employed in a conflict shapes possibilities for the growth or downfall of social capital and civil institutions. In the east, the massacres, disappearances, and identifications undermined social fabric, breaking down trust between individuals and the potential for developing relationships based on reciprocity. In the absence of these two key components of social capital, trust and reciprocity, not only was civic engagement dampened, but opportunistic behaviour was encouraged. In Jaffna, the mode of warfare differed dramatically, with wartime costs during this period being largely associated with the economic blockade. Society was not fractured from within, and solidarity and a sense of community were maintained to some degree. Equally important, in the absence of the state, the LTTE provided a strong set of alternative structures, giving society a stable, if not democratic, framework. In such an environment, repeated and predictable economic and social exchanges were able to continue—connecting people to one another in numerous overlapping relationships, or building social capital—despite the continuation of the conflict. As a result, opportunistic behaviour continued to have a real cost, that of exclusion from the system of exchange and networks. Moreover, given this environment, civic and other institutions were able to operate, providing specific services which decreased the material need to engage in crime, fraud, or the like.

Thus both the mode of warfare and the maintenance of a societal framework governing transactions, whether from the state or from other sources, affect the development or regeneration of social capital and networks of civic engagement that can help supplement civil entitlements. At the same time, the mode of warfare, in causing economic dislocation, by moving the society from a 'trust equilibrium' to an 'opportunistic equilibrium', can increase the costs of war by making it much harder to maintain market entitlements, and to guarantee the fair provision of public services. By countering moves towards such an opportunistic equilibrium, alternative structures can mitigate the costs of war.

Ultimately, the experience of Sri Lanka has important implications for other countries at war, as well as for those in the international community who seek to aid them. As the above conclusions reveal, the government maintains an important responsibility in supporting household entitlements, even in the face of difficult policy choices. At the same time, international actors should not overlook the possibility that alternative

---

[80] For an overview of the civil society debate which covers this strain as well as others, see The *Brookings Review* (1997) Special Issue on Civil Society (Fall).

structures and NGOs can be similarly effective in alleviating war costs. Furthermore, government responsibility goes beyond fiscal matters and extends to the means by which the war is conducted. By minimizing warfare that breeds suspicion in factioned societies like the Eastern Province of Sri Lanka, governments will also find that their social expenditure is more effective. Perhaps while the international community pressures countries at war to structure their expenditure in such a way as to limit human and developmental costs where possible, it can also influence governments to employ modes of warfare that are less destructive of the trust which ties a society together, both economically and socially.[81]

Sadly, these conclusions suggest that the most recent stage of the Sri Lankan conflict, Eelam War 3 (1995 to the present time), is likely to be the most costly episode of Sri Lanka's war thus far.[82] The eviction by the government of the LTTE from Jaffna in late 1995, the ensuing offensives, and the subsequent huge influxes of refugees has rendered ineffective the well-developed network provided by both the government and alternative structures to buttress entitlements in the north. In Jaffna, although a semblance of normality is maintained under the Sri Lankan army, insecurity is pervasive as the number of disappearances climbs and civilian harassment continues at army checkpoints. Government suspicion of NGOs working in the conflict region—both local and international—has mounted and these organizations are now operating under increasingly difficult and precarious conditions.[83] Predictably, social capital will be destroyed, rather than augmented in such an environment. While the government has continued to provide shipments of food and medicine to internally displaced people, the relief effort has been greatly constrained both by the government's unwillingness to allow NGOs to operate freely in the region and its reluctance to acknowledge the extent of the refugee crisis. Reportedly, intense fighting and political manœuvring on both sides has in some cases halted efforts to supply even the most basic relief to displaced people. Moreover, the efforts of the LTTE to provide relief are hindered by diminishing resources as opportunities for taxing the population have evaporated and the organization has been forced to cut its civilian workforce considerably (US Committee for Refugees 1997: 26). Ongoing fighting in the multi-ethnic east promises much more of the divisive type of warfare that has been observed to be the most damaging. Finally, in addition to affecting how people in the northeast have secured entitlements, recent government budgets which cut Sri Lanka's social spending in order to finance the exploding costs of the war indicate that human welfare *outside* the war area will soon also suffer.

---

[81] This could involve a variety of measures—from discouraging the use of landmines to encouraging combatants to honour international treaties concerning warfare and human rights.

[82] See Van Brabant, (1996, 1997*b*) for more details on conditions during Eelam War 3.   [83] See ibid.

8

Sudan: Conflict and Rationality

DAVID KEEN

1 Introduction

Warfare, particularly civil warfare, has commonly been depicted as irrational. Recent civil wars, including the war in Sudan, have often been seen as the result of tribalism, of mindless violence, religious rivalries or some combination of the three. Related to this 'irrationalist' tendency in the discussion of war has been a tendency to portray wars as exogenous—as something superimposed on society, rather than something that emerges from relationships within society. Wars have frequently been dissociated from the economic and political relationships that exist in 'normal times', and war has tended to be portrayed as an absolute departure from peacetime—the sudden ascendancy of violence over non-violence.

The widely accepted, commonsensical view is that war is an essentially senseless outbreak of violence with a number of 'innocent victims' but no clear beneficiaries or functions. Famine is portrayed in a similar manner, as an event that disrupts normal social relations and economic activity—that creates only victims and ignores the possibility of there being beneficiaries (Rangasami 1985; Sen 1990).

Civil war in Sudan can more usefully be seen as a deepening of exploitative processes that exist in 'normal' times, a continuation and exaggeration of long-standing conflicts over resources (such as labour, cattle, grain, land, and oil). It is also a means—for certain groups—of maximizing the benefits of economic transactions through the exercise of various kinds of force against groups depicted as 'fair game' in the context of civil, or 'holy' war. 'Winning the war' was not the sole, or even the most important, objective of many of those engaging in violence. The primary goal for many was to manipulate violence in ways that achieved economic goals. The repeated victimization of politically powerless groups in resource-rich areas suggested that wealth and fertility may be a source of vulnerability to famine, just as much as poverty and drought.

Far from war constituting an absolute 'break' with peacetime, the outbreak and nature of warfare in Sudan have been driven and shaped by Sudan's peacetime political economy, and by the particular set of economic interests within this political economy. Moreover, Sudan's peacetime political economy has itself been profoundly shaped by warfare; it is not simply something that 'disrupts' the economy, but shapes, and is shaped by, economic relationships.

In both peacetime and wartime, the distribution of economic resources has been profoundly influenced not only by custom and by market forces but also by violence (legal and illegal, actual and threatened, past and present). Although ethnic and religious rivalries have played a significant role in fuelling conflict in Sudan, much of the violence can realistically be depicted as rational. Ethnic and religious tensions have been greatly exacerbated by government policy, as successive governments have attempted to prop up a highly inequitable political economy through a policy of divide and rule. Meanwhile, war has been used to define groups which lie outside Sudan's political community and can therefore legitimately be exploited.

In the run-up to Sudan's second civil war in 1983, exploitative transactions (themselves underpinned by violence) fuelled resistance, which in turn tended to increase exploitation and to promote further resistance. No government in Sudan has ever been all-powerful. Successive regimes have attempted to manipulate local conflicts and resentments. An enduring theme has been the state's granting to powerful groups of some kind of licence—either a legal right, or immunity to prosecution in practice—which allows them to exploit natural or human resources, through the use of legal or illegal violence. The efficacy of emergency aid has been powerfully shaped by these political and economic processes. Although Amartya Sen (1991) was right to point out in his essay 'War and Famines' that war may discourage democratic government, which in turn tends to discourage famine relief, he overlooks the crucial point that famines (and the obstruction of relief) may be actively encouraged by governments, even by democratic governments, such as the formally 'democratic' government of Sudan of 1986–9.

Sudan is a vast country, with an area of 2.5 million sq. km populated by Aran and Nubian, mainly Moslem peoples in the north, and Nilotic and Negro people in the south, generally Animist or Christian. The official language is Arabic and Islam is the state religion.

This chapter focuses on the 'border' area between north and south Sudan, particularly northern Bahr el Ghazal and southern Kordofan, an area of intense suffering, particularly, during the period 1986–8.

2   The Roots of Violence: Winners and Losers in Uneven Development

2.1   *From the 1820s to the 1920s*

Under the Turko-Egyptian regime, during the Mahdist revolution and Khalifate of the 1880s and 1890s, and during the early years of the Anglo-Egyptian Condominium that followed, the peoples of southern Sudan stood, in effect, outside the Sudan's political community. They were not deemed deserving of, or entitled to, the protection of the law. Instead of the protection of the government, they were subject to periodic raids by government-supported forces.

After the conquest of much of the Sudan in 1820–1 by the Egyptian ruler Mohamed Ali, southern Sudan was effectively treated as the hinterland of the Turko-Egyptian state. It was a source of government revenue, plunder and labour, and an outlet for the energies of potentially rebellious Egyptian groups. Slave labour came to underpin the social, agricultural and commercial life of northern Sudan (Gray 1961, p. 5; O'Fahey

Map 8.1 Sudan

1973: 137; Paulding 1982: 11; Sanderson and Sanderson 1981: 10). In effect, the south was no more than a 'dependency' of the Turko-Egyptian state, a 'reservoir of outsiders' (James 1988: 133), its largely non-Muslim people having virtually no political rights or means of representation within the state apparatus. The pattern of economic exploitation of a politically impotent south had been set. It has never fully receded.

As British rule was extended over Sudan in the late nineteenth and early twentieth centuries, Britain invested only relatively small material and manpower resources. As elsewhere in the British Empire, imperial rule was possible only with the collaboration of local elites, which in the case of Sudan, primarily meant northern elites. British strategic concerns (notably, the protection of the Nile waters) dictated that priority be given to appeasing the northern interests behind the Mahdist revolt that began in 1881.

This meant appeasing the Baggara and tolerating, to a large extent, their continued exploitation of the south. In addition, British officials argued that these Baggara raids on the Dinka were to be tolerated as the Dinka were resisting the Anglo-Egyptian government (Henderson 1939: 71). In the Nuba Mountains area of southern Kordofan, local Baggara Arabs were used by the British in punitive expeditions against rebel Nuba groups (Ibrahim 1988: 35).

2.2   From the 1920s to Independence

By the early 1920s, British administrators began to address the vulnerability of the southern Sudanese to exploitation and violence from the north (Collins 1983; Johnson 1989: 463–86; Sanderson and Sanderson 1981). This shift in policy was brought about by the threat of wholesale rebellion by the Dinka of Bahr el Ghazal in 1922, which left British administrators severely shaken (Collins 1983: 33–7; Sanderson and Sanderson 1981: 121–2). The policy of quelling 'rebellious' peoples in southern Sudan with punitive raids (including those that created famine) no longer worked. Strong government security forces were recruited from both the Baggara and the Dinka to reduce warfare in the Bahr el Arab area (Collins 1971: 189). Meanwhile the Closed Districts Ordinance of 1922 resticted the access of Arab traders and priests to areas deemed non-Arab (including the south, the Nuba Mountains, and parts of Darfur and Blue Nile). These newly powerful tribal chiefs, together with local authorities and security forces, created a system to regulate grazing and minimize tribal disputes. Thus, a system of legal protection limited the use of violence to obtain economic resources.

This system of protection depended to a large extent on continued British rule. Although there was some missionary education, the British had largely neglected education in the south, and British officials saw the solution to 'the southern problem' in terms of continued British tutelage rather than the emergence of political self-help (Sanderson and Sanderson 1981: 283). The Dinka were, therefore, generally poorly placed to fill vacant posts under 'Sudanization' in the early 1950s, and after Independence in 1956 (Mawson 1989: 85). Moreover, with Egypt pressing a residual claim of sovereignty over Sudan, the British carved out few safeguards for the south in hasty negotiations over Independence (Alier 1990: 18–22).

2.3   Uneven Development after Independence

Sudan's pattern of highly uneven extractive and export-oriented economic development—with resources concentrated in the central-eastern area both before and after independence—fuelled the resentment of factions, such as the Baggara in the west and the southern Sudanese. In addition, this pattern of development created an impulse to exploit the resources of the south, which gave rise to conflict.

2.3.1   Marginalization of the south

In the years following independence, the Arabization of southern bureaucracy and education provoked resentment in the south. A new generation of Dinka increasingly favoured resistance to the north, which they saw as progressively oppressing non-Muslims. The Nuba too, suffered widespread discrimination in educational opportunities, and the resulting frustration was a reason that youths joined the rebel Sudan People's Liberation Army (SPLA) founded in 1983 (African Rights 1995: 35).

The state-run Mechanized Farming Corporation, established in 1968, used the law to intimidate smallholders. According to the 1970 Unregistered Land Act, unregistered land was to go to the state and entitlement could no longer be acquired by long-standing use (African Rights 1995: 40–1). The Mechanized Farming Corporation acted as the conduit for major World Bank loans to enable the clearing and cultivation of millions of hectares of land. Together with loans from the state-owned Agricultural Bank of Sudan, this allowed mechanized farming to spread from Kassala and Blue Nile provinces to southern Kordofan, Upper Nile, and other areas of Sudan (Barnett and Abdelkarim 1991: 29; Shepherd 1984). The total registered mechanized farming land rose from 2 million hectares in 1968 to some 8 million in 1986, a quarter of this land in southern Kordofan (African Rights 1995: 41). New agricultural estates sprang up along the Bahr el Arab river, often funded with Middle Eastern money. These were subject to incursions by Dinka, resentful at their loss of land, and the owners found it necessary to guard the estates by arming nomadic groups, mainly from the Rizeigat. Many Dinka were killed by these guards in repeated conflicts over land (Prunier 1986: 32–3).

Land was not the only bone of contention. Another was the developing cattle trade. Merchants who bought cattle in the south for sale in the north enjoyed an oligopolistic position. These merchants came from a limited number of experienced, wealthy northern Sudanese families. Meanwhile, the Dinka's lack of capital, agents, and necessary family ties made it practically impossible for them to join the privileged ranks of those moving cattle to northern markets. The livestock trade, although bringing additional cash into the south, became the focus of considerable resentment. By the 1980s, this trade had come under attack from elements of the Ngok Dinka. Meanwhile, army personnel also began to acquire an increasing interest in livestock trade, as they were bribed into giving special protection to the northern merchants (Ateeg 1983; El Khalifa, Ford, and Khogali 1985: 213; Niamir, Huntington, and Cole 1983: 1–33).

2.3.2 *Marginalization of the Baggara*

Although in certain respects British colonial rules favoured the Baggara, in others they were disadvantaged. British administrators tended to draw sharp boundaries between potentially conflicting ethnic groups, and for the most part these were considered to be the Baggara groups (including the Messiriya). In the post-independence period, political and economic power was concentrated in the hands of a northern riverain elite from today's Blue Nile, Northern, and Khartoum provinces. This elite was able to manipulate traditional religious loyalties (notably those of the Baggara) in order to maintain its hold on political power and its near monopoly on the most profitable commercial enterprises (Ibrahim 1985; Khalid 1990; Mahmoud 1984; Niblock 1987: 204–32).[1]

---

[1] Many Ngok perceived that the Abboud take-over had put them on an even footing with the Humr.

Since the 1950s, the pressure on grazing among the Baggara had increased dramatic-ally as a result of the rise in the number of cattle. Increased remittances from migrant labour in the 1960s were invested in animals (El Sammani 1986: 90). Increasing insecurity of crop production, particularly with the expansion of mechanized farming, encouraged peasants to hold more livestock (Suliman 1993: 106). Together with the rapidly rising human population, the rise in livestock numbers contributed to the degra-dation of the land (El Sammani 1986: 54, 76; Karam 1980: 5, 37; Wilson 1977: 500–4). At the same time the total area available for grazing was restricted by the increased area under cultivation, often of export crops. (Davey *et al.* 1976 i. 27; El Sammani 1986: 86, 99–100; Karam 1980: 5). Particularly damaging to the Baggara were the expanding mechanized farms in southern Kordofan and, to a lesser extent, southern Darfur. The growth of cultivation in the Lagawa area, southern Kordofan, threatened the Messiriya Baggara nomads, many of whom were accustomed to spending the dry season in the area (Saeed 1982: 155). Their southerly migration routes were cut off by the new agri-cultural schemes (Ibrahim 1988: 120). The problem was made worse by the exhaustion of mechanized farming land within some 15 years of initial cultivation, because of the lack of rotation and fertilizer, and the pattern of 'strip-mining' that characterised com-mercial agriculture in much of Sudan (Ibrahim 1988: 110). This fuelled the land-hunger of the mechanized farming sector.

M. A. Mohame Sali, a Sudanese scholar noted in 1987 and quoted in African Rights (1995: 48):

It is estimated that 80 per cent of the 350,000 pastoralists and agro-pastoralists of Southern Kordofan province are seriously affected by the expansion of large-scale mechanized schemes.

Further to the south, the Baggara found their access to grazing under threat from the newly confident southern politicians, from southern army units—which ex-Anyanya (rebel) guerrillas had joined, and from southern police units—increasingly staffed by southern Sudanese.

As a result of government restrictions on access to grazing land, and the inability of the Baggara to stand up to the state during the 1970s, many Baggara viewed the Dinka groups as 'their immediate antagonists' (Saeed 1982: 387). Meanwhile, other Baggara, finding their migration routes restricted, allowed their animals to pasture on Nuba farms, undermining a formerly cordial relationship. Mechanized farms were well-defended, but Nuba smallholdings were usually not (African Rights 1995: 49). These ethnic tensions were frequently encouraged by central government in an attempt to 'divide and rule'.

The 'traditional leadership' of the Baggara, Dinka, and Nuba proved unable to con-trol their younger, discontented members and failed to secure significant state resources or protection against calamity, including violence and famine for their own people.

2.3.3 *Winners in uneven development*

The partial economic integration of the south into the Sudanese economy brought some benefits to southerners, although these were offset by the new dependence on northern grain and, more especially, by the creation of powerful vested interests in the north. The prosperity of these northern groups depended increasingly on their ability to exploit the resources of the south (whether these took the form of land, cheap labour, cheap livestock, or cash exchanged for northern grain). Dependence on southern labour was encouraged by a common distaste for agricultural labour among Arab groups who associated it with slave labour. Bahr el Ghazal became, in the 1960s and 1970s, an important source of labourers for southern Darfur and southern Kordofan (Shepherd 1984: 83). Indeed, in the course of the first civil war from 1955 to 1971, migrant labourers became, in the words of one police report, 'an indispensable factor for the farmers and townspeople in places like Al Fula, Al Muglad, and Babanousa' (Saeed 1982: 213). In the aftermath of the first civil war, northern commercial interest in Dinka cattle increased considerably. By the late 1970s, what one report referred to as a 'bonanza' was to be made from purchasing southern cattle in Abyei, southern Kordofan, which created a powerful interest in maintaining, even expanding, this trade among the merchants involved.

The rapid expansion of mechanized farming in the land between Sudan's semi-arid zone and the rich savannah provided important profits for merchants and their Islamic bank backers. New leases for mechanized farms went to well-connected civil servants, traders, officers, and absentee landlords, not the local 'small farmers' who were supposed to be favoured (African Rights 1995: 40–1). As under British rule, the state granted cheap leases and privileged access to cheap inputs to win political support (Ali 1988: 187; Ibrahim 1988: 187). Little or no compensation was made to the previous users (Shepherd 1984: 89). Further, Suliman (1993: 7) noted that, following a 1974 initiative to divert some of the Nile waters into a new 'Jonglei Canal' for the benefit, primarily, of northern Sudan and Egypt, 'Northern elites now coveted not only the water to use downstream but also the vast expanse of fertile marsh land, an area the size of England, that the canal would drain'.

2.3.4   Erosion of political protection

The period from the late 1950s saw the erosion of the system of protection against violence, exploitation, and famine that had been built up from the mid-1920s. This was not a steady erosion; the departure of the British and the first civil war left the Dinka increasingly exposed, but the system of Native Administration provided a measure of protection at local level. Moreover, the early years under Nimeiri helped restore some measure of protection for southern Sudanese at the centre, as the south became an important power base for Nimeiri following his break with the Communists in 1970–1.[2] The Addis Ababa agreement of 1972 included a provision to incorporate members of the Anyanya into the national army, and stipulated that half the army's Southern Command should be filled with southern Sudanese. These measures offered important protection for southern Sudanese (Alier 1990: 66, 152).

However, protection for the peoples of southern Sudan was dangerously dependent on Nimeiri's manœuvrings in Khartoum, and fell apart when, in the late 1970s, he began to reconstruct his power base, turning away from the south and towards the

---

[2] On this break, see Niblock (1987: 249–56).

Islamic fundamentalist interests and the traditional religiously based parties—the Umma Party and the Democratic Unionist Party (DUP).[3]

During the first civil war (1955–71), the Baggara lacked close ties with Khartoum. When the Messiriya Baggara appealed to central government for arms, claiming that the Anyanya rebels were spearheading attacks on them, support within the government administration was limited (Saeed 1982: 221–2). However, after the first civil war, the Baggara began to acquire increasing numbers of automatic weapons, from Libya and from the arms markets created by wars in Uganda and Chad (de Waal 1990*b*: 5). Increasingly well-armed, but still largely excluded from the organs of the Sudanese state, the Ansar, vanguard of the Mahdist revolt of the 1880s and drawing critical support from the Baggara of Darfur and Kordofan, made repeated attempts to overthrow Nimeiri's secular government. In July 1976, the Ansar, backed by Libya, came close to overthrowing Nimeiri.

3 Divide and Rule: The Second Civil War

War in Sudan has often been presented as an essentially religious dispute exacerbated by southern discontent at the underdevelopment of the south. However, this portrayal ignores the role of underdevelopment in western Sudan, and the active coveting of southern resources by an alliance of northern interests seeking to benefit economically from violence. In the course of a peacetime struggle over the allocation of resources, such as land, oil, and trading profits, increasingly southerners and non-Arab groups realized that they were being deprived of any representation within the organs of the Sudanese state, that might have allowed them to stake an effective claim to these resources. When significant numbers were moved to violence, a shifting coalition of northern Sudanese interests (including elements of the neglected Baggara in the west) labelled whole sections of the southern and non-Arab population as 'rebels'—people who were undeserving of the state's protection, who could legitimately be subjected to extreme exploitation, deprived of famine relief, and any redress against violence. Khartoum was able to use the labour and abundant natural wealth of the south and the Nuba Mountains to reward supporters at the expense of these non-Arab populations deemed (as in the nineteenth century) to be outside Sudan's political community and outside the protection of the law. Thus, while some groups were effectively placed 'above the law', others were effectively positioned 'below' the law.

In the course of violence and famine, the state did not so much collapse, as attempt to compensate for its economic weakness by dividing and manipulating civil society. At the same time, the violence, far from being completely irrational, served a range of mundane functions not only for central government but also for the Baggara, who stood

---

[3] Army ties with the Unionists had never been entirely severed by Nimeiri. The DUP, formed in 1967 from a merger of the old Nationalist Unionist Party and the People's Democratic Party, was closely linked with the Khatmiyya sect. Many army officers came from the geographical stronghold of the Khatmiyya, north of Khartoum, where education opportunities were relatively abundant. Khatmiyya officers had been important supporters of the previous military regime (1958–64) under General Abboud.

to gain from access to grazing land, stolen cattle, and the cheap (or even free) labour of southern Sudanese captives and famine migrants. As has been seen more recently in the conflict in Sierra Leone and elsewhere, rich local resources helped to sustain the war where the government attempted to make war largely 'self-financing'.

An important element underpinning this exploitative and destructive system has been a major infusion of remittances from abroad (notably from the Gulf to Khartoum) in the 1980s and 1990s. This helped successive destructive governments to survive despite the collapse of production in large areas affected by the war, and despite a persistent inability to exploit the oil resources in the conflict zone.

The fact that many non-Arabs considered themselves to be outside the protection of the government even prior to the outbreak of the second civil war in 1983, is suggested by the way one Nuba man analysed conflict in his home area of Tira el Akhdar (African Rights 1995: 49):

In the Tira area, our big problem in the late 1970s and early '80s was the Government of Sudan policy of taking fertile land for mechanised farms. They drove the local people off. . . When our youth in Khartoum and the northern towns saw these things, they began to know that the Sudan Government is not our government.

As a result, many turned to the rebel Anyanya II movement in Ethiopia in 1981–2. In the early 1980s in particular, the Nuba felt they were unable to obtain a fair and impartial decision when disputes over resources (such as access to land and legal compensation) were considered in court or at inter-tribal conferences (African Rights, 1995: 26–8).

After the outbreak of war, these decisions helped to give legitimacy to exploitation. This is illustrated by the experience of one Nuba agricultural worker in Gedaref in the 1980s:

At the end of the contract, when we had finished . . . they gave us less money than we had agreed. When we complained, they said, 'You do not have the right to complain as you are rebels.' Being in the bush, those merchants had the means to eliminate us without trace. So we submitted (African Rights 1995: 52).

The narrowness of Nimeiri's escape at the hands of the Ansar in 1976 prompted him to seek a reconciliation with Sadiq el Mahdi, leader of the Ansar and Umma Party, and Hassan el Turabi, leader of the modern fundamentalist Muslim Brothers, who were supported by the Islamic revivalist movements elsewhere in the Middle East. Partly in order to cut off Nimeiri from his political support in the south, in 1983, the northern parties pressured him into abrogating the Addis Ababa agreement, that had provided a measure of protection and autonomy for the south after the first civil war (Alier 1990: 235–6). The three regions of the south to which power was now ostensibly 'devolved' were actually granted very limited powers and sources of revenue. Revenues from the large deposits of oil that had been discovered in the south in 1978, were in future to accrue to central government.

This constitutional initiative, part of a wider diminution in southern political representation, created the conditions for widespread violence without redress. By the mid-1980s, there was no significant southern representation in northern Sudan, either at central government level in Khartoum (where southern Ministers were marginalized) or at local level in southern Kordofan. Meanwhile, the balance of power within the army had been shifting, as southern Sudanese troops were transferred to the north (the immediate spark for the second civil war in 1983) and northern troops were transferred to the south, notably to the oil-rich Bentiu area (Alier 1990: 223, 234, 242, 246). Government attempts to control, and even eliminate, the educated Dinka and Nuba were part of a deliberate strategy to deprive these groups of representatives or spokesmen.

Facing pressure to repay escalating international debts and unable to afford a large, salaried army, the Sudan government resorted to a strategy of turning the dissatisfaction of economically marginalized Baggara against the Dinka and the Nuer. In these circumstances, the arming and encouragement of Baggara militias (as well as the largely Nuer Anyanya II militias in the Upper Nile) offered central government a cheap means of quelling southern opposition (Africa Watch 1990; Amnesty International 1989). The Messiriya militias had been created partly to protect landowning interests and partly to protect Chevron's oil installations (African Rights 1995: 60). The government provided militias with immunity from prosecution for theft, killings, and other violations of the law (Africa Watch 1990: 78–97; Alier 1990: 256; Amnesty International 1989, section 4.1; Oxfam-UK 1986a: 1; *Sudan Times*, 25 Oct. 1988). Significantly, it was elected politicians (under the Sadiq el Mahdi administration of 1986–9) who engineered much of the worst militia raiding.

The government did nothing to prevent famine, indeed famine was arguably induced. This strategy offered the prospect of depopulating potentially oil-rich lands and decimating the Dinka, seen as the principal supporters of the rebel SPLA. In addition, it offered an opportunity to confuse the international community, and to deflect recriminations away from the Sudan government. When government-held areas began to fall to the SPLA in 1988 and 1989, there was a feeling in some quarters that Prime Minister, Sadiq el Mahdi, was intent on building up the militias, while allowing an inadequately equipped army and the SPLA to exhaust one another fighting in the south (Alier 1990: 288; Khalid 1990: 357).

This militia strategy also offered a counter to SPLA hopes of recruiting the Baggara into rebellion. Some of the SPLA saw the government as struggling on behalf of all marginalized peoples against the *jellaba*, the northern merchants who were seen as dominating Sudan's political economy (Suliman 1993: 108). As late as May 1985, after the overthrow of Nimeiri, John Garang, leader of the SPLA, appealed to the Baggara (and other groups in the north 'who have always been neglected') to join the revolt against Sudan's privileged elite (Garang 1987: 61). Whereas the Baggara's economic marginalization might in other circumstances have led them to join in an opposition to Sudan's riverain elites, their discontent was to a large extent deflected towards the south.

Increasingly through the 1980s, the rebellion was used by a coalition of politicians, traders, soldiers, and discontented Baggara to portray the Dinka, the Nuba, and other non-Arab groups as rebels, and as people who could therefore legitimately be attacked and exploited. The fact that the raids in late 1985 south of the Bahr el Arab took place some two years before a major SPLA presence in the area, suggested that the economic motive for the raiding was more important, at least initially, than any counter-insurgency motive (de Waal 1990a: 10; Oxfam-UK 1986a: 1).

Initially, the northern Dinka—Ngok, Malwal, and Twic—had held aloof from the conflict, resisting cattle-raiding by the Raik Dinka, who had close links with the SPLA. It is clear that the raids themselves prompted thousands of people to join the SPLA, including aloof Dinka groups (Mahmud and Baldo 1987: 19; interview with Melvyn Almond, Oxfam-UK, Khartoum, 10 Nov. 1988).[4] In this sense, the raids (for which economic motivation was critical) actually provided their own military justification, by stimulating the growth of the enemy. In 1988–9, there was apparently a shift in the *murahaleen* strategy. Growing risks and diminishing returns discouraged raiding into Bahr el Ghazal, but there was increased emphasis on plundering (and killing) famine migrants as they headed north (Africa Watch 1990: 82).[5] Just as raiding preceded SPLA strength in the south, so the SPLA's growing strength discouraged raiding—again the opposite of what one might expect if the war were simply being driven by antipathy to the SPLA.

The Nuba's increasingly marginal position within the Sudanese political economy attracted them to the SPLA. Earlier violent attacks on groups of Nuba, often in connection with land disputes, also drove them to support the SPLA and defend themselves. Attacks on the Nuba became routine from July 1985. After a Messiriya attack in 1987, a Nuba delegation went to Khartoum and protested publicly through the newspapers. One member explained: 'We made it clear that if there was no government protection or assistance, we would protect ourselves' (African Rights, 1995: 31). In 1989 the arrival of the SPLA's New Kush Division led to a ferocious over-reaction from the army and government-sponsored militias (African Rights 1995: 7, 81–3). Government-sponsored attacks on mosques in the Nuba Mountains underlined the hypocrisy of portraying the conflict as a *jihad*, or holy war.

Both during and before the period of widespread raiding in the Nuba Mountains, the manipulation of scarce resources played a key role in securing a degree of Nuba collaboration and cooperation with the government authorities who were oppressing them. On the one hand, the government had been able to deprive the majority of Nuba of critical resources, often to the point of famine; on the other, the government selectively rewarded a few persons (for example, with mechanized-farming concessions), as well as providing a minimum level of emergency relief, education, and health services to people in government-controlled 'peace camps', and, more particularly, to those who cooperated with the demands of their captors. These demands included sex, conversion to Islam, forced labour, and conscription. Conscription of young men into the 'Popular Defence Forces' militia (created in 1989) has helped to renew the cycle of violence and deprivation as the Nuba were coerced into attacking their own people (African Rights 1995: 3, 16, 90–5).

An important economic motive for depopulation in northern Upper Nile and northern Bahr el Ghazal was the land hunger generated by Sudan's pattern of horizontally expanding mechanized agriculture. In mid-1988, with raiding opportunities drying up in Bahr el Ghazal, many Baggara Arabs from south Darfur joined a growing wave

---

[4] The Ngok Dinka had remained largely aloof prior to 1985–6 dry-season raids on them (Oxford-UK, 1986*a*: 1).

[5] These groups were also plundered by the army and militias when they began to return to Bahr el Ghazal in 1989.

of raiding on the Fur of Darfur (*News from Africa Watch*, 6 Apr. 1990). The economic benefits from these raids were considerable and many cattle were stolen (Africa Watch 1990: 85). The Fur were not only Muslims, but they had shown their loyalty to Khartoum and their religious affiliations by rejecting SPLA appeals for support, and by returning fifteen Umma Party MPs in the 1986 election. There was no threat of insurrection from the Fur, but this did not protect them. Before long, the search for land and booty led to severe raiding on, and displacement of, the Nuba in the Nuba Mountains of southern Kordofan.

The role of conflict over oil in underpinning the war was critical. Following the discovery of oil in 1978, the idea of a 'Unity Region' was proposed in government circles: this region would embrace the major oil-rich areas of the Bentiu and Gogrial area councils in the south, and the Abyei area council (where additional oil deposits had been discovered), and other parts of southern Kordofan (Alier 1990: 216). These were the areas (together with the garrison towns of Aweil and Wau which served as a refuge for those displaced by militia attacks) most severely affected by famine in 1986–8. This was more than a coincidence. The Bentiu area, with the richest oil reserves, was where the initial raiding had been concentrated, and where both government and SPLA troops continued to be stationed in large numbers.

4 Economics and Distorted Markets

A variety of market transactions were distorted by the conflict and the use of various kinds of force. Indeed, 'forced markets' might be said to have played a more significant role in driving famine than 'market forces'. Force played a key role in creating high grain prices, which in turn helped to create famine. In part, the cutting off of southern garrison towns—and the persistence of very high grain prices within Bahr el Ghazal—was due to the SPLA, which attempted to place government-held garrison towns like Aweil and Wau under siege. But another major problem was the manipulation of supply by northern Sudanese. This strategy of exploitative trading was facilitated by the south's dependence on northern grain. One of the main groups to benefit from the high grain prices in the south were army officers. In many parts of the south, officers cooperated with merchants to shape grain markets, and restrict grain movements to their mutual advantage. For example, both merchants and army officers were involved in delivering commercial goods to Aweil by train, and by restricting the quantities delivered they were able to maintain high prices. The composition of the trains from Babanousa was decided by local merchants, the town councils in Babanousa and Muglad, and the army.

Livestock markets were also powerfully influenced by the use of force. Intimidation in the market place by soldiers meant that cattle were exchanged in Abyei in July–August 1987 for no more than a single sack of grain. The potential profits for those able to sell grain and buy cattle (later sold for meat) were very great. The cattle/grain price ratio in El Obeid, the major livestock and grain market of Kordofan (calculated from Ministry of Agriculture (1987) data), was around 27 : 1 at this time. Thus, the grain-purchasing power of those with cattle was 27 times better in El Obeid than in Abyei. Any Dinka seeking to take advantage of this price differential by moving cattle north faced overwhelming security obstacles from northern militias and the army. It is clear that the livestock traders, who benefited from the livestock price changes, provided finance for the Baggara militia raids. For example, merchants in Ed Daien—one of the two biggest cattle markets in the Darfur region in the far west and an important market for stolen cattle—provided money for guns and ammunition for the Rizeigat militias (Mahmud and Baldo 1987: 2; Oxfam-UK 1986b: 5).[6]

The presence of Dinka famine migrants appears to have helped relieve certain economic pressures in the north by reducing outlays on portering, wood-collecting, and other low-status tasks.[7] There were reports of widespread involvement in forced labour/slavery by groundnut farmers. Keen (1991) includes sixteen first-hand accounts of Dinka who were subjected to some form of slavery. Captured Dinka were used for a variety of unpaid herding, farming, and domestic work. Often, they were subjected to violence and sexual abuse. One boy, whose face was horribly burnt, said he was burnt while sleeping in the cattle byre. He believed he was burnt by somebody, but said his 'masters' tried to convince him he had been burnt by the cows.

The potential value of the famine migrants to resident farmers was underlined by Dinka reports that they had been told by Sudanese Arab farmers not to try to return to Bahr el Ghazal (Ryle 1989a: 10). Further, famine migrants were sometimes forcibly removed from camps in southern Kordofan, often to work for no money. One woman told me that three of her children—aged 9, 5 and 3-and-a-half—had been taken from Meiram camp in this way. She said she did not know where they were, but added: 'If I knew, I would go there and get them back, or be killed myself.' Clearly, wartime violence not only shaped the price at which commodities were sold, but also the concept of what might legitimately count as a 'commodity'. In the political and security context of south Kordofan in 1988, wages could even be negative. For example, a Sudanese Arab farmer took a Dinka man from Aweil to work for him once they reached the farmer's home area. However, the Dinka had to pay his employer (20 Sudanese pounds) for protection en route. Whilst initially the second civil war disrupted the merchants' economic strategy when the supply of southern cattle and labour dried up, the large-scale forced sale of labour and livestock that accompanied mass out-migration provided important profits.

Transport was another 'forced market'. For famine migrants from the south, moving by foot was hazardous, and subject to official control. Both merchants and army officers profited from the high price of travel on 'authorized' lorries (de Waal 1990a: 23), while policemen and soldiers made substantial profits from the famine migrants seeking a train ride north from Aweil to Babanousa (Wannop 1989: 9). Counter-insurgency strategies seemed to require these restrictions on movements. There were also economic benefits, for the more that non-market strategies were constricted, the more necessary it became for famine migrants to enter into exploitative market transactions.

[6] Ed Daien merchants were also heavily involved in the grain trade (Mahmud and Baldo 1987: 2), benefiting from 'famine' prices and from aid agency purchases.

[7] Noted in Muglad by Concern Worldwide (1988).

The influence of political factors on the success or otherwise of market and non-market strategies (as well as on vulnerability to asset-theft in the north) is clearly illustrated by comparing the experience of the Dinka with that of the Nuer groups affiliated to the government-backed Anyanya II in Upper Nile, and who had been driven into southern Kordofan by the SPLA. Many Nuer family members were protected by safe passes provided by the government, and many of them were armed. In Abyei, young Nuer men had a machine-gun emplacement pointing directly into the Abyei market place, confirming that markets were not governed by 'market forces' alone (*New York Times*, 16 Oct. 1988; Ryle 1989*b*: 88).

5 Humanitarian Intervention

Violence and famine created powerful obstacles to effective relief; Darfur, Kordofan, and the Eastern regions received the bulk of relief grain administered in 1986–8 while the southern regions of Equatoria, Upper Nile, and Bahr el Ghazal, although more severely affected by famine, received far less. Considerable light is thrown on the issue of 'access' by investigating the movement of trains from Babanousa, southern Kordofan, to Aweil, Bahr el Ghazal. Original evidence on the frequency and composition of these trains was obtained by the writer at Babanousa railway station. Only small amounts of relief were delivered to Aweil by train in 1986, despite the fact that SPLA was at that time a weak force in Bahr el Ghazal, and there were only minor security obstacles to getting grain by train to Aweil. The SPLA continued to have only a weak presence in Bahr el Ghazal for most of 1987 (Africa Watch 1990: 82–4), and the accessibility of Aweil was demonstrated by the passage of trains at various points throughout the year. Nevertheless, relief trains were infrequent.

A Sudan Railways Corporation worker provided a detailed breakdown of the contents of the three March 1988 Aweil trains. His information tallies broadly with information given at aid coordination meetings. There were 71 wagons, excluding an unspecified number carrying merchants' goods on the second train. Only 17 carried relief for the citizens of Aweil. Fifteen wagons carried grain for the army; 21 wagons carried soldiers and military goods; and a further 18 (plus the unspecified number on the second train) carried merchants' goods, of which 8 also carried a small number of railway workers. And yet these March 1988 trains carried greater quantities of relief food than any trains from Aweil between March 1986 and April 1989. The pattern of relief operations to the south helped to create the security obstacles which were then cited by the government to excuse the inadequacy of relief. In particular, the direction of relief exclusively to government-held areas, and the use of 'relief' trains for military and commercial purposes, caused SPLA antagonism. As Africa Watch (1990: 188–90) revealed, the mixing of military and relief goods, and discrimination against rebel areas encouraged rebel attacks in Ethiopia.

Meanwhile, at the height of the famine in the summer of 1988, 23 wagons of grain consigned to Aweil were 'discovered' in Babanousa railyard by NGO staff. Ten had been waiting there for a year, and 8 for two or more years (Concern Worldwide 1988 and Interview with Mark Cunningham, Concern, Khartoum, 2 Nov. 1988). The government blamed a six-week delay in the dispatch from Babanousa of a train carrying relief on the lack of a military escort, yet there had actually been no SPLA activity within 100 miles of the town (de Waal 1990*a*: 11–12). Moreover, trains on a military mission were moving freely to Meiram and beyond: for example, at the beginning of August, a train was reported travelling through Meiram on its way to Bahr el Arab to collect soldiers.[8] These shipments could be organized rapidly, in contrast to the delays affecting relief trains. A Sudan Railways Corporation worker, with direct experience of the patterns of train movements on the line from Babanousa to Aweil, revealed that soldiers from Meiram and Bahr el Arab (both on the rail line to Aweil) sent messages to the Babanousa railway authorities when they required bullets and food. He added, 'If they (the railway authorities) receive a message at evening time, the train will start at night time.' It was widely rumoured that Meiram was one of the centres where the Messiriya militias obtained arms, and that much of the ammunition for these arms came by train from Babanousa.

High grain prices were dependent on the absence of substantial relief.[9] The control over commodity flows to garrison towns that was exerted by merchants and army personnel—both profiting from high prices in the towns—also extended to relief, as was clear from the large proportion of 'relief' shipments devoted to military and commercial goods. International donor representatives who had sometimes been reluctant to counter the vested interests opposing relief, particularly in the period 1985–8, in 1989 tackled the problems affecting relief operations. Bryan Wannop, Resident Representative of the UNDP and UN Special Coordinator for Emergency and Relief Operations (1989: 9), played an active role in trying to get unescorted relief-only trains to Aweil under Operation Lifeline, and his account describes the system of profit and exploitation that was threatened by relief operations:

We were aware that we were stepping on toes by pushing through an unarmed and unescorted train which would carry relief goods only. The local policemen and soldiers who generally profit from their escort duties by carrying with them large amounts of commercial goods which they then dispose of at a significant profit in Aweil stood to be adversely affected by the concept of a successful unescorted train. Similarly, their opportunity to purchase wood, hides and handicrafts in Aweil to sell on their return was being eliminated as was the money they made from 'allowing' the displaced to travel on the train to 'sanctuary' in northern Sudan. Of course, the commercial traders were also not keen to see increased tonnages of relief food going in that would depress the usually high prices in Aweil, especially when the train would not carry commercial goods for them. We were introducing a pattern which was dangerous to the traditional groups involved because it eliminated profiteering.

---

[8] Interview with Marc Lejars, MSF-France, Khartoum, 25 Oct. 1988. At end–August, Babanous officials told aid workers there was a weekly supply train to Meiram, although it does not seem to have run every week, at least in August (minutes of aid coordination meeting, 25 Aug. 1988, at Kordofan Regional Officers in El Obeid, 2).

[9] These high prices were sometimes boosted by the purchase of grain for relief purposes from local merchants, when significant relief had failed to arrive.

Wannop (1989: 9) emphasized the strength of both military and economic opposition:

The strength of the forces opposed to a dedicated relief train, especially one carrying food into SPLA-controlled territory, had not been fully realized and it seemed to us that the more determined we became to get the train to move, the more determined the forces opposed to it became.

The inadequacy of relief increased the benefits derived by merchants and army officers from Dinka cattle, labour and, potentially, land and oil. In 1987, the army used its control over relief supplies stored within its own compound at Raga, Bahr el Ghazal, to organize large-scale looting of relief intended for the people of Wau to the east.

Relief agencies were frequently criticized for creating labour shortages by distributing relief to displaced people. For example, farmers in Meiram complained that the Dinka constituted their sole potential labourers, and that, ever since relief distribution began, the Dinka had not wanted to work (interviews with farmers in Meiram market, November 1988).

Local government and the civil service had few resources and given the sharply falling real earnings of government officials, who often had to go unpaid for months, and given the otherwise-limited opportunities for merchants in a context of economic downturn, high inflation, high interest rates, and a need for a quick return on investments, the temptation to profit from sales of relief goods was considerable (Duffield 1990*a*: 22; de Waal 1989: 53; Minear 1991: 19; Republic of Sudan/UNDP/and ODA 1984: 71; Shepherd 1988: 64). Indeed, the selling of official supplies was reported to be sometimes the only way that provincial government officials could subsist (*Sudan Times*, 18 July 1988). Wartime shortages made such action particularly profitable.

Extensive local 'diversion' of relief was routinely matched, at central government level, by more subtle tactics, for example, by manipulating exchange rates and allowing the government to 'cream off' a large proportion of international resources intended for relief (Duffield 1992: 10). When relief did arrive at its destination, the power of the army and local Messiriya, and an absence of effective registration or monitoring by outside agencies, encouraged the widespread, officially sanctioned 'diversion' of relief away from the intended beneficiaries. Aid workers Oxfam-UK (1988) visiting famine-stricken Meiram, southern Kordofan, at the beginning of September reported that:

Recently the following pattern has emerged at distribution times. At 4 am the army surrounds the camp and then proceeds to supervise the distribution, however, on more than one occasion, following the 'distribution' there is hardly any food to be found in the camp. It is understood that children are sent into the camp by the army and other Arabs to collect food during the distribution.

According to an MSF-France (1988) report, 'entire columns of grain-carrying Dinka could be seen leaving the camp for the Arab town or the army headquarters'.

There was no effective counter to such abuses in Meiram. Symptomatic of a wider political impotentence was the fact that there were no Dinka on the Meiram relief committee. Until the end of 1988, the lobbying power of the Dinka (and other victims of violence and famine) within donor organizations was scarcely greater than their lobbying power within Sudanese institutions.

6   Sudan in the International Context

Since the early-1970s and President Nimeiri's break with the Communists, Sudan had been an important ally of Western governments, notably the USA. It offered access to the Red Sea, a key channel for Middle Eastern oil supplies, and a base for the USA's rapid deployment force. Following the outbreak of the second civil war, the rebel SPLA was seen in the USA as having dangerous links with Communism, through its ties with Ethiopia. To quote Kenneth Brown, Deputy Assistant Secretary for African Affairs, Department of State (USA): 'The Soviets, of course, are the primary supporters of Ethiopia. The Ethiopians are the primary supporters of the SPLA' (US Congress 1990: 51). As with the near silence on the government's failure to provide food to famine victims, the lack of public criticism of the government's prosecution of the civil war was acknowledged by American diplomats to be linked with a desire not to push Prime Minister el Mahdi towards Libya (*New York Times*, 14 Mar. 1989). Sudan's strategic importance was reflected in substantial economic support from Western donors. Despite a reduction in aid, from the USA in particular, in the mid-1980s, Western donors still provided roughly half the recurrent government expenditure in Sudan in the winter of 1988–9 (*Financial Times*, 24 Feb. 1989). While this gave donors considerable potential leverage in relation to the Sudan government, they appeared more worried about driving Sudan into the arms of Libya, and about favoured economic reforms, than about policy abuses in the south.

Donor officials tended to argue that 'conditionality'—linking aid to human rights issues and effective relief—would constitute unwarranted interference in Sudanese sovereignty.[10] Yet donors were prepared to link continued non-emergency aid with reforms in the Sudanese government's economic policies, in line with the structural adjustment programmes promoted by the World Bank and the IMF. Donor references to 'sovereignty' were less common in this context.

5.1   The 1988 Famine

Violence leading to devastating famine in southern Sudan in the late-1980s was typically depicted by the Sudan government—and to a large extent by the US State Department —as arising from 'long-standing ethnic hostility' between the Arab-speaking Baggara peoples of the north and the Dinka and Nuer in the south. Superimposed on this misleading portrayal was the emphasis in the international media on the religious origins of a civil war between the 'Islamic north' and the 'Christian south'. What was damagingly absent was any coherent account of the role of the Sudan government in supplying arms, and immunity to prosecution to northern Baggara militias, who were encouraged to attack southern Sudanese occupying areas that were rich in fertile land and, critically, oil.

As the famine worsened, donors remained unwilling to challenge government definitions of when and where relief distributions were acceptable and possible. At the height of a famine in which perhaps 250,000 died, and at a time when NGOs were seeking

---

[10] See, for example, Minear (1991: 115) on the importance attached by donors to this argument.

major financial support from the EC, an EC-funded official announced that the numbers of 'unacceptably malnourished that we are able to reach is limited to small groups, possibly totalling several hundred only' (RRC/EC 1988). Roger Winter, Director of the US Committee on Refugees attempted to mobilize support for relief to the south. He admitted to the author that:

In mid-1988 when I returned from the SPLA zone with video and photos of starving people in that sector, I was told flatly by a key AID official that their position was that the areas I visited were 'the empty quarter—there is no-one there.'

Donors tended to define famine (sometimes implicitly, sometimes explicitly) in terms of nutritional crises and famine mortality. As malnutrition and mortality became severe only in the final stages of famine, these definitions tended to encourage and justify a lack of significant intervention during the earlier stages of famine. Allied with the concept of famine as a nutritional crisis was a donor focus on 'numbers in need'. Little attention was paid to the processes by which people had become and were becoming needy, or to how these processes might be slowed or reversed, by addressing the manipulation of violence by various groups (including the Sudan government). Instead, donors tended to regard 'civil war' as a given, an unalterable external imposition (like drought) whose negative side effects they were seeking to ameliorate.

Some NGOs felt that donors regarded asset loss as in some respects, a sign of progress. When Oxfam was lobbying the EC for a substantial relief response in the spring of 1987, Oxfam's Country Representative (Oxfam-UK, 1987b: 7) noted:

When tackled on the question of nutritional indicators not being helpful in relation to pastoralists, [the EC official] replied that to make good a claimed food deficit when people still have livestock could cause dependency. . . . In his view, pastoralism was, in any case, non-viable and in decline all over the region . . . It is important to note that USAID, UNICEF and EEC have all recently expressed similar views concerning pastoralism in the South, that it is on the way out and in twenty years would have disappeared anyway.

The potential for relief to slow down forcible asset transfers by removing the need for forced sales or reducing the need for out-migration was reduced by the failure to get significant relief to the south. Donors' concern to avoid creating 'dependency' with relief distributions hardly helped in this respect. A lack of adequate monitoring or supervision of relief deliveries and distribution tended to play into the hands of those manipulating violence and famine. The Sudan representative of MSF-France even suggested that neither the EC nor the RRC was interested in what happened to their food, unless news of abuses leaked out into the public domain (Interview with Christopher Carr, MSF-France, Khartoum, 20 Nov. 1988).

Donors' public statements commonly referred to 'insecurity' and 'civil strife' (see, for example, UNOEA 1988: 5), but they paid little attention to the government's role in promoting it. Although the 'Famine Early Warning System' reports put out by USAID described one of their aims as being to isolate the 'proximate causes' of nutritional emergencies (USAID 1987: i), these generally omitted any mention of the critical importance of the government-sponsored militias. USAID Khartoum staff later recalled that the organization had required information (from NGOs) on:

the numbers of displaced, their location, where they were from, their nutritional status, local food availability, external assistance already in place, and the relationship between the displaced and the local residents.

There was no mention of the need for information on why people had been displaced. As late as November 1988, the key UN document which claimed to address the issue of the displaced contained only one reference to militias (UNOEA 1988).

When militias were mentioned, their links with the government were for a long time overlooked,[11] and their role was generally portrayed as defensive. Kenneth Brown, of the Bureau of African Affairs, US State Department, noted at a July 1988 Congressional hearing that militias had been armed by the government 'for the purpose of protecting [population unspecified] against the SPLA' (US Congress 1988: 26).

There is no doubt that there were gaps in donors' information: these could have been filled to a large extent by talking to displaced people in the capital, Khartoum, where large numbers of southern Sudanese had fled from militia attacks (and many from the SPLA). Donors' 'science' of humanitarian intervention in effect disqualified certain speaking subjects (Clay, Steingraber, and Niggli 1988: 1; Foucault 1981: 85). Limited definitions of 'what was to be known' (including who was to be consulted) helped to underpin a narrow definition of 'what was to be done' (Foucault 1981: 5). In so far as violence appeared on donors' agendas, the focus was on its consequences rather than its causes.

Although donor criticism of, and pressure on, the government increased substantially in 1989 (particularly when it supported Iraq during the Gulf war), the west has refrained from exerting full pressures on the el Beshir military regime, which came to power in a 1989 coup. The USA continued to provide aid through multilateral institutions (US Congress 1990: 62). Programme food aid has also been provided. But other forms of leverage that might have been introduced were a major expansion of cross-border relief operations independently of Sudan government consent, a drive for the complete diplomatic isolation of Sudan (on the lines of Iraq), and a concerted campaign to high-light the continuing human rights abuses and the obstruction of relief in Sudan.

International neglect of the suffering Dinka has been accompanied by a deeply damaging international neglect of the Nuba. SPLA-controlled areas of the Nuba Mountains have been consistently deprived of relief, while some international donors have been drawn into providing relief in adjacent government-controlled towns (African Rights, 1995: 4, 147). Violence and the manipulation of relief continue to be used as tools of depopulation and exploitation. The pace of displacement of small-holders and pastoralists has increased under the military government of el Beshir. African Rights (1995: 50–1) reported that:

The present military government has been far more draconian in its land policies than any of its predecessors. The expropriation of land for mechanised farming has accelerated, based upon legislation that gives the government unlimited power over land allocation.

---

[11] State Department Country Reports for 1986 and 1987 referred to militias and slavery but made no mention of government involvement (Africa Watch 1990: 164).

Finally, in any peace agreement, it will be vital to look critically at the political economy that produced the violence, and not simply to return to the *status quo ante*. This means addressing inequalities and underdevelopment (including the problem of mechanized farming) in the north as well as the south. Even if there were a constitutional settlement that divided Sudan this would not necessarily protect the Nuba (trapped in the north), or remove the likelihood of renewed northern violence against an autonomous south.

9

Uganda: The Social and Economic Costs of Conflict

JOHN MARY MATOVU AND FRANCES STEWART

1 Introduction

In 1908 Churchill wrote: 'Uganda is a fairy tale. You climb up a railway instead of a beanstalk and at the top is a wonderful new world.'[1] It is a fertile, landlocked area, with a good climate and adequate rainfall. Yet since the country gained independence in 1962, there has been political violence for at least half the period, with a total of 1 million or more killed. Persistent conflict led to economic regression and worsening human indicators so that in the first half of the 1990s per capita income was little more than in 1962, food availability per capita was below that of 1965, the infant mortality rate was 113 per 1,000, compared with 61 in neighbouring Kenya.

Uganda has had a harsh, conflict-ridden history since 1962. These conflicts were the outcome of a complex interaction between ethnic, regional, and religious divisions. Underlying these distinctions are entrenched economic differences. Economic and political factors both reinforced the ethnic, regional, and religious divisions and transformed the tensions into violent conflict.

This chapter explores the economic and social consequences of the conflicts in Uganda. The next section reviews Uganda's political history, which provides the context for economic developments. The following sections explore the economic and social costs imposed by Uganda's disturbances. Section 3 examines macroeconomic performance; Section 4 assesses the meso–consequences and considers some aggregate indicators of household well-being; Section 5 looks at the unevenness of developments across different regions of the country. Section 6 focuses on the effects of conflict on people most centrally affected, reviewing the findings of a small survey of people who lived in the Luwero triangle in the 1980s, the region worst affected by conflict, and Section 7 presents some general conclusions.

The Uganda story shows how heavy the costs of conflict can be: on one estimate the cumulative income loss between 1965 and 1994 amounted to half 1995 GDP, while the excess infant mortality due to conflict was 295,000 taking the period as a whole, or 2 per cent of the 1995 population.[2] Any estimates of this kind are inevitably crude, dependent

This study was financed with the generous support of the Swedish International Development Agency. We are grateful to Meghan O'Sullivan and an anonymous referee for very helpful comments on an earlier draft.

[1] Churchill 1908, quoted in Hansen and Twaddle 1988: 4.

[2] Chap. 4, Vol. I. The method adopted for these rather crude estimates is to compare actual GDP/infant mortality with the rate that would have been achieved had Uganda improved its performance at the average rate for sub-Saharan Africa as a whole.

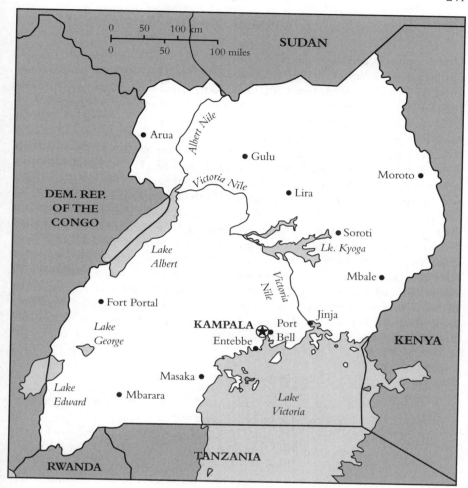

Map 9.1 Uganda

on weak statistics and on assumptions about the counterfactual. We are well aware of these issues in the analysis that follows. None the less, while accurate estimates of costs can never be realized, we are confident that the broad magnitudes and direction we have identified are correct. Uganda suffered very heavy costs, made worse, compared to many other countries at war,[3] by the near collapse of the government machinery and services, but somewhat ameliorated by people's ability to retreat into subsistence production.

---

[3] See the comparisons in Chaps. 4 and 5, Vol. I.

2   A Political Overview

Ugandan post-independence political history falls into four distinct periods: Obote's first period of power from 1962–71 (Obote I); the Amin era (1971–9); transition followed by Obote's second regime, 1980–5, (Obote II); transition, then Museveni's rule (1986+). There has been political violence in each era. It was relatively minor in Obote I, although 2,000 people were killed when the Kabaka's palace was attacked. The Idi Amin era was characterized by state-inspired violence, culminating in the invasion of Uganda by a combined Tanzanian and Uganda rebel force in 1979 which overturned the regime. In the course of the Amin era over 300,000 people were killed, mainly by government troops. Violence was at least as bad in the second Obote regime, as the army wrought uncontrolled havoc, especially in the Luwero triangle of Buganda, in part in reaction to the efforts of the National Resistance Army and other rebellious forces which culminated in victory for Museveni and the National Resistance Army and Movement. Perhaps 500,000 people died violently over this period. Many more deaths were caused indirectly, as the collapse of health services led to rising mortality. Rebellions in the north and the north-west have persisted throughout Museveni's regime, although at a low level. Deaths are estimated at between five and ten thousand. Below we provide a brief overview of events in each period, before analysing the economic dimensions of violence. Although the focus is on post-independence Uganda, it is essential to start by looking at the Colonial legacy.

2.1   The Colonial Period and Legacy

The colonial period is of enormous importance as it shaped post-independence developments. Six features need to be emphasized:

First is the special position of Buganda. Buganda is located in the centre of Uganda (Kampala) and accounts today for about 30 per cent of the population. The kingdom's history can be traced over at least four hundred years. In the last quarter of the nineteenth century, British Protestants and French Catholics fought for control over Buganda. The Protestants won political control following a battle in 1892. Catholics and Moslems remained in Buganda but in less-privileged positions. The British Protectorate, established in a series of agreements with Buganda, gave the Baganda a special role, including land rights to the Kabaka and major chiefs. Administration in the Protectorate relied on indirect rule by chiefs from Buganda whom the Colonials viewed as superior people: 'The Baganda are a Bantu race of intelligence and general capacity far beyond any other inhabitants of Central Africa' (Mullins 1904: 17).

A second colonial heritage was religious divisions and discrimination. The colonial bias was towards Protestants, who were allocated land, and privileged access to resources and authority.

Third, the system of indirect rule adopted by the British strengthened ethnic divisions, since administrative units followed ethnic lines. The colonial period completely failed to create any sense of nation in the territory that became Uganda. No common language, other than English, developed. The central government was viewed as a remote arbiter of disputes, while most areas regarded themselves as distinct entities.[4] There were few economic links between areas. As Andrew Cohen, a progressive Governor in the 1950s, stated describing the administration: 'It was a system which looked at the problems and interests of each given area or tribe. It was not conceived in the framework of building up a state or nation' (Cohen 1959: 26–7).

In contrast to many other African colonies, no national independence movement developed, and at independence there was no national leader, like Kenyatta in Kenya or Nkrumah in Ghana. The Baganda expected independent status. They refused to participate in the pre-independence legislative council and mostly boycotted the 1961 elections. Independence was rushed, leading to divisive jockeying for power among groups.

Fourth, substantial inequalities developed during the colonial period, especially between the north and south. Development efforts were all focused on the south, including education, the development of cash crops, the provision of infrastructure and the locus of administration. The northern and western areas were to provide labour for the centre and south.[5] Later they started to grow cotton in the north, but it was much less remunerative than coffee. The same attitudes were believed to have carried on in government policies in the early independence era: 'What I know the government does think about the West Nile is to keep it as a human zoo, and get cheap labourers from it to work in places like Kakira . . .' (Okello).[6]

The Baganda became unpopular with the rest of the country, owing to their political and administrative role and their economic privileges. The central role of Buganda, physically, including and surrounding Kampala, as well as economically, together with the attitudes of the Baganda to the rest of Uganda and of others to them, has left a deep fault line in the centre of the Ugandan polity.

Fifth, there was a deliberate policy of ethnic imbalance in the army which was made up almost entirely of northerners and easterners. A theory of 'ethnofunctionalism' developed, that people from the north and east were naturally martial; this was still being argued after independence.[7] Much of the army was illiterate. At independence consequently, there were few Ugandan officers with experience and education.[8]

Sixth, there were very limited economic opportunities for Africans in the colonial era. Africans had been excluded from most activities other than farming up to the 1950s (Brett 1993); they were mainly restricted to peasant agriculture, petty trade, and government. Asians dominated small and medium-size business. At the beginning of

---

[4] The Wallis Report noted that each administrative area wanted independence for itself (Mudoola 1992).

[5] In 1925 the Director of Agriculture reprimanded a District Officer who had been encouraging the growth of cotton in the West Nile, telling him 'to refrain from actively stimulating the production of cotton or other economic crops in outlying districts' from which the country 'is dependent on a supply of labour for the carrying out of essential services in the central or producing areas' (quoted in Mamdani 1976: 52).

[6] Uganda Parliamentary Debates (1964), Entebbe: Government Printer, xxxv. 3, 135–6.

[7] For example, it was stated that 'some sections of the population just cannot fight, even if they are soldiers' (H. Makmot in the National Consultative Council Debates (1965), iv. 755).

[8] Before independence Amin (himself only semi-literate) beat up a Turkana village community so brutally that he would have been court-martialled, but this was stopped because he was one of only two African commissioned officers.

the 1960s, securing state favours of one kind or another was virtually the only way to advance economically, making gaining political power more important than in countries with more diverse opportunities.

2.2   Situation at Independence in 1962

Together these six elements formed an explosive mix when independence was granted in 1962. At independence, Uganda's population totalled 7.7 million. There were 15 major tribes, speaking an estimated 63 languages or dialectics, broadly divided between Bantu (south) and non–Bantu (north) languages (a classification created by Europeans, not previously recognized by Africans), while the Nilotic (West Nile) formed a third group. Regional and ethnic differences largely coincided with economic inequalities: the southerners were privileged in education and resources; northern and western areas were extremely poor and underdeveloped. Yet the northerners dominated the army. Religious differences partly coincided and partly cut across these regional, ethnic and economic divisions. Moslems and traditional religions were stronger in the north. Catholics and Protestants were to be found throughout the country. The numerical majority were Catholics; but the favoured elite in Buganda, to whom the British gave privileges, including land rights and administrative jobs, were Protestant; Moslems, smaller in number, tended to be economically deprived.

There were virtually no national movements before independence. Political parties were organized along religious and ethnic lines. Control of government offered great rewards, particularly since there were few alternative sources of income; securing and sustaining political power therefore became of overwhelming importance.

2.3   Obote I: 1962–71

In the 1962 elections, in order to gain power, Obote (a Langi from the north) formed an alliance between the Protestant (and anti-Buganda) Ugandan People's Congress (UPC) and the Baganda Kabaka Yeki (KY) which aimed for more autonomy for Buganda. Obote became Prime Minister of the independent country and as a quid pro quo for the support of the KY, the Kabaka was made President.

Once Obote no longer needed KY support, as some members of parliament moved from the Catholic Democratic Party (DP) to the UPC, government hostility to Buganda emerged. He returned land to Bunyoro which had been taken by Buganda in the early years of the Protectorate. The consequent riots in Buganda were put down harshly, with a number of deaths.

In 1964 the armies mutinied throughout East Africa about pay and conditions. Obote reacted by raising pay significantly, increasing equipment and promoting army officers. He thus enhanced the power of the army in Uganda, in contrast to the reactions in Kenya and Tanzania where political control over the military was increased.[9] From this

---

[9] In Kenya the army was kept small, and firmly under political control; Tanzania converted its army into a people's militia.

time, Obote relied increasingly on the support of the army, purging it of Bantu officers in 1965. In February 1996, after opposing members of the cabinet set up an enquiry into malfeasance by Obote and Amin related to the army's Congo operation, Obote arrested five cabinet members and the commander of the army and suspended the constitution, assuming the presidency himself and deposing the Kabaka. The Buganda parliament reacted by asking the central government to move from Buganda (Karugire 1980). Government troops attacked the King's palace. An estimated 2,000 were killed, including many civilians. This was the first major bloodbath in independent Uganda. From that time, Obote incurred the hatred of the Buganda. Obote's actions showed that he would sacrifice constitutional law and democratic rights in order to sustain his power.

Obote became increasingly authoritarian, alienating many groups by abuses of human rights and promotion of his own people, while relying on the army for support. From 1969 he proscribed political parties, and proposed that the presidency should be his for life. He aimed to restore his popularity by his 'Move to the Left' and 'People's Charter', but he had alienated the Baganda; antagonized the Catholics by discriminating policies towards education; offended some Protestants by Church appointments; and annoyed one section of Moslems by backing another section (Mudoola 1992).

A state of emergency, declared in Buganda in early 1966, was extended to other parts of the country in 1969. The last years of Obote's rule saw an increasing erosion of human rights. Leaders of political parties and religious organizations were arrested, while prominent businessmen, lawyers, teachers, and doctors were periodically detained. The scale of violence, however, was modest compared with later developments.

By 1969, Obote had divided the army into two factions, one under Amin, which was Nilotic, like Amin, and one composed of northerners (Acholi and Langi). The army was thus divided between Obote and Amin, and each camp planned the elimination of the other. Amin was supported by many of those whom Obote had alienated, including foreigners such as the British and Israelis, who were suspected of supporting the Amin coup in January 1971, which occurred during a visit abroad by Obote.

2.4 *The Amin Regime 1971*

Initially, there was considerable jubilation about the successful coup among the many sections of the population who had been antagonized by Obote. Amin's behaviour soon after the coup seemed directed towards national reconciliation. He released detainees, and brought back the body of the Kabaka, who had died in exile in London, granting him a state funeral. This ensured Baganda support for the regime (Kiwanuka 1979).

Yet simultaneously, the Acholi and Langi in the army were ruthlessly attacked and many killed. Members of these tribes, who dominated the army, were allies of Obote, giving Amin a strong sense of insecurity.[10] Then he initiated attacks on others: first

---

[10] Most of the killings in the army during the first twenty months took place in four incidents. The first was when a coup to topple Amin was attempted in July 1971 and Acholi and Langi soldiers were massacred at Ganga, Maratha, and Mbarara barracks; the second was at Mutukula on the Uganda–Tanzania border in February 1972; the third was during another attempted coup in June 1972; and the fourth coincided with the departure of the Asians in June 1972.

the Israelis and then the Asians were expelled. In April 1972, all Israelis were expelled on the grounds that they were sabotaging the Ugandan economy and the country's security. After this, the regime received support from the Arabs states, including finance and arms.

One reason Amin gave for overthrowing Obote was the prevailing economic hardship (Kumar 1989). Yet after one year of his rule, there was no improvement. So he turned upon the wealthy Asian community and distributed the fruits to his supporters. The expulsion of 50,000 Asians, who together owned and controlled perhaps half of the country's wealth, allowed the state to acquire their assets without payment. Amin described the expulsion of the Asians as 'economic war' intended 'to make an ordinary Ugandan master of his own economic destiny'.[11] In December 1972, the economic war was extended to British interests with the take-over of a number of British companies.

The powers of the military police were increased by a 1973 decree allowing them to arrest people without a court order or an arrest warrant (Bwengye 1985). After attempted coups in 1973 and 1974, Amin reorganized the army, bringing it directly under his control. He created a Defence Council which increasingly encroached on the duties of the cabinet. In essence, he moulded the army into a state instrument for the consolidation of his power. The army increasingly took over the role of the police in effecting arrests. Violence and murder became institutionalized. Many prominent people were killed including those of leading personalities such as the Archbishop Janani Luwum. The Chief Justice, Ben Kiwanuka, was dragged from his chambers in broad daylight and disappeared. Disappearances became common and summary executions were frequent. Many people, particularly the highly educated, fled to other countries.

In October 1978, Amin invaded part of Tanzania, claiming it belonged to Uganda. Amin's soldiers penetrated deep into Tanzania, leaving a trail of rapes, murders, and looting. After two months, the Tanzanian Peoples Defence Forces together with Ugandan opposition groups attacked central and western Uganda, defeating Amin's army.

2.5   The Era of the Uganda National Liberation Front (UNLF) 1979–80

The UNLF which acquired power after the liberation was composed of a number of groups with a variety of ideologies and aspirations, whose one common goal had been to remove Amin. It established a military commission to take the major political decisions. In the two years after Amin was overthrown, three administrations held office as different groups gained power. Throughout the Tanzanians remained powerful behind the scenes, retaining a sizeable military force in the country. During this confusion, Acholi and Langi soldiers in the UNLA proceeded to carry out acts of revenge for the massacres of Amin, with indiscriminate killings in West Nile, Idi Amin's home area, destroying most of the town of Arua. According to the UNHCR, over a quarter of a million refugees from West Nile fled to neighbouring countries like Sudan and Zaire (Karugire 1980).

---

[11] Amin speech to university students, 1972.

After three administrations were successively displaced by the military commission[12] a general election was called. It was fought by the traditional political parties—UPC led by Obote, and the DP—as well as a new political party, the Uganda Patriotic Movement (UPM), led by Yoweri Museveni. The election results were clearly rigged. Although it appears clear that the DP won the majority of votes, Milton Obote was declared the winner by the military commission, a decision approved by Commonwealth observers.[13]

2.6 Obote II Regime, 1980–5

In December 1980, Milton Obote was sworn in to his second presidency. The National Resistance Army (NRA), along with some other opposition groups, immediately launched an armed struggle against the government because of the fraudulence of the elections and to remove a repugnant system of government: 'We went to the bush to oppose murder, tribalism and any other form of sectarianism' (Museveni 1992: 31). The NRA established themselves in parts of central Uganda, particularly in the region immediately surrounding the capital known as the 'Luwero Triangle'. The majority of the NRA were Baganda, who were particularly victimized by the UNLA.

The Obote government's response was brutal, not discriminating between the guerillas—who were elusive and rarely captured—and civilians, who were arbitrarily detained, tortured, raped, and killed. Conservative estimates are that about 300,000 people may have been killed during these years and another 500,000 displaced in Buganda alone (Mutibwa 1992). Many commentators suggest that the extent of human rights abuse under Obote II exceeded that in the Amin years.

By mid-1985 the strength of the UNLA had been undermined by its lack of military success against the NRA. Obote's support had dwindled, and he was replaced by a military council headed by Major-General Tito Okello. But the security situation continued to deteriorate, with rival armed bands controlling different parts of Kampala, while mass killings persisted in the Luwero Triangle. Meanwhile, the NRA consolidated its control over the rural areas of south-west Uganda, also capturing military garrisons in the major towns to the west of Kampala. The NRA took over Kampala in January 1986, and their leader, Yoweri Museveni, became President.

2.7 Museveni: from 1986

The government appointed by Museveni was broad-based politically and ethnically. Prominent members of the various political parties, and the different regions and religions in the country, gained positions in the administration, although the balance

---

[12] The chairman was Paulo Muwanga a veteran UPC politician supported by the Tanzanians.

[13] The early results strongly favoured the DP, whereupon Muwanga announced that all further results would be declared by the military commission; a decree was issued that anyone who talked about the results would be subject to imprisonment. From then on the UPC and Obote were declared the winners. (Mudoola 1988.)

favoured the Western and Central regions. The NRM government held power without elections for ten years. In May 1996, elections—without political parties—were held, resulting in an easy victory for Museveni.

On taking power the NRM aimed to incorporate all the various military forces into a single national army (NRA), with a balanced ethnic composition (Mudoola 1988). As a consequence of this policy of incorporation the NRA grew from a small, tightly disciplined guerilla force into one of the largest armies in Africa, comprising more than 100,000 soldiers.

Within a few months of coming to power the NRM government faced armed opposition in the West Nile, the north and north-east from supporters of Amin and Obote. Rebels among West Nilers, led by Moses Ali, a former Amin minister, soon surrendered and Ali was given a job in the government. Armed opposition continued, at a fairly low level, under the leadership of Jumar Oris, also a former minister of Amin. Support was provided by Zaire and Sudan.

In early 1986, former ULNA troops who had fled to Sudan returned to northern Uganda, initiating conflict in Gulu and Kitgum districts. By the end of 1986, at least two insurgent groups were operating in the north and north-eastern areas inhabited by the Acholi—the Uganda People's Democratic Army and the Holy Spirit Movement led by Alice Lakwena. Peace agreements were reached with many of these rebels, but some violent opposition continued under the leadership of Joseph Kony (his group was named the United Democratic Christian Army (UDCA)). This Northern insurgency has continued, at varying levels of ferocity, receiving support from the Sudanese government in retaliation for Ugandan support for Sudanese opposition groups.

In the course of efforts to suppress the northern rebellion, many thousands of people were forced to leave their villages and take refuge in camps. At least 70,000 were in camps in 1988 (UHRA 1988). The NRA burned huts, granaries, and crops in villages, in their search for rebels and to prevent food supplies getting into rebel hands. The same strategies were used in Kumi and Soroti districts where around 120,000 people were moved from their homes. These strategies were effective militarily and by October 1990 the majority of civilians had been allowed to return to their homes.

However, the group led by Joseph Kony continued to fight, instituting many arbitrary killings. Some of the victims were elected members of resistance committees, but most were ordinary villagers with no formal connection to the government. Some civilians were abducted and forced to join the rebels. The NRA responded with violence against civilians as well as guerrillas, in villages alleged to support the rebels. The episodes of political violence are summarized in Table 9.1.

The ongoing violence in many parts of the periphery of Uganda is connected with the politics of the region as a whole, with the war in southern Sudan, the situation in Rwanda and the Congo. Uganda's welcome to refugees from all three countries, her support for opposition in Sudan, for the Tutsi invasion of Rwanda, of Kabila's take-over (again with Tutsi support) in the Congo, and subsequently for anti-Kabila forces in the Congo, has meant that opposition to these forces have supported violent anti-Museveni groups within Uganda. It is difficult to estimate the scale of the violence. It undoubtedly has heavy human costs and diverts resources to the military.

Table 9.1 Episodes of political violence, 1962–1996

Episodes		Estimated deaths
Obote I		
1964	Riots of Buganda after referendum on 'lost counties': Nakulabye massacre followed with Bagandans killed by Obote troops.	100s
1966	Kabaka deposed. Battle of Mengo. Baganda killed.	2,000
Amin		
1971–9	Amin terror: against Acholi and Langi; then randomly.	300,000
Military Commission (Three Presidents)		
1979–80	UNFLA against West Nilers.	3,000 (260,000 refugees)
Obote II		
1980–6	Obote and UNFLA against Baganda in Luwero Triangle.	300,000+
Museveni		
1986–99	Rebellion in north-west in north-east.	10,000?

Sources: Bwengye 1985; Karugire 1980; Mudoola 1988; Reuters News Service.

3   The Economic and Social Costs of Conflict

A general framework for considering the economic and social costs of conflict was presented in Chapter 1, Volume I of this study. This chapter explores how far the expectations about the costs of conflict analysed there were borne out in the Uganda case.

The differing conditions in war-affected countries, in terms of the nature of conflict and of the economies in which they occur, make it difficult to generalize about the consequences. But our earlier analysis suggests that, broadly, the following effects seem likely in conflict-ridden economies compared with what might have been expected in the absence of conflict: at a macrolevel reduced GDP per capita, reduced export earnings and probably reduced imports, a lower investment ratio and probably savings ratio, reduced government revenue and expenditure, higher budget deficits, and higher inflation. At a mesolevel, a switch to government expenditure on the military from economic and social would be expected; and within economic activity, a switch from tradables to non-tradables, from production which is exchanged to subsistence production, and from formal to informal sectors. At a microlevel, average levels of entitlements of all kinds are likely to decline, sometimes with catastrophic consequences for human survival. Indicators of well-being of all sorts are likely to worsen.

We should emphasize that in predicting the consequences of conflict, as with natural disasters, there are two types of effect: the immediate consequences of the conflict, and the reactions to these direct effects. Humans are very ingenious, and while it is fairly straightforward to predict the immediate consequences, the reactions can be large, unexpected and often have positive effects, as has been shown in the realm of natural disasters (see Albala-Bertrand, 1993).

3.1   *The Macroeconomic Record*

Data for the major macroeconomic variables are mainly derived from two sources: Government of Uganda publications and World Bank data sets. The data were compiled for 1960–92, with a few variables up to 1994. Similar variables were compiled for Kenya for comparison purposes.

Growth rates were quite high in the 1960s, more than 4 per cent a year on average, while in the second decade this was reversed with the worst situation between 1978 and 1980 when the invasion from Tanzania occurred. In 1984 output fell by 4.7 per cent, again at a time when the country was wracked by civil war. Since 1986, the growth rate has on average been 5 per cent a year.

The investment ratio (investment as a percentage of GDP) reveals a similar pattern, with a sharp decline between the years 1975 to 1982 and 1984 to 1989. Inflation between the years 1960 to 1968 was in general less than 10 per cent. But after 1972, it accelerated rapidly under Amin. From 1972 to 1978, the minimum inflation rate was 24 per cent while the maximum was 88 per cent. The trend of inflation worsened further during the subsequent decade, reaching a maximum of 200 per cent in 1987.

The macro data are presented in charts, showing changing trends, and a comparison with Kenya over the same period. The Ugandan growth performance was considerably worse than that of Kenya (Figure 9.1). Uganda's growth rate was negative in years of conflict, that is 1977–80 and 1983–5 and was also close to zero in the Amin years. There is clear evidence from Figure 9.2 that investments were badly affected by instability. Kenya and Uganda had identical investment ratios in 1964, but while the ratio increased in Kenya until the late 1980s, in Uganda it fell substantially from 1970, recovering only after political stability was restored in 1986. By 1985, the investment ratio in Uganda had fallen to just 5 per cent of GDP, compared to nearly 25 per cent in Kenya. The trends in absolute terms are even worse in Uganda (Figure 9.3) showing a precipitous decline from 1972 to 1980, whereas in Kenya there was a trend rise over these years. The savings ratio (Figure 9.4) reveals a similar trend falling throughout the Amin regime, and plunging to below zero in the 1979–80 period. In contrast, the savings ratio in Kenya has been on a rising trend. The obverse of this is shown by the consumption ratio (Figure 9.6) which rose during political crises. (It should be noted, however, that data for savings are likely to be particularly unreliable).

Figures 9.14 and 9.15 reveal the behaviour of exports and imports as a percentage of GDP. They show a somewhat different trend. The decline in the export ratio started as early as 1964, but there was some recovery between 1977 and 1979. After 1982, when it reached a peak of nearly 25 per cent, it again fell sharply, only beginning to recover again in the late 1980s. Since then the ratio has tended to rise. Of course, it must be noted that these are ratios of exports to GDP: in absolute terms exports were declining, especially during instability, when GDP was declining (Figure 9.15), falling to about one fifth of their value from 1969 to 1989. The import ratio behaved in a similar way to

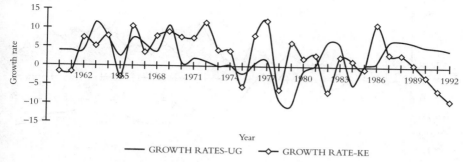

Figure 9.1 Growth rate of Kenya and Uganda, %

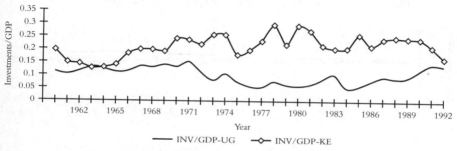

Figure 9.2 Investments as % of GDP in Kenya and Uganda

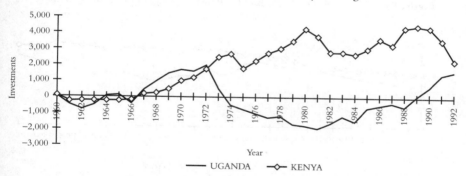

Figure 9.3 Investments in Kenya and Uganda (absolute terms), constant prices

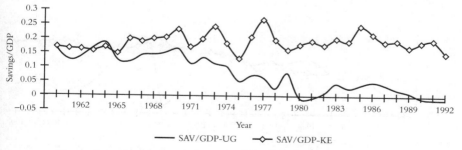

Figure 9.4 Savings as % of GDP for Kenya and Uganda, constant prices

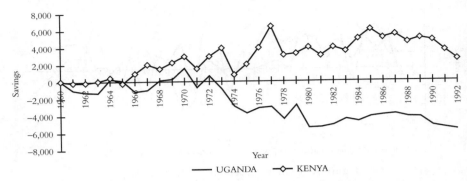

Figure 9.5 Savings in Kenya and Uganda (absolute values), constant prices

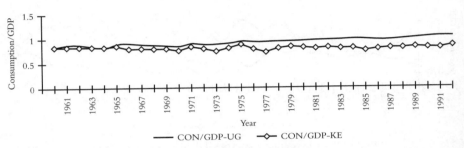

Figure 9.6 Total consumption as % of GDP by Kenya and Uganda, constant prices

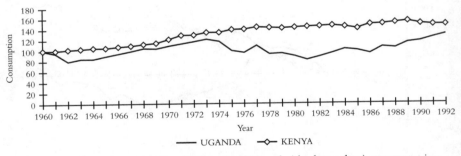

Figure 9.7 Total consumption for Kenya and Uganda (absolute values), constant prices

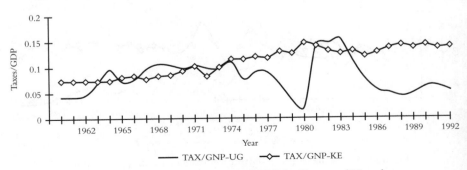

Figure 9.8 Tax revenues as % of GDP for Kenya and Uganda

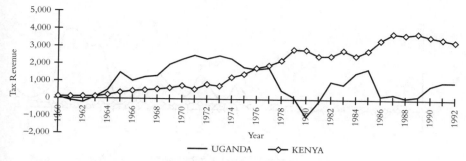

Figure 9.9 Tax revenues for Kenya and Uganda (absolute values), constant prices

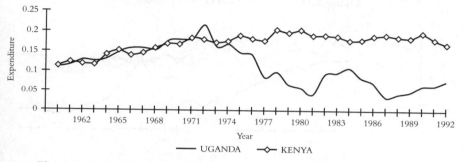

Figure 9.10 Total government expenditure as % of GDP for Kenya and Uganda

Figure 9.11 Total government expenditure in Kenya and Uganda (absolute values), constant prices

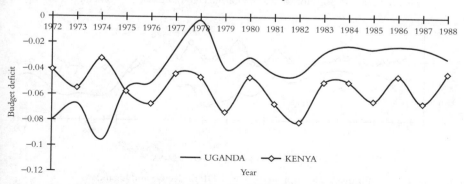

Figure 9.12 Budget deficit as % of GDP for Kenya and Uganda

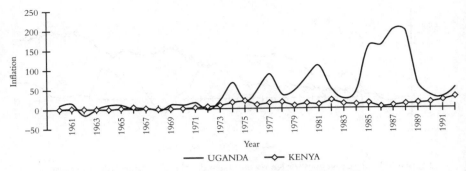

Figure 9.13   Inflation rise in Uganda and Kenya, %

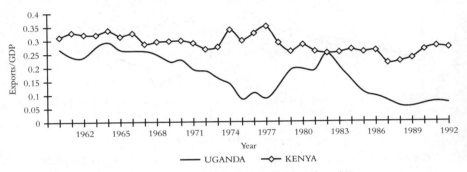

Figure 9.14   Exports as % of GDP for Uganda and Kenya

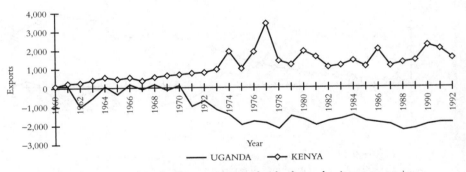

Figure 9.15   Exports for Kenya and Uganda (absolute values), constant prices

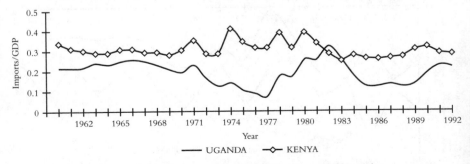

Figure 9.16   Imports as % of GDP for Kenya and Uganda

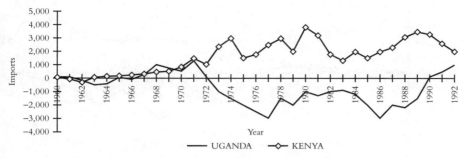

Figure 9.17 Imports for Kenya and Uganda (absolute values), constant prices

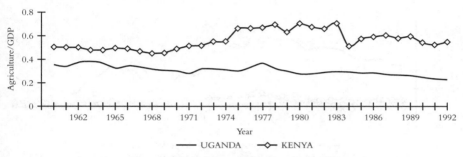

Figure 9.18 Agricultural production as % of GDP for Kenya and Uganda

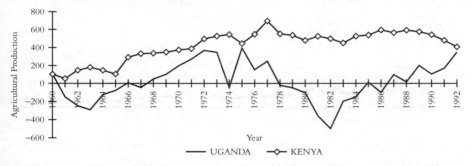

Figure 9.19 Agriculture production in Kenya and Uganda (absolute values), constant prices

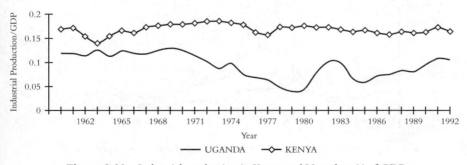

Figure 9.20 Industrial production in Kenya and Uganda as % of GDP

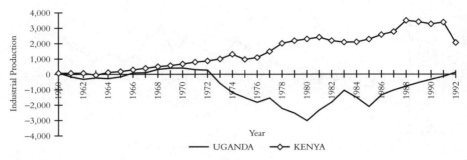

Figure 9.21 Industrial production in Kenya and Uganda (absolute values), constant prices

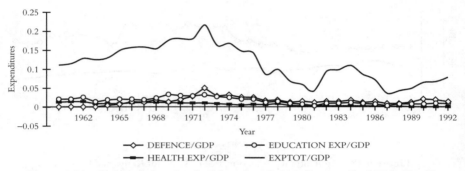

Figure 9.22 Defence, education, health, and total expenditures as % of GDP, Uganda

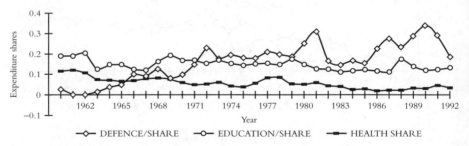

Figure 9.23 Shares of defence, education, and health in total government expenditure, Uganda

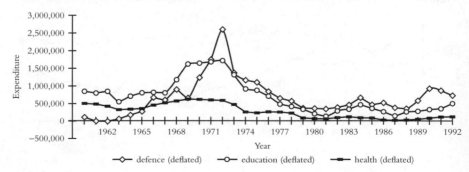

Figure 9.24 Expenditure on defence, education, and health, Uganda (absolute values)

exports, but was generally higher, indicating a trade deficit. The import ratio fell during the Amin era, recovering in the early 1980s as Obote II secured agreements with the IMF and other international donors, but then fell precipitously from 1982 to 1986, at the time of the civil war. In absolute terms (Figure 9.17) imports fell sharply from 1971 to 1977, and again between 1983 and 1985. Imports recovered from 1988, financed by renewed agreements with the international community. The decline in international trade during the Amin period is probably largely due to the expulsion of skilled manpower (particularly Asians and Israelis). Amin's 'economic war' contributed to the poor performance of the economy, as well as the civil disturbances. Kenya, in contrast, has generally managed to sustain exports and imports over the three decades (Figures 9.15 and 9.17).

During the years when Uganda was politically unstable, its revenue collection dwindled sharply from 11 per cent of GDP in the peak year (1974) to about 2 per cent of GDP in 1980 (Figure 9.8). It rose quite sharply in the early years of Obote II, but fell dramatically between 1984 and 1986. In contrast, Kenya's revenues rose fairly steadily over the whole period. While from 1960 to 1974, the taxes collected as a percentage of GDP in Uganda were greater than Kenya's, a huge gap emerged in the 1970s and again in the 1980s. The Amin instability and the war years had a significant effect in depleting the tax base. Although the period since 1986 has been broadly stable in economic terms, especially in the most productive regions, it may take some time for the tax base to recover to the levels of the 1960s.

Total government expenditure as a percentage of GDP also declined sharply in the years of political instability associated with the Amin period, and especially over 1979 and 1984–7 (Figure 9.14). In contrast in Kenya, the expenditure ratio held up until 1976; it declined after that but was very much higher than that of Uganda throughout, never falling below 20 per cent of GDP. Although owing to budget deficits, expenditure did not reach as low levels as revenue in Uganda, it was only 4 per cent of GDP in 1981 and a similar level in 1987. These low levels of expenditure put limits on the budget deficit, which from 1975 was notably higher in Kenya than Uganda. It rose during the 1979–80 war but was little affected by the 1983–5 war (Figure 9.11). Despite fairly low budget deficits, the inflation rate, which had been very low during the 1960s (Figure 9.13), rose, with fluctuations, from 1970, peaking in 1988 at a rate of over 200 per cent. Although inflation rose during political instability, it did not appear to be closely associated with it. However, the inflation rate in Uganda greatly exceeded that of Kenya.

These charts all tell a similar story. Uganda and Kenya were at a similar level as regards their macroeconomic performance in the 1960s, and from then on diverged widely. The comparison with Kenya and the timing of downward movements in Uganda, strongly suggest that Amin's instability and the civil wars had a direct negative effect on GDP growth, and on investment and savings ratios, revenue collection and government expenditure as a proportion of GDP. The unstable environment also contributed to declining export and import ratios and to rising inflation, although the timing indicates that these were less immediately affected. In Uganda, it was not only the large-scale outright violence that occurred at the end of the 1970s and the early-middle 1980s, but also Amin's 'economic war' that undermined economic performance.

3.2   Impact of Conflict Regression Analysis

Economic growth is expected to be negatively affected by civil wars and political instability. The most obvious effect is through the disruptions to productive activities due to the unfavourable environment during war. A second effect may follow from increased defence expenditures, as the government attempts to control the violence, so that resources are crowded out from other more productive activities. On the other hand, military expenditures may increase expectations of security and hence promote private investment and growth. A third indirect effect occurs as the production and trade disruptions reduce exports and hence finance for and the availability of imports, which in turn has a negative effect on economic production. This effect could be countered by additional external finance.

The overview of performance in Uganda over time, and compared with Kenya, suggests that many of these negative effects did take place in Uganda. There were three types of disturbance: first, general political instability associated with Amin which continued until Museveni took over in 1986. Second, the invasion from Tanzania of 1979 and the subsequent war; and third, the civil war between Obote and the NRA which peaked during 1983–5. We shall adopt dummy variables for each of these to see whether their effects can be detected econometrically. In the regressions, the three events are defined as follows: war-1979/80 is the 1979–80 war between Uganda and Tanzania; war-1983/5 is the 1983–5 war between the NRA and Obote II's government; political instability during the regimes of Amin and Obote II from 1972–85 is represented by (POLINST).

Equations 2(1) to 2(5) (Table 9.2) estimate the relationship between these three measures of disturbance and the growth rate (without any time-lags). Both the 1983–5 war and the 1972–85 political instability (POLINST) have strong and significant negative effects on the growth rate, showing in every equation where the variables are included. The negative effects of the 1983–5 war appear even when POLINST, encompassing the war years of 1983–5, is included. However, in contrast, the 1979–80 war did not have significant negative effects whether POLINST was included or not. In equation 2(6) some economic variables are added to the investment ratio, defence expenditure, and the international terms of trade. This reduces the significance of the political variables (which are now significant at only the 20 per cent level). The investment ratio is also significant at the same level, but the other economic variables do not show any significance. However, this may not be the right way of assessing the effects of either political or economic variables, since the political variables can be expected to affect the economic variables, which in turn affect the growth rate. An equation including both as independent variables would not capture this process.

Table 9.3, therefore, examines the direct impact of the political variables on the economic variables, expressed as a percentage of GDP. It also includes defence expenditure as a percentage of GDP as an explanatory variable. We see from equations 2(1) to 2(3) that each of the three types of disturbance and defence expenditure had significant negative effects on the investment ratio, but the 1979–80 war effects were only significant if POLINST was omitted. There were fewer significant effects on the savings ratio,

Table 9.2 Impact of civil wars and political instability on economic growth
(Dependent variable: Growth of GDP)

	2(1)	2(2)	2(3)	2(4)	2(5)	2(6)
Constant	2.903****	3.250****	5.563****	3.559****	5.563****	1.502
	(3.183)	(4.049)	(6.013)	(4.231)	(6.311)	(0.311)
War 1979–80	−2.435			−3.093	−0.443	−0.976
	(−0.818)			(−1.163)	(−0.158)	(−0.335)
War 1983–5		−9.219****		−9.528****	−6.127***	−4.709*
		(−2.871)		(−2.974)	(−2.173)	(−1.539)
Political instability			−6.164***		−5.406****	−3.161*
			(−4.561)		(−3.735)	(−1.578)
Changes in terms of trade						1.937
						(0.72)
Investment as % of GDP						47.317*
						(1.456)
Defence expenditure as % of GDP						−37.201
						(−1.091)
Defence expenditure Squared						109.12
						(1.122)
R-sq	0.215	0.2359	0.499	0.564	0.578	0.550
F-value	8.243	4.476	9.329	9.432	9.545	9.320

**** significant at 1% level.
*** significant at 5% level.
** significant at 10% level.
* significant at 20% level.
Figures in parentheses are t-ratios.

Notes: War 1979–80 is a dummy variable for the years 1979 and 1980 to represent the war between Tanzania and Uganda which overthrew Amin. War 1983–5 is a dummy variable for the years 1983 to 1985 to represent the civil war between the NRA guerilla movement and Obote's UPC government. Political instability (POLINST) is a dummy variable to represent the years from 1972 to 1985 (inclusive) when Uganda was continuously subject to political instability.

with only POLINST showing any significant negative effect (3(4) and 3(6)). As noted earlier, theoretical analysis is not clear as to whether savings should fall as incomes fall below life-time expectations, or rise because of increased uncertainty.

There were no significant effects on tax revenue as a proportion of GDP (3(7) to 3(9)) from any of the political variables. The fall in revenue observed was correlated with the fall in GDP which in turn was associated with the wars/political disturbances, but no additional negative effect was observed. Government expenditure as a ratio to GDP was *positively* affected by the war-1983–5 and POLINST (3(10) and 3(12)). Although we have not estimated the effects on the budget deficit, the combined effects of a zero effect on the revenue ratio and a positive effect on the expenditure ratio imply a positive effect on the budget deficit. As far as inflation is concerned, 3(13) to 3(15), the 1979–80 war had a slight positive effect, while the 1983–5 war and POLINST did not, but there was a strong positive correlation between defence expenditure as a ratio of GDP and inflation. The export and import ratios were only affected by defence expenditure, which had a negative impact on both the export and import ratios, but were not affected directly by the war/disturbance variables (3(16) to 3(21)). However, estimates of the effects of the wars and political instability on defence expenditure as a percentage of GDP in Table 9.5 (equations 5(9) to 5(11)) show that POLINST had some positive effect, but the two wars did not. Hence POLINST may indirectly have had some negative effect on export and import ratios via the effects in raising the defence expenditure ratio.

Table 9.3 Impact of wars and political disturbance on major macroeconomic variables as a ratio to GDP (Dependent variable as % of GDP)

	3(1) Investment	3(2) Investment	3(3) Investment	3(4) Savings	3(5) Savings	3(6) Savings	3(7) Tax revenue
Constant	0.127**** (11.83)	0.132**** (14.18)	0.129**** (14.09)	0.085**** (7.05)	0.096*** (6.27)	0.097**** (6.42)	0.117**** (5.38)
War 1979–80	−0.037*** (−2.31)	−0.0187 (−1.206)		−0.047 (−1.019)	−0.030 (−0.614)		−0.002 (−0.031)
War 1983–5	−0.0386** (−1.986)	−0.0233* (−1.292)		−0.046 (−0.987)	−0.028 (−0.583)		−0.089 (−1.07)
Political instability		−0.028*** (−2.915)	−0.0352**** (−4.05)		−0.0292* (−1.187)	−0.037** (−1.68)	
Defence expenditure as % of GDP	−0.116*** (−2.14)	−0.0739** (−1.474)	−0.0704* (−1.41)				
R–Squared	0.395	0.537	0.448	0.15	0.16	0.086	0.10
F–Value	4.28	6.68	11.78	1.34	1.51	2.829	1.02

	3(8) Tax revenue	3(9) Tax revenue	3(10) Government expenditure	3(11) Government expenditure	3(12) Government expenditure	3(13) Annual Inflation (%)	3(14) Annual Inflation (%)
Constant	0.126**** (4.52)	0.125*** (4.607)	0.123** (1.72)	0.099** (1.43)	0.123** (1.52)	−15.73*** (−0.80)	−13.05 (−0.66)
War 1979–80	−0.012 (−0.16)		0.012 (0.71)	0.009 (0.61)		33.39 (1.09)	47.24* (1.43)
War 1983–5	−0.074 (−0.843)		0.072* (1.72)	0.062* (1.51)		−4.656 (−0.13)	7.00 (0.18)
Political instability	−0.022 (−0.49)	−0.0302 (−0.758)		0.042* (1.43)	0.134* (1.57)		−21.48 (−1.03)
Defence expenditure as % of GDP						367.17**** (3.56)	399.25**** (3.71)
R–Squared	0.11	0.0188	0.13	0.211	0.23	0.329	0.35
F–value	1.03	0.574	2.10	4.77	4.01	4.59	3.719

	3(15) Annual Inflation (%)	3(16) Exports	3(17) Exports	3(18) Exports	3(19) Imports	3(20) Imports	3(21) Imports
Constant	−9.714	0.161***	0.279****	0.277*****	0.186***	0.234***	0.234****
	(−0.497)	(10.43)	(13.21)	(12.92)	(15.71)	(9.69)	(9.88)
War 1979–80		−0.0103	−0.033		0.002	0.0439	
		(−0.214)	(−0.98)		(0.052)	(0.994)	
War 1983–5		0.0277	0.048		0.016	0.041	
		(0.470)	(1.23)		(0.347)	(0.90)	
Political instability	−9.967		0.020	0.0137		−0.0083	−0.0025
	(−0.541)		(0.964)	(0.717)		(−0.328)	(−0.117)
Defence expenditure as % of GDP	376.19**		−0.709****	−0.694*****	−0.068**	−0.256**	−0.265***
	(3.55)		(−6.36)	(−6.141)	(−1.81)	(−1.82)	(−2.087)
R–Squared	0.307	0.12	0.635	0.578	0.13	0.288	0.243
F-Value	6.411	1.34	8.72	19.21	1.39	2.023	2.894

***** significant at 1% level.
*** significant at 5% level.
** significant at 10% level.
* significant at 20% level.
Figures in parentheses are t-ratios.

Table 9.4 Impact of civil wars and political disturbance on major macroeconomic variables, absolute values (Dependent variables)

	4(1) Investment level	4(2) Savings level	4(3) Tax revenue level	4(4) Govt. expenditure level	4(5) Exports level	4(6) Imports level
Constant	3.745e+3****	3.016e+4*****	1.965e+4****	3.145e+4****	6.622e+4*****	7.352e+4****
	(14.39)	(3.876)	(7.344)	(6.123)	(6.898)	(12.93)
War 1979–80	1.588e+3	−1.314e+3	−8.755e+3*	−6.432e+3**	3.024e+3	5.927e+3
	(0.237)	(−0.065)	(−1.277)	(−1.79)	(0.123)	(0.406)
War 1983–5	1.416e+3	−6.539e+3	1.0594e+3**	−5.894e+3**	2.621e+3	1.058e+4
	(0.248)	(−0.384)	(1.811)	(−1.81)	(0.124)	(0.851)
Political instability	−2.976****	−2.161e+3***	−4.493e+3***	−7.234e+3**	−3.033e+10***	−3.848e+4***
	(−8.148)	(−1.988)	(−1.201)	(−1.73)	(−2.262)	(−4.844)
Defence expenditure as % of GDP	0.0236****	0.0187**	0.0175****	0.0113***	0.0156*	0.0204***
	(7.418)	(1.972)	(5.361)	(2.34)	(1.332)	(2.945)
R-Squared	0.799	0.232	0.574	0.599	0.193	0.506
F-Value	27.87	2.117	9.42	10.11	1.695	7.173

**** significant at 1% level.
*** significant at 5% level.
** significant at 10% level.
* significant at 20% level.
Figures in parentheses are t-ratios.

Table 9.3 is concerned with estimating the impact of conflict on values as a percentage of GDP, that is on the allocation of GDP. Table 9.4 estimates the effects on *absolute values* of the same variables. POLINST has a negative effect on investment levels (4(1)) and defence expenditure, a positive effect. Similar results obtain for savings (4(2)). The 1979–80 war and POLINST had negative effects on tax revenue in absolute terms, while defence expenditure had a positive effect. However, the 1983–5 war unexpectedly appears to have had a positive effect on tax revenue (4(3)). But this seems to be a matter of time-lags, as the revenue ratio fell from 1983 to 1989, only recovering in the 1990s (Figure 9.8). All three variables for political disturbance had a significant negative impact on levels of government expenditure (4(4)), and defence expenditure had a positive effect. POLINST also had a negative effect on exports and imports in absolute values (equations (4(5) and 4(6)). POLINST had a positive effect on defence expenditure in absolute terms, while both the wars had a negative effect.

The regression estimates together, shown in Tables 9.3 and 9.4, suggest that the political disturbances had a negative impact on investment, savings, tax revenue, government expenditure, exports and imports, and a positive effect on defence expenditures. The impact of the specific war episodes was much less than the prolonged disturbance, although these events do, of course, form part of the prolonged disturbance. Anticipation of these outbreaks of war, and, in the case of the 1979–80 conflict, some lagged effects, are picked up in the longer period estimates.

3.3 Conclusion on Macroeconomic Effects

The fact that the various approaches adopted for estimating the impact of conflict and political instability on macro performance in Uganda give similar results, permits some confidence in the conclusions. The most definite conclusion is that there was a strong negative effect from the conflicts and political instability on economic growth. This was partly due to direct disruptions of production, partly to indirect effects resulting from increased defence expenditure, reduced availability of imports due to constraints on finance following declines in exports, and reduced investment because of the weakened confidence and shortage of imports. Inflation accelerated and tax revenue fell as a proportion of GDP, although there was no statistical association between the timing of this fall and the timing of instability.

We should note, however, that the post-1986 period has generally seen some economic recovery despite the persistence of some conflict. This is probably due to the location of the post-1986 conflicts, mainly concentrated in marginal, rather unproductive areas of the country, in contrast to the 1979 and 1983–5 conflict which was centrally located and threatened the stability of the government itself.

4 Economic Costs of Conflicts: A Meso Analysis

To understand how these negative macro effects translated into effects on individual or household well-being, meso analysis is needed. The meso analysis examines both the

sectoral reallocation, mainly determined through the market, and changes in the allocation of government expenditures.

4.1   A Sectoral Reallocation due to Conflict

Wars tend to change the production activities of households and firms. In general, one
would expect non-tradable production to rise relative to tradables; and subsistence
activities in particular to increase given the disruptions in national and international
markets and rising transaction costs. In the Ugandan context, this would suggest a shift
towards subsistence agriculture and away from industrial activities. The evidence suggests that this is what occurred in relative terms, even though agriculture as well as
industry suffered absolutely from the conflict.

Agriculture is likely to be adversely affected by war, as the population is displaced,
while people search for a more secure environment, and households lose their entitlements to land. Moreover, with market disruptions it becomes more difficult to gain
access to fertilizer, to hired labour and markets to which to send produce. But because
levels of output are likely to decline in every sector due to the breakdown in markets
and migration, the share of agriculture in GDP might be expected to rise, and industrial
production to fall since the latter is more dependent on market transactions and
imported inputs. This seems to have been the case in Uganda. Agricultural production
as a proportion of GDP rose during political instability, from just under half of GDP
in 1970 to over 70 per cent in the worst war years of 1970 and 1983. Meanwhile, manufacturing as a percentage of GDP declined from 7 per cent in 1975 to 2 per cent in
1981; and industrial production showed a similar trend. Despite the rise in agriculture
as a proportion of GDP from 1969 to 1983, which contrasts with the trend fall in Kenya
(Figure 9.18), data for agricultural production as a whole in volume terms (Figure 9.19),
and for selected food crops, shown in Table 9.5, showed a large drop in production
from 1977 to 1981. Production of plantains, cereals, and root crops fell particularly
sharply in 1979 and 1980. Indeed the year 1980 witnessed a famine in most parts of the
country, and production of plantains and cereals did not full recover until the late 1980s
although root crops recovered more quickly.

Figures 9.20 and 9.21 show how industrial production fell both as a proportion of
GDP, and in absolute terms during the political instability and conflict, while it rose
for most of the period in Kenya. In 1969, industrial production as a proportion of GDP
was 12 per cent, which was considerably higher than that of Kenya at 8 per cent.
But between 1969 to 1979, this ratio declined consistently to 4 per cent, while in Kenya
it continued to increase. The difference may be explained by the politically unstable
environment, the expulsion of the Asians, and the migration of technically skilled
Ugandans. Shortly after the 1979 war, the industrial production to GDP ratio increased
again until 1983, when conflict again caused it to decrease until 1986. Since 1986, with
political stability in most of the country, this ratio has been on the increase. A similar
performance was shown by the ratio of manufacturing to GDP, although the decline
was even more precipitous, and up to 1992 there was little sign of recovery.

	5(1) Manufacturing as % of GDP	5(2) Manufacturing as % of GDP	5(3) Manufacturing as % of GDP	5(4) Manufacturing output level	5(5) Agriculture as % of GDP	5(6) Agriculture as % of GDP
Constant	0.0988**** (14.78)	0.099**** (14.39)	0.098**** (13.61)	2.119e+4***** (8.93)	0.423**** (11.00)	0.411*** (11.56)
War 1979–80	-0.025*** (-2.40)	-0.0256*** (-2.19)		-3.668e+3 (-0.602)	0.065 (1.11)	0.0057 (0.096)
War 1983–85	-0.0118 (-0.928)	-0.0121 (-0.896)		-3.065e+3 (-0.590)	0.089 (1.23)	0.0386 (0.554)
Political instability		-0.001*** (-0.095)	-0.0066 (-0.975)	-1.139**** (-3.436)		0.093*** (2.50)
Defence expenditure as % of GDP	-0.218**** (-6.148)	-0.219**** (-5.81)	-0.209*** (-5.35)	0.0106** (3.640)	0.714***** (3.53)	0.575**** (2.97)
R–Squared	0.653	0.620	0.549	0.502	0.37	0.49
F–Value	15.26	11.04	17.69	7.056	5.49	6.46

	5(7) Agriculture as % of GDP	5(8) Agriculture output level	5(9) Defence as % of GDP	5(10) Defence as % of GDP	5(11) Defence as % of GDP	5(12) Defence level
Constant	0.410**** (11.99)	1.797e+7***** (21.95)	0.165*** (9.73)	0.144*** (6.80)	0.145**** (6.97)	5.0833e+5*** (4.271)
War 1979–80		9.505e+5 (0.452)	-0.009 (-0.181)	-0.0402 (-0.59)		-5.334e+5** (-1.414)
War 1983–85		-5.148e+4 (-0.028)	0.0589 (0.897)	0.0279 (0.414)		-4.823e+5** (-1.509)
Political instability	0.099**** (3.084)	-2.134e+6*** (-1.865)		0.0510* (1.501)	0.049** (1.625)	5.103e+5*** (2.687)
Defence expenditure as % of GDP	0.582***** (3.144)	5.383**** (5.38)				
R–Squared	0.483	0.531	0.08	0.101	0.081	0.214
F–Value	13.55	7.94	0.91	1.045	2.64	2.63

**** significant at 1% level.
*** significant at 5% level.
** significant at 10% level.
* significant at 20% level.
Figures in parentheses are t-ratios.

The regression analysis, presented in Table 9.5, generally confirms these sectoral effects. Significant results are that agriculture as a share of GDP was positively affected by POLINST (5(6) and 5(7)); and manufacturing as a share of GDP was negatively affected by the 1979–80 war (equations 5(1) and 5(2)); while defence expenditure as a share of GDP was negatively related to manufacturing and positively related to agriculture. However, the absolute effects of the political disturbances were negative for *both* agriculture and manufacturing (5(8) and 5(4)), while defence expenditure as a share of GDP, which, as noted above, itself appeared to be positively affected by the political disturbances, had a significant positive effect on the level of agricultural and manufacturing output.

Micro studies confirm the reallocation of production towards subsistence agriculture in both rural and urban areas during the political disturbances, with a fall in production of cash crops in the rural areas and a rise in urban farming (see Bigsten and Kayizzi-Mugwera 1992 and 1995; Maxwell, 1995). Both industry and markets were badly affected by the 'economic war'—this in turn had negative effects on agriculture as markets were disrupted.

The fall in production associated with the instability had negative effects on welfare. The worst consequences arose from the agricultural decline. For the most part, particular crops are grown in distinct areas due to climatic factors, with cereals mainly grown in the north and eastern regions, while plantains are grown in the southern and western parts of the country. Hence a decomposition of crop production may give a better idea of the effects of the wars on agricultural production in particular areas. As shown in Table 9.6, production of plantain crops was relatively stable between 1970 and 1978.[14] However, due to the war in 1979, there was a drop in the production of plantains from 6,090 to 5,699 tonnes, as the war between Tanzania and Uganda led to displacements of people in search of security. Other crops also declined—the production of cereals from 1,505 tonnes in 1978 to 1,078 tonnes in 1980, and root crops production from 3,716 tonnes to 3,382 tonnes. Cereal production was adversely affected by the war from 1984 to 1986, which took place in the south. Other crops, grown elsewhere, were less badly affected in those years.

Being an agricultural subsistence economy, a decline in production of these subsistence crops has adverse effects on household welfare. Moreover, the agricultural sector employs the majority of the population, providing both employment and food, any excess being sold to buy other essential commodities. Data for food production per capita show a decline of over 40 per cent between 1975 and 1980. Estimates of calorie availability per person indicate a decline from 2,096 in 1970 (then 90 per cent of estimated requirements) to 1,778 in 1980 (80 per cent of requirements on average), with a recovery to 2,180 by 1990.

The decline in industrial production was much larger than the fall in agricultural output. The decline in the early years of the 1970s is not to be attributed to fighting. Rather it was due to a poor political environment which discouraged investment at that time. The period was characterized by the nationalization of private industrial enterprises (which resulted in reduced inflows of foreign capital) and made worse by the expulsion

---

[14] The crops referred to in Table 9.6 do not include cash crops such as coffee, cotton, or tea.

Table 9.6 Production of selected food crops ('000 tonnes)

Year	Plantains	Cereals	Root crops
1970	7,657	1,633	4,148
1971	7,557	1,419	3,842
1972	7,634	1,513	3,874
1973	8,126	1,448	3,364
1974	8,879	1,366	4,136
1975	9,106	1,719	4,945
1976	8,137	1,640	4,840
1977	8,531	1,488	4,651
1978	8,844	1,505	3,716
1979	6,090	1,150	3,382
1980	5,699	1,078	3,438
1981	5,900	1,165	4,509
1982	6,596	1,093	4,810
1983	6,487	1,399	5,291
1984	6,250	944	4,731
1985	6,468	1,171	4,532
1986	6,565	1,058	4,863
1987	7,039	1,220	4,960
1988	7,293	1,398	5,177
1989	7,469	1,637	5,474
1990	7,842	1,580	5,337
1991	8,080	1,576	5,268
1992	7,806	1,743	5,069
1993	8,222	1,880	5,417
1994	9,000	1,986	4,577
1995	9,519	2,080	5,246

Sources: Republic of Uganda, *Statistical Abstracts* (various years).

of the Asians who had dominated the sector. Together with the low managerial skills of those allocated the deported Asians' properties and businesses, this led to a substantial decline in both production and maintenance in these sectors.[15] Another important factor leading to mismanagement of the industrial sector was job insecurity among managers.

The decline in industrial production caused shortages of commodities and led to rising prices. During the 1970's some goods, including sugar, were rationed resulting in the emergence of parallel markets supplied by goods smuggled from neighbouring countries.[16]

[15] Those who benefited from the deported Asians' property were mainly political self-seekers without any managerial skills.

[16] This may also widen income distribution as there would be some individuals who benefited from the rents accrued to the 'magendo' business. During the period 1970–80 there was a growing affluent middle-class group which derived most of its income from business activities.

The fall in industrial production also had a negative effect on employment opportunities, mainly affecting skilled and unskilled labourers located in major towns, especially Jinja and Kampala. However, because of the small size of the sector, the number of people affected was not high.

4.2   Changing Allocation of Government Expenditures

We noted above that one macro effect of conflict was a decline in revenue. Taxes as a percentage of GDP fell to as little as 2.1 per cent in 1980 from 10.7 per cent in 1968. Tax revenue recovered in 1983 to 15.5 per cent of GDP, but then again fell sharply with the renewal of conflict. It was only 4.4 per cent of GDP in 1988. In absolute terms the situation was even worse because of the decline in GDP over the 1970s. Regression analysis showed that both political instability and the 1979–80 war had negative effects on the absolute levels of government revenue although not on the revenue ratio, which may be due to the fact that time-lags were not included. As expected government expenditure fell less drastically, as deficit financing increased. As a percentage of GDP expenditure was 14.8 per cent in 1970, falling to 6.3 per cent in 1979 and only 4.3 per cent in 1980. It rose to over 11 per cent in 1983, but then fell back, with the conflict, to 6.6 per cent in 1985.

4.2.1   Social Expenditure on Health, Education and Defence
The most direct impact of the government on household welfare is through its expenditure on social services. With declining revenues and expenditure, government expenditure on social services was also adversely affected. Moreover, there is a clear indication in Figures 9.22 and 9.23 that there was a reallocation of resources from the health and education sectors to the defence sector.

Figure 9.22 shows the shares of defence, education, and health as a percentage of GDP for the past three decades. As might be expected, defence expenditure crowded out expenditure on the social services so that there was a steady decline in both education and health as a percentage of GDP from the early 1970s onwards, with an especially sharp decline in 1979 for both. Education and health expenditures had fallen to almost nothing by 1987. The same trend is revealed by the shares of total government expenditure (Figure 9.23). In 1961 the share of defence expenditure was almost zero, but health and education were 20 and 10 per cent respectively; defence expenditures have been on the increase since then, peaking in 1971, 1981, and 1990; health expenditure had been on a consistent downward trend falling to below 2 per cent of total government expenditure in 1986, with some recovery since then. Education also generally showed a downward trend, but less steep.

Translating these declining shares of social services into absolute figures (Figure 9.24) shows a decline for both health and education over the period from the late 1960s, with especially sharp declines during the two war periods. When further deflated to allow for population growth, expenditure per head diminished to less than 7 per cent of the 1970 level in 1981 in the case of education, and to 8.3 per cent in the case of health.

Table 9.7 Social developments in Uganda, 1962–1990s

Year	Calories per person	Calories as % required	Primary school enrolment (%)	Secondary school enrolment (%)	Persons per doctor	Population with safe water (%)	Adult literacy (%)	IMR
1960	2,383	na	49	3	15,050	na	25	133
1970	2,096	90	54	4	9,210	35	44	117
1980	1,778	80	50	5	26,810	16	43	113
1990 (or near)	2,180	93	67	11	21,681	34	54	114

Sources: UNDP 1996; *Human Development Reports* (various editions); World Bank 1989*a*, 1996*a*; *World Development Reports* (various years).

4.3   Growth, War, and Household Welfare

Falling GDP is obviously likely to lead to worsening household incomes and welfare. But although the conflicts in Uganda in the 1970s and 1983–5, which were associated with falling GDP, predisposed to falling welfare, the current regime has faced persistent rebel activities in the north and yet has achieved good macroeconomic performance, so war does not inevitably lead to worsening aggregate welfare.

Social indicators are needed to ascertain how households were affected during war periods. One direct indicator would be the poverty level, but the data needed, which would include detailed household data sets collected at various points in time during the periods of conflict, are not available. However, other social indicators are available, which are summarized in Table 9.7. The table shows that most indicators worsened over the war period, while in contrast in Kenya most indicators improved or remained relatively stable. Calorie intake per person deteriorated in the period 1970–80 in Uganda, while there was an increase in calorie intake per person between 1980–90.[17] All other social indicators also suggest there was a negative impact on the welfare of households during the period 1970–80. For example, primary enrolment fell, the available doctors per person decreased; and the population with access to safe water decreased.

4.4   Conclusion on Meso Performance and Household Well-being

During the conflicts of the 1970s and 1980s, there was a negative effect on macroeconomic performance with consequent knock-on effects on both private and public entitlements. Though agriculture increased its share and subsistence activities rose, household's well-being was negatively affected as shown by the decline in income per capita. In the 1970s, consumption per head is estimated to have declined by 4 per cent a year, while in Kenya it increased by 1.5 per cent a year. Declining tax revenue as a share of GDP and a rising share of military in total expenditure compounded the situation, so households also had reduced access to public entitlements. However, the post-1986 conflicts have had less severe adverse effects, except in the immediate vicinity of the conflict. In

[17] This increase may be difficult to explain since it comprises both a period of civil unrest—1981–5, and a period of relative stability—1986–90. Attributing the increase in the calorie intake per person to any particular period would require some time series of this data.

aggregate since 1986, income per capita has been rising as have public entitlements for health and education services. None the less, there is evidence of rising poverty over this period. Comparisons of the earlier (geographically widespread) and the later (localized) conflicts suggest the latter had less adverse effects on the economy as a whole on average Uganda-wide household welfare, although they had negative effects on economic development and welfare in the districts where they were concentrated.

5   Regional Imbalances

The effects of instability were not uniform throughout the country. In the days of Amin and Obote the south suffered most, while from 1986 it was the north, the west and to a certain extent the east which was directly affected by fighting. Indirect effects may be located outside the war zones: for example, the cuts in public expenditure or import shortages normally affect the whole country. This section records regional imbalances in important economic and social dimensions, attempting to identify which areas were particularly badly affected by the political instability. However, there were other factors besides conflict affecting regional imbalances, notably market trends and government policy, and it is difficult to disentangle these various influences.

Regional inequalities in Uganda date back to pre-colonial times; they were accentuated by the colonial regime which favoured the southern part of the country.[18] However, there is some evidence of a narrowing of some of the infrastructural differentials, particularly as between the south and the north, due both to the negative effects of the war, which was concentrated in the south, and to government policy particularly under Obote and Amin, both northerners. None the less, economic opportunities remain heavily concentrated in the south. The disruptions of war affected market activities particularly badly, but the effects appear to have been temporary.

5.1   Infrastructure

The economic and social infrastructure is concentrated in the central and southern parts of the country, while the northern regions remain the most deprived. But the gap between the north, and the rest of the country appears to have narrowed since independence. Part of this is due to destruction of facilities in the south—due to conflict —while the north generally saw some improvements.

5.2   Water

The Central and Eastern Regions were most favoured in 1961, with one borehole for about 20,000 people compared with over 30,000 in the Western and Northern Regions (see Table 9.8). But from then on, the other Regions were favoured—the

---

[18] The 'southern' and the 'south' part of Uganda is to be understood as including the Central and Western regions, and may be used interchangeably, while the 'northern' part normally includes both the Northern and Eastern regions.

Table 9.8 Regional distribution of boreholes

Region	1961		1969		1990s				Change in number of boreholes (%)		
	No. of boreholes	Population per borehole[a]	No. of boreholes	Rural population per borehole	No. of boreholes	Population per borehole	Rural population covered (%)[b]	Population with safe water	1961–9	1969–94	1961–94
Central	919	19,900	424[c]	53,540	1,588	2,307	24	28	–54	273	72
Eastern	897	20,910	1,894	13,910	2,504	1,520	40	25	111	32	179
Northern	586	31,470	1,205	13,210	3,521	847	42	28	106	192	501
Western	465	32,270	725	32,430	2,149	1,923	47	22	56	196	362

[a] Total population, including urban.

[b] By all sources including protected springs, boreholes, shallow wells, and gravity flow schemes.

[c] The decline in boreholes in Central Region is due to reclassification of some boreholes, as they were not local authority controlled, and a transfer from Central to Western region.

Sources: Republic of Uganda 1966b, 1996; UNDP 1996.

Table 9.9   Regional distribution of medical facilities

Region	Population per bed		Population per doctor, 1991	Population per nurse, 1991	Rural population to primary health–care centre (average km), 1992–3
	1971	1991			
Central	500	920	12,720	7,360	9.3
Eastern	780	1,600	35,130	12,970	7.4
Northern	1,040	930	57,950	18,300	11.3
Western	1,040	1,690	74,120	24,310	7.7
Uganda	750	1,200	27,140	12,480	8.8

Sources: Republic of Uganda 1972; World Bank 1993; Republic of Uganda, MFEP 1996.

Table 9.10   Regional distribution of education (%)

Region	Population by education level attained, 1969				Primary enrolment		Secondary enrolment 1990
	No. at school	P1–6	S5–6	University	1968	1990	
Central	56.2	35.9	0.11	0.17	38.2	68.8	11.4
Eastern	77.9	17.4	0.04	0.03	35.0	78.6	11.8
Northern	75.7	20.0	0.08	0.03	36.9	85.4	7.7
Western	75.8	21.2	0.05	0.02	31.3	67.7	9.4

P1–6: first six levels of Primary School.
AS5–6: last two years of Secondary School.

Source: Republic of Uganda 1973; World Bank 1993.

Eastern and Northern in the 1960s and, subsequently, the Western and Northern, so that by the 1990s rural coverage was least good in the Central Region at only 24 per cent, compared to over 40 per cent in the Western and Northern Regions.

5.3   Health Facilities

In 1971 the distribution of hospital and clinics favoured the Central Region, with the Northern and Western Regions having less than half as many beds per person. From 1971 to 1991 the situation deteriorated in all regions except the North. By 1991, the Northern and Central Regions had the most beds per person, the other two regions were in a considerably worse position (Table 9.9). The Central Region remained in the most favourable situation with respect to doctors and nurses.

5.4   Education

In 1969, the Central Region had the highest levels of educational attainments at every level, with little difference among the other regions. By 1990 there were improvements in all Regions, particularly in the Northern Region. At primary level, the Northern Region achieved the highest enrolment rate, while the Central Region had sunk to near the bottom (Table 9.10). But the Northern Region was the worst in terms of

Table 9.11 Distribution of land, cultivable land, soil quality, and crops by region

	Central Region	Eastern Region	Northern Region	Western Region
Cultivable land (km²)	34,458	26,638	68,241	38,261
% cultivable	92	95	83	77
Population per km², 1991 (rural)	106	143	44	72
% of Rural Council areas with unused land available for cultivation, 1992–3	28.0	27.7	37.7	48.2
Soil quality	I–II	II–III	II–III–IV	I–II–III
Proportion of area[a], 1990s:				
small-scale/subsistence	41.3	63.5	34.6	38.0
large-scale	7.0	5.4	0.4	5.2
Proportion of agricultural revenue from:				
cash crops	9.7	5.9	4.6	3.8
coffee	9.3	2.6	0.2	2.6

I: very good quality; II: good quality; III: poor quality; IV: very poor quality.
[a] Excluding land covered by water.
Source: Republic of Uganda, MFEP, 1996a; Republic of Uganda, 1971a; World Bank, 1996b.

gender balance, with the ratio of girls to boys at 0.58, compared to 0.8 as the national average. At secondary level, the Eastern Region had caught up with Central, and the Northern was still the lowest. Current human resources reflect past imbalances in educational opportunities: the Northern Region continues to lag behind the rest of the country as indicated by the adult literacy rate.

5.5   Land and Agriculture

The development potential of Uganda, both nationally and regionally, is heavily dependent on its agricultural resources. Although, in general, all regions can potentially provide for their own subsistence and for cash crops, the Northern Region is the worst endowed, in terms of quality of land and its use, while the Central and Western regions are the most fertile. Cash-crop agriculture is more developed in the south, and the crops, especially coffee, are more profitable than those, such as cotton, which are grown in the north.

Data for the early 1990s (Table 9.11) show that the Eastern and Central Regions have the highest proportion of land devoted to farmland; the Central Region has the most large farms and obtains the greatest revenue from cash crops. The Northern Region has the smallest proportion of farmland and of large-scale farms, indicating relative deprivation.

Southern and Central Region agriculture was particularly badly affected by conflict in the 1970s and mid-1980s, because cash crops were most affected by disrupted

Table 9.12   Regional distribution of employment, 1962–1991

| Region | Employment, 1970 (1962 = 100) | | | 1970–91 change as ratio to aggregate change |
	Total	Public	Private	Total
Central	177	168	185	2.2
Eastern	185	163	213	0.67
Northern	132	127	137	0.39
Western	156	137	173	0.71
Uganda	161	147	176	1.0

Sources: Republic of Uganda, *Statistical Abstracts* (various years); 1991 Population and Housing Census.

markets. In addition the fighting caused massive flight and household insecurity which radically disrupted farming (see Section 6). The post-1986 fighting affected the north, but it was generally sporadic and most farming continued. However, the insecurity delayed any modernization.

5.6   Employment

In 1962, recorded employment was fairly equally distributed among the population as between the Central, Eastern, and Northern Regions, with each accounting for about 20 per cent, but there was a disproportionate concentration in the Western Region in both public and private sectors. From 1962 to 1970, the Central and Eastern Regions benefited most from the rapid expansion in employment, with the Northern Region lagging behind. It was particularly weak in the public sector, where employment grew by only 28 per cent compared to a national expansion of 47 per cent.

From the early 1970s to the mid-1980s statistical data are scant, but in the late 1980s and early 1990s the employment was even more concentrated in the Central Region than in the 1960s, with the Eastern and especially the Northern Regions lagging (Table 9.12). For example in 1991, the proportion of employment in the Central Region was more than one-and-a-half its share of population, while the Northern share was only 56 per cent of its population share. The disparity is greater in terms of quality jobs, the Central Region had 54 per cent of male managerial jobs and 59 per cent of male employed professionals, compared to only 29 per cent of the population, and the Northern Region with 19 per cent of the population had 11 per cent of managerial jobs and 10 per cent of professional ones.

5.7   Business Enterprises and Employment

A survey of businesses employing more than five people in the early 1990s showed that the Central Region, had 60 per cent of total establishments, which provided 75 per cent of the employment and 84 per cent of the value-added. In contrast, the Northern and

Table 9.13 Incomes and poverty

Region	Distribution of taxpayers (rural), 1969		Average household expenditure, 1992 (Uganda average = 100)	Poverty levels			Distribution of income, cumulative (%) 1992–3
				1989–90 Total	1990–1		
	% <1,000 sh. pa	% >2,500 sh. pa			Rural	Urban	Lowest/highest quartile
Central	50	9.1	139.3[a]	51.1[b]	50.9	3.1	17/34
Eastern	84.9	3.7	84.3	61.3	84.7	20.9	29/19
Northern	90.8	3.1	81.5	68.2	93.8	65.1	39/13
Western	80.1	5.3	88.2	44.2	46.3	12.6	18/31
Major towns	16.3	43.9	na	na	na	na	na

[a] Includes Kampala. For 1989–90, Kampala was 105.8, and Central, excluding Kampala, 173.9 of Uganda average.
[b] Excludes Kampala

Sources: Republic of Uganda 1972; World Bank 1993; Department of Statistics, MFEP; UNDP 1996.

Western Regions together, accounted for 46.4 per cent of the total population, had 25 per cent of business establishments, 13 per cent of employment generated by these establishments, and 5 per cent of the value-added.[19] In contrast, a survey of small-scale and family enterprises showed that these were concentrated in the Eastern and Northern Regions, relative to their share of the population. Non-agricultural enterprises were disproportionately found in the Northern Region, which also had a higher proportion of hired labour.[20]

Taken together the surveys indicate that the large-scale formal business sector was disproportionately concentrated on the Central and, to a lesser extent, the Western Region, compared to the Northern Region which had a larger proportion of household agricultural activities, typically associated with lower incomes. For Uganda as a whole, value-added per employee in business enterprises in 1989 was 584,000 sh., while the value-added per employee in small-scale and household enterprises 1992–3 was 124,000 sh. Adjusting for price changes between these years would make the difference even greater. Although there is no direct evidence on the impact of conflict, the sizeable negative effect the instability of the 1970–86 period had on industrial production and government revenue would strongly suggest that the Central Region should have been most severely affected. However, it is clear from recent evidence that these effects were not long-lasting, as the region has recovered its predominance in formal-sector activities. This may have been helped by the endemic conflict in other regions in the later period.

5.8 Living Standards

Evidence on the regional distribution of incomes and poverty, summarized in Table 9.13, shows that in 1969 the rural Central Region was on average the best-off and had the lowest poverty levels, followed by the Western Region, with the Northern Region

[19] Evidence from Republic of Uganda 1996.   [20] Evidence from Republic of Uganda, MFEP, 1996.

being the worst-off. This pattern continued into the early 1990s. In 1969, according to the data for graduated taxpayers, 91 per cent of rural taxpayers in the Northern Region had annual incomes below 1,000 sh. compared to 50 per cent in the Central Region. A similar disparity is indicated by later data, with the Eastern and Northern Regions showing far higher poverty rate than the other regions. The Western Region seems to have caught up the Central Region; in the early 1990s, rural poverty in the Northern Region was estimated at over 90 per cent.

Data for regional GDP per capita adjusted for purchasing power parity (PPP), estimated by UNDP, shows that the Central Region had the highest income, with the Western Region just second, and the Northern Region had the lowest income, though PPP adjustment reduces the gaps between regions.

5.9   Social Indicators

Social indicators reveal similar disparities: the Central Region is ranked top for adult literacy, infant and child mortality rates, and life expectancy, and the Northern Region consistently ranked bottom (Tables 9.14 and 9.15). These differences, already apparent in the 1960s, continued into the 1990s for the only indicator—infant mortality rates (IMR)—available on a regional basis throughout the period (Table 9.13). But the impact of war from 1969 to 1991 is revealed by the sharp *rise* in IMR in the areas worst affected—that is, Central and Western Regions, while the rate in the Northern Region remained unchanged and the Eastern Region's rate continued to improve, although more slowly.

Social and economic indicators are calculated in the UNDP's Human Development Index (HDI) (Table 9.14). The gap between the North and Central Region is marked. The HDI of the Northern Region was 80 per cent of the Uganda average in 1992—this is eleven places lower than Uganda as a whole and eighth from the world's worst ranking, while the Central Region was 120 per cent of the Uganda average (up 15 ranks in world terms) and the Eastern and Western Regions were fairly close to the national average.

Table 9.14   Trends in infant mortality

	Central Region	Eastern Region	Northern Region	Western Region
IMR, 1959	150	178	170	163
IMR, 1969	99	139	142	121
IMR, 1991	105	122	141	125
Under-5 mortality, 1989–90	187[a] (174)	207	211	179

[a] Excludes Kampala; Kampala in parentheses.

Sources: Protectorate of Uganda 1961; Republic of Uganda 1971; World Bank 1993; Republic of Uganda 1996*b*.

Table 9.15 Human Development Index (HDI) by region, 1991

	Central Region	Eastern Region	Northern Region	Western Region
Adjusted real GDP per capita	155.5	82.6	75.1	83.0
Adult literacy	67.2	49.9	43.2	51.0
Educational attainment index[a] (Uganda average = 100)	111.8	94.6	84.9	95.9
Life expectancy (years)	49	49	43.6	48.9
HDI, 1992 (Uganda average = 100)	119.2	97.9	80.8	95.9

[a] Includes adult literacy plus average years of schooling.
Source: UNDP 1996.

Table 9.16 Northern war districts' performance

	Arua	Gulu	Kitgum	Northern Region	Uganda
IMR	137	172	165	141	122
Literacy (%)	46	49	39	43	54
Access to water (%)	23	54	29	42	31
Primary enrolment, 1989	69	53	102	72	72
Secondary enrolment, 1989 (%)	11	8	6	8	14
Population per government health unit, 1991 (000s)	17.3	21.1	17.6	16.2	19.5
Population per doctor, 1991 (000s)	52.1	42.3	38.9	57.9	27.1
Share of bottom quartile of population	33	38	64	43	25

Sources: UNDP 1996; World Bank 1996; Bigsten 1995.

There seems to have been some closing of the gap between the Regions over the years, partly the result of policy, partly the conflict. We have shown above that the gap between the north and the rest narrowed with respect to the provision of a number of services, including education and water. It is more difficult to assess economic differences. But comparing estimates by Jamal (1991*b*) for 1970 with data for 1992 suggests disparities had narrowed.[21] District data for areas especially affected by conflict in the 1990s (Table 9.16) indicates very poor economic levels, though not markedly worse than for the Northern Region as a whole.

[21] Jamal estimated that the south which accounted for 35–40% of the population had 75–80% of national income in 1970. Estimates for 1992, show that the Central Region with 28% of the population had 44% of the income.

Table 9.17   Characteristics of households interviewed

No. of respondents	56
Gender:	
Female	26
Male	30
Average household size	7
Marital status:	
Married	20
Divorced	5
Never married	6
Widowed	25
Average age of household head	52
Education of respondents:	
No education	27
Primary	23
Secondary	5
Tertiary	1

6   Survey of Semuto in the Luwero Triangle

It is not possible fully to determine the effects of conflict on households and individuals from macro or meso analysis. Moreover, no household surveys were available during the time of conflict to provide information at microlevel.[22] We therefore carried out a survey in one of the Ugandan areas affected by war for five years—Semuto in the Luwero Triangle—which borders the Kampala and Mpigi districts. As a result of the formation of the NRA which opposed the outcome of the 1981 elections, fighting started in the Semuto district and it continued to be a central location of conflict from 1981 to 1985/6. The operations and movements of the rebels within the district were rather ad hoc, which helped determine the impact on those living in the area.

In order to understand what happens to individual households in such an environment, we designed a questionnaire which covered different aspects of the effects of war: the demographic composition of the households; production activities within the household; market accessibility before and after the war; effects on income and nutrition; entitlements to assets and livestock during the war; displacement and the consequences; accessibility to social services; and a final section in which respondents could comment on any aspect of the war. Fifty-six respondents from three different sub-counties of Semuto were chosen for interview, one of the worst-affected counties. Only persons aged over 30 years at the time of conflict were interviewed. Some characteristics of the sample interviewed are presented in Table 9.17. The provision of social services was

---

[22] Household surveys conducted five or more years after the war ended provide some indication of the effects of war by showing how activities even years after the war were still apparently affected by it: e.g. Bigsten and Kayizzi-Mugwera, 1992, 1995; Maxwell 1995.

Table 9.18 Factors reported as impeding productive activities

Factors reported	Number	%
No cultivation because of movements of people	34	60.7
No operational markets	7	12.5
No communication/transport	6	10.7
Uncertainty discouraged agricultural activity	1	1.8
Disincentive due to crime/stealing of food	5	8.9

also investigated by interviewing staff members in two primary schools and one health centre. Most of the questions were open-ended in order to capture a broad view from respondents of the consequences of the conflict for their activities and well-being.

The main findings of the survey are presented below. Overall the survey showed that all effects of the conflict on households were negative. Production and money-generating activities were adversely affected, markets were distorted or ceased to exist, people lost their entitlements to assets such as land, as a result of displacement, the provision of social services in the health and education sectors stopped, and in general living conditions deteriorated drastically.

6.1 Production Activities and Collapse of Markets

Being a predominantly agricultural area almost all the inhabitants were farmers. Even those involved in other money-generating activities complemented these with farming. A wide range of crops were grown, including cash crops and crops for own consumption. The food crops grown for own consumption included plantains, cassava, sweet potatoes, beans, maize, yams, and groundnuts, while coffee was the main cash crop and some cotton was also grown. The three most important food crops for most households were bananas, sweet potatoes, and cassava—in some households the surplus production of these crops was sold.

All production activities in the area were affected negatively. All respondents indicated that the war either greatly reduced or halted their farming activities. Due to the prevailing war environment, plantations and gardens were left fallow for the following reasons:

1. Most respondents indicated that it was difficult to carry out any farming activities as they were preoccupied with how to survive the war. This was the main reason given by respondents (61 per cent). As people were always on the move and uncertain of how long they would stay in a given place, it was not possible to do much farming.

2. Output was difficult to sell due to the lack of any operational markets. Hence, there was almost no incentive to engage in agricultural activities for cash. Of the 56 respondents asked about the factors that most paralysed their agricultural activities, 12.5 per cent responded that lack of markets was the biggest factor. Previously, cash crops had been bought mainly by traders from Kampala. The coffee-processing plants in the area became inoperative, so that the market for the major cash crop was largely paralysed.

Table 9.19   Other activities generating income apart from agriculture

	Number	%
Not involved in any other activity	28	50.0
Business	16	28.5
Government	5	8.9
Private enterprise	7	12.5

3. Labour input on farms was reduced. Hired labourers were difficult to get during the war, and even if hired labour was available, there was no money to pay for it, due to the lack of markets.

4. Vandalism by government soldiers in the area was another reason given for the fall in production. Nine per cent of respondents indicated that this was one of the main problems affecting agricultural activities. In a number of cases, plantations were set on fire on the pretext of searching for rebels.

5. Respondents were asked whether the fall in production could be attributed to the limitation of services provided by agricultural extension workers. They indicated that these services were generally limited before the war, but during the war there was no provision of such services at all.

6. Lack of agricultural fertilizers was among the factors that led to a reduction in output according to 82 per cent of respondents; only 3.5 per cent had any access; and 14 per cent indicated that they had not used fertilizers before the war. Since the area was isolated from the other regions of the country, virtually no trade took place with Luwero, and this led to the lack of fertilizers.

Respondents were asked whether family members were engaged in other money-generating activities apart from farming. For those involved in small business trade activities, respondents indicated that the situation was analogous to farming:

- It was difficult to get new stock mainly due to the series of roadblocks mounted by soldiers from Kampala, the main source of merchandise for the Luwero district. The roadblocks were intended to check everyone entering the area, but in the process many people were victimized as being rebels and sometimes killed.
- It was also difficult to sell merchandise given the prevailing poverty in the area. This indicates how interlinked the markets are in the area—adverse effects on the production activities of farmers had a knock-on effect on other markets.
- Activities such as building houses were halted by the prevailing vandalism.
- It was difficult to carry out business activities during the war period as there were few regular customers because nearly everyone was living in a temporary location.
- It was difficult to get capital during the war. The formal credit market was generally non-existent as credit societies in the region had virtually collapsed. Both the suppliers and recipients of credit were reluctant to carry out any transactions during the conflict because of the uncertain conditions.

Table 9.20 Main factors which contributed to the collapse of markets during the war

	Number	%
Restricted movements by government soldiers	15	26.7
Unavailability of new stock	12	21.4
Low demand/poor buyers	29	51.7

Table 9.21 Factors that led to the inadequacy of income during war period

	Number	%
No longer working	28	50.0
Assets destroyed	12	21.4
Frequent displacements/uncertainty	15	26.8

A few respondents worked with government agencies, especially at county and sub-county levels and hospitals and schools. Government employees were affected because the area was sealed off from contact with other government agencies, and there was a lack of communication facilities such as vehicles and telephones.

With the collapse of market structures in the area, the key question was how the inhabitants survived. Without money, people resorted to barter. They exchanged basic items such as 'salt' for 'crops'. This appears to have worked at the beginning of the war period, although it was not sustainable over fairly long war periods because of a lack of commodities to exchange. Some respondents also indicated that it was risky to carry out cash transactions, as soldiers were likely to take the money, arguing that otherwise it might be used to fund rebel activities.

A further reason hindering the existence and operations of markets, was that respondents' movements were frequently restricted by government soldiers. Most people moved at night in search of safer places to stay, generally on foot. Table 9.21 shows the main factors that led to the collapse of markets during the war.

Respondents were asked whether the price of basic necessities such as paraffin, salt, sugar, and soap changed greatly during the war. Replies were contradictory. Some indicated that there were big price differentials between Luwero and other districts, particularly for basic essentials. Many respondents said that it was difficult to get access to traders selling such items, because traders were often killed on their way to collecting merchandise. This created excess demand for any available commodities. Others indicated that prices were very low for most commodities as people were generally so poor. Thus a shortage of supplies may not wholly explain the lack of access to such goods. The massive unemployment and prevailing poverty led to an inability to afford the basic items. The implications of the shortage of goods included unhygienic conditions and a lack of essential medicines, at times resulting in death.

Table 9.22   Types of property lost

	Number	%
House unroofed	9	16.1
Furniture stolen.destroyed	5	8.9
Animals and livestock stolen	5	8.9
All assets–including houses, furniture, livestock	37	66.1

6.2   Income, Assets Entitlement and Nutrition

The destruction of markets reduced production activities and caused a fall in household incomes, which were inadequate even before the war. The adverse effects on incomes were attributed to a number of factors:

- 50 per cent of respondents attributed their fall in income to the fact that they were no longer involved in money-generating activities. Uncertainty about the unpredictable war environment reduced the incentive to invest in money-generating activities.
- 27 per cent of respondents attributed their inadequate incomes to their frequent displacement which meant that people had continually to resettle in new places. As a result of displacement, people lost their entitlements to assets such as land and livestock. And given the unplanned nature of their movements, it was difficult to carry out any agricultural activity.
- The nutrition status of households is strongly related to income. Being an agricultural area, before the war households did not buy basic foods. But after displacement and loss of entitlements to land, fewer individuals were producing food themselves or hiring labour to produce it for them.
- Another reason given for the poor nutrition standards in the area was that people were concentrated in particular 'safe' areas such as the Lukoola. This led to excess demand for food in that area which the fragmented markets could not easily cater for. In some cases, individuals resorted to stealing.

The deaths that occurred in Luwero were not only be due to physical attacks, but also to a lack of basic necessities, including food and health services. Respondents suggested that the old and young were particularly vulnerable.

All respondents indicated that they lost their household property and other assets, such as livestock. Two-thirds of the respondents lost virtually everything as shown in Table 9.22. In most cases their cattle were stolen by soldiers. Their houses were unroofed or bombed and other household property such as bicycles and furniture was stolen or vandalized by soldiers. Some items had to be abandoned when moving.

The loss of entitlement to assets also reduced income-generating potential. This phenomenon may well have had far more long-term effects than any physical fighting. While almost all respondents indicated that they had managed to replace some of their assets by the time of the interview in February, 1997—over ten years after the end of the conflict nearly 60 per cent indicated that they were still worse off compared to the pre-war period.

Table 9.23 Distance and period of displacement from original place of residence

Miles	Number	%	Length of time (years)	Number	%
0–50	20	35.6	Up to one	12	21.4
51–100	15	26.8	One to three	27	48.2
101–50	5	8.9	Three to five	10	17.9
150 +	6	10.7	More than five	5	8.9

6.3 Displacement

All the respondents interviewed had been displaced from their original place of residence. We tried to establish the distance they moved during the war. But this was a difficult question for respondents, who indicated that they had no fixed destination. For those who gave a precise distance of displacement from their original place of residence, it was on average 68 miles, with a distribution given in Table 9.23.

It was noted that there was no established refugee camp which could be used as a safety net for the people of this area. Only 10 per cent of respondents had stayed in a refugee camp. One alternative was to stay with relatives, though this was used by only 15 per cent of respondents. The majority of the 'displaced' (74 per cent of respondents) lived in the bush, which had two implications for their security and survival: first, government troops found it difficult to differentiate civilians from rebels in the bush, and second, it was difficult for the NGOs, such as the Red Cross to find and supply essential commodities, such as food, given the ad hoc movements of the affected groups and their undefined place of residence.

The major problems mentioned by the displaced are as follows:

- The biggest problem, mentioned by 54 per cent of respondents, was getting food. This was accentuated by the frequent movements to different places in search of security.
- The second problem was the deficient accommodation in the new destination. Essentially they stayed in grass thatched huts, which were very temporary structures, and at times with no structure at all for fear of being recognized by government soldiers. Respondents indicated that this made life particularly difficult during the rainy season.
- Water was very scarce especially during the dry season. People used to walk fairly long distances in search of water. In the rainy season, they drank stagnant water, which presented serious health hazards. Indeed some indicated that water was one of the factors that led to their frequent moving. Being overcrowded in a destination resulted in a scarcity of water, which was generally only available from springs. The unhygienic conditions and the lack of safe drinking water were among the major causes of sickness during the war.
- Sickness without treatment was another problem mentioned by 32 per cent of respondents. Below we show what happened to the provision of social services.

Respondents were also asked for how long they were displaced. The overall average period of displacement was 3 years, 4 months. Almost all respondents interviewed went back to their original place of residence after the war.

6.4   Health, Education and Agricultural Extension Services

Health, education, and agricultural extension services were all adversely affected during the war. To start with the health sector: before the war there were health centres in every county of the Luwero district, mainly government-funded. In addition, there were health clinics and other private hospitals owned and operated by NGOs. Even before the war the provision of these services was often poor, particularly in the government health centres. These health centres were completely vandalized during the war and ceased to exist. For instance, the iron sheets which formed the roof of the health Centre at Semuto were taken by government troops.

There was virtually no medical personnel and the supply of drugs to health centres was hampered by the difficulty of communicating with Kampala, the source of supply. The health workers, including doctors, nurses, and medical assistants, abandoned their work as they were often accused by government troops of treating injured rebels. The few who still worked privately were expensive and lacked medicines and equipment.

As a result of the destruction of these facilities, the frequency of clinic and hospital visits fell. Most people resorted to the use of traditional herbs. Because of the poor health services, even minor illnesses that could easily have been cured with modern drugs resulted in death. Indeed as pointed out earlier, sickness and the lack of treatment was a major problem experienced by the inhabitants of the area during the war period.

It was even worse when people moved to more isolated places. The only health services that might have been feasible would have been mobile health clinics, but these could only have been provided by government; and the government already categorized all people in the area as being involved in rebel activities.

Schools were also badly affected. All primary and secondary schools were unroofed by soldiers. The teachers like other villagers were also displaced. The consequences of this were that:

- Most children were not in school. With the appalling state of schools and unavailability of teachers it was very difficult to study. The frequent mobility in search of safer places also meant that children dropped out of school. This affected the continuity of the students' education cycle, and in the end many of them abandoned schooling permanently.
- Many children joined the rebel groups in the area. There were two reasons given for this by the parents interviewed. First, it was easier to survive within a rebel group than as a civilian. Indeed, basic facilities like food, medicine, and water were available for the rebels in contrast to the civilians. Second, as school facilities were not available and children were idle, they chose to join the rebel groups.

Agricultural extension services also ceased during the war. Though the services had been poor before, they deteriorated further during the war for two main reasons. First,

Table 9.24 Main problems in resettling after the war

	Number	%
Replacing house	10	17.9
Replacing plantations	11	19.6
Immediate availabilty of food/basic necessities	30	53.5
Paying fees for children's education	5	8.9

there was less need as people were no longer involved in farming; and second, the situation was not conducive to the normal activities of extension workers.

6.5   Resettling and Replacement of Assets Destroyed during the War

Respondents were asked to comment on the difficulty of replacing what had been destroyed during the war. In general, the inhabitants had endeavoured to replace what was destroyed, but older people lacked the physical strength to rebuild or replace what they had lost. Good quality houses were particularly difficult to replace. We noted that many households which had had iron-roofed houses before the war were in grass-thatched houses.

It was particularly difficult to resettle immediately after the war. There was no income-generating activity that could be undertaken by the majority of people. Farming—the main occupation—takes a while to obtain returns. The most pressing problem was to get access to food and other basic necessities; this was coupled with the need to replace assets, as shown in Table 9.24. However, respondents indicated that the NRM government and NGOs assisted them, especially with food and essential medical facilities.

Another major problem was getting young people back into education. Some chose to remain in the army, while others engaged in small informal business activities or farming. After the war, there were long-term effects especially on education and health. Indeed some individuals mentioned that they had never resettled.

6.6   General Comments

In the questionnaire, respondents were asked for general comments on their welfare, access to markets, social services, as well as their opinion on the suffering endured during the war.

- On the question of general suffering, respondents indicated that a massive number of people were killed by the UNLF soldiers. Others died of secondary effects, such as hunger, lack of access to health services and so on.
- On the whole, respondents stated by 1997 that they were generally better off than during the war, although they were still not as well off as before the war. Some indicated that they had not received as much help from government as promised,

especially help to replace their houses. Some felt that the Luwero district had been less rewarded than expected.

- Respondents indicated that the incentive to invest in productive activities had been restored with the greater political stability. Market structures had recovered. This is reflected in the greater availability of goods and the reduction in price differentials between Luwero and other districts.
- Schools had been renovated, especially by NGOs, and the education system had greatly improved since the end of the war. However, they indicated that despite the renovation of health centres, these facilities were still inadequate, and they still had to pay for drugs. Government facilities were supplemented by private clinics, which had increased as compared to the pre-war situation.

6.7 Conclusions from the Micro Survey

This micro survey of the effects of the wars on households graphically underlined the negative effects, already identified in the earlier analysis. The survey emphasizes the linkages which mean that the total effects extend to beyond the immediate visible consequences, for example, the destruction of communications and markets undermines people's ability to sell their output or buy essentials. Many of the indirect effects not only lower living standards, but may lead to death.

This survey found *only* negative effects, it also found that these were all-embracing, covering all respondents in almost all dimensions. In this respect, the survey does not support the findings of other contributors to this book—for example, Keen or Chingono—who noted some positive effects for select groups, for example through the adoption of new income-earning opportunities created by war. One reason for this more negative view is that this survey was conducted in an area at the heart of the conflict, whereas other enquiries covered larger areas, including some outside the immediate area of conflict. It is well known that the Luwero Triangle suffered immense hardship, with up to half a million deaths, which is one-fifth of the Baganda population. Any positive effects from the conflict would have been likely to occur outside the most directly affected area.[23]

Micro surveys conducted in other rural and urban districts in Uganda five or more years after the war ended also noted the negative impact of conflict. A rural study, by Bigsten and Kayizzi-Mugwera (1995), showed that people suffered from reduced remittances and agricultural inputs, and that rural employment had been adversely affected, with a consequent shift towards subsistence agriculture and Maxwell (1995) found an increase in urban farming and a shift into the informal sector in Kampala.

However, other studies in Uganda noted more positive household survival strategies to cope with political disturbance and conflict. For example, Green (1981) identified a thriving informal economy in the early 1980s, although much of it appeared to be occupied with trade and smuggling rather than production. Similar findings were made

---

[23] Chingono's more positive evidence for Mozambique is based on an urban survey outside the locus of fighting.

for north-western Uganda (which was a conflict centre at the time) in the late 1980s by Meagher (1990). Each of these studies identified household strategies which moderated the harsh effects of conflict, but in none did the outcome appear to be one of net gains.

7 Conclusions of the Uganda Study as a Whole

Political instability and war in Uganda had very heavy economic costs, in addition to the high number of deaths resulting from the fighting. Both private and public entitlements were undermined during the Amin period, 1979–80 and the NRM war of the early 1980s.

In the period from 1972 to 1986, Uganda exemplified most of the negative effects predicted in the general framework in Volume I. The effects were particularly severe with respect to *public* entitlements; as for *private* entitlements, people's ability to retreat into subsistence activities provided some sort of protection, but not, as noted in the micro survey, where the fighting was most severe, and people's own farming activities were thoroughly disrupted, often by displacement

Most of the costs followed the direction expected, according to the analysis presented in Volume I. As predicted there, at a macrolevel there was a fall in GDP per capita during the period of war and political disturbance compared with what might have been expected in the absence of conflict, together with reduced export earnings and imports, lower investment and savings ratios and reduced government revenue and expenditure. The inflation rate accelerated, although the budget deficit as a proportion of GDP did not rise to a very large level. In Uganda, there was an unusually severe contraction of government revenue and expenditure, so that the government effectively ceased to perform any functions that might have offset the harsh human effects.

At the mesolevel, as anticipated there was a switch of government expenditure to the military away from the economic and social sectors. Theory predicts a switch from tradables to non-tradables; from marketed production to subsistence production; and from the formal to the informal sector. There was strong evidence that this occurred in Uganda, with a rise in the proportion of agricultural output, and within agriculture of subsistence activities. Moreover, micro studies showed that an informal 'magendo' economy developed which permitted smuggling and exchange so that probably more economic activity (including the sale of coffee across borders) occurred than the official data suggest.[24] This meant that outside the worst areas of fighting, people were partly able to protect their private incomes. But with the collapse of virtually all state medical and educational facilities, people were left to fend for themselves. In this respect, the Uganda wars were worse than in some other countries, such as Sri Lanka (Ch. 8 this volume), where government or rebel authorities were able to sustain services, food rations and so on. At a microlevel, entitlements of all kinds declined, sometimes with catastrophic consequences for human survival. This was borne out by data for incomes,

---

[24] Official data normally include some estimates of informal-sector activities, but these are usually taken as a fixed proportion of formal activities and estimates are not enlarged to allow for wartime developments.

government expenditure on social sectors, and worsening social indicators shown above. But the most graphic illustration of these negative developments was provided by results of the micro survey in the Luwero district.

Since 1971, Uganda has been subjected to an almost continuous period of strong political disturbance or outright war. Our analysis suggests that the political disturbances of 1971 to 1985 that were associated with a stronger negative impact on the economy and human welfare than the specific outbreaks of civil war in 1979–80 or 1983–5. This does not mean that these wars did not badly affect their particular localities—and indeed their effects are incorporated in the costs of political instability of the period 1972–85 as a whole—but rather that the effects were largely confined to the localities where they occurred, while generalized political disturbance in the centre of the country, undermining government authority and functions had worse aggregate effects.

The post-1986 conflicts have had far less serious effects at a nationwide level, and indeed they have coincided with a general economic and social recovery, including the restoration of government capacity. But these more localized conflicts have had very serious costs for those living in the areas affected, including loss of life, assets, education and health services and displacement. And, at a macrolevel, there has been a significant diversion of resources into military expenditure, accounting for 20 per cent of government recurrent expenditure in 1995/6, compared to 8 per cent for education, 3 per cent for health. The costs of the ongoing conflict should not be overlooked even though they are far smaller than the costs of earlier conflicts.

REFERENCES

ABRAHAMSSON, H. and NILSSON, A. (1995), *Mozambique: The Troubled Transition*, London: Zed Books.

ACEVEDO, A. and NEIRA, O. (1992), *El final de la hiperinflación prolongada*, Managua: CRIES.

Afghanistan Outlook (1999), Office of the UN Coordinator, New York: UN.

AFRICA WATCH (1990), *Denying the 'Honor of Living': Sudan, A Human Rights Disaster*, New York; Washington; London: Africa Watch Committee.

AFRICAN RIGHTS (1995), *Facing Genocide: The Nuba of Sudan*, London: African Rights.

Agence France-Presse (various), News reports available at http://www.reliefweb.int.

ALBALA-BERTRAND, J. (1993), *The Political Economy of Large Natural Disasters*, Oxford: Clarendon Press.

ALI, T. M. A. (1988), 'The State and Agricultural Policy: In Quest of a Framework for Analysis of Development Strategies', in T. Barnett and A. Abdelkarim (eds.), *Sudan: State, Capital and Transformation*, London: Croom Helm.

ALIER, A. (1990), *Southern Sudan: Too Many Agreements Dishonoured*, Reading: Ithaca Press.

AMNESTY INTERNATIONAL (1989), *Sudan: Human Rights Violations in the Context of Civil War*, London: Amnesty International.

—— (1995a), *Sierra Leone: Human Rights Abuses in a War against Civilians*, London: Amnesty International.

—— (1995b), *Women in Afghanistan: A Human Rights Catastrophe*, London: Amnesty International.

ARANA, M. (1990), 'Nicaragua: Estabilización, ajuste y estrategia económica', in M. Arana, R. Stahler-Sholk, and C. Vilas (eds.), *Políticas de ajuste en Nicaragua: Reflexiones sobre sus implicaciones estratégicas*, Managua: CRIES.

ASIAN DEVELOPMENT BANK (various years), *Key Economic Indicators of Developing Asian and Pacific Countries*, Manila: Asian Development Bank.

ATEEG (1983), 'A Critical Analysis of Livestock and Meat Marketing in Sudan', Ph.D. thesis, London University.

ATHUKORALA, P. (1995), 'Foreign Direct Investment and Manufacturing for Export in a New Exporting Country: The Case of Sri Lanka', *World Economy*, 18/4.

AVIRGAN, T. and HONEY, M. (1982), *War in Uganda*, Dar es Salaam: Tanzania Publishing House.

BANCO DE MOÇAMBIQUE (1995), *Boletim Estatístico*, 3, Maputo.

BARKER, P. (1999), 'Making a Difference for Afghan Women', *Journal of Humanitarian Assistance*, http://www.reliefweb.int (May).

BARNETT, T. and ABDEL KARIM, A. (1991), *Sudan: The Gezira Scheme and Agricultural Transition*, London: Cass.

BARRACLOUGH, S. (1982), *A Preliminary Analysis of the Nicaraguan Food System*, Geneva: UNRISD.

BARRO, R. J. (1990), 'Government Spending in a Simple Model of Endogenous Growth', *Journal of Political Economy*, 98: 103–25.

BARROWS, W. (1976), *Grassroots Politics in an African State: Integration and Development in Sierra Leone*, New York and London: Africana.

BARRY, D. (1985), 'La Guerra de Baja Intensidad', *Pensamiento Propio*, 21.

BAUMEISTER, E. (1985), 'The Structure of Nicaraguan Agriculture and the Sandinista Agrarian Reform', in R. Harris and C. Vilas (eds.), *A Revolution under Siege*, London: Zed Books.

BAUMEISTER, E. and NEIRA, O. (1987), 'La conformación de una economía mixta: Estructura de clases y política estatal en la transición nicaragüense', in J. L. Coraggio and C. D. Deere (eds.), *La Transición Difícil*, México: Siglo XXI/CRIES.

BERG-SCHLOSSER, D. and SIEGLER, R. (1990), *Political Stability and Development: A Comparative Analysis of Kenya, Tanzania and Uganda*, Boulder, Colo. and London: Lynne Rienner.

BHADURI, A. and SKARSTEIN, R. (1996), 'Short-period Macroeconomic Aspects of Foreign Aid', *Cambridge Journal of Economics*, 20/2.

BIGSTEN, A. (1995), 'Uganda 1995: Boom and Poverty in Uganda', *Macroeconomic Studies*, Stockholm: SIDA.

—— and KAYIZZI-MUGWERA, S. (1992), 'Adaption and Distress in the Urban Economy: A Study of Kampala Households', *World Development*, 20/10: 1423–42.

—— —— (1995), 'Rural Sector Responses to Economic Crisis in Uganda', *Journal of International Development*, 7/2: 181–210.

BIONDI-MORA, B. (1990), *Revolución y Política Alimentaria: un Análisis Crítico de Nicaragua*, México: Siglo XXI/CRIES.

BOOTHBY, N., UPTOM, P., and SULTAN, A. (1991), *Children of Mozambique: The Cost of Survival*, Durham NC.: Duke University.

Bradbury, M. (1995), 'Rebels Without a Cause? An Exploratory Report on the Conflict in Sierra Leone', Council of Churches in Sierra Leone, *Relief Secretariat*, 1 (April).

BRETT, E. A. (1993), *Providing for the Rural Poor: Institutional Decay and Transformation in Uganda*, Kampala: Fountain Publishers.

BRITISH AGENCIES AFGHANISTAN GROUP (BAAG) (1996a), *Exile and Return: Report on a Study on Coping Strategies among Afghan Refugees in Iran and Returnees to Afghanistan*, London: The Refugee Council.

—— (1996b), *Living in Exile: Report on a Study of Economic Coping Strategies among Afghan Refugees in Pakistan*, London: The Refugee Council.

—— (1997a), *A Population on the Move: A Study of the Socio-economic Manifestations of Displacement in Relation to Kabul, Afghanistan*, London: The Refugee Council.

—— (1997b), 'Return and Reconstruction: Report on a Study of Economic Coping Strategies Among Farmers in Farah Province, Afghanistan', London: The Refugee Council.

BROCHMANN, G. and OFSTAD, A. (1990), *Mozambique: Norwegian Assistance in a Context of Crisis*, Fantoft: Chr. Michelsen Institute.

BRÜCK, T. (1996), *The Economic Effects of War*, M.Phil. thesis, University of Oxford.

—— (1997), 'Macroeconomic Effects of the War in Mozambique', QEH Working Paper Series, 11, Oxford: Queen Elizabeth House (http://www.qeh.ox.ac.uk/ftprc.html).

—— (1998), Guerra e Desenvolvimento em Moçambique, *Análise Social*, 23/149: 1019–51.

—— FITZGERALD, E. V. K., and GRIGSBY, A. (2000), *Enhancing the Private Sector to Post-War Recovery in Poor Countries*, Report Prepared for the UK Department for International Development, Oxford: Queen Elizabeth House (http://www.qeh.ox.ac.uk/ftprc.html).

BRUNDENIUS, C. (1987), Industrial Development Strategies in Revolutionary Nicaragua, in R. Spalding (ed.), *The Political Economy of Revolutionary Nicaragua*, London: Allen & Unwin.

BRZOSKA, M. (1995), 'The Arms Trade', in R. A. Hinde and H. E. Watson (eds.), *War: A Cruel Necessity? The Bases of Institutionalized Violence*, London: Tauris Academic Studies.

BWENGYE, F. L. (1985), *The Agony of Uganda: From Idi Amin to Obote: Repressive Rule and Bloodshed*, London: Regency Press.

CARE (1996), *Key Facts on Afghanistan*, Atlanta, http://www.care.org/newscenter/pr/afghan4.html.

CASTEL-BRANCO, C. N. (ed.) (1994), *Moçambique: Perspectivas Económicas*, Maputo: Universidade Eduardo Mondlane and Fundação Friedrich Ebert.

CASTILLO, M. (1989), 'El sector industrial de la economía nicaragüense', *Revolución y Desarrollo*, 5 (July).

CATHOLIC RELIEF SERVICES (CRS) (1995), *Chronology of Events Leading to the Closure of the ULIMO Demobilization Project*, Baltimore and Freetown: Catholic Relief Services.

CENTRAL BANK OF SRI LANKA (various years), *Annual Report on the Economy*, Colombo: Central Bank.

CEPAL (1981), *Nicaragua: El impacto de la Mutación Política*, Santiago: Comisión Económica para América Latina.

—— (1988), *Damage Caused by Hurricane Joan in Nicaragua*, Santiago: Comisión Económica para América Latina.

CHINGONO, M. F. (1996a), *The State, Violence and Development: The Political Economy of War in Mozambique, 1975–1992*, Aldershot: Avebury.

—— (1996b), 'War, Economic Change and Development in Mozambique: The Grass-roots War Economy of Manica Province', Queen Elizabeth House, Oxford (mimeo).

CHURCHILL, W. (1908), *My African Journey*, repr. 1990, London: Mandarin.

CIERA (1984), *Informe Final del Proyecto Estrategia Alimentaria*, i–iv, Managua: CIERA/PAN/ CIDA.

—— (1988), *El Debate Sobre la Reforma Económica*, Managua: CIERA.

—— (1989), *La Reforma Agraria Nicaraüense*, 1979–1989, i–ix, Managua: CIERA.

CLAY, J. W., STEINGRABER, S., and NIGGLI, P. (1988), *The Spoils of Famine: Ethiopian Famine Policy and Peasant Agriculture*, Cambridge, Mass.: Cultural Survival Inc.

CLIFF, J. and NOORMAHOMED, A. R. (1988), 'Health as a Target: South Africa's Destabilization of Mozambique', *Social Science and Medicine*, 27: 717–22.

COHEN, A. (1959), *British Policy in Changing Africa*, London: Routledge & Kegan Paul.

COLBURN, F. (1986), *Post-revolutionary Nicaragua*, Los Angeles: University of California Press.

COLEMAN, J. (1990), *The Foundations of Social Theory*, Cambridge, Mass.: The Belknap Press of Harvard University Press.

COLLIER, P. (1995), 'Civil War and the Economics of the Peace Dividend', CSAE Working Paper Series 8, Centre for the Study of African Economies, Oxford, 95–8.

—— and GUNNING, J. (1995), 'War, Peace and Private Portfolios', *World Development*, 23/2: 233–41.

COLLINS, R. O. (1971), *Land Beyond the Rivers: The Southern Sudan, 1898–1918*, New Haven, and London: Yale University Press.

—— (1983), *Shadows in the Grass: Britain in the Southern Sudan, 1918–1956*, New Haven and London: Yale University Press.

COMISSÃO NACIONAL DO PLANO (1987), *Informação Estatística 1986*, Maputo: Comissão Nacional do Plano.

—— (1989), *Informação Estatística 1988*, Maputo: Comissão Nacional do Plano.

—— (1990), *Estatísticas dos Transportes e Comunicações 1989*, Maputo: Comissão Nacional do Plano.

—— (1991), *Anuário Estatístico 1991*, Maputo: Comissão Nacional do Plano.

—— (1993a), *Anuário Estatístico 1992*, Maputo: Comissão Nacional do Plano.

—— (1993b), *Plano de Reconstrução Nacional 1994–96*, Maputo: Comissão Nacional do Plano.

—— (1995), *Anuário Estatístico 1994*, Maputo: Comissão Nacional do Plano.

CONCERN WORLDWIDE (1988), 'Situation Report on Relief Operations', Dublin: Concern Worldwide.

CORAGGIO, J. L. and DEERE, C. D. (eds.) (1987), *La Transición Difícil*, México: CRIES/Siglo XXI.

CRAMER, C. (1999), 'Can Africa Industrialize by Processing Primary Commodities? The Case of Mozambican Cashew Nuts', *World Development*, 27/7: 1247–66.

—— and PONTARA, N. (1998), 'Rural Poverty and Poverty Alleviation in Mozambique: What's Missing from the Debate?', *Journal of Modern African Studies*, 36/1: 101–38.

D'SOUZA, F. (1984), *The Threat of Famine in Afghanistan: A Report on Current Economic and Nutritional Conditions*, London: Afghan Aid Committee, UN Department of Humanitarian Affairs (DHA) (1997).

DAVEY, K., GLENTWORTH, G., KHALIFA, M. O., and IDRIS, M. S. (eds.) (1976), *Local Government and Development in the Sudan: The Experience of Southern Darfur Province*, i and ii, Khartoum and Birmingham: University of Birmingham.

DE SILVA, K. M. (1995), *The 'Traditional Homelands' of the Tamils: Separatist Ideology in Sri Lanka: A Historical Appraisal*, Kandy: International Centre for Ethnic Studies.

DE SOTO (1989), *The Invisible Revolution in the Third World*, New York: Harper and Row.

DE WAAL, A. (1989), *Famine that Kills: Darfur, Sudan 1984–5*, Oxford: Clarendon Press.

—— (1990*a*), 'Starving Out the South: Famine, War and Famine, 1983–9', (mimeo).

—— (1990*b*), 'Armed Militias in Contemporary Sudan', (mimeo).

—— (1997), *Famine Crimes, Politics of the Disaster Relief Industry in Africa*, Oxford: James Currey.

DEPARTMENT OF CENSUS AND STATISTICS (various years), *Economic and Social Statistics of Sri Lanka*, Colombo: Central Bank.

—— (various years), *Labour Force and Socio-Economic Survey, Sri Lanka*, Colombo: Central Bank.

DI ADDARIO, S. (1997), 'Estimating the Economic Costs of Conflict: an Examination of the Two-Gap Estimation Model', *Oxford Development Studies*, 25/1.

DIJKSTRA, A. G. (1990), 'La industria en la economía mixta de Nicaragua', *Cuadernos de Pensamiento Propio*, Managua: CRIES.

DODGE, C. P. and WEIBE, P. D. (eds.) (1985), *Uganda: The Breakdown of Health Services*, Oxford: Pergamon Press.

DONINI, A. (1996*a*), *The Policies of Mercy: UN Coordination in Afghanistan, Mozambique, and Rwanda*, Occasional Paper, no. 22, Providence, RI: Thomas J. Watson Jr. Institute for International Studies.

—— DUDLEY, E., and OCKWELL, R. (1996*b*), *Afghanistan: Coordination in a Fragmented State: A Lessons Learned Report*, New York: UN Department of Humanitarian Affairs.

DUFFIELD, M. (1990*a*), 'Sudan at the Crossroads: From Emergency Preparedness to Social Security', Institute of Development Studies Paper, Sussex University, DP275 (May).

—— (1990*b*), 'War and Famine in Africa', Oxfam Research Paper, no. 5, Oxford.

—— (1992), 'NGOs, Disaster Relief and Asset Transfer in the Horn: Political Survival in a Permanent Emergency', Paper presented to 1992 Annual Conference of the Development Studies Association, 16–18 Sept., University of Nottingham.

—— (1999), *Globalisation and War Economies: Promoting Order or the Return of History*, Paper prepared for the Fletcher Forum of World Affairs on the Geography of Confidence: Environments, Populations, Boundaries, Birmingham.

DUMAZERT, P. (1987), 'Centroamerica: Macroeconomía de los cambios estructurales', *Cuadernos de Pensamiento Propio*.

DUPREE, L. (1980), *Afghanistan*, Princeton: Princeton University Press.

ECONOMIST INTELLIGENCE UNIT (EIU) (1976), *Quarterly Economic Review of Pakistan, Bangladesh and Afghanistan*, Annual Supplement, London: EIU.

—— (1989), *Afghanistan Country Profile 1989–90*, London: EIU.

—— (1998), *Afghanistan Country Profile 1997–98*, London: EIU.

EDIRISINGHE, N. (1987), *The Food Stamp Scheme in Sri Lanka: Costs, Benefits, and Options for Modification*, Washington: International Food Policy Research Institute.

EDWARDS, S. (1989), *Real Exchange Rates, Devaluation and Adjustment: Exchange Rate Policy in Developing Countries*, Cambridge, Mass.: MIT Press.

EL KHALIFA, E., FORD, R., and KHOGALI, M. M. (1985), *Sudan's Southern Stock Route: An Environmental Impact Assessment*, Khartoum and Worcester, Mass.: Institute of Environmental Studies.

ELLIS, F. (1993), *Peasant Economics* (2nd edn.), Cambridge: Cambridge University Press.

EL SAMMANI, M. O. (ed.) (1985), *El Khuwei–Mazroub–Tinna Study Area, North-Central Kordofan and Messeriya Study Area, Southern Kordofan*, Institute of Environmental Studies/Khartoum University/USAID (project no. 698-0427).

—— (1986), *Kordofan Rehabilitation Development Strategy*, i, Ministry of Finance and Economic Planning/UNDP/Khartoum University.

ENRIQUEZ, L. and SPALDING, R. (1987), 'The Banking System and Revolutionary Change', in R. Spalding (ed.), *The Political Economy of Revolutionary Nicaragua*, London: Allen & Unwin.

ENVIO (1985), 'Los campesinos nicaragüenses dan un giro a la reforma agraria', 4/51, Managua: IHCA.

—— (1987), 'Cooperativas: un nuevo giro', 6/72, Managua: IHCA.

—— (1989), 'La organización campesina', 8/93, Managua: IHCA.

—— (1992), 'The economic plan's feet of clay', Managua: IHCA.

FALLA, R. (1981a), 'Las bandas contrarevolucionarias', Managua (mimeo).

—— (1981b), 'Las clases sociales en Jinotega', Managua (mimeo).

FANON, F. (1968), *Wretched of the Earth*, New York: New Grove.

FAUNE, A. (1989), 'Organización y participación popular en el campo', *Revolución y Desarrollo*, 5 (July).

FENDRU, I. (1985), 'The Rural Question and Democracy in Uganda', *Mazuro*, 6/1: 55–75.

FIDA (1980), *Informe de la misión especial de progamación a Nicaragua*, Rome: Food and Agricultural Organisation.

FINNEGAN, W. (1992), *A Complicated War: The Harrowing of Mozambique*, Berkeley: University of California Press.

FITZGERALD, E. V. K. (1985), 'Agrarian Reform as Model of Accumulation: The Case of Nicaragua since 1979', *Journal of Development Studies*, 22/1.

—— (1987), 'An Evaluation of the Economic Costs of Nicaragua of US Aggression 1980–84', in R. Spalding (ed.), *The Political Economy of Revolutionary Nicaragua*, London: Allen & Unwin.

—— (1989), 'Problems in Financing a Revolution: Accumulation, Defence and Income Distribution in Nicaragua, 1979–96, in E. V. K. FitzGerald and R. Vos (eds.), *Financing Economic Development: A Structuralist Approach to Monetary Policy*, Aldershot: Gower.

—— (1993), *The Macroeconomics of Development Finance*, London: Macmillan.

—— (1994), 'The Economic Dimension of the Social Development and Peace Process in Cambodia', in P. Utting (ed.), *Between Hope and Insecurity: The Social Consequence of the Cambodian Peace Process*, Geneva: UNRISD.

—— (1997), 'Paying for the War: Macroeconomic Stabilization in Poor Countries under Conflict Conditions', *Oxford Development Studies*, 25/1, 43–64.

—— (2000), 'Global Linkages, Vulnerable Economies and the Outbreak of Conflict', in E. W. Nafziger and R. Väyrynen (eds.), *War and Destitution: The Prevention of Humanitarian Emergencies*, London: Macmillan.

—— and CROES, E. (1988), 'The Regional Monetary System and Economic Recuperation in Central America', in G. Irvin and S. Holland (eds.), *Central America: The Future of Economic Integration*, Boulder Colo.: Westview Press.

FITZGERALD, E. V. K. and GRIGSBY, A. (1997), *Nicaragua: The Political Economy of Social Reform and Armed Conflict*, Oxford: Queen Elizabeth House and Stockholm: Swedish International Development Cooperation Agency.

—— and F. STEWART (1997), 'Editors' Introduction', *Oxford Development Studies*, 25/1: 5–11.

FOOD AID ADMINISTRATION, KORDOFAN REGION (1988), 'Distribution of 11,790 Tons of Dura Donated by the Ministry of Finance', El Obeid, Sudan: Food Aid Administration.

FOOD AND AGRICULTURE ORGANISATION (FAO) (1997), *Afghanistan*, Rome: FAO, Internet.

—— (FAO) (various years), *Food Production Yearbook*, Rome: FAO.

FOUCAULT, M. (1981), 'Questions of Method: An Interview with Michel Foucault', *Ideology and Consciousness*, 8 (Spring).

—— (1988), *Power/Knowledge: Selected Interviews and Other Writings, 1972–1977*, in C. Gordon (ed.), Brighton: Harvester Press.

FRELIMO FIFTH CONGRESS (1989), *Mozambique: Documents (1), Statutes and Programmes*, Maputo: Frelimo.

FURLEY, O. (1989), 'Britain and Uganda: From Amin to Museveni', in K. Rupesinghe (ed.), *Conflict Resolution in Uganda*, Oxford: James Currey.

GARANG, J. (1987), *John Garang Speaks*, London: Kegan Paul International.

GEFFRAY, C. (1991), *A Causa das Armas*, Porto: Edições Afrontamento.

GERSOVITZ, M. (1983), Savings and Nutrition at Low Incomes, *Journal of Political Economy*, 91/5: 841–55.

GIBSON, B. (1987), 'Structural Overview of the Nicaraguan Economy', in R. Spalding (ed.), *The Political Economy of Revolutionary Nicaragua*, London: Allen & Unwin.

GRAY, J. R. (1961), *A History of the Southern Sudan, 1939–1989*, Oxford: Oxford University Press.

GREEN, R. (1981), 'Magendo in the Political Economy of Uganda: Pathology, Parallel System or Dominant Sub-mode of Production', IDS Discussion Paper 164, Institute of Development Studies Sussex.

GRIGSBY, A. (1987), 'Nicaragua: Adjustment Policies and Constraints', M.Phil. diss., Institute of Development Studies, University of Sussex.

—— (1996), 'Es viable la integración Sur-Sur?', *Pensamiento Propio No 2*, Segunda Época: Nicaragua.

GROBAR, L. and GNANASELVAM, S. (1993), 'The Economic Effects of the Sri Lankan Civil War', *Economic Development and Cultural Change* (Jan.).

GURDIAN, G. (1989), 'La cuestión étnico-nacional en Nicaragua a diez años de revolución, *Revolución y Desarrollo*, 5 (July).

GUTIÉRREZ, H. R. (1989), 'La política económica de la revolución (1979–1989)', *Revolución y Desarrollo*, 5 (July).

HALL, M. and YOUNG, T. (1997), *Confronting Leviathan: Mozambique since Independence*, London: Hurst & Company.

HANLON, J. (1984), *Mozambique: the Revolution under Fire*, London: Zed.

—— (1991), *Mozambique: Who Calls the Shots?*, Oxford: James Currey.

—— (1996), *Peace without Profit: How the IMF Blocks Rebuilding Mozambique*, Oxford: James Currey.

HANSEN, H. B. and TWADDLE, M. (eds.) (1988), *Uganda Now: Between Decay and Development*, Oxford: James Currey.

HARDING, J. (1996), 'The Mercenary Business', *London Review of Books*, 1 Aug.

HARRIS, R. and VILAS, C. (eds.) (1985), *Nicaragua: A Revolution under Siege*, London: Zed Books.

HENDERSON, K. D. D. (1939), 'A Note on the Migration of the Messiriya Tribe into South-West Kordofan', *Sudan Notes and Records*, 22/1.

HERMELE, K. (1988), *Country Report: Mozambique*, Stockholm: SIDA.

HEWITT, K. (ed.) (1983), *Interpretations of Calamity*, London: Allen & Unwin.

HODSON, R. (1995), *Report on the Visit to Jaffna District by the Humanitarian Adviser to the United Nations Resident Coordinator*, Colombo: United Nations.

HOILE, D. (1989), *Mozambique: A Nation in Crisis*, London: Claridge.

HUMPHREYS, F. P. (1996), 'A Cross-Country Statistical Analysis of the Effects of War on Developing Countries', M.Sc. thesis in Economics for Development, University of Oxford.

IBRAHIM, A. R. A. (1985), 'Regional Inequality and Underdevelopment in Western Sudan', Ph.D. thesis, Sussex University.

IBRAHIM, H. (1988), 'Agricultural Development Policy, Ethnicity and Socio-political Change in the Nuba Mountains, Sudan', Ph.D. thesis, University of Connecticut.

ICG (International Crisis Group) (1996), *Report on Sierra Leone*, Brussels: ICG.

ILO/JASPA (1988), *Employment Promotion in the Informal Sector in Africa: Report of a Regional Seminar*, Addis Ababa: JASPA.

IMF (1998), *Republic of Mozambique: Selected Issues, IMF Staff Country Report, 98/59*, Washington: International Monetary Fund.

—— (various years), *Government Finance Statistics Yearbook*, Washington: International Monetary Fund.

—— (various years), *International Financial Statistics*, Washington: International Monetary Fund.

INSTITUTO NACIONAL DE ESTATÍSTICA (1997a), *Anuário Estatístico 1997*, Maputo: Instituto Nacional de Estatística.

—— (1997b), *Estimativas e Projecções Anuais da População, País, Províncias e Distritos: 1990–2000*, Maputo: Instituto Nacional de Estatística.

INTERNATIONAL INSTITUTE FOR STRATEGIC STUDIES (IISS) (various editions), *The Military Balance*, London: IISS.

INTERNATIONAL ORGANISATION FOR MIGRATION (1994), *Assistance Programme for Internally Displaced Vulnerable Groups in Mozambique*, Maputo: International Organization for Migration.

JAMAL, V. (1991a), 'The Agrarian Context of the Ugandan Crisis', in H. B. Hansen and M. Twaddle (eds.), *Changing Uganda*, Oxford: James Currey.

—— (1991b), 'Inequalities and Adjustment in Uganda', *Development and Change*, 22: 321–37.

JAMES, W. (1988), 'Perceptions from an African Slaving Frontier', in L. Archer (ed.), *Slavery and Other Forms of Unfree Labour*, London: Routledge and Kegan Paul.

JOHNSEN, V. (1992), 'Artisanal Fishermen and Intermediaries in Mozambique', in I. Tvedten and B. Hersoug (eds.), *Fishing for Development: Small-Scale Fisheries in Africa*, Uppsala: Scandinavian Institute of African Studies, 115–32.

JOHNSON, C. (1997), *Afghanistan: A Land in Shadow*, Oxford: Oxfam.

JOHNSON, D. H. (1989), 'Political Ecology in the Upper Nile', *Journal of African History*, 30/3.

Journal of the American Medical Association (JAMA) (1998), 'Women's Health and Human Rights in Afghanistan', abstracts, http://www.ama-assn.org (5 Aug.).

KAIMOWITZ, D. (1986), 'Nicaraguan Debates on Agrarian Structure and their Implications for Agricultural Policy and the Rural Poor', *Journal of Peasant Studies*, 14/1 (Oct.).

—— (1988), 'Nicaragua's Experience with Agricultural Planning: From State-centred Accumulation to the Strategic Alliance with the Peasantry', in E. V. K. FitzGerald and M. Wuyts (eds.), *Markets within Planning: Socialist Economics Management in the Third World*, London: Frank Cass.

KANAGARATNAM, N. (1994), 'Acute Services Access', Jaffna Hospital, Medical Institute of Tamils (Conference proceedings).

KAPLAN, R. (1994), 'The Coming Anarchy', *Atlantic Monthly* (Feb.).

KARAM, K. M. (1980), 'Dispute Settlement among Pastoral Nomads in the Sudan', thesis, M.Soc.Sci., University of Birmingham.

KARUGIRE, S. (1980), *A Political History of Uganda*, Nairobi: Heinemann Educational Books.

KEEN, D. (1994), *The Benefits of Famine: A Political Economy of Famine and Relief in Southwestern Sudan, 1983–1989*, Princeton: Princeton University Press.

KELEGAMA, S. (1994), *The Impact of the Two Hundred Garment Factory Programme on the Sri Lankan Economy*, Colombo: Institute of Policy Studies.

—— (1997), 'The Economic Cost of the North-East Conflict in Sri Lanka', *Lanka Outlook* (Winter 97/98), 8–12.

—— TIRUCHELVAM, N. and MANIKAWASAKAR, K. (1995), 'The Economic Cost of the North-East Conflict in Sri Lanka', Colombo: Institute of Policy Studies.

KHALID, M. (1990), *The Government They Deserve: the Role of the Elite in Sudan's Political Evolution*, London and New York: Kegan Paul International.

KHIDDU-MAKABUYA, E. (1989), 'Paramilitarism and Human Rights', in K. Rupesinghe (ed.), *Conflict Resolution in Uganda*, Oxford: James Currey.

—— (1991), 'The Rule of Law and Human Rights in Uganda: The Missing Link', in H. B. Hansen and M. Twaddle (eds.), *Changing Uganda*, London: James Currey.

KILLICK, T. (1995), *The Flexible Economy: Cause and Consequences of the Adaptability of National Economies*, London: Routledge.

KIWANUKA, S. (1979), *Amin and the Tragedy of Uganda*, Munich: Weltforum Verlag.

KUMAR, R. (1989), *Conflict Resolution in Uganda*, Ohio: Ohio University Press.

LUCAS, R. E. (1988), 'On the mechanics of Economic Development', *Journal of Monetary Economics*, 99: 3–42.

MCLACHLAN, F. (1992), *Life During Wartime: Afghan Women and Conflict*, Oxford: Oxfam.

MACHEL, S. (1977), *Our Sophisticate Weapon*, Maputo, repr. speech.

MACKINTOSH, M. (1988), 'Mozambique', in C. Harvey (ed.) *Agricultural Pricing Policy in Africa: Four Country Case Studies*, London: Macmillan.

MAHMOUD, F. B. (1984), *The Sudanese Bourgeoisie: Vanguard of Development?*, London: Zed Books, and Khartoum: Khartoum University Press.

MAHMUD, U. A. and BALDO, S. A. (1987), *Al Daien Massacre: Slavery in the Sudan*, Khartoum: Human Rights Violations in the Sudan.

MALDIDIER, C. and MARCHETTI, P. (1996), *El Campesino Finquero*, Managua: Nitlapan.

MALEY, W. (1996), 'Women and Public Policy in Afghanistan: A Comment', *World Development*, 24/1.

MAMDANI, M. (1976), *Politics and Class Formation in Uganda*, London: Monthly Review Press.

—— (1988), 'NRA/MRM: Two Years in Power', Lecture at Makerere University, 3 March.

—— (1996), *Citizen and Subject: Contemporary Africa and the Legacy of Late Colonialism*, Princeton: Princeton University Press.

MANICKAVASAGAR, K. (1994), *Special Report on the Situation in the Jaffna District*, London: Medical Institute of Tamils.

MANOGARAN, C. (1987), *Ethnic Conflict and Reconciliation in Sri Lanka*, Honolulu: University of Hawaii Press.

MARSDEN, P. (1998), 'Afghan Episodes', *New Routes*, 3/2: 11–14.

MAWSON, A. M. M. (1989), 'The Triumph of Life: Political Dispute and Religious Ceremonial among the Agar Dinka of the Southern Sudan', Ph.D. thesis, Cambridge University.

MAXWELL, D. (1995), 'Alternative Food Security Strategy: A Household Analysis of Urban Agriculture in Kampala', *World Development*, 3/10: 1669–82.

MAXWELL, S. and SINGER, H. (1979), 'Food Aid to Developing Countries: A Survey, *World Development*, 7: 225–47.

MEAGHER, K. (1990), 'The Hidden Economy: Informal and Parallel Trade in Northwestern Uganda', *Review of African Political Economy*, 47: 64–83.

MEDAL, J. L. (1985), *La Revolución Nicaragüense: Balance Económico y Alternativas Futuras*, Managua: CINASE.

—— (1988), *Política Económica y Cambio Social*, Managua: CINASE.

MEDICAL INSTITUTE OF TAMILS (1994), *Victims of War in Sri Lanka: Conference Proceedings*, London: Medical Institute of Tamils.

MEDIPAZ (1994), 'Guerra de baja intensidad: efectos y consecuencias', Managua: Médicos para la Paz (mimeo).

MILWARD, A. S. (1970), *The Economic Effects of the Two World Wars on Britain*, London: Macmillan.

—— (1979), *War, Economy and Society: 1939–45*, London: Macmillan.

MINEAR, L. (1991), *Humanitarianism under Siege: A Critical Review of Operation Lifeline, Sudan*, Trenton: Red Sea Press, and Washington: Bread for the World.

MINISTÉRIO DE EDUCAÇÃO (1994), *Impacto da Guerra na Educação 1983–1992*, Maputo: Ministério de Educação.

MINISTRY OF AGRICULTURE AND FISHERIES AND WORLD BANK (1998), *Cashew Production and Marketing among Smallholders in Mozambique: A Gender-Differentiated Analysis Based on Household Survey Data*, Maputo: World Bank.

MINISTRY OF EDUCATION AND HIGHER EDUCATION (1993), *Educational Statistics of Sri Lanka*, Colombo: Ministry of Education.

MINISTRY OF FINANCE, PLANNING, ETHNIC AFFAIRS AND NATIONAL INTEGRATION AND THE UNICEF (1995), *Progress Towards Mid-Decade Goals in Sri Lanka, 1995*, Colombo: UNICEF.

MINISTRY OF HEALTH (various years), *Annual Health Bulletin*, Colombo: Ministry of Health.

MINISTRY OF INDUSTRY, TRADE AND TOURISM (1997), *Cashew Marketing Liberalisation Impact Study Mozambique*, Maputo: Ministry of Industry, Trade, and Tourism.

MINISTRY OF SHIPPING, PORTS, REHABILITATION AND RECONSTRUCTION (1995), *Performance, Policy, Strategies and Programmes*, Colombo: Government of Sri Lanka.

MIPLAN (1980), *Programa de Reactivación Económoca en Beneficio del Pueblo*, Managua: Ministerio de Planificación.

MITTLEMAN, J. (1988), *Mozambique: Out From Underdevelopment*, New York: Monthly Review Press.

MOGHADAM, V. M. (1994), 'Building Human Resources and Women's Capabilities in Afghanistan: A Retrospect and Prospects', *World Development*, 22/6.

MSF-FRANCE (1988), 'El Meiram, Situation Brief, IV', Paris.

MUDOOLA, D. (1988), 'Political Transitions since Amin: A Study in Political Pathology', in H. B. Hansen and M. Twaddle (eds.) (1988), *Uganda Now: Between Decay and Development*, Oxford: James Currey.

—— (1992), 'Interest Groups and Institution Building Processes in Uganda, 1962–71', Kampala: Makerere Institute of Social Research.

—— (1995), *Religion, Ethnicity and Politics in Uganda*, Kampala: Fountain Publishers.

MUKHERJEE, R. (1956), *The Problem of Uganda: A Study in Acculturation*, Berlin: Akademie-Verlag.

MULLINS, J. D. (1904), *The Wonderful Story of Uganda*, London: Church Missionary Society.

MUSEVENI, Y. (1992), *What is Africa's Problem?*, Kampala: NRM Publications.

MUTIBWA, P. (1992), *Uganda Since Independence: A Story of Unfulfilled Hopes*, Kampala: Fountain Publishers.

NABUDERE, D. W. (1988), 'External and Internal Factors in Uganda's Continuing Crisis', in H. B. Hansen, and M. Twaddle (eds.), *Uganda Now: Between Decay and Development*, Oxford: James Currey.

NATCHINARKINIAN, C. S. (1994), 'Current Patterns of Health Care and Resource Allocation', Medical Institute of Tamils.

NATIONAL RESISTANCE MOVEMENT SECRETARIAT (NRM) (1987), 'The Political Programme of the NRM: Two Years of Action', Kampala: NRM.

NEF, J. (1950), *War and Human Progress*, Cambridge, Mass.: Harvard University Press.

NEIRA, O. (ed.) (1996), *ESAF: Condicionalidad y Deuda*, Managua: CRIES.

—— and RENZI, M. (1996), 'La Herencia Económica de la Administración Barrios de Chamarro', *Pensamiento Propio*.

NEWITT, M. (1995), *A History of Mozambique*, London: Hurst.

NIAMIR, M., HUNTINGTON, R., and COLE, D. C. (1983), 'Ngok Dinka Cattle Migrations and Marketings: A Missing Piece of the Sudan Mosaic', Development Discussion Paper no. 155, Harvard University, Cambridge Mass.

NIBLOCK, T. (1987), *Class and Power in Sudan: The Dynamics of Sudanese Politics, 1898–1985*, London: Macmillan.

NILSSON, A. (1990), *Unmasking the Bandits: The Face of MNR*, London: Ecasaama.

NORTH, D. C. (1990), *Institutions, Institutional Change and Economic Performance*, Cambridge: Cambridge University Press.

NORTH-EAST PROVINCIAL SECRETARIAT (1994), *Statistical Information of the North-East Province*, Trincomalee: North-East Provincial Council.

NSIBAMBI, A. (1989), 'The Land Question and Conflict', in K. Rupesinghe (ed.), *Conflict Resolution in Uganda*, Oxford: James Currey.

NUÑEZ, O. (1995), *La Guerra y el Campesinado en Nicaragua*, Managua: CIPRES.

OCAMPO, J. A. (1991), 'Collapse and Incomplete Stabilization of the Nicaraguan Economy', in R. Dornsbusch and S. Edwards (eds.), *The Macroeconomics of Populism in Latin America*, Chicago: Chicago University Press.

O'FAHEY, R. S. (1973), 'Slavery and the Slave Trade in Darfur', *Journal of African History*, 14/1.

OKOTH, P. (1996), 'The Historical Dimensions of Democracy in Uganda: A Review of the Problems and Prospects', in J.Oloka-Onyango, K. Kiowana, and C. Maina Peter (eds.), *Law and the Struggle for Democracy in East Africa*, Nairobi: Claripress.

OPALA, J. A. (1994), *Ecstatic Renovation: Street Art Celebrating Sierra Leone's 1992 Revolution*, Freetown: Sierra Leone Adult Education Association.

ORTEGA, M. (1990), 'The State, the Peasantry and the Sandinista Revolution', *Journal of Peasant Studies*, 26.

O'SULLIVAN, M. L. (1994), 'Economics and Ethnic Strife: The Case of Sri Lanka', M.Sc. thesis, University of Oxford.

—— (1997), 'Household Entitlements during Wartime: the Experience of Sri Lanka', *Oxford Development Studies*, 25/1.

OXFAM-UK (1986a), 'The Economic War against the Dinka of Bahr el Ghazal', Oxford, 4 June.

—— (1986b), 'Ed Daien Tour Report', Oxford, 18 June.

—— (1987), *Country Representative's Report (Sudan)*, Oxford: Oxfam.

PAUL, L. (1997), 'Women in Danger in Afghanistan', *Peace Magazine*, http://www.peacemagazine.org (Sept.).

PAULDING, J. (1982), 'Slavery, Land Tenure and Social Class in the Northern Turkish Sudan', *International Journal of African Historical Studies*, 15/1.

PHYSICIANS FOR HUMAN RIGHTS (PHR) (1998), 'Physician Group's Unprecedented Study Calls Taleban War on Women a Health and Human Rights Crisis in Afghanistan', press release, http://www/reliefweb.int, 5 Aug.

PIZARRO, R. (1987), 'The New Economic Policy: A Necessary Readjustment', in R. Spalding (ed.), *The Political Economy of Revolutionary Nicaragua*, London: Allen & Unwin.

PROTECTORATE OF UGANDA (1961), *Uganda Census 1959*, Entebbe: Government Printer.

PRUNIER, G. (1986), 'From Peace to War: The Southern Sudan 1972–1984', Occasional Paper no. 3, Department of Sociology and Social Anthropology, Hull University.

PUTNAM, R. (1993), *Making Democracy Work*, Princeton: Princeton University Press.

RANGASAMI, A. (1985*a*), 'Failure of Exchange Entitlements', *Economic and Political Weekly*, 20/41 (12 Oct.).

—— (1985*b*), 'Theory of Famine: A Response', *Economic and Political Weekly*, 20/42 (19 Oct.).

RATILAL, P. (1990), *Using Aid to End the Emergency*, New York: UNDP.

RATNESWARAN, S. (1995), *Health Care in the Northeast Province Area: Notes from a Visit to Jaffna*, London: Tamil Information Centre.

RENO, W. (1995), *Corruption and State Politics in Sierra Leone*, Cambridge: Cambridge University Press.

REPUBLIC OF SUDAN/UNDP/ODA (1984), 'Decentralization: Management and Development Issues', Report of the Inter-regional Seminar held in Juba, 21–3 Nov.

REPUBLIC OF UGANDA (1966*a*), *Statistical Abstract 1996*, Department of Statistics, Entebbe: MFEP.

—— (1966*b*), *Work for Progress: Uganda's Second Five Year Plan*, Entebbe: Government Printer.

—— (1971*a*), *Statistical Abstract 1971*, Department of Statistics, Entebbe: MFEP.

—— (1971*b*), *The Birth of the Second Republic*, Entebbe: Government Printer.

—— (1971*c*), *Report on the 1969 Population Census*, Entebbe: Government Printer.

—— (1972), *Uganda's Third Five Year Development Plan 1971/2– 1975/6*, Entebbe: Government Printer.

—— (1973), *Report on the 1969 Population Census*, iii, Entebbe: Government Printer.

—— (1996*a*), *Cabinet Committee Reporting on 'Land Disputes in Kasese District'*, Kampala: Government Printer.

—— (1996*b*), *Statistical Abstract 1996*, Department of Statistics, Kampala: Government Printer.

—— MINISTRY OF FINANCE AND ECONOMIC PLANNING (MFEP) (1996*c*), *Report on the Uganda National Integrated Household Survey, 1992–3*, iii, Kampala: MFEP.

Reuters News Service, courtesy of SLNet (Internet Service), 1995–6.

RICHARDS, P. (1995), 'Rebellion in Liberia and Sierra Leone: A Crisis of Youth?', in O. Furley (ed.), *Conflict in Africa*, London: I. B. Tauris.

ROBERTS, S. and WILLIAMS, J. (1995), *After the Guns Fall Silent: The Enduring Legacy of Landmines*, Washington: Vietnam Veterans of America Foundation.

ROEMER, M. (1989), 'The Macroeconomics of Counterpart Funds Revisited', *World Development*, 7: 795–807.

RRC/EC (1988), 'Note to the Acting Delegate', from Adviser, 10 June.

RUBIN, B. (1997), *Afghanistan: The Last Cold War Conflict, The First Post-Cold War Conflict*, Helsinki: WIDER.

—— (1996), *Afghanistan: The Forgotten Crisis: Update March–November*, WRITENET Country Papers, http://www/unhcr.org (Dec.).

RUCCIO, D. (1987), 'The State and Planning in Nicaragua', in R. Spalding (ed.), *The Political Economy of Revolutionary Nicaragua*, London: Allen & Unwin.

RYLE, J. (1989*a*), *Displaced Southern Sudanese in Northern Sudan with Special Reference to Southern Darfur and Kordofan*, London and Khartoum: Save the Children.

—— (1989*b*), 'The Road to Abyei', *Granta*, 26 (Spring), London: Granta Publications.

SAEED, A. (1982), 'The State and Socioeconomic Transformation in the Sudan: The Case of Social Conflict in Southwest Kordofan', Ph.D. thesis, University of Connecticut.

SAFERWORLD (1994), *The True Costs of Conflict*, London: Macmillan.

SAITH, A. (ed.) (1985), *The Agrarian Question in Socialist Transitions*, London: Cass.

SANDERSON, L. P. and SANDERSON, N. (1981), *Education, Religion and Politics in Southern Sudan, 1899–1964*, Reading: Ithaca Press, and Khartoum: Khartoum University Press.

SAUL, J. (1985), *A Difficult Road: The Transition to Socialism in Mozambique*, New York: Monthly Review Press.

SEABRIGHT, P. (1986), 'Effects of Conflict on the Economy in Northern Sri Lanka', *Economic and Political Weekly*, 21: 78–83.

SEN, A. K. (1981), *Poverty and Famines: An Essay on Entitlement and Deprivation*, Oxford: Clarendon Press.

—— (1990), 'Individual Freedom as a Social Commitment', *New York Review of Books* (14 June).

—— (1991), 'Wars and Famines: On Divisions and Incentives', STICERD, Discussion Paper 33, London: LSE.

SESAY, M. A. (1993), Interdependence and Dependency in the Political Economy of Sierra Leone, Ph.D. thesis, University of Southampton.

SHEPHERD, A. W. (1984), 'Nomads, Farmers and Merchants: Old Strategies in a Changing Sudan', in E. Scott (ed.), *Life Before the Drought*, London: Allen & Unwin.

—— (1988), 'Case Studies of Famine: Sudan', in D. Curtis, M. Hubbard, and A. Shepherd (eds.), *Preventing Famine: Policies and Prospects for Africa*, London and New York: Routledge.

SIVARAJAH, N. (1992), *Report on the Current Nutritional Status of the People of the Jaffna District*, Jaffna: Council of Non-Governmental Organisations.

—— (1994), *Maternal and Child Care*, London: Medical Institute of Tamils.

SIVARD, R. L. (1985; 1993), *World Military and Social Expenditures*, Washington: World Priorities.

SPALDING, R. (ed.) (1987), *The Political Economy of Revolutionary Nicaragua*, London: Allen & Unwin.

—— (1994), *Capitalists and Revolution in Nicaragua*, Chapel Hill, NC: The University of North Carolina Press.

SPOOR, M. (1995), *The State and Domestic Agricultural Markets in Nicaragua*, New York: St Martin's Press.

SPP (1987), *Plan Económico 1987*, Managua: Secretaría de Progrmación y Presupuesto.

SRISHNAMUGARAJAH, M. (1994), *An Overview of the Effects of War in North East Sri Lanka*, London: Medical Institute of Tamils.

STAHLER-STOCK, R. (1987), 'Foreign Debt and Economic Stabilization Policies in Revolutionary Nicaragua', in R. Spalding (ed.), *The Political Economic of Revolutionary Nicaragua*, London: Allen & Unwin.

STEPHENS, J. (1994), *The Political Economy of Transport in Mozambique: Implications for Regional Development*, Ph.D. thesis, University of Sussex.

STEWART, F. (1985), *Planning to Meet Basic Needs*, London: Macmillan.

—— (1993), 'War and Underdevelopment: Can Economic Analysis Help Reduce the Costs?', *Journal of International Development*, 5/4: 357–80.

—— (1995), 'Groups for Good or Ill', *Oxford Development Studies*, 24: 9–25.

—— HUMPHREY, F. and LEE, N. (1997), 'Civil Conflict in Developing Countries over the Last Quarter of a Century: An Empirical Overview of Economic and Social Consequences', *Oxford Development Studies*, 25: 11–41.

STOCKHOLM INTERNATIONAL PEACE RESEARCH INSTITUTE (SIPRI) (various years), *SIPRI Yearbook: Armaments, Disarmaments and International Security*, Stockholm: SIPRI.

STRASBERG, P., MOLE, P., and WEBER, M. T. (1998), *Analysis of Smallholder (Family Sector) Cashew Tree Ownership, Production and Marketing Patterns in Mozambique Using TIA96 Data*, Maputo: MAP/DE/FSP/MSU.

SULIMAN, M. (1993), 'Civil War in the Sudan, from Ethnic to Ecological Conflict', *The Ecologist*, 23/3: 104–9.

SWEDISH COMMITTEE FOR AGRICULTURE (SCA) (1988), *Agricultural Survey of Afghanistan*, Peshawar: Pakistan.

TAMIL INFORMATION CENTRE (1993), *Economic Blockade*, London: Tamil Information Centre.

TAMIL REHABILITATION ORGANIZATION (various issues), *Information Bulletin* and *Future Quarterly Newsletter*.

TIBANA, R. J. (1994), *Mozambique Commodity and Policy Shocks: Terms of Trade Changes, The 'Socialist Big Push', and the Response of the Economy (1975–1986)*, Oxford: Centre for the Study of African Economies, Working Paper Series 18.

TSCHIRLEY, D. L. and WEBER, M. T. (1994), Food Security Strategies under Extremely Adverse Conditions: The Determinants of Household Income and Consumption in Rural Mozambique, *World Development*, 22/2: 159–73.

UN DEPARTMENT OF HUMANITARIAN AFFAIRS (DHA) (1997), 'Report of the DHA Mission to Afghanistan 30 March–5 May', DHA, New York, http://www/reliefweb.int (15 June).

UNCTAD (various editions), *Handbook of Trade and Development Statistics*, Geneva: UNCTAD.

—— (various editions), *The Least Developed Countries*, Geneva: UNCTAD.

UNDP (1993), *Afghanistan Rehabilitation Strategy: Action Plan for Immediate Rehabilitation*, i–vi, Kabul: UNDP.

—— (1995), 'The Humanitarian Situation in Sierra Leone, January–March 1995', Freetown: UNDP.

—— (1996), *Uganda's Human Development Report*, Kampala: UNDP.

—— (1998), *Mozambique National Human Development Report 1998*, Maputo: UNDP.

—— (various editions), *Human Development Report*, New York: UNDP.

UNDPI (1999), 'Poverty Impairs Access to Food in Pakistan and Afghanistan, UN Officials Say', http://www.reliefweb.int (14 May).

UNESCO (1995), *UNESCO Statistical Yearbook, 1995*, Paris: UNESCO.

UNHCR (1997), *Refugees Magazine: Afghanistan: The Unending Crisis*, Geneva: UNHCR, http://www.unhcr.ch.

—— (1999), *Country Update: Afghanistan*, Geneva: UNHCR, http://www.relief.int (10 March).

UNICEF (1990), *A Profile of the Sri Lankan Child in Crisis and Conflict*, Colombo: United Nations Children's Fund.

—— (1991), *Children and Women in Sri Lanka: A Situation Analysis*, Colombo: United Nations Children's Fund.

—— (various editions), *State of the World's Children*, New York: UNICEF.

UNITED NATIONS (1996a), *Consolidated Inter-Agency Appeal Emergency for Afghanistan*, October 1995–September 1996, New York: UN Department of Humanitarian Affairs, http://www/reliefweb.int.

—— (1996b), *Consolidated Inter-Agency Appeal Emergency for Afghanistan, Supplement*, New York: UN Department of Humanitarian Affairs.

—— (UNSYB) (1997), *UN Statistical Yearbook 1997*, New York: United Nations.

—— (1998), *1998 Consolidated Appeal Emergency for Afghanistan*, New York: UN Department of Humanitarian Affairs, http://www.reliefweb.int.

UNITED STATES STATE DEPARTMENT, COUNTER-TERRORISM DEPARTMENT (1995), *Annual Report on Patterns of Global Terrorism*, Washington: Department of State.

UNIVERSITY GRANTS COMMISSION (various years), *Statistics on Higher Education in Sri Lanka*, Colombo, Division of Planning and Research: UGC.

UNOEA (1988), *The Emergency Situation in Sudan: Urgent Humanitarian Requirements*, Khartoum: UNOEA.

UNOHAC (1994), *UNOHAC Map Series*, Maputo: UNOHAC.

US COMMITTEE FOR REFUGEES (1995), *The Usual People*, Washington: US Committee for Refugees.

—— (1997), *Conflict and Displacement in Sri Lanka*, Washington: Immigration and Refugee Services of America.

US CONGRESS (1990), 'Emergency Situations in Sudan and Liberia', Hearing before the Subcommittee on African Affairs of the Committee on Foreign Relations, US Senate, Washington, 27 Nov.

USAID (1987), 'Country Report: Sudan', *FEWS* (June).

UTTING, P. (1987), 'Domestic Supply and Food Shortages, in R. Spalding (ed.), *The Political Economy of Revolutionary Nicaragua*, London: Allen & Unwin.

—— (1988), 'The Peasant Question and Development Policy in Nicaragua', Discussion Paper no. 2, Geneva: UNRISD.

—— (1992), *Economic Adjustment under the Sandinistas: Policy Reform, Food Security and Livelihood in Nicaragua*, Geneva: UNRISD.

VAN BRABANT, K. (1996), 'Banned, Restricted or Sensitive: Workings with the Military in Sri Lanka', *Relief and Rehabilitation Network Newsletter*, London: Overseas Development Institute (June), 4–6.

—— (1997*a*), 'NGO–Government Relations in Sri Lanka', in J. Bennett (ed.), *NGOs and Governments: A Review of Current Practice for Southern and Eastern NGOs*, Oxford: INTRAC Publications, 161–72.

—— (1997*b*), 'The Coordination of Humanitarian Action: The Case of Sri Lanka', *Relief and Rehabilitation Network Newsletter*, London: Overseas Development Institute, (Dec.).

VAN DER LAAN, H. L. (1965), *The Sierra Leone Diamonds*, Oxford: Oxford University Press.

VERGARA, R., CASTRO, J., and BARRY, D. (1986), 'Nicaragua país sitiado', *Cuadernos de Pensamiento Propio*, 4, Managua: CRIES.

VINES, A. (1996), *Renamo: From Terrorism to Democracy in Mozambique?*, Oxford: James Currey.

WALLIS, C. (1953), *Report of an Inquiry into African Local Government in the Protectorate of Uganda*, Entebbe: Government Printer.

WANNOP, B. (1989), *Report on the First Muglad-Aweil Relief Train, 20 May to 28 May*, Khartoum: UNDP.

WEEKS, J. (1992), *Development Strategy and the Economy of Sierra Leone*, New York: St Martin's Press.

WHITE, H. (1992), 'The Macroeconomics of Aid: A Critical Survey', *Journal of Development Studies*, 28: 163–240.

—— and WIGNARAJA, G. (1992), 'Exchange Rates, Trade Liberalisation and Aid: The Sri Lankan Experience', *World Development*, 20/10.

WILSON, K. (1992), *Internally Displaced Refugees and Returnees from Mozambique*, SIDA/Refugee Studies Programme, Oxford, Report No. 1.

WILSON, R. T. (1977), 'Temporal Changes in Livestock Numbers and Patterns of Transhumance in Southern Darfur, Sudan', *Journal of Developing Areas* (July).

WORLD BANK (1977), *World Bank Development Indicators*, CD-ROM, Washington: World Bank.

—— (1989*a*), *African Economic and Financial Data*, Washington: World Bank.

—— (1989*b*), *Mozambique: Transport Sector Review*, Washington: World Bank.

—— (1990), *Mozambique: Restoring Rural Production and Trade*, Washington: World Bank.

—— (1992), *Mozambique: Second Public Expenditure Review*, Washington: World Bank.

—— (1993), *Uganda: Social Sectors*, Washington: World Bank.

—— (1995), *Sri Lanka Poverty Assessment*, Washington: World Bank.

—— (1996*a*), *African Development Indicators 1996*, Washington: World Bank.

—— (1996*b*), *Uganda: The Challenge of Growth and Poverty Reduction*, Washington: World Bank.

—— (1999), *World Development Indicators*, CD-ROM, Washington: World Bank.

—— (various years), *Social Indicators of Development*, Washington: World Bank.

—— (various years), *World Development Report*, Washington: World Bank.

—— (various years), *World Tables*, Baltimore: Johns Hopkins University Press.

WORLD FOOD PROGRAMME (1996), *Tackling Hunger in a World Full of Food: Tasks Ahead for Food Aid*, New York: WFP, http://www.wfp.org/info/policy/hunger.

WUYTS, M. (1989), *Money and Planning for Socialist Transition*, Aldershot: Gower.

—— (1996), Foreign Aid, Structural Adjustment, and Public Management: The Mozambican Experience, *Development and Change*, 27/4: 717–49.

ZACK-WILLIAMS, A. (1995), *Tributors, Supporters and Merchant Capital*, Aldershot: Avebury.

INDEX